ENGLISH LANGUAGE SERIES

TITLE NO 9

Cohesion in English

ENGLISH LANGUAGE SERIES
General Editor: Randolph Quirk

Cohesion in English

M. A. K. HALLIDAY
Professor of Linguistics
University of Sydney

RUQAIYA HASAN
Associate Professor
School of English and Linguistics
Macquarie University

Longman

An imprint of **Pearson Education**

Harlow, England · London · New York · Reading, Massachusetts · San Francisco
Toronto · Don Mills, Ontario · Sydney · Tokyo · Singapore · Hong Kong · Seoul
Taipei · Cape Town · Madrid · Mexico City · Amsterdam · Munich · Paris · Milan

Pearson Education Limited
Edinburgh Gate, Harlow,
Essex CM20 2JE, England
and Associated Companies throughout the world

Visit us on the World Wide Web at:
http://www.pearsoneduc.com

First published 1976

ISBN 0-582-55041-6

20 19 18 17
04 03 02 01 00

Printed in Malaysia (LSP)

Foreword

Throughout more than a century of outstanding progress in linguistics – and especially from the time of the *Junggrammatiker* – the most impressive and apparently most abiding successes have been in work at the elemental end of language structure: the description and relation of phonological units. Nor, when they were pressed into reluctant service, did the categories and insights evolved for phonology get us far in explicating linguistic organization at other 'levels', the morphological and syntactic. Moreover, even in the fruitful renaissance of syntactic studies during the third quarter of this century, work has been virtually confined to relations within the sentence. This limitation, though to some extent vigorously defended on theoretical grounds, has not in general been because no relevance to linguistic structure was seen in the relations between sentences, in the connections which resulted in the impression of well-formed paragraphs or longer stretches of discourse. But as with semantics – another and indeed closely related area which linguists have hesitated to enter, often justifying their dissociation on closely-argued theoretical grounds – it was not unreasonably held that relations 'beyond the sentence' involved a complex interplay of linguistics with other concerns such as rhetoric, aesthetics, and pragmatics, for which the theoretical foundations and framework were too shaky to support ambitious model building. And that in any case linguists had enough on hand to get their sentential house furnished.

Meanwhile, literary critics (for whom of course text structure has been a traditional concern) and social anthropologists (for whom text and tale constitute fundamental evidence) began themselves to look at the constructs evolved by de Saussure, the Prague School, and other linguists. One thinks for example of Lévi-Strauss, Dell Hymes, Roland Barthes, as outstanding exponents of structuralism in broad-scale textual analysis. And among linguists, there have always been those who have persisted in the venture to subserve literary and other humanistic disciplines by extending their work to embrace stylistics and other aspects of textual studies. In this movement, Michael Halliday and Ruqaiya Hasan have long been especially active. The prose of Golding and the verse of Yeats are among the material subjected to valued linguistic scrutiny by the former, while the latter has made 'cohesion' her special field, beginning with a doctoral dissertation at the University of Edinburgh and continuing with influential papers while she worked for several fruitful years in the Communication Research Centre at University College London. During the whole of this period, the two authors have worked in close cooperation and mutual influence, acutely aware of areas in English studies of profound interest for both linguists and critics but rigorously explored to a large extent by neither.

We are singularly fortunate that we are able to correct some of these grave deficiencies in the description of English with the work of so uniquely equipped a team. As English has increasingly come into world-wide use, there has arisen a correspondingly increasing need for more information on the language and the ways in which it is used. The English Language Series seeks to meet this need and to play a part in further stimulating the study and teaching of English by providing up-to-date and scholarly treatments of topics most relevant to present-day English – including its history and traditions, its sound patterns, its grammar, its lexicology, its rich variety and complexity in speech and writing, and its standards in Britain, the USA, and the other principal areas where the language is used.

University College London   RANDOLPH QUIRK
May 1975

Preface

This book originated as one of a series of studies of the English language and modern English texts which were undertaken by the *Nuffield Programme in Linguistics and English Teaching* at University College London. The aim of these studies was to provide an account of aspects of contemporary English which would be both founded on theory and also applicable in practice: a description of the system, but one which, since it was based on evidence from texts of different varieties, including both spoken and written, would be useful in application to further text studies.

A relatively neglected aspect of the linguistic system is its resources for text construction, the range of meanings that are specifically associated with relating what is being said .or written to its semantic environment. The principal component of these resources is that of cohesion. Cohesive relations are relations between two or more elements in a text that are independent of the structure; for example between a personal pronoun and an antecedent proper name, such as *John . . . he*. A semantic relation of this kind may be set up either within a sentence or between sentences; with the consequence that, when it crosses a sentence boundary, it has the effect of making the two sentences cohere with one another. The various kinds of cohesion had been outlined by M. A. K. Halliday in his writings on stylistics, and the concept was developed by Ruqaiya Hasan in her University of Edinburgh doctoral thesis.

The earlier chapters of this book were first published as *Grammatical Cohesion in Spoken and Written English, Part I*, by Ruqaiya Hasan, Communication Research Centre (University College London) and Longmans, Green & Co, *Programme in Linguistics and English Teaching: Papers*, No. 7, 1968. This contained Chapters 1, 2 and 3 in their original form. The later chapters were written in collaboration by Ruqaiya Hasan and M. A. K. Halliday, and were prepared for publication in the follow-up series (*Schools Council Programme in Linguistics and English Teaching: Papers*

Series II). However, instead of issuing this part separately, it was decided to revise the earlier chapters and to publish the two halves together as a book. The revision was undertaken by M. A. K. Halliday, who also added the last two chapters.

We should like to express our gratitude to several individuals and institutions for their cooperation and help. The Nuffield Foundation financed the original project within which the earlier part of the work was written. The Schools Council financed the successor project (*Schools Council Programme in Linguistics and English Teaching*, 1967–71); although the later part was not written directly under their auspices, since Ruqaiya Hasan had by then left the team, it had been planned to publish it in the series of papers emanating from this project, and we are grateful to them for allowing it to be withdrawn and published in its present revised form. The final version was written by M. A. K. Halliday during his tenure of a fellowship at the Center for Advanced Study in the Behavioral Sciences, Stanford, California, and we are most grateful to the Center for providing this opportunity.

We wish to thank Stephen Lushington, General Editor of the *Schools Council Programme in Linguistics and English Teaching: Papers Series II*, and a former colleague in the project, for his valuable help and comments throughout the preparation of the original manuscript. Other members of the Nuffield team – Kenneth Albrow, Eirian Davies, Peter Doughty, David Mackay and Brian Thompson – provided stimulating discussion, as did our colleagues on another related research project, Rodney Huddleston, Richard Hudson and Eugene Winter. To Marcia Insel we express our appreciation for her research and bibliographical assistance during the final revision. Students at the Linguistic Society of America's Linguistic Institute, at the University of Michigan, Ann Arbor, in summer 1973, made numerous helpful observations in the context of a course based on this material.

We much appreciate the interest shown by Randolph Quirk, friend, former colleague, and General Editor of the present series; and would like to take this opportunity of referring to the debt owed by everyone in the field of contemporary English to the work done by him and by his colleagues at the Survey of English Usage. Finally we thank the many people who have kindly enquired after the progress of the book. Their continuing concern has been a most valuable source of encouragement.

University of Essex   MAKH
May 1975   RH

Acknowledgments

We are grateful to the following for permission to reproduce copyright material:

Author's agents for the sonnet 'The Bad Thing' by John Wain; Gerald Duckworth & Company Ltd for 'The Hippopotamus' from *The Bad Child's Book of Beasts* by Hilaire Belloc; Granada Publishing Ltd for extracts from *Class, Codes and Control* Vol 1 by Basil Bernstein, published by Paladin Books; The Proprietor of The Greenwich Bookshop for extracts from *Royal Greenwich* by Olive and Nigel Hamilton, The Greenwich Bookshop 1969; the Author for an extract from the article 'Meeting Wilfred Pickles' by Frank Haley from *The Dalesman* September 1973; Author's agents for extracts from 'An Inspector Calls' from *The Plays of J. B. Priestley* Vol 3 published by William Heinemann Ltd. Reprinted by permission of A. D. Peters and Company and Author's agents, M. B. Yeats, Miss Anne Yeats, Macmillan of London & Basingstoke, Macmillan of Canada and Macmillan Publishing Company Inc for an extract from *The Autobiography of William Butler Yeats*. Copyright © 1916, 1935 by Macmillan Publishing Co Inc, renewed 1944, 1963 by Bertha Georgie Yeats.

Table of Contents

3 Substitution

Chapter 1

Introduction

1.1 The concept of cohesion

1.1.1 Text

If a speaker of English hears or reads a passage of the language which is more than one sentence in length, he can normally decide without difficulty whether it forms a unified whole or is just a collection of unrelated sentences. This book is about what makes the difference between the two.

The word TEXT is used in linguistics to refer to any passage, spoken or written, of whatever length, that does form a unified whole. We know, as a general rule, whether any specimen of our own language constitutes a TEXT or not. This does not mean there can never be any uncertainty. The distinction between a text and a collection of unrelated sentences is in the last resort a matter of degree, and there may always be instances about which we are uncertain – a point that is probably familiar to most teachers from reading their students' compositions. But this does not invalidate the general observation that we are sensitive to the distinction between what is text and what is not.

This suggests that there are objective factors involved – there must be certain features which are characteristic of texts and not found otherwise; and so there are. We shall attempt to identify these, in order to establish what are the properties of texts in English, and what it is that distinguishes a text from a disconnected sequence of sentences. As always in linguistic description, we shall be discussing things that the native speaker of the language 'knows' already – but without knowing that he knows them.

A text may be spoken or written, prose or verse, dialogue or monologue. It may be anything from a single proverb to a whole play, from a momentary cry for help to an all-day discussion on a committee.

A text is a unit of language in use. It is not a grammatical unit, like a clause or a sentence; and it is not defined by its size. A text is sometimes envisaged to be some kind of super-sentence, a grammatical unit that is larger than a sentence but is related to a sentence in the same way that a sentence is related to a clause, a clause to a group and so on: by CON-STITUENCY, the composition of larger units out of smaller ones. But this is misleading. A text is not something that is like a sentence, only bigger; it is something that differs from a sentence in kind.

A text is best regarded as a SEMANTIC unit: a unit not of form but of meaning. Thus it is related to a clause or sentence not by size but by REALIZATION, the coding of one symbolic system in another. A text does not CONSIST OF sentences; it is REALIZED BY, or encoded in, sentences. If we understand it in this way, we shall not expect to find the same kind of STRUCTURAL integration among the parts of a text as we find among the parts of a sentence or clause. The unity of a text is a unity of a different kind.

1.1.2 Texture

The concept of TEXTURE is entirely appropriate to express the property of 'being a text'. A text has texture, and this is what distinguishes it from something that is not a text. It derives this texture from the fact that it functions as a unity with respect to its environment.

What we are investigating in this book are the resources that English has for creating texture. If a passage of English containing more than one sentence is perceived as a text, there will be certain linguistic features present in that passage which can be identified as contributing to its total unity and giving it texture.

Let us start with a simple and trivial example. Suppose we find the following instructions in the cookery book:

[1:1] Wash and core six cooking apples. Put them into a fireproof dish.

It is clear that *them* in the second sentence refers back to (is ANAPHORIC to) the *six cooking apples* in the first sentence. This ANAPHORIC function of *them* gives cohesion to the two sentences, so that we interpret them as a whole; the two sentences together constitute a text. Or rather, they form part of the same text; there may be more of it to follow.

The texture is provided by the cohesive RELATION that exists between *them* and *six cooking apples*. It is important to make this point, because we shall be constantly focusing attention on the items, such as *them*, which typically refer back to something that has gone before; but the cohesion is effected not by the presence of the referring item alone but by the presence of both the referring item and the item that it refers to. In other words, it is not enough that there should be a presupposition; the presupposition must also be satisfied. This accounts for the humorous effect produced by the radio comedian who began his act with the sentence

[1:2] So we pushed him under the other one.

This sentence is loaded with presuppositions, located in the words *so*, *him*, *other* and *one*, and, since it was the opening sentence, none of them could be resolved.

What is the MEANING of the cohesive relation between *them* and *six cooking apples?* The meaning is that they refer to the same thing. The two items are identical in reference, or COREFERENTIAL. The cohesive agency in this instance, that which provides the texture, is the coreferentiality of *them* and *six cooking apples*. The signal, or the expression, of this coreferentiality is the presence of the potentially anaphoric item *them* in the second sentence together with a potential target item *six cooking apples* in the first.

Identity of reference is not the only meaning relation that contributes to texture; there are others besides. Nor is the use of a pronoun the only way of expressing identity of reference. We could have had:

[1:3] Wash and core six cooking apples. Put the apples into a fireproof dish.

Here the item functioning cohesively is *the apples*, which works by repetition of the word *apples* accompanied by *the* as an anaphoric signal. One of the functions of the definite article is to signal identity of reference with something that has gone before. (Since this has sometimes been said to be its only function, we should perhaps point out that it has others as well, which are not cohesive at all; for example none of the instances in (a) or (b) has an anaphoric sense:

[1:4] a. None but the brave deserve the fair.
  b. The pain in my head cannot stifle the pain in my heart.

For the meaning of *the*, see 2.4.2 below.)

1.1.3 Ties

We need a term to refer to a single instance of cohesion, a term for one occurrence of a pair of cohesively related items. This we shall call a TIE. The relation between *them* and *six cooking apples* in example [1:1] constitutes a tie.

We can characterize any segment of a text in terms of the number and kinds of ties which it displays. In [1:1] there is just one tie, of the particular kind which we shall be calling REFERENCE (Chapter 2). In [1:3], there are actually two ties, of which one is of the 'reference' kind, and consists in the anaphoric relation of *the* to *six cooking apples*, while the other is of a different kind and consists in the REPETITION of the word *apples*, a repetition which would still have a cohesive effect even if the two were not referring to the same apples. This latter type of cohesion is discussed in Chapter 6.

The concept of a tie makes it possible to analyse a text in terms of its cohesive properties, and give a systematic account of its patterns of texture. Some specimen analyses are given in Chapter 8. Various types of question can be investigated in this way, for example concerning the difference between speech and writing, the relationship between cohesion and the organization of written texts into sentences and paragraphs, and the possible differences among different genres and different authors in the numbers and kinds of tie they typically employ.

The different kinds of cohesive tie provide the main chapter divisions of the book. They are: reference, substitution, ellipsis, conjunction, and lexical cohesion. A preliminary definition of these categories is given later in the Introduction (1.2.4); each of these concepts is then discussed more fully in the chapter in question.

1.1.4 Cohesion

The concept of cohesion is a semantic one; it refers to relations of meaning that exist within the text, and that define it as a text.

Cohesion occurs where the INTERPRETATION of some element in the discourse is dependent on that of another. The one PRESUPPOSES the other, in the sense that it cannot be effectively decoded except by recourse to it. When this happens, a relation of cohesion is set up, and the two elements, the presupposing and the presupposed, are thereby at least potentially integrated into a text.

This is another way of approaching the notion of a tie. To return to example [1:1], the word *them* presupposes for its interpretation something other than itself. This requirement is met by the *six cooking apples* in the preceding sentence. The presupposition, and the fact that it is resolved, provide cohesion between the two sentences, and in so doing create text.

As another example, consider the old piece of schoolboy humour:

[1:5] Time flies.
    – You can't; they fly too quickly.

The first sentence gives no indication of not being a complete text; in fact it usually is, and the humour lies in the misinterpretation that is required if the presupposition from the second sentence is to be satisfied. Here, incidentally, the cohesion is expressed in no less than three ties: the elliptical form *you can't* (Chapter 4), the reference item *they* (Chapter 2) and the lexical repetition *fly* (Chapter 6).

Cohesion is part of the system of a language. The potential for cohesion lies in the systematic resources of reference, ellipsis and so on that are built into the language itself. The actualization of cohesion in any given instance, however, depends not merely on the selection of some option from within these resources, but also on the presence of some other element which resolves the presupposition that this sets up. It is obvious that the selection of the word *apples* has no cohesive force by itself; a cohesive relation is set up only if the same word, or a word related to it such as *fruit* (see Chapter 6), has occurred previously. It is less obvious, but equally true, that the word *them* has no cohesive force either unless there is some explicit referent for it within reach. In both instances, the cohesion lies in the relation that is set up between the two.

Like other semantic relations, cohesion is expressed through the stratal organization of language. Language can be explained as a multiple coding system comprising three levels of coding, or 'strata': the semantic (meanings), the lexicogrammatical (forms) and the phonological and orthographic (expressions). Meanings are realized (coded) as forms, and forms are realized in turn (recoded) as expressions. To put this in everyday terminology, meaning is put into wording, and wording into sound or writing:

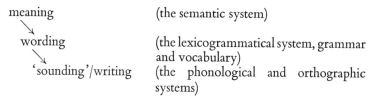

meaning	(the semantic system)
wording	(the lexicogrammatical system, grammar and vocabulary)
'sounding'/writing	(the phonological and orthographic systems)

The popular term 'wording' refers to lexicogrammatical form, the choice of words and grammatical structures. Within this stratum, there is no hard-and-fast division between vocabulary and grammar; the guiding principle in language is that the more general meanings are expressed through the grammar, and the more specific meanings through the vocabulary. Cohesive relations fit into the same overall pattern. Cohesion is expressed partly through the grammar and partly through the vocabulary.

We can refer therefore to GRAMMATICAL COHESION and LEXICAL COHESION. In example [1:3], one of the ties was grammatical (reference, expressed by *the*), the other lexical (reiteration, expressed by *apples*). The types of cohesion dealt with in Chapters 2–4 (reference, substitution and ellipsis) are grammatical; that in Chapter 6 is lexical. That dealt with in Chapter 5 (conjunction) is on the borderline of the two; mainly grammatical, but with a lexical component in it. The distinction between grammatical and lexical is really only one of degree, and we need not make too much of it here. It is important to stress, however, that when we talk of cohesion as being 'grammatical or lexical', we do not imply that it is a purely formal relation, in which meaning is not involved. Cohesion is a semantic relation. But, like all components of the semantic system, it is realized through the lexicogrammatical system; and it is at this point that the distinction can be drawn. Some forms of cohesion are realized through the grammar and others through the vocabulary.

We might add as a footnote here that certain types of grammatical cohesion are in their turn expressed through the intonation system, in spoken English. For example, in

[1:6] Did I hurt your feelings? I didn't mean to.

the second sentence coheres not only by ellipsis, with *I didn't mean to* presupposing *hurt your feelings*, but also by conjunction, the adversative meaning 'but' being expressed by the tone. Phonologically this would be:

//.2. did I / hurt your / FEELINGS // 4 ∧ I / didn't / MEAN / to //

the second sentence having the rising-falling tone 4. For an explanation of the intonation system, see section 5.4 and the references cited there.

1.2 Cohesion and linguistic structure

1.2.1 Texture and structure

A text, as we have said, is not a structural unit; and cohesion, in the sense in which we are using the term, is not a structural relation. Whatever relation there is among the parts of a text – the sentences, or paragraphs, or turns in a dialogue – it is not the same as structure in the usual sense, the relation which links the parts of a sentence or a clause.

Structure is, of course, a unifying relation. The parts of a sentence or a clause obviously 'cohere' with each other, by virtue of the structure. Hence they also display texture; the elements of any structure have, by definition, an internal unity which ensures that they all express part of a text. One cannot change text in mid-sentence, so to speak; or rather, if one does, there will always be a break in the structure, with something being interpolated which is not structurally a part of the same sentence, as in Hamlet's

[1:7] Then I will come to my mother by and by –
      they fool me to the top of my bent – I will come by and by.

or, more conversationally,

[1:8] . . . But what I want to know is – yes, some ice, please – what this government think they're doing when they spend all that money on building new schools. What's wrong with the old ones?

In general, any unit which is structured hangs together so as to form text. All grammatical units – sentences, clauses, groups, words – are internally 'cohesive' simply because they are structured. The same applies to the phonological units, the tone group, foot and syllable. Structure is one means of expressing texture.

If every text consisted of only one sentence, we should not need to go beyond the category of structure to explain the internal cohesiveness of a text: this could be explained simply as a function of its structure. But texts are usually not limited to one sentence; on the contrary, texts consisting of one sentence only are fairly rare. They do exist; there are public notices, proverbs, advertising slogans and the like, where one sentence by itself comprises a complete text, for example

[1:9] a. No smoking.
     b. Wonders never cease!
     c. Read The Herald every day.

But most texts extend well beyond the confines of a single sentence.

In other words, a text typically extends beyond the range of structural relations, as these are normally conceived of. But texts cohere; so cohesion within a text – texture – depends on something other than structure. There are certain specifically text-forming relations which cannot be accounted for in terms of constituent structure; they are properties of the text as such, and not of any structural unit such as a clause or sentence. Our use of the term COHESION refers specifically to these non-structural text-forming relations. They are, as we have suggested, semantic relations, and the text is a semantic unit.

1.2.2 Cohesion within the sentence?

Since cohesive relations are not concerned with structure, they may be found just as well within a sentence as between sentences. They attract less notice within a sentence, because of the cohesive strength of grammatical structure; since the sentence hangs together already, the cohesion is not needed in order to make it hang together. But the cohesive relations are there all the same. For example

> [1:10] If you happen to meet the admiral, don't tell him his ship's gone down.

Here the *him* and *his* in the second half have to be decoded by reference to *the admiral*, just as they would have had to be if there had been a sentence boundary in between. Similarly:

> [1:11] Mary promised to send a picture of the children, but she hasn't done.

Here *done* equals *sent a picture of the children*, and it is quite irrelevant to this whether the two are in the same sentence or not.

Cohesive relations have in principle nothing to do with sentence boundaries. Cohesion is a semantic relation between an element in the text and some other element that is crucial to the interpretation of it. This other element is also to be found in the text (*cf* 1.2.4 below); but its location in the text is in no way determined by the grammatical structure. The two elements, the presupposing and the presupposed, may be structurally related to each other, or they may not; it makes no difference to the meaning of the cohesive relation.

However, there is a sense in which the sentence is a significant unit for cohesion precisely because it is the highest unit of grammatical structure: it tends to determine the way in which cohesion is EXPRESSED. For example, if the same entity is referred to twice within the same sentence, there are rules governing the form of its realization. These are the rules of pronominalization. It is the sentence structure which determines, within limits, whether at the second mention the entity will be named again or will be referred to by a pronoun. For example, we cannot say

> [1:12] John took John's hat off and hung John's hat on a peg.

Assuming that there is only one 'John' here, and only one 'hat', then this identity of reference must be expressed by the use of pronominal forms: *John took his hat off and hung it on a peg.*

This sort of thing can be accounted for by reference to sentence structure; the relation between an item and another one that presupposes it could be explained as a structural relation. In the preceding sentence, for example, the words *one* and *it* both, in different ways, presuppose the word *item*; and this presupposition could be incorporated into the structure of the sentence. But this would be misleading. Only certain instances of cohesion could be treated structurally, and only when the two items, the presupposing and the presupposed, happened to occur within the same sentence. But, as we have seen, the question whether the two fall within the same sentence or not is irrelevant to the nature of the cohesive relation; cohesion is a more general notion, and one that is above considerations of structure.

Moreover only certain kinds of cohesive relation are governed by such rules; mainly those involving identity of reference, which under certain conditions must be signalled by a reference item (Chapter 2). Cohesion that is expressed through substitution and ellipsis (Chapters 3 and 4) is unaffected by the sentence structure; and so is lexical cohesion (Chapter 6). In the case of conjunction (Chapter 5), there are special forms to express the various conjunctive relations where these are associated with grammatical structure; compare [1:13a], which is non-structural, with its structural counterpart [1:13b]:

[1:13] a. It's raining. – Then let's stay at home.
       b. Since it's raining, let's stay at home.

Regardless of the presence or absence of a structural link, the semantic relation that provides cohesion, namely that of cause, is the same in both.

For these reasons cohesion within the sentence need not be regarded as essentially a distinct phenomenon. Cohesion is a general text-forming relation, or set of such relations, certain of which, when incorporated within a sentence structure, are subject to certain restrictions – no doubt because the grammatical condition of 'being a sentence' ensures that the parts go together to form a text anyway. But the cohesive relations themselves are the same whether their elements are within the same sentence or not.

As a general rule, the examples cited in this book will be of cohesion across sentence boundaries, since here the effect is more striking and the meaning is more obvious: cohesive ties between sentences stand out more clearly because they are the ONLY source of texture, whereas within the sentence there are the structural relations as well. In the description of a text, it is the intersentence cohesion that is significant, because that represents the variable aspect of cohesion, distinguishing one text from another. But this should not obscure the fact that cohesion is not, strictly speaking, a relation 'above the sentence'. It is a relation to which the sentence, or any other form of grammatical structure, is simply irrelevant.

1.2.3 Cohesion and discourse structure

It will be clear from what has been said above that cohesion is not just another name for discourse structure. Discourse structure is, as the name implies, a type of structure; the term is used to refer to the structure of some postulated unit higher than the sentence, for example the paragraph, or some larger entity such as episode or topic unit.

The concept of cohesion is set up to account for relations in discourse, but in rather a different way, without the implication that there is some structural unit that is above the sentence. Cohesion refers to the range of possibilities that exist for linking something with what has gone before. Since this linking is achieved through relations in MEANING (we are excluding from consideration the effects of formal devices such as syntactic parallelism, metre and rhyme), what is in question is the set of meaning relations which function in this way: the semantic resources which are drawn on for the purpose of creating text. And since, as we have stressed, it is the sentence that is the pivotal entity here – whatever is put together within one sentence is *ipso facto* part of a text – we can interpret cohesion, in practice, as the set of semantic resources for linking a SENTENCE with what has gone before.

This is not to rule out the possibility of setting up discourse structures, and specifying the structure of some entity such as a paragraph or topic unit. It is clear that there is structure here, at least in certain genres or registers of discourse. But it is doubtful whether it is possible to demonstrate generalized structural relationships into which sentences enter as the realization of functions in some higher unit, as can be done for all units below the sentence. The type of relation into which sentences enter with each other differs from that which holds among the part or sub-parts of a sentence. We cannot show, for example, that there is any functional relation between the two sentences of [1:1] above, such that the two form a configuration of mutually defining structural roles. (It may on the other hand be possible to show something of the kind precisely by invoking the concept of cohesion; *cf* Chapter 5.) Whereas within the sentence, or any similar unit, we can specify a limited number of possible structures, such as types of modification or subordination, transitivity or modal structures and the like, which define the relations among the parts, we cannot in the same way list a set of possible structures for a text, with sentence classes to fill the structural roles. Instead we have to show how sentences, which are structurally independent of one another, may be linked together through particular features of their interpretation; and it is for this that the concept of cohesion is required.

1.2.4 *Cohesion as a semantic relation*

To say that two sentences cohere by virtue of relations in their meaning is not by itself very precise. Practically any two sentences might be shown to have something to do with each other as far as their meaning is concerned; and although in judging whether there is texture or not we certainly have recourse to some feeling about how much the sentences do actually interrelate in meaning, we could not give any very explicit account of the degree of relatedness that is needed or how it is to be measured.

But there is one specific kind of meaning relation that is critical for the creation of texture: that in which ONE ELEMENT IS INTERPRETED BY REFERENCE TO ANOTHER. What cohesion has to do with is the way in which the meaning of the elements is interpreted. Where the interpretation of any item in the discourse requires making reference to some other item in the discourse, there is cohesion.

Consider the example

[1:14] He said so.

This sentence is perfectly intelligible as it stands; we know what it means, in the sense that we can 'decode' it semantically. But it is UNINTERPRETABLE, because we do not know who 'he' is or what he said. For this we have to refer elsewhere, to its 'context' in the sense of what has gone before.

Now it is also true that, given just the sentence

[1:15] John said everything.

we do not know who 'John' is, or what he said, either. But there is an important difference between examples [1:14] and [1:15]. In [1:14], the items *he* and *so* contain in their meaning an explicit signal that the means of their interpretation is available somewhere in the environment. Hearing or reading this sentence, we know that it links up with some other passage in which there is an indication of who 'he' is and what he said. This is not the case with *John* or *everything*, neither of which necessarily presupposes any such source of further interpretation.

We now come to the more complex part of the picture. It is easy enough to show that *he* and *so* are cohesive; there is no means of interpreting them in their own right, and we are immediately aware of the need to recover an interpretation from elsewhere. There are systematically related questions which express this: *Who said so? What did he say?* By the same token we can readily recognize the cohesive effect of a sentence such as:

[1:16] Lying on the floor.

Here there is no explicit signal of presupposition, in the form of a word like *he* or *so*; the cohesion is provided by what is left out, and again we can ask the relevant question *Who is?* Notice however that there is now some ambiguity as regards the information to be supplied; the actual text might have been

> [1:17] What was John doing when you came in?
>   Lying on the floor.

in which case *lying* would have to be interpreted as *was lying* not *is lying*. And there are still further possibilities as illustrated by:

> [1:18] What is your favourite pastime?
>   Lying on the floor.

These show that cohesion is a relational concept; it is not the presence of a particular class of item that is cohesive, but the relation between one item and another.

This point emerges very clearly with another type of cohesion, which would otherwise be difficult to explain. We said with reference to example [1:15] that there is nothing presupposing about the item *John*; the sentence *John said everything* does not in itself confer the automatic right to ask for an interpretation of *John*, as *he said everything* does with regard to *he*. But we may have a sequence such as:

> [1:19] I was introduced to them; it was John Leathwall and his wife. I
>   had never met John before, but I had heard a lot about him and
>   had some idea what to expect.

Here *John* does have a cohesive function – because it is reiterated. This form of cohesion is lexical (Chapter 6); it consists in selecting the same lexical item twice, or selecting two that are closely related. The two instances may or may not have the same referent; but the interpretation of the second will be referable in some way to that of the first. Compare what was said about example [1:3] above. Another example would be:

> [1:20] Jan sat down to rest at the foot of a huge beech-tree. Now he was
>   so tired that he soon fell asleep; and a leaf fell on him, and then
>   another, and then another, and before long he was covered all
>   over with leaves, yellow, golden and brown.

Here *leaf* ties with *beech-tree*. The two are clearly not identical in reference, since *tree* and *leaf* are not synonymous; but the interpretation of *leaf* depends on *beech-tree* – we 'know' that the leaf was a beech-leaf, and if the sentence had continued *before long he was covered all over with oak-leaves* we should have rejected it as a mistake. This illustrates the force of cohesion; and it also illustrates the fact that cohesion depends not on the presence of explicitly anaphoric items like *so* and *he*, but on the establishment of a semantic relation which may take any one of various forms.

One other form it may take is that of conjunction, expressed by means of items such as *but, later on, in that case* (Chapter 5). Here the cohesion resides in an abstract relation between one proposition and another. This may be a matter of the CONTENT of the propositions, how they are related to each other as phenomena; for example

[1:21] First, he took a piece of string and tied it carefully round the neck of the bottle. Next, he passed the other end over a branch and weighted it down with a stone.

Or it may be a matter of their role in the discourse, how they are related in the perspective of the speaker or writer, for example

[1:22] First, he has no experience of this kind of work. Next, he showed no sign of being willing to learn.

Here *next* refers to succession in the argument, not to any sequence of events in time. A very large number of different words and phrases occur as expressions of conjunction; but they all fall into a few sets representing very general types of logical relation.

Thus the concept of cohesion accounts for the essential semantic relations whereby any passage of speech or writing is enabled to function as text. We can systematize this concept by classifying it into a small number of distinct categories – reference, substitution, ellipsis, conjunction, and lexical cohesion; categories which have a theoretical basis as distinct TYPES of cohesive relation, but which also provide a practical means for describing and analysing texts. Each of these categories is represented in the text by particular features – repetitions, omissions, occurrences of certain words and constructions – which have in common the property of signalling that the interpretation of the passage in question depends on something else. If that 'something else' is verbally explicit, then there is cohesion. There are, of course, other types of semantic relation associated with a text which are not embodied in this concept; but the one that it does embody is in some ways the most important, since it is common to text of every kind and is, in fact, what makes a text a text.

1.3 Cohesion and linguistic context

1.3.1 The domain of cohesive relations

The simplest form of cohesion is that in which the presupposed element is verbally explicit and is found in the immediately preceding sentence; for example

[1:23] Did the gardener water my hydrangeas?
    – He said so.

We shall treat this as the norm for purposes of illustration and discussion; not only because it is simpler in practice but also because it is, as we have suggested, the paradigm case of cohesion from a theoretical point of view, since the boundary between two sentences represents a minimal break in structural continuity.

There are two kinds of departure from this norm. First, the presupposed element may be located elsewhere, in an earlier sentence, perhaps, or in the following one; secondly, it may not be found in the text at all. Let us consider these in turn.

Cohesion as we have said is not a structural relation; hence it is unrestricted by sentence boundaries, and in its most normal form it is simply the presupposition of something that has gone before, whether in the preceding sentence or not. This form of presupposition, pointing BACK to some previous item, is known as ANAPHORA. What is presupposed anaphorically may be in the sentence immediately preceding, but it may also be in some earlier sentence; in the following example, *he* refers back to *Henry:*

[1:24] The first years of Henry's reign, as recorded by the admiring Hall, were given over to sport and gaiety, though there was little of the licentiousness which characterized the French Court. The athletic contests were serious but very popular. Masques, jousts and spectacles followed one another in endless pageantry. He brought to Greenwich a tremendously vital court life, a central importance in the country's affairs and, above all, a great naval connection.★

Or it may be the whole of some longer passage; here the *such* presupposes everything that precedes:

[1:25] Travelling with huge retinues of staff and servants, medieval monarchs demanded a series of houses to take care of their needs.

★ Olive and Nigel Hamilton, *Royal Greenwich,* The Greenwich Bookshop.

Their requirements were large. Government went where they went – (it was still the King's government) – with all its attendant staff and visitors. They were responsible for a large number of followers, and visitors had to be entertained in style. They were expected to dispense patronage and to entertain on a lavish scale. During the winter festival of Çhristmas, lasting twenty days, they nominally kept open house. Richard II, notoriously prodigal, entertained over ten thousand every day at his palaces, and even more over Christmas.

No single home could possibly cope with the organization and material products needed on such a scale.*

As might be expected, the tendency is different with different types of cohesion. Where the cohesive element is something like *he* or *one*, which coheres by direct reference to, or substitution for, another item, the presupposed element is typically a specific item in the immediately preceding sentence. This is the most usual pattern in the case of reference and substitution. Characteristically these intances also tend to form COHESIVE CHAINS, sequences in which *it*, for example, refers back to the immediately preceding sentence – but to another *it* in that sentence, and it is necessary to go back three, four or more sentences, stepping across a whole sequence of *it*s, before finding the substantial element. An example of this is [1:25] above, which has a cohesive chain *medieval monarchs . . . their . . . they . . . they . . . they . . . they*, leading finally to *Richard II* as a specific instance of a medieval monarch. Here is another example in which three such cohesive chains intertwine, initiated by *Short, Johnson over Jordan* and *Johnson:*

[1:26] Short places *Johnson over Jordan* squarely in the tradition of expressionist drama. He says that Johnson is a 'typical Briton', an 'English Everyman'. He regards the play as an imaginative presentation of the mind of a man who has just died. But, he adds, Priestley is more interested in Johnson living than in Johnson dead. In this the play is expressionist in its approach to theme. But it is also so in its use of unfamiliar devices – the use of masks, the rejection of the three or four act lay-out of the plot. And, finally, he points to the way in which Johnson moves quite freely in and out of chronological time.†

It may be helpful to tabulate the ties forming these three chains:

---

* Olive and Nigel Hamilton, *Royal Greenwich*, The Greenwich Bookshop.

† Gareth Lloyd Evans, *J. B. Priestley – The Dramatist*, Heinemann.

	(i) Short	(ii) *Johnson over Jordan*	(iii) Johnson
Sentence 1:	Short	*Johnson over Jordan*	Johnson (in *J over J*)
Sentence 2:	he	↓	Johnson
Sentence 3:	he	the play	a man who has just died
Sentence 4:	he	↓	Johnson (2×)
Sentence 5:	⏐	the play . . . its	⏐
Sentence 6:	↓	it . . . its	↓
Sentence 7:	he		Johnson

Where the cohesion takes the form of conjunction, with expressions like *but, so, in that case, later on,* the presupposition typically involves a passage longer than a single sentence. This hardly needs illustrating, but here is one example, a passage of Carlyle in which the conjunction *on the other hand* clearly relates to the whole of the preceding paragraph:

[1:27]   How much is still alive in England; how much has not yet come into life! A Feudal Aristocracy is still alive, in the prime of life; superintending the cultivation of the land, and less consciously the distribution of the produce of the land, the adjustment of the quarrels of the land; judging, soldiering, adjusting; everywhere governing the people, – so that even a Gurth, born thrall of Cedric, lacks not his due parings of the pigs he tends. Governing; – and, alas, also game-preserving, so that a Robin Hood, a William Scarlet and others have, in these days, put on Lincoln coats, and taken to living, in some universal-suffrage manner, under the greenwood tree!
   How silent, on the other hand, lie all Cotton-trades and such like; not a steeple-chimney yet got on end from sea to sea!

Lexical cohesion differs again, in that it regularly leaps over a number of sentences to pick up an element that has not figured in the intervening text:

[1:28]   I screamed, and my scream went wafting out on the night air! And some neighbours who – they were my nearest neighbours, but they were still some distance away – came rushing along. They were awfully good, and they said afterwards they thought I'd been being murdered. Well, I couldn't've made more noise if I had been! But I'd surprised myself – really, the sound that

went floating out on the air I didn't know I had it in me, and they said it would make my fortune if I sent it to Hollywood. And I may say it surprised the thief sufficiently that he dropped my handbag and fled. Fortunately I wasn't between him and the door, so there was no harm done and I didn't lose anything.
– Fortunately for him, or fortunately for you?
– Oh, for me; they generally carry knives.
– I know; someone was murdered in the main hotel quite recently.
– Oh yes, yes, although people did say that there were wheels within wheels in that. But you get between a fleeing thief and his exit, and he's bound to be carrying a knife. But anyhow, the only thing I lost was my voice. I couldn't speak for a week afterwards.

Here *lost* (in *lost . . . my voice*) resumes the *lose* (in *didn't lose anything*), the resumption being signalled by the conjunctive item *anyhow*; and *voice* relates back to *scream, noise* and *sound*. Resumptions of this kind can span large passages of intervening text, especially in informal conversation.

So far we have considered cohesion purely as an anaphoric relation, with a presupposing item presupposing something that has gone before it. But the presupposition may go in the opposite direction, with the presupposed element following. This we shall refer to as CATAPHORA.

The distinction only arises if there is an explicitly presupposing item present, whose referent clearly either precedes or follows. If the cohesion is lexical, with the same lexical item occurring twice over, then obviously the second occurrence must take its interpretation from the first; the first can never be said to point forward to the second. If *John* follows *John*, there is no possible contrast between anaphora and cataphora. But an item such as *this* and *here* CAN point forward, deriving its interpretation from something that follows, for example:

[1:29] This is how to get the best results. You let the berries dry in the sun, till all the moisture has gone out of them. Then you gather them up and chop them very fine.

The presupposed element may, and often does, consist of more than one sentence. Where it does not, the cataphoric reference is often signalled in writing with a colon: but although this has the effect of uniting the two parts into a single orthographic sentence, it does not imply any kind of structural relation between them. The colon is used solely to signal the cataphora, this being one of its principal functions.

There remains one further possibility, namely that the information required for interpreting some element in the text is not to be found in the text at all, but in the situation. For example, given

[1:30] Did the gardener water those plants?

it is quite possible that *those* refers back to the preceding text, to some earlier mention of those particular plants in the discussion. But it is also possible that it refers to the environment in which the dialogue is taking place – to the 'context of situation', as it is called – where the plants in question are present and can be pointed to if necessary. The interpretation would be 'those plants there, in front of us'.

This type of reference we shall call EXOPHORA, since it takes us outside the text altogether. Exophoric reference is not cohesive, since it does not bind the two elements together into a text. One might reason that, metaphorically speaking, the plants form part of the text; but this seems rather pointless, because there could be no significant contrast here between the presence of cohesion and its absence – one would have to assume that, in the absence of cohesive reference to them, the plants would have comprised a text on their own. But exophora is of interest at several points in the discussion, particularly with reference to the definite article as a text-forming agent, and it will be brought up where relevant.

The line between exophoric and anaphoric reference is not always very sharp. In dramatic dialogue, for example, the mere presence or absence of a stage direction would change the picture, *eg*

[1:31]   How sweet the moonlight sleeps upon this bank!
         Here will we sit, and let the sound of music
         Creep in our ears.

If the stage directions specify something like 'a grassy bank', then for the reader *this* and *here* become anaphoric; otherwise, they were exophoric. The significance of the exophoric potential is that, in instances where the key to the interpretation is not ready to hand, in text or situation, the hearer or reader CONSTRUCTS a context of situation in order to supply it for himself. So we supply the grassy bank in our imagination, and the producer need not put one on the stage. This is an essential element in all imaginative writing.

It may be helpful here to draw attention to the distinction between cohesion as a relation in the system, and cohesion as a process in the text. 'Cohesion' is defined as the set of possibilities that exist in the language for making text hang together: the potential that the speaker or writer has at his disposal. This is a purely relational concept, and directionality comes into it only if one of the elements in the cohesive relation is BY ITS NATURE cohesive, in that it is inherently 'pointing to' something else; in this case there is a logical dependence, and hence a significant opposition IN THE SYSTEM between pointing back (anaphora) and pointing forwards (cataphora). But cohesion is also a process, in the sense that it is the instantiation of this relation in a text. A text unfolds in real time, and directionality is built into it; hence of the two elements embodying the cohesive relation, one always follows the other.

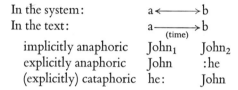

In the system:	a ⟷ b	
In the text:	a ⟶ b (time)	
implicitly anaphoric	John₁	John₂
explicitly anaphoric	John	:he
(explicitly) cataphoric	he:	John

In the text it is natural for the element occurring second to depend for its interpretation on the one occurring first; hence, anaphora is the unmarked and cataphora is the marked term in the opposition. Cataphora occurs only as an EXPLICIT relation, with the first element always being one that is inherently presupposing. Thus cohesion as a process always involves one item pointing to another; whereas the significant property of the cohesive relation, as we have stressed above, is the fact that one item provides the source for the interpretation of another.

1.3.2 Text and situation

We should now say a little more about the nature of a text, and its relation to a context of situation. Let us begin with an example:

[1:32]   Although the light was on he went to sleep. Although the house was unfurnished the rent was very high. Although he was paid a high salary he refused to stay in the job.

These three sentences clearly have something in common; they are not just three sentences picked at random from a corpus of written English. What they have in common is a certain degree of grammatical similarity: parallel structures, with repetition of the item *although*. They could, however, be written in any other sequence without disturbing the organization of the passage as a whole, such as it is; whatever it is that gives unity to this 'text' it does not depend on the order in which the sentences are arranged.

This sort of grammatical parallelism is not irrelevant to internal cohesion; it is a common feature not only of poetry but of many other kinds of discourse as well. But by itself it does not make a string of sentences into a text. The sentences in [1:32] could be said to form a text, but if so it is a text of a very special kind: a text about language, in which the sentences are CITATION FORMS – that is, items introduced for the purpose of saying something about them. A set of citation forms that are related ONLY by their grammatical parallelism is a familiar feature of texts about language; and [1:32] is in fact taken from a textbook of Chinese for English-speaking students. The sentences in it, together with their Chinese equivalents, form part of a drill.

The passage illustrates, in an extreme form, a general principle concerning decisions about what is and what is not a text. We do not, in fact, evaluate any specimen of language – and deciding whether it does or does not constitute text is a prerequisite to any further evaluation of it – without knowing something about its context of situation. It is the context of situation of this passage, the fact that it is part of a language textbook, that enables us to accept it as text. A set of sentences that in any other environment would not constitute a text is admissible as such in the restricted context of a book about language. Since the present book will be full of citation forms we need not discuss them further here; the effect of their occurrence in a situation to which they are inappropriate can be seen in Ionesco's play *The Bald-headed Primadonna*. But they illustrate the general principle that the hearer or reader, when he is determining, consciously or unconsciously, the status of a specimen of language, invokes two kinds of evidence, the external as well as the internal: he uses not only linguistic clues but also situational ones. Linguistically, he responds to specific features which bind the passage together, the patterns of connection, independent of structure, that we are referring to as cohesion. Situationally, he takes into account all he knows of the environment: what is going on, what part the language is playing, and who are involved.

The internal and the external aspects of 'texture' are not wholly separable, and the reader, or listener, does not separate them when responding unconsciously to a passage of speech or writing. But when the linguist seeks to make explicit the basis on which these judgments are formed, he is bound to make observations of two rather different kinds. The one concerns relations within the language, patterns of meaning realized by grammar and vocabulary; the other concerns the relations BETWEEN the language and the relevant features of the speaker's and hearer's (or writer's and reader's) material, social and ideological environment. Both these aspects of a text fall within the domain of linguistics. The linguistic patterns, which embody, and at the same time also impose structure on, our experience of the environment, by the same token also make it possible to identify what features of the environment are relevant to linguistic behaviour and so form part of the context of situation. But there are two sets of phenomena here, and in this book we are concerned with the LINGUISTIC factors that are characteristic of texts in English. The situational properties of texts, which are now beginning to be studied in greater detail and with greater understanding, constitute a vast field of enquiry which lies outside our scope here. Some of the factors of most immediate relevance are summarized in the paragraphs that follow.

The term SITUATION, meaning the 'context of situation' in which a text is embedded, refers to all those extra-linguistic factors which have some bearing on the text itself. A word of caution is needed about this concept. At the moment, as the text of this Introduction is being composed, it is a typical English October day in Palo Alto, California; a green hillside is visible outside the window, the sky is grey, and it is pouring with rain. This might seem part of the 'situation' of this text; but it is not, because it has no relevance to the meanings expressed, or to the words or grammatical patterns that are used to express them. The question is, what are the external factors affecting the linguistic choices that the speaker or writer makes. These are likely to be the nature of the audience, the medium, the purpose of the communication and so on. There are types of discourse in which the state of the weather would form part of the context of situation, for example, language-in-action in mountaineering or sailing; but writing a book about language is not one of them.

As a rule, the features of the situation are relevant at a rather general level. That is to say, if we think of the example of a lecture on current affairs to an adult evening class, what matters is not that it is John Smith talking to Messrs Jones, Robinson, Brown and others on a particular Tuesday evening in Burnley, but that it is a lecturer addressing a gathering of adult students within the framework of a given social institution. This is not to deny either the individual characteristics of speakers or writers or the importance of studying the distinctive quality of a particular author's style. It is merely to emphasize that many of the features of a text can be explained by reference to generalized situation types.

1.3.3 Components of the context of situation, and register

The concept of CONTEXT OF SITUATION was formulated by Malinowski in 1923, in his supplement to Ogden and Richards' *The Meaning of*

Meaning, and subsequently elaborated by Firth, particularly in a paper written in 1950 called 'Personality and language in society'. It has been worked over and extended by a number of linguists, the best-known treatment being perhaps that of Hymes in 'Models of interaction of language and social setting'. Hymes categorizes the speech situation in terms of eight components which we may summarize as: form and content of text, setting, participants, ends (intent and effect), key, medium, genre and interactional norms. It will be noted that, in this view of the matter, the text itself forms part of the speech situation.

A more abstract interpretation, intended as a basis for DERIVING the features of the text from the features of the situation, had been offered by Halliday, McIntosh and Strevens in *The Linguistic Sciences and Language Teaching*. They had proposed the three headings FIELD, MODE, and TENOR (to adopt the terminology preferred by Spencer and Gregory in *Linguistics and Style*). These are highly general concepts for describing how the context of situation determines the kinds of meaning that are expressed. The FIELD is the total event, in which the text is functioning, together with the purposive activity of the speaker or writer; it thus includes the subject-matter as one element in it. The MODE is the function of the text in the event, including therefore both the channel taken by the language – spoken or written, extempore or prepared – and its genre, or rhetorical mode, as narrative, didactic, persuasive, 'phatic communion' and so on. The TENOR refers to the type of role interaction, the set of relevant social relations, permanent and temporary, among the participants involved. Field, mode and tenor collectively define the context of situation of a text (see the further discussion in Halliday's *Language and Social Man*).

The linguistic features which are typically associated with a configuration of situational features – with particular values of the field, mode and tenor – constitute a REGISTER. The more specifically we can characterize the context of situation, the more specifically we can predict the properties of a text in that situation. If we merely name the subject-matter, or the medium, it will tell us very little; we could talk of a 'register of marine biology' or a 'newspaper register', but this hardly enables us to say anything of interest about the types of text in question. But if we give some information about all three categories of field, mode, and tenor, we begin to be able to make some useful observations. For instance, if we specify a field such as 'personal interaction, at the end of the day, with aim of inducing contentment through recounting of familiar events', with mode 'spoken monologue, imaginative narrative, extempore' and tenor 'intimate, mother and three-year-old child', we can reconstruct a great deal of the language of this kind of bedtime story, especially if we go further and describe the CONTEXT OF CULTURE (another of Malinowski's concepts) which will tell us, among other things, what are the familiar events in the life of a child with the given socio-cultural background. The register is the set of meanings, the configuration of semantic patterns, that are typically drawn upon under the specified conditions, along with the words and structures that are used in the realization of these meanings. The fact that we can say of any given text, with some assurance, whether or not it satisfies a description of the context of situation such as the one just given, shows how real the notion of register is.

In general, if a passage hangs together as a text, it will display a consistency of register. In other words, the texture involves more than the presence of semantic relations of the kind we refer to as cohesive, the dependence of one element on another for its interpretation. It involves also some degree of coherence in the actual meanings expressed: not only, or even mainly, in the CONTENT, but in the TOTAL selection from the semantic resources of the language, including the various interpersonal (social-expressive-conative) components – the moods, modalities, intensities, and other forms of the speaker's intrusion into the speech situation.

The concept of COHESION can therefore be usefully supplemented by that of REGISTER, since the two together effectively define a TEXT. A text is a passage of discourse which is coherent in these two regards: it is coherent with respect to the context of situation, and therefore consistent in register; and it is coherent with respect to itself, and therefore cohesive. Neither of these two conditions is sufficient without the other, nor does the one by necessity entail the other. Just as one can construct passages which seem to hang together in the situational-semantic sense, but fail as texts because they lack cohesion, so also one can construct passages which are beautifully cohesive but which fail as texts because they lack consistency of register – there is no continuity of meaning in relation to the situation. The hearer, or reader, reacts to both of these things in his judgment of texture.

Under normal circumstances, of course, we do not find ourselves faced with 'non-text', which is 'non-sense' of a rather esoteric kind. Texture is a matter of degree. It is almost impossible to construct a verbal sequence which has no texture at all – but this, in turn, is largely because we insist on interpreting any passage as text if there is the remotest possibility of doing so. We assume, in other words, that this is what language is for; whatever its specific function may be in the particular instance, it can serve this function only under the guise of text. If one can imagine a situation in which someone is faced with a string of words picked at random from a dictionary, but which has been made to look or sound as if it was structured, then it is safe to predict that he will go to great lengths to interpret it as text, and as related to some accessible features of the situation. The nearest we get to non-text in actual life, leaving aside the works of those poets and prose writers who deliberately set out to create non-text, is probably in the speech of young children and in bad translations.

Two further points are worth making, in connection with the text and its context of situation. One is that the relation of text to situation is very variable, in terms of the relative weight which the text has to bear. There are certain types of situation in which the non-linguistic factors clearly dominate and the language plays an ancillary role: for example, a non-verbal game, like football, in which there are a few verbal instructions from player to player; or joint operations on objects, building, assembling, cooking, cleaning and the like. Here it is impossible to interpret what is said or written without situational information; one must know what is going on. At the other end of the scale are types of activity in which the language is the whole story, as in most formal or informal discussion on abstract themes, such as those of business, politics and intellectual life. Here the language may be totally self-sufficient and any relevant situational factors are derivable from the language itself. The quality of texture, and the forms of cohesion which provide it, differ very much as between these two poles. One question on which a great deal of further study is needed is the relation between texture and situation type: the different ways in which texts of different kinds are constructed so as to form semantic wholes.

The second point concerns what Ellis calls DELICACY OF FOCUS in situational analysis. We obviously cannot draw a clear line between 'the same situation' and 'different situations'; any two contexts of situation will be alike in some respects and not in others, and the amount of detail needed to characterize the situation will vary according to what we are interested in – what distinctions we are trying to make between one instance and another, what features of the text we are trying to explain and so on. Questions like 'are these two texts in the same register?' are in themselves meaningless; we can only ask in what respects the texts, and the situations, are alike and in what respects they differ. If a child turns around from talking to his father and starts talking to his uncle, we are not called on to decide whether the situation has changed or not; but we shall be interested to note whether there are linguistic signals of the difference in personal relationships. This affects our notion of a text. Up to now we have been discussing this on the assumption of an all-or-nothing view of texture: either a passage forms text, or it does not. In real life we so seldom meet non-text that we can afford to adopt such a deterministic view: we are not required in practice to decide where a text begins and ends. But in fact there are degrees of texture, and if we are examining language from this point of view, especially spoken language, we shall at times be uncertain as to whether a particular point marks a continuation of the same text or the beginning of a new one. This is because texture is really a 'more-or-less' affair. A partial shift in the context of situation – say a shift in one situational factor, in the field of discourse or in the mode or tenor – is likely to be reflected in some way in the texture of the discourse, without destroying completely the continuity with what has gone before.

It is worth pointing out in this connection that continuity of subject-matter is neither a necessary nor a sufficient condition for the creation of texture. Subject-matter is neither more nor less important than other features of the context of situation as a determinant of text; it is simply one of the factors that enters into the picture. And where there is continuity of subject-matter within a text, as we typically find it, the texture is not necessarily the result of this ; the following example is about mathematics, but cohesion is provided, especially in the last sentence, more by the lexical patterns of *complicated . . . difficult . . . easy* and *greater time . . . long . . . short* than by any linking of specifically mathematical concepts:

> [1:33] Throughout the long history of mathematics, men have always wished that they could calculate more quickly. As each mathematical discovery was made and knowledge advanced a little the calculations facing mathematicians became more and more complicated and demanded an even greater time. There are some people who like doing long and difficult arithmetic, but most of us do not and are eager to finish our sums in the shortest and easiest way.*

A text, then, can be thought of as the basic unit of meaning in language. It is to semantic structure what the sentence is to lexicogrammatical structure and the syllable to phonological structure. It is a unit of situational-semantic organization: a continuum of meaning-in-context, constructed around the semantic relation of cohesion. According to the particular situational-semantic configuration, or REGISTER, of the text, so the forms taken by the cohesive relation will differ: texture in informal conversation

---

* F. B. Lovis, *Computers I* (Contemporary School Mathematics, First Series), Edward Arnold.

is quite unlike that in formal written language, which is one reason why the former looks strange when written down and the latter sounds odd when read aloud. A text therefore normally has continuity of register; it 'fits' a given set of situational features, a pattern formed by the nature of the communicative event (field), the place assigned to language acts within the event (mode) and the role-relationships of those who are participating (tenor). This fit does not by itself ensure the kind of continuity we associate with texts; we often feel, in looking at children's writing for example, that it OUGHT to hang together precisely because it is making sense in the situation, but in fact it does not. This reveals the existence of the other aspect of texture, which is cohesion. The meaning relations which constitute cohesion are a property of text as such, and hence they are general to texts of all types, however much they may differ in the particular form they take in one text or another.

Texture results from the combination of semantic configurations of two kinds: those of register, and those of cohesion. The register is the set of semantic configurations that is typically associated with a particular CLASS of contexts of situation, and defines the substance of the text: WHAT IT MEANS, in the broadest sense, including all the components of its meaning, social, expressive, communicative and so on as well as representational (see 1.3.4 below). Cohesion is the set of meaning relations that is general to ALL CLASSES of text, that distinguishes text from 'non-text' and interrelates the substantive meanings of the text with each other. Cohesion does not concern what a text means; it concerns how the text is constructed as a semantic edifice.

1.3.4 *The place of cohesion in the linguistic system*

Table 1 summarizes the main components in the linguistic system, show- · ing where cohesion comes in relation to the rest.

There are three major functional-semantic components, the IDEA-TIONAL, the INTERPERSONAL and the TEXTUAL. The IDEATIONAL component is that part of the linguistic system which is concerned with the expression of 'content', with the function that language has of being ABOUT something. It has two parts to it, the experiential and the logical, the former being more directly concerned with the representation of experience, of the 'context of culture' in Malinowski's terms, while the latter expresses the abstract logical relations which derive only indirectly from experience. The INTERPERSONAL component is concerned with the social, expressive and conative functions of language, with expressing the speaker's 'angle': his attitudes and judgments, his encoding of the role relationships in the situation, and his motive in saying anything at all. We can summarize these by saying that the ideational component represents the speaker in his role as observer, while the interpersonal component represents the speaker in his role as intruder.

There is a third component, the TEXTUAL, which is the text-forming component in the linguistic system. This comprises the resources that language has for creating text, in the same sense in which we have been using the term all along: for being operationally relevant, and cohering within itself and with the context of situation.

In part, the textual component operates like the other two, through systems associated with particular ranks in the grammar (see 7.4.1 below). For example, every clause makes a selection in the system of THEME, a selection which conveys the speaker's organization of the clause as a message and which is expressed through the normal mechanisms of clause structure. But the textual component also incorporates patterns of meaning which are realized outside the hierarchical organization of the system. One of these is INFORMATION structure, which is the ordering of the text, independently of its construction in terms of sentences, clauses and the like, into units of information on the basis of the distinction into GIVEN and NEW: what the speaker is treating as information that is recoverable to the hearer (given) and what he is treating as non-recoverable (new). This aspect of the meaning of the text is realized in English by intonation, the information unit being expressed as one TONE GROUP.

The remaining part of the textual component is that which is concerned with cohesion. Cohesion is closely related to information structure, and indeed the two overlap at one point (see 5.8.2 below); but information structure is a form of structure, in which the entire text is blocked out into elements having one or other function in the total configuration – everything in the text has some status in the 'given-new' framework. Cohesion, on the other hand, is a potential for relating one element in the text to another, wherever they are and without any implication that everything in the text has some part in it. The information unit is a structural unit, although it cuts across the hierarchy of structural units or constituents in the grammar (the 'rank scale' of sentence, clause and so on); but there are no structural units defined by the cohesive relation.

Cohesion, therefore, is part of the text-forming component in the linguistic system. It is the means whereby elements that are structurally unrelated to one another are linked together, through the dependence of one on the other for its interpretation. The resources that make up the cohesive potential are part of the total meaning potential of the language, having a kind of catalytic function in the sense that, without cohesion, the remainder of the semantic system cannot be effectively activated at all.

1.3.5 The meaning of cohesion

The simplest and most general forms of the cohesive relation are 'equals' and 'and': identity of reference, and conjoining. We shall discuss the meanings of these and of the other forms of cohesion, and related meanings in other parts of the linguistic system, in a rather summary way in Chapter 7, after the detailed discussion of each type. The means of expressing these various types of cohesion are, as we have seen, drawn from a number of areas of the lexicogrammatical system, which have in common merely the fact that they contribute to the realization of cohesion. The personal pronoun *he*, the verb substitute *do* and the adjunct *nevertheless* would not be likely to appear on the same page in a description of English grammar; still more remote would be any reference to the phenomena of ellipsis or to the repetition of lexical items. But these do come together in this book, because they are all text-forming agencies. A sentence displaying any of these features is an invitation to a text. If the invitation is taken up – if there is in the environment another sentence containing the required key to the interpretation – the text comes into being.

We have noted the significance of the sentence, as the highest structural unit in the grammar. The relation among the elements within the sentence, together with the order in which the elements occur (which is one of the means of realizing these relations), is determined by the structure. Between sentences, however, there are no such structural relations; and there are no grammatical restrictions on the sequence in which sentences are put together. Hence the sentences of [1:32] could follow each other in any order, without in any way affecting the total meaning of the passage.

The sentences of a text, however, are related to each other both substantively and by cohesion; and it is a characteristic of a text that the sequence of the sentences cannot be disturbed without destroying or radically altering the meaning. A text has meaning as a text, whereas a passage consisting of more than one text has no meaning as a whole; it is simply the sum of its parts. Within a text the meaning of each sentence depends on its environment, including its cohesive relations with other sentences. When we consider cohesion, therefore, we are investigating the

Table 1: The place of COHESION in the description of English

Functional components of the semantic system

Ideational		Interpersonal	Textual		(non-structural)
Experiential	Logical		(structural)		
By rank:	All ranks:	By rank:	By rank:	Cross-rank:	**Cohesion**
Clause: transitivity	Paratactic and hypotactic relations (condition, addition, report)	Clause: mood, modality	Clause: theme	Information unit: information distribution, information focus	Reference
Verbal group: tense		Verbal group: person	Verbal group: voice		Substitution
Nominal group: epithesis		Nominal group: attitude	Nominal group: deixis		Ellipsis
Adverbial group: circumstance		Adverbial group: comment	Adverbial group: conjunction		Conjunction
					Lexical cohesion

linguistic means whereby a text is enabled to function as a single meaning-ful unit.

To round off this general introduction, let us look at one further example, with a brief discursive commentary on its cohesion:

[1:34]   The Cat only grinned when it saw Alice.
'Come, it's pleased so far,' thought Alice, and she went on. 'Would you tell me, please, which way I ought to go from here?'
'That depends a good deal on where you want to get to,' said the Cat.
'I don't much care where –' said Alice.
'Then it doesn't matter which way you go,' said the Cat.
'– so long as I get *somewhere*,' Alice added as an explanation.
'Oh, you're sure to do that,' said the Cat, 'if you only walk long enough.'

Starting at the end, we find the words *do that* occurring as a verbal sub-stitute for *get somewhere;* this in turn relates by lexical cohesion to *where you want to get to* and thence to *which way I ought to go.* The form *oh* is a con-junction relating the Cat's answer to Alice's preceding remark; and in similar fashion the Cat's interruption is related to *I don't much care where* by the conjunction *then.* The elliptical form *where* presupposes (*I*) *get to;* and *care,* in *I don't much care,* is lexically related to *want.* The reference item *that,* in *that depends,* presupposes the whole of Alice's question; and the *it* in Alice's first remark presupposes *the Cat,* also by reference. Finally both the proper names *Alice* and *the Cat* form cohesive chains by repetition, leading back to the first sentence of the passage.

A systematic analysis of cohesion in a number of other passages is given in the final section of Chapter 8. Table 1 shows where cohesion belongs in relation to the grammar of the language as a whole.

Chapter 2

Reference

2.1 Endophoric and exophoric reference

There are certain items in every language which have the property of reference, in the specific sense in which we are using the term here; that is to say, instead of being interpreted semantically in their own right, they make reference to something else for their interpretation. In English these items are personals, demonstratives and comparatives.

We start with an example of each:

[2:1] a. Three blind mice, three blind mice.
       See how they run! See how they run!
    b. Doctor Foster went to Gloucester in a shower of rain.
       He stepped in a puddle right up to his middle and never went there again.
    c. There were two wrens upon a tree.
       Another came, and there were three.

In (a), *they* refers to *three blind mice*; in (b) *there* refers to *Gloucester*; in (c) *another* refers to *wrens*.

These items are directives indicating that information is to be retrieved from elsewhere. So much they have in common with all cohesive elements. What characterizes this particular type of cohesion, that which we are calling REFERENCE, is the specific nature of the information· that is signalled for retrieval. In the case of reference the information to be retrieved is the referential meaning, the identity of the particular thing or class of things that is being referred to; and the cohesion lies in the continuity of reference, whereby the same thing enters into the discourse a second time. In *See how they run!*, *they* means not merely 'three blind mice' but 'the same three blind mice that we have just been talking about'. This is sometimes expressed by the formula that all reference items 'contain the definite article', since the definite article is the item that, in English, carries the meaning of specific identity or 'definiteness' in its pure form (see 2.4.2. below). But this is putting it in unnecessarily concrete terms; there is no need to imagine a *the* lurking in every reference item. It is enough to say that reference has the semantic property of definiteness, or specificity.

In principle this specificity can be achieved by reference to the context of situation. By contrast to substitution, which is a grammatical relation (see Chapter 3 below), reference is a semantic relation. One of the consequences of this distinction, as we shall see, is that substitution is subject to a very strong grammatical condition: the substitute must be of the same grammatical class as the item for which it substitutes. This restriction does not apply to reference. Since the relationship is on the semantic level, the reference item is in no way constrained to match the grammatical class of the item it refers to. What must match are the semantic properties. But these need not necessarily have been encoded in the text; they may be retrievable from the situation, as in

[2:2] For he's a jolly good fellow
And so say all of us.

where the text does not make it explicit who *he* is, although *his* identity is not in doubt to those who are present.

It has been suggested in fact that reference to the situation is the prior form of reference, and that reference to another item within the text is a secondary or derived form of this relation. This seems quite plausible, even though it is not entirely clear what it means; is the priority a historical one, or is it in some sense logical? It is certainly possible that, in the evolution of language, situational reference preceded text reference: in other words, that the meaning 'the thing you see in front of you' evolved earlier than the meaning 'the thing I have just mentioned'. Being present in the text is, as it were, a special case of being present in the situation. We tend to see matters the other way round; the word CONTEXT, for example, means literally 'accompanying text', and its use in the collocation CONTEXT OF SITUATION seems to us a metaphorical extension. But it is fairly easy to see that there is a logical continuity from naming (referring to a thing independently of the context of situation), through situational reference (referring to a thing as identified in the context of situation) to textual reference (referring to a thing as identified in the surrounding text); and in this perspective, situational reference would appear as the prior form.

We shall find it useful in the discussion to have a special term for situational reference. This we are referring to as EXOPHORA, or EXOPHORIC reference; and we could contrast it with ENDOPHORIC as a general name for reference within the text:

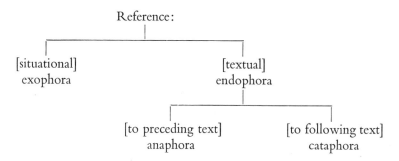

Reference:

[situational]
exophora

[textual]
endophora

[to preceding text]
anaphora

[to following text]
cataphora

As a general rule, therefore, reference items may be exophoric or endophoric; and, if endophoric, they may be anaphoric or cataphoric (cf 1.9 above). This scheme will allow us to recognize certain distinctions within the class of reference items, according to their different uses and 'phoric' tendencies.

Exophora is not simply a synonym for referential meaning. Lexical items like *John* or *tree* or *run* have referential meaning in that they are names for some thing: object, class of objects, process and the like. An exophoric item, however, is one which does not name anything; it signals that reference must be made to the context of situation. Both exophoric and endophoric reference embody an instruction to retrieve from elsewhere the information necessary for interpreting the passage in question; and taken in isolation a reference item is simply neutral in this respect – if we hear a fragment of conversation such as

[2:3] That must have cost a lot of money.

we have no means of knowing whether the *that* is anaphoric or exophoric. The previous speaker might have said, 'I've just been on holiday in Tahiti', or the participants might be looking at their host's collection of antique silver; and if both these conditions hold good, the interpretation will remain doubtful. Ambiguous situations of this kind do in fact quite often arise.

What is essential to every instance of reference whether endophoric (textual) or exophoric (situational) is that there is a presupposition that must be satisfied; the thing referred to has to be identifiable somehow.

One of the features that distinguish different REGISTERS is the relative amount of exophoric reference that they typically display. If the situation is one of 'language-in-action', with the language playing a relatively small and subordinate role in the total event, the text is likely to contain a high proportion of instances of exophoric reference. Hence, as Jean Ure has demonstrated in her studies of different registers, it is often difficult to interpret a text of this kind if one only hears it and has no visual record available.

It is important to make this point, and to emphasize that the special flavour of language-in-action is not a sign that it is ungrammatical, simplified, or incomplete. It is often highly complex, although we have no very convincing measures of structural complexity; and if it appears ungrammatical or incomplete this is largely due to the preponderance of reference items used exophorically, which seem incomplete because their presuppositions are unresolved. A high degree of exophoric reference is one characteristic of the language of the children's peer group. When children interact with each other, especially young children, they do so through constant reference to things; and since the things which serve as reference points are present in the immediate environment they are typically referred to exophorically. In the same way the adult is expected to pick up the necessary clues from the context of situation, as in this exchange between one of the present authors and her three-year-old son:

[2:4] Child: Why does THAT one come out?
Parent: That what?
Child: THAT one.
Parent: That what?
Child: That ONE!
Parent: That one what?
Child: That lever there that you push to let the water out.

It did not occur to the child that he could point to the object in question, presumably because it did not occur to him that what was in HIS focus of attention was not also in everyone else's, a limitation that is characteristic of the egocentric phase of interaction.

Bernstein has shown that one characteristic of speech that is regulated by RESTRICTED CODE is the large amount of exophoric reference that is associated with it; and the researchers in his team have found abundant evidence of this. He characterizes it in terms of dependence on the context of situation: exophoric reference is one form of context-dependence, since without the context we cannot interpret what is said. Let us quote one of Bernstein's passages in which this point is brought out.

We can distinguish between uses of language which can be called 'context bound' and uses of language which are less context bound. Consider, for example, the two following stories which Peter Hawkins, Assistant Research Officer in the Sociological Research Unit, constructed as a result of his analysis of the speech of middle-class and working-class five-year-old children. The children were given a series of four pictures which told a story and they were invited to tell the story. The first picture showed some boys playing football; in the second the ball goes through the window of a house; the third shows a woman looking out of the window and a man making an ominous gesture, and in the fourth the children are moving away. Here are the two stories:

(1) Three boys are playing football and one boy kicks the ball and it goes through the window and the ball breaks the window and the boys are looking at it and a man comes out and shouts at them because they've broken the window so they run away and then that lady looks out of her window and she tells the boys off.

(2) They're playing football and he kicks it and it goes through there it breaks the window and they're looking at it and he comes out and shouts at them because they've broken it so they run away and then she looks out and she tells them off.

With the first story the reader does not have to have the four pictures which were used as the basis for the story, whereas in the case of the second story the reader would require the initial pictures in order to make sense of the story. The first story is free of the context which generated it, whereas the second story is much more closely tied to its context.

There is nothing ungrammatical about the second version of the story, nor is it any simpler in its structure; but it is 'context-bound' because it depends on exophoric reference – *he, she, they* and *there* have no possible interpretation without the pictures. Notice that in the other version we do not get any significantly greater AMOUNT of information. The equivalents of *they, he, he* and *she* are *three boys, one boy, a man* and *that lady*; but we know the sex from the pronouns, and we could have guessed which were children and which were adults from the story. And it is not hard to infer that *through there* means *through the window*. The significant difference between the two versions is that *three boys, one boy* and *a man* do not presuppose anything else. They are not very specific in themselves; but they carry no implication that any further specification is available from elsewhere, and hence they are not context-bound. (On the other hand *that lady* does contain an exophoric *that*; if Hawkins had wanted to be totally consistent he would have had to write *a lady*. For the interesting case of *the* in *through the window* see 2.4.2 below.)

If children's speech is characterized by a tendency towards exophoric reference, this is because it is neighbourhood speech, the language of the children's peer group. We know very little about neighbourhood speech; but it seems likely that it is highly exophoric, no doubt because of the way children tend to relate to things, and to relate to each other through things. Typically in peer group interaction the context of situation is the material environment – the 'things' are there in front of one – and there is also a reservoir of shared experience, a common context of culture; so exophoric reference poses no problems and, in fact, any more explicit naming would be unnatural. The 'restricted code' nature of neighbourhood language is a positive feature; one should not be misled by the word 'restricted', which is an abstract technical term referring to the highly coded, non-redundant properties of speech in this semantic mode. Such speech is characteristic not only of the neighbourhood but of all close-knit social groups; for example, to quote from one of Bernstein's descriptions,

> 'prison inmates, combat units of the armed forces, criminal subcultures, the peer group of children and adolescents, and married couples of long standing'.

It becomes RESTRICTING if it is transferred to contexts in which it is inappropriate; if Bernstein has emphasized the damaging consequences of restricted code in the context of formal education, this is not because of any deficiency in restricted code as such but because the educational context is one to which neighbourhood and peer group semantic styles are not relevant. The problem lies as much in the nature of formal education as in the nature of restricted code.

There are of course many other aspects to restricted code than a high frequency of exophoric reference. But one of the principal characteristics of restricted code is dependence on the context, and the exophoric use of reference items is one form such dependence takes.

A reference item is not of itself exophoric or endophoric; it is just 'phoric' – it simply has the property of reference. Any given INSTANCE of reference may be either one or the other, or it may even be both at once. We shall see in this chapter that there are tendencies for particular items or classes of items to be used exophorically or endophorically; but the reference relation is itself neutral: it merely means 'see elsewhere'. On the other hand, as we have emphasized already, only endophoric reference is cohesive. Exophoric reference contributes to the CREATION of text, in that it links the language with the context of situation; but it does not contribute to the INTEGRATION of one passage with another so that the two together form part of the SAME text. Hence it does not contribute directly to cohesion as we have defined it.

For this reason we shall take only little account of exophoric reference, not attempting to describe it in detail but bringing it in where it relates to and contrasts with reference within the text. We shall treat 'endophoric' reference as the norm; not implying by this that it is the logically prior form of the reference relation, but merely that it is the form of it which plays a part in cohesion, and which therefore has priority in the context of the present study. At the same time, however, where we identify TYPES OF REFERENCE and REFERENCE ITEMS in the language, we do so on the criterion of reference potential without regard to the endophoric/exophoric distinction. A reference item is any one which has this potential, and a systematic account of the different types of reference and their place in the linguistic system has to be based on the generalized concept of reference and not on the particular concrete form that it takes when incorporated into the text.

2.2 Types of reference

There are three types of reference: personal, demonstrative, and comparative.

Personal reference is reference by means of function in the speech situation, through the category of PERSON (Table 2).

Demonstrative reference is reference by means of location, on a scale of PROXIMITY (Table 3).

Comparative reference is indirect reference by means of IDENTITY or SIMILARITY (Table 4).

Grammatically, all reference items except the demonstrative adverbs, and some comparative adverbs, function within the nominal group (noun phrase). It will be necessary therefore to give a brief account of the struc-

Table 2: Personal reference

Semantic category	Existential	Possessive	
Grammatical function	Head		Modifier
Class	noun (pronoun)	determiner	
Person:			
speaker (only)	I me	mine	my
addressee(s), with/without other person(s)	you	yours	your
speaker and other person(s)	we us	ours	our
other person, male	he him	his	his
other person, female	she her	hers	her
other persons; objects	they them	theirs	their
object; passage of text	it	[its]	its
generalized person	one		one's

For categories of grammatical function and class, see below.

Table 3: Demonstrative reference

Semantic category	Selective		Non-selective
Grammatical function	Modifier/Head	Adjunct	Modifier
Class	determiner	adverb	determiner
Proximity:			
near	this these	here [now]	
far	that those	there then	
neutral			the

Table 4: Comparative reference

Grammatical function	Modifier: Deictic/Epithet (see below)	Submodifier/Adjunct
Class	adjective	adverb
General comparison: identity general similarity difference (ie non- identity or similarity)	same identical equal similar additional other different else	identically similarly likewise so such differently otherwise
Particular comparison:	better, more etc [comparative adjectives and quantifiers]	so more less equally

ture of the nominal group, in order to explain the grammar of reference in more explicit terms.*

The logical structure of the nominal group is one of modification; it consists of a HEAD, with optional MODIFIER. The modifying elements include some which precede the head and some which follow it; the distinction in the relative position of modifying elements is semantically

---

* The analysis of the nominal group follows that of Halliday; versions of it have appeared in various unpublished sources, eg: English System Networks (1964). For its use in textual studies see Ruqaiya Hasan, 'A linguistic study of contrasting features in the style of two contemporary English prose writers', University of Edinburgh Ph.D thesis, 1964; also G. J. Turner and B. A. Mohan, A Linguistic Description and Computer Program for Children's Speech, London, Routledge & Kegan Paul, 1970. For a related interpretation see J. McH. Sinclair, A Course in Spoken English: Grammar, London, Oxford U.P., 1972. A detailed account of the present version will appear in M. A. K. Halliday, Meaning of Modern English, London, Oxford U.P. (forthcoming).

We retain the term NOMINAL GROUP in preference to the more usual NOUN PHRASE, partly because it has been used throughout Halliday's writings and related publications, having originally been taken over by Halliday (1956) from W. S. Allen (1951), but more because, although noun phrase and nominal group are more or less equivalent, Halliday's VERBAL GROUP is very different from the verb phrase, so that the term verbal group has to be retained in any case, and, by the same token, nominal group belongs in a somewhat different conceptual framework from noun phrase.

significant, so it is useful to make it terminologically explicit, and we shall
refer to modification preceding the head by the term PREMODIFIER and
to that following the head by the term POSTMODIFIER. Thus in

[2:5] The two high stone walls along the roadside

the Head is *walls*, the Premodifier is formed by *the two high stone* and the
Postmodifier by *along the roadside*.

The Head is typically expressed by a common noun, proper noun or
pronoun. Usually only common nouns accept modification; pronouns
and proper nouns tend to occur alone (see below).

Simultaneously the nominal group is structured along another dimension, the experiential – that is, in terms of the function that language has
of expressing (the speaker's experience of) phenomena of the real world
(*cf* 1.3.4 above). This has the effect of introducing subdivisions within the
Modifier, although these are not in fact subcategories of Modifier but, as
we have said, structural roles deriving from a different functional component within the semantics. The elements of this structure are DEICTIC,
NUMERATIVE, EPITHET, CLASSIFIER, QUALIFIER, and what we shall
call THING.

The structural analysis of [2:5] is now as follows; the last line shows the
classes of word (or, in one case, rankshifted group) which realize the
functions in question. These are the typical classes associated with each
function.

	the	two	high	stone	walls	along the roadside
Structures: logical	Premodifier				Head	Postmodifier
experiential	Deictic	Numera- tive	Epithet	Classifier	Thing	Qualifier
Classes	deter- miner	numeral	adjec- tive	noun	noun	[prepositional group]

As far as the 'experiential' structure is concerned, the Deictic is normally a determiner, the Numerative a numeral or other quantifier, the
Epithet an adjective and the Classifier a common or proper noun; but the
correspondence of class and function is far from being one to one – adjec-

tives, for example, regularly function both as Deictic and as Classifier, *eg*

their	*famous*	*old*	*red*	*wine*
Deictic	Deictic	Epithet	Classifier	Thing
determiner	adjective	adjective	adjective	noun

(whereas *famous* in *a famous victory* and *red* in *red paint* are both functioning as Epithet). The Qualifier is normally a rankshifted relative clause or prepositional phrase. Apart from the Thing, all elements in the experiential structure may occur more than once; note that this does NOT refer to co-ordination, since coordinate items function as single units – in *boys and girls* there are two nouns but only one Thing, and in *hot or cold tea* there are two adjectives but only one Epithet.

The logical structure is somewhat different; here there is always a Head, but it may be of any class, and may be mapped on to any of the experiential functions. This can best be explained by illustration:

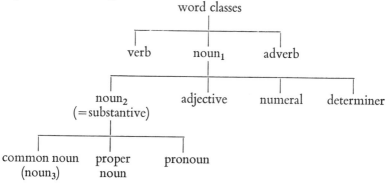

these	two	custo-mers	these	two	these
Modifier		Head	Modi-fier	Head	Head
Deictic	Numerative	Thing	Deictic	Numerative	Deictic

Similarly in *the old* we have the function of Head combined with that of Epithet, and in *the red* (in the sense of 'the red wine', *eg* in *I'll take the red*) Head combined with Classifier. Where the Head is a noun, it may be not only a common noun, as in [2:5], but also a proper noun or pronoun. (To avoid the confusion usually inherent in the use of the word NOUN, let us represent its meaning as follows:

word classes

verb   noun₁   adverb

noun₂   adjective   numeral   determiner
(=substantive)

common noun   proper   pronoun
(noun₃)   noun

We shall avoid as far as possible the use of NOUN in the sense of noun₁, that of 'nominal word' in the most generalized scheme of word classes. In almost all cases its use will correspond to noun₂, 'nominal word that is the typical exponent of a Thing': EXCLUDING adjective, numeral (quantifier) and determiner but INCLUDING pronoun and proper noun as well as common noun. When it is necessary to indicate common or proper noun, but excluding pronoun, the locution COMMON OR PROPER NOUN will be used; since proper nouns in many ways resemble pronouns rather than common nouns, there is no particular reason for using noun in just this sense. Occasionally, where the context makes it clear, NOUN will be used in the sense of noun₃, 'common noun' only. All other uses of noun, those in which it refers to elements higher than words – phrases, clauses, nominalizations of any kind, are avoided altogether.)

If the Head is a proper noun or pronoun, it usually occurs without modification. It is beyond our scope here to go further into the analysis and interpretation of the nominal group; but for purposes of cohesion it is important to clarify and explain the structure up to this point. Common nouns designate classes of things; so they are liable to be further specified, and the general meaning of the functions Deictic, Numerative, Epithet, Classifier and Qualifier is that of SPECIFICATION. The Deictic specifies by identity, non-specific as well as specific (*which train?*, *a train*, *all trains*) and including identity based on reference (*this train*, *my train*); the Numerative by quantity or ordination (*two trains*, *next train*); the Epithet by reference to a property (*long trains*); the Classifier by reference to a subclass (*express trains*, *passenger trains*); and the Qualifier by reference to some characterizing relation or process (*trains for London*, *train I'm on*). These functions are introduced into the nominal group through the logical structure of modification, being mapped on to the function of Modifier; hence, common nouns are typically modified. But pronouns and proper names are not as a rule susceptible of further specification. The category of pronoun is a mixed bag; but it comprises PERSONAL and INDEFINITE pronouns, of which the personals, as we have seen, are reference items and therefore take over the specificity of whatever it is they are presupposing, while the indefinites (*eg: something*, *everybody*) already embody a non-specific deictic component in their meaning and cannot be specified further. Proper names designate individuals, and are therefore fully specified in their own right. Proper names can accept DESCRIPTIVE modification, as in *that Charlie Brown*, *beautiful Buttermere*; this is a derived function of the modifying structure and one which differs in certain significant ways (for example, descriptive modifiers do not admit of ellipsis; see Chapter 4).

But the normal pattern is: with Modifier if the Head is a common noun, without Modifier if the Head is proper noun or pronoun.

Finally there is the structural relation of SUBMODIFICATION, by which a Modifier is itself further modified. Submodifiers are typically adverbs, such as *very, equally, too;* they may also be rankshifted prepositional groups, like *in every way* in *an in every way valiant attempt.* Submodifiers are most frequent within the Epithet, though they can be found elsewhere.

It will be necessary to refer to the structure of the nominal group at frequent points in the discussion of cohesion. To cite one example, it is a regular source of ellipsis, and we can define an elliptical nominal group as one in which there is no overt Thing and the Head is therefore combined with some other function. What distinguishes reference from other types of cohesion, however, is that reference is overwhelmingly nominal in character. With the exception of the demonstrative adverbs *here, there, now,* and *then,* and some comparative adverbs, all reference items are found within the nominal group. They may have any of the functions in the 'experiential' structure except those of Classifier and Qualifier. It is not that these elements cannot also incorporate cohesive reference – they can, but if so the reference item functions as something else, typically as Deictic, in a rankshifted nominal group, *eg: that* referring to *box* in

[2:6] It's an old box camera. – I never had one of that kind.

The classification of reference items is not, however, based on their function in the nominal group; it is based on the type of reference involved. This is a semantic classification and cuts across the classification according to grammatical function. At the same time the type of reference is not unrelated to the form which it takes in the grammar, and to the classes of word which function as reference items. This will be discussed and exemplified where necessary in what follows.

2.3 Personal reference

The category of PERSONALS includes the three classes of personal pronouns, possessive determiners (usually called 'possessive adjectives'), and possessive pronouns. There is no general name for this category in traditional grammar, because the members of it belong to different classes with diverse structural roles; but in fact they represent a single system, that of PERSON:.

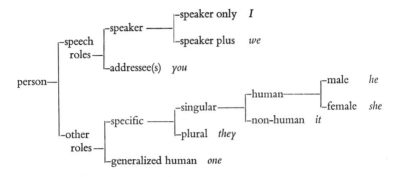

In tabular form:

	Speech roles		Other roles		
			Specific		Generalized Human
	Speaker	Addressee	Human	Non-human	
one	I me mine my	you you	he him his his ——— she her hers her	it it [its] its	one one – one's
more than one	we us ours our	yours your	they them theirs their		

These items are all reference items; they refer to something by specifying its function or role in the speech situation. This system of reference is known as PERSON, where 'person' is used in the special sense of 'role'; the traditionally recognized categories are FIRST PERSON, SECOND PERSON and THIRD PERSON, intersecting with the NUMBER categories of SINGULAR and PLURAL. The actual system found in the semantics of languages is nearly always a departure in some way from this 'ideal' type; that of English is as set out above, with one or two further complexities which will be brought up in the discussion – including the so-called impersonal uses of *we*, *you* and *they*.

The term PERSON might seem a little misleading, as the system includes not only 'impersonal' meanings (which are actually still personal, *ie* human; they are merely not individualized) but also reference that is truly non-personal, reference to objects. But most grammatical terms have fuzzy edges; they express the central or typical meaning of the category in question, and are justified by being in this way simple and easy to remember. The alternatives would be either to use purely abstract labels, such as letters and numbers, which have no mnemonic value; or to attempt more accurate designations, which would soon become cumbersome and syntactically recalcitrant. The technical term itself is not part of any linguistic theory; it is simply an 'address' for easy recovery.

2.3.1 *Semantic distinctions in the personal system*

The significance of the PERSON system is that it is the means of referring to RELEVANT persons and objects, making use of a small set of options centring around the particular nature of their relevance to the speech situation. The principal distinction is that between the PERSONS DEFINED BY THEIR ROLES IN THE COMMUNICATION PROCESS, on the one hand, and all other entities on the other. The former we shall call SPEECH ROLES; they are the roles of SPEAKER and ADDRESSEE. These are the two roles assigned by the speaker; and we use 'addressee' in preference to 'hearer' or 'listener' in order to suggest the meaning 'person DESIGNATED BY THE SPEAKER AS recipient of the communication' – as distinct from one who chooses to listen or happens to hear. The latter, which we shall call simply OTHER ROLES, include all other relevant entities, OTHER THAN speaker or addressee. In terms of the traditional categories of person, the distinction is that between first and second person on the one hand (*I, you, we*) and third person on the other (*he, she, it, they, one*).

Each of these personal forms enters into the structure in one of two guises: either as participant in some process, or as possessor of some entity. If the former, it falls into the class NOUN, subclass PRONOUN, and functions as Head – and sole element – in the nominal group; it then has one form when that nominal group is the Subject (*I, you, we, he, she, it, they, one*) and in most cases a different form when it is anything other than subject (*me, you, us, him, her, it, them, one*). If the latter, it falls into the class DETERMINER, and then functions either as Head (*mine, yours, ours, his, hers, [its], theirs*) or as Modifier (*my, your, our, his, her, its, their, one's*). Examples:

(a) I had a cat   *I:*   participant;

                                     Subject   pronoun   Head

(b) the cat pleased me   *me:*   participant;
                                   non-Subject   pronoun   Head
(c) take mine   *mine:* possessor   determiner   Head
(d) my plate's empty   *my:*   possessor   determiner   Modifier

Note that *one* never occurs as possessor/Head, although it docs as possessor/ Modifier: we can say *Do they pay one's debts?* but not *Do they only pay their own debts, or do they also pay one's?* There is a reason for this, which will appear later. The form *its* is also rare as Head, although there seems to be no very clear reason for this restriction and, in fact, instances do occur, *eg*

[2:7] You know that mouse you saw? Well that hole there must be its.

Within each of the two major categories of personals, further distinctions are built into the system. Within the speech roles, the English person system recognizes only speaker *I* and addressee *you*, making no distinction according to the number of addressees or according to the social hierarchy or the social distance between addressee and speaker.* It does however comprise a third form *we* representing the speaker together with some other person or persons, among whom the addressee(s) may or may not be included.†

As far as the remaining items are concerned, those which refer to other roles, not to speaker or addressee, the distinctions are fairly clearcut. There is a generalized personal form with human referent, *one*, perhaps 'borrowed' from French *on* although it is not restricted to functioning as Subject as *on* is; in the following example, only the second of the four could have *on* in French translation:

[2:8] They couldn't do a thing like that to one. – One never knows, does one? – It makes one think, though.

* Elizabethan English distinguished *thou* (singular, familiar) from *you* (plural; or singular showing respect or distance), much like the French distinction of *tu* and *vous* today. The distinction was lost in all varieties of English except some northern rural dialects, in which it is now fast dying out. The Quaker use of *thee* is a later imitation and does not directly reflect original usage.

† It should be noted that a separate system of 'person' operates in imperative clauses. The Subject of an imperative clause is always a 'personal' element; but in this case the addressee is always included, and the option is plus or minus the speaker. In other words the contrast is between (*you*) *go!* and *let's go!*, where *let's* always includes 'you'. So *let's* is not equivalent to *let us*, in which *us* is part of the ordinary person system and may exclude the addressee. The form *let's try* is a form of the imperative of *try*; but *let us try* contains the imperative of *let* (as in *let John try*, etc) and means '(you) allow us to try', where *us* may, and in such instances typically does, exclude the person being spoken to.

There is a difference between British and American English as regards repetition of *one* within the sentence: British English retains *one* in second and subsequent occurrences, where American English normally substitutes *he:*

> [2:9] One can hardly be expected to reveal one's/his innermost secrets to the first casual enquirer, can one/he?

The rest of the 'other roles' are non-generalized: they make specific reference to persons or things, and the categories are familiar to every student of English from lesson one: plural, with no distinction of persons and things, *they;* singular, human, male *he*, female *she*, non-human *it*. Animals are treated sometimes as persons and sometimes as things; the lower orders of creation are referred to as *it*, the higher orders either as *it* or as *he/she* depending on a whole number of variables, primarily the speaker's relationship to the species in question (farmer and farm animal, pet owner and pet, for example), but also on his individual preference. If the reference is to a single human being, but with the sex unknown or unspecified, the form used is *he*, as in:

> [2:10] If the buyer wants to know the condition of the property, he has to have another survey carried out on his own behalf.*

This means that, as in many languages, the masculine is the syntactically unmarked form. This is a matter of concern to some, since they see in it another manifestation of the subjection of women and want to insist on *he or she* (or presumably *she or he*) in such instances. Not all languages enforce the sex distinction; in Chinese there is only one word meaning both *he* and *she*, just as there is only the one word *they* (as contrasted with *ils* and *elles*) for the plural in English. And it cannot be denied that, whatever the origins of the 'unmarked masculine' – they lie far back in the history of Indo-European – the use of *he* has its problems. The authors of the *Breakthrough to Literacy Teacher's Manual* used *he* to refer to a child but *she* to refer to a teacher, on the grounds that infant teachers are more often female – a reasoning that might equally be objected to:

> [2:11] It is most important to note that a child who tells his teacher an imaginative story which she subsequently writes down for him is not engaged in creative *writing;* but in creative speaking.

No doubt the authors were glad to be able to avoid the possible ambiguities that might arise if both child and teacher were referred to by identical personal forms.

---

* *The Legal Side of Buying a House*, Consumers' Association.

2.3.2 Speech roles and other roles

The use of personal forms as reference items with a cohesive function is so all-pervading in English that it hardly needs illustrating. The following is from Alice's conversation with the flowers:

> [2:12] 'Aren't you sometimes frightened at being planted out here, with nobody to take care of you?'
> 'There's the tree in the middle,' said the Rose. 'What else is it good for?'
> 'But what could it do, if danger came?' Alice asked.
> 'It could bark,' said the Rose.
> 'It says "Bough-wough!"' cried a Daisy: 'that's why its branches are called boughs!'

Four occurrences of *it*, and one of *its*, refer anaphorically to *the tree*. To appreciate the effect of the use of personals, and cohesive items of all kinds, WITHOUT appropriate referents, see the verses read out by the White Rabbit as evidence in *Alice in Wonderland*, Chapter 12, beginning

> [2:13] 'They told me you had been to her
> And mentioned me to him.'

The whole poem is an excellent example of a pseudo-text.

There is a distinction to be made, however, between the speech roles (first and second person) and the other roles (third person). Only the third person is inherently cohesive, in that a third person form typically refers anaphorically to a preceding item in the text. First and second person forms do not normally refer to the text at all; their referents are defined by the speech roles of speaker and hearer, and hence they are normally interpreted exophorically, by reference to the situation. This is an important distinction in principle: there is a major division within the person system between the third person, which as far as the speech situation is concerned is not a 'person' – not a role – at all (it can only be defined negatively as 'not first or second'), and the first and second persons which are defined as roles in the speech situation. The first and second person forms essentially refer to the situation, whereas those of the third person essentially refer anaphorically or cataphorically to the text.

Hence the absence of any verbal reference for *I* and *you* does not normally lead to any sense of incompleteness. In written language they are anaphoric when they occur in quoted ('direct') speech, as opposed to those instances where the writer is addressing his readers; so in [1:34] *I* and *you* have as verbal referents *Alice* and *the Cat*. Compare

[2:14] There was a brief note from Susan. She just said, 'I am not coming home this weekend.'

where *I*, in the quoted clause, refers back, like the preceding *she*, to *Susan* in
the first sentence. These are instances of anaphora, albeit indirect anaphora;
I still refers to the speaker, but we have to look in the text to find out who
the speaker is. In general however *I* and *you* are given by the situation;
other than in cases of quoted speech, if we are 'in on' the text at all we are
usually ourselves occupying one or other of the speech roles.

Conversely, a third person form does normally imply the presence of a
referent somewhere in the text; and in the absence of such a referent the
text appears incomplete. The meaning 'male person other than speaker or
addressee' is hardly specific, so that an occurrence of *he* typically presupposes a singular human masculine common or proper noun somewhere
in the vicinity. At the same time, just as the first and second person forms,
while typically exophoric, may refer anaphorically, so also the third person forms, while typically anaphoric, may refer exophorically to some
person or thing that is present in the context of situation. An example such
as the following could occur as a complete text.

[2:15] Oh, he's already been? – Yes, he went by about five minutes ago.

The nature of the reply shows that the identity of *he* is clear to the respondent, at least to his own satisfaction. As we have emphasized already,
'present in the context of situation' does not necessarily mean physically
present in the interactants' field of perception; it merely means that the
context of situation permits the identification to be made. The setting of
the above example might be some event at which a collection is being
taken, where the first speaker, money in hand, notices that those around
him are no longer proffering contributions; by this time the steward, the
he of the dialogue, is in fact well out of sight, but it is obvious to both
speakers who is in question. We may be inclined to speculate, as with
other reference items, that the original mode of reference of third person
forms was actually situational, and that endophoric reference is ultimately
derived from exophoric. There are reasons for thinking that reference is
primarily a situational RELATION, whereas substitution is a textual one
(see Chapter 3). Be that as it may, the typical INSTANCE of third person
reference is textual, and therefore cohesive; and in many texts the third
person forms constitute the most frequent single class of cohesive items.

Finally there is the 'mixed' personal *we*. This may refer just to speaker
and addressee ('you and I'), and so include in its meaning only the speech

roles; but it may extend to a third person or persons (either with or without the addressee, *ie* 'he/she/they and I' or 'he/she/they and you and I'), in which case it is mixed and demands a referent for the 'other role'. This may be exophoric, as when the leader of a delegation uses *we* to refer to himself plus the group of which he is acting as spokesman – who may or may not be forgathered around him: again the concept of 'situation' is an abstract one defined not by the physical presence of the participants but by the institutional framework, in this case the concept of a spokesman 'one who speaks on behalf of (himself and) others'. Or it may be anaphoric, as in

[2:16] My husband and I are leaving. We have seen quite enough of this unpleasantness.

To summarize: personals referring to the speech roles (speaker and addressee) are typically exophoric: this includes *I* and *you*, and *we* meaning 'you and I'. They become anaphoric, however, in quoted speech; and so are normally anaphoric in many varieties of written language, such as narrative fiction. In narration the context of situation includes a 'context of reference', a fiction that is to be constructed from the text itself, so that all reference within it must ultimately be endophoric. Somewhere or other in the narrative will be names or designations to which we can relate the *I* and *you* of the dialogue. A written text as a whole, however, still has its outer context of situation, in which the writer may refer exophorically either to himself, as *I* or *we*, or to his reader(s), as *you*, or to both. This happens in letter-writing, in first person narrative, in advertising, in official documents addressed to the public, and in notices; for example:

[2:17] a. Dear Carrie: How are you? I had a strange dream about you last night – we were wandering together through a dense forest . . .

b. I suppose my face must have given me away, for suddenly she swept across and kissed me, but fortunately for my good resolutions she didn't linger close to me but promptly returned to her chair.

c. Look around you. Just how much of YOU is projected into your environment, and how much of IT is projected at you?

d. The Medical Director thanks you for your attendance at the X-Ray Unit and is happy to inform you that your film is satisfactory. YOU SHOULD KEEP THIS LETTER AND TAKE IT WITH YOU WHENEVER YOU HAVE AN X-RAY IN FUTURE.

e. You have been warned!

Personals referring to other roles (persons or objects other than the speaker or addressee) are typically anaphoric; this includes *he*, *she*, *it* and *they*, and also the 'third person' component of *we* when present. They may be exophoric, however, wherever the context of situation is (judged by the speaker to be) such as to permit identification of the referent in question.

As has been pointed out, it is only the anaphoric type of reference that is relevant to cohesion, since it provides a link with a preceding portion of the text. When we talk of the cohesive function of personal reference, therefore, it is particularly the third person forms that we have in mind. But we shall find instances of these which are not cohesive, as well as instances of the first and second person forms which are. In spoken English, especially in contexts of 'language-in-action', those registers in which the verbal activity is closely interwoven with non-verbal activity, it is quite common for third person forms to function exophorically; but in writing an explicit referent will normally be required, and even in speech the hearer is sometimes constrained to demand one – so we hear exchanges such as: *They're here! – Who are?* In other words, a third person form is assumed to be anaphoric unless the context of situation makes it quite unambiguous. With the first and second person forms, on the other hand, the assumption is the other way round. In spoken language *I* means the speaker and *you* means the addressee unless there is positive indication to the contrary in the form of a clause introducing quoted speech; and quoted speech, although common enough, is largely associated with certain particular types of narrative, such as gossip and joke-telling. In written language the exophoric use of *I* as writer and *you* as audience is restricted to certain registers; but even in writing we find some form of explicit signal (quotation marks, or 'inverted commas') to tell us when they are not being used in this way.

	Speech roles *I, you, we* ('*you and I*')	Other roles *he, she, it, they, we* ('*and other(s)*')
typically:	exophoric (non-cohesive): speaker, addressee(s); writer, reader(s)	anaphoric (cohesive): person(s) or thing(s) previously referred to
secondarily:	anaphoric (cohesive): speaker, addressee in quoted speech	exophoric (non-cohesive): person(s) or thing(s) identified in context of situation

Note finally that it is characteristic of third person forms that they may be cumulatively anaphoric. One occurrence of *John* at the beginning of a text may be followed by an indefinitely large number of occurrences of *he, him* or *his* all to be interpreted by reference to the original *John*. This phenomenon contributes very markedly to the internal cohesion of a text, since it creates a kind of network of lines of reference, each occurrence being linked to all its predecessors up to and including the initial reference. The number and density of such networks is one of the factors which gives to any text its particular flavour or texture.

2.3.3 *Some special kinds of personal reference*

2.3.3.1 EXTENDED REFERENCE, AND TEXT REFERENCE

The word *it* differs from all other personals in that it may refer not only to a particular person or object, some entity that is encoded linguistically as a 'participant' – a noun or nominal expression – but also to any identifiable portion of text. This actually comprises two rather distinct phenomena, both of which are illustrated in the following example:

> [2:18] [The Queen said:] 'Curtsey while you're thinking what to say. It saves time.' Alice wondered a little at this, but she was too much in awe of the Queen to disbelieve it.

In the first instance, *It saves time, it* refers to *curtsey*[*ing*] *while you're thinking what to say;* the reference is still to a 'thing', but not in the narrow sense of a participant (person or object) – it is a whole process or complex phenomenon which is in question. Only *it* has the property of EXTENDED REFERENCE of this kind: consider for example an eye-witness's description of an accident, concluding with the remark *It all happened so quickly.*

In the second instance, . . . *to disbelieve it*, the *it* refers not to a THING but to a FACT: [*that*] *curtsey*[*ing*] *while you're thinking what to say* . . . *saves time.* This is an instance of TEXT REFERENCE. Whereas extended reference differs from usual instances of reference only in extent – the referent is more than just a person or object, it is a process or sequence of processes (grammatically, a clause or string of clauses, not just a single nominal) – text reference differs in kind: the referent is not being taken up at its face-value but is being transmuted into a fact or a report. Perhaps the best way to convey the distinction is through ambiguity:

> [2:19] It rained day and night for two weeks. The basement flooded and everything was under water. It spoilt all our calculations.

Either the phenomenon of heavy rains and flooding, the EVENT itself, destroyed our records; or the 'metaphenomenon', the FACT that it rained so much, upset the weather pattern that we had predicted. In addition to *it*, the demonstratives *this* and *that* frequently occur in both extended reference and text reference. One of the striking aspects of cohesion is the ability of hearers and readers to identify the relevant portion of text as referent, when they are faced with *it*, *this* or *that* in these uses. Clearly one of the factors that enables them to do this is the internal cohesion within the passage that is being presupposed.

2.3.3.2 GENERALIZED EXOPHORIC REFERENCE

Not only the generalized personal *one* but also *we, you, they* and *it* all have a generalized exophoric use in which the referent is treated as being as it were immanent in all contexts of situation. (i) *You* and *one* mean 'any human individual', as in *you never know, one never knows;* and often by implication 'any self-respecting individual', 'any individual I would approve of', particularly in the combination of *one* plus a verbal modulation as in *one must accept certain standards.* (ii) *We* is used in similar fashion but more concretely, implying a particular group of individuals with which the speaker wishes to identify himself, as in *we don't do that sort of thing here.* In addition there are various other intermediate uses of *we*: royal and editorial, *eg: we consider it our duty* . . ., with an assumption of status behind it; medical *we*, from doctor to patient as in *how are we today?*, implying 'you in your role as patient, with whom I seek to identify myself'; impersonal *we* used in expository writing (for example in this book), *eg: we conclude therefore that* . . ., simply because English demands a subject and an excess of passives soon becomes tiresome. (iii) *They* is used to mean 'persons unspecified'; often those with responsibility, 'the authorities', but also simply 'persons adequately specified for purposes of discussion by the context', as in *they're mending the road out there.* (iv) *It* occurs as a universal meteorological operator in a few expressions such as *it's snowing, it's hot today.* All these are exophoric, but with a kind of institutionalized exophora; they make it possible to conform to the structural requirements of the clause, which demands a nominal in various places – for this reason they are often untranslatable, since other languages make different requirements.

Exophoric reference makes no contribution to the cohesion of a text. But it is worth noting, perhaps, that this 'institutionalized' exophora makes no demands either on the verbal context or on the context of situation. Confronted with the old verse

[2:20] They're digging up Grandpa's grave to build a sewer

the hearer does not feel obliged to ask 'Who are?' – the message is complete. If a personal form cannot be interpreted institutionally, either because it does not make sense in the context or because it is one such as *he* which is never used in this way, then the hearer must seek the necessary evidence for interpreting it. If he finds such evidence in the situation, he can accept the passage in question as a complete text. If not, he has to seek textual evidence, and therefore to assume that the original passage is related to some preceding piece by cohesion – otherwise, he can only regard it as incomplete. It is not suggested that he performs these operations as a systematic search in this or any other order. The important fact is that the hearer typically assumes that any passage which for external reasons OUGHT to be a text (as opposed to something that he knows to be a fragment, such as one end of a telephone conversation) *is* in fact a text; and he will go to enormous lengths to interpret it as complete and intelligible. This is an aspect of the very general human tendency to assume in the other person an intention to communicate, an assumption which is no doubt of very great value for survival.

2.3.4 *Personal pronouns, possessive determiners and possessive pronouns*

All that has been said about the personal pronouns applies equally to the other two categories of personal, namely the possessive determiners and possessive pronouns. Neither the syntactic function of the personal itself, nor the syntactic function of its referent, has any bearing on the anaphoric relation between the two; in this respect reference is quite unlike substitution (Chapter 3). In [2:21] below, the personal reference item *he* is a pronoun functioning as Head; this refers back to *John* equally well whether *John* is non-possessive proper noun as Head as in (a), possessive as Deictic as in (b), or possessive as Head as in (c):

[2:21] a. John has moved to a new house. ⎫
        b. John's house is beautiful.   ⎬ He had it built last year.
        c. That new house is John's.   ⎭

Likewise the other personal forms, both possessive determiners (*my, your,* etc) and possessive pronouns (*mine, yours,* etc), may refer without restriction to a referent having any of the functions of *John* in [2:21], or indeed any other syntactic function that is open to nominals. So we could have any combination of the following:

[2:22] a. John has moved to a   ⎤ ⎡x. He had it built last year.
   new house.
  b. John's house is beautiful. ⎬ y. His wife must be delighted with
               it.
  c. That new house is John's. ⎦ ⎣z. I didn't know it was his.

where (x) has personal pronoun *he*, (y) has possessive determiner *his* and
(z) has possessive pronoun *his*.

Moreover the referent may be embedded deep in a complex sentence;
there is still no difficulty in identifying *John* as the referent of *his* in [2:23]:

> [2:23] You really ought to ask Sally not to tell a story like that to all
> those friends of hers if she thinks they might be going to be
> working with John, unless she can be quite sure it's not going to
> go any further. I hardly think it would appeal to his sense of
> humour.

There is however one respect in which possessive pronouns differ from
other personal reference items as regards their anaphoric function. Whereas the other personals require only one referent for their interpretation,
possessive pronouns demand two, a possessor and a possessed. The difference can be seen in [2:24]:

> [2:24] a. John's is nice.
>   b. His house is nice.
>   c. His is nice.

Given (a), we need the answer to 'John's what?'; given (b), the answer to
'whose house?'; but given (c) we need the answer to 'whose what?'. So
any occurrence of a possessive pronoun involves two ties, only one of
which is a form of reference; the other is present with any possessive
nominal, such as *John's* or *my father's*, whenever it is functioning as Head.
This is in fact an instance of ellipsis (Chapter 4). Possessive pronouns, in
other words, are doubly anaphoric because they are both referential and
elliptical: they are anaphoric (i) by reference, to the possessor, and (ii) by
ellipsis, to the thing possessed. So in [2:25] only (c) satisfies the presuppositions of the second sentence:

> [2:25] a. Can you find another programme? ⎤
>   b. Can you help Mary?   ⎬ Hers has got lost.
>   c. Can you hand Mary a programme? ⎦

The possessive pronoun *hers* presupposes *Mary* by reference and *programme* by ellipsis.

2.3.5 Cataphoric reference

So far no mention has been made of cataphoric personal reference. Personals can refer cataphorically, as in

[2:26]   He who hesitates is lost.

where *he* does not presuppose any referent in the preceding text but simply refers forward to *who hesitates*. Unlike demonstratives, however, which do refer cataphorically in a way that is genuinely cohesive – they refer FORWARD to succeeding elements to which they are in no way structurally related (see 2.4 below) – personals are normally cataphoric only within a structural framework, and therefore do not contribute to the cohesion of the text. The reference is within the sentence, and is determined by the structure of the sentence.

It may be helpful nevertheless to summarize the cataphoric structural functions of the personal forms – in which only the personal pronouns participate, never the possessive forms. (i) Third person pronouns other than *it* may refer cataphorically to a defining relative clause, as in [2:26]. This usage is felt to be somewhat archaic; it is found in proverbs and aphorisms, and in some rhetorical, literary and liturgical styles. Such cataphoric reference is also found occasionally with *we* and *you*, as in *you who doubt my word* (meaning 'those among you who doubt my word'; note that there is no cataphora in forms which are non-defining, such as *you, who used to be so tolerant*). (ii) All third person pronouns occur cataphorically as 'substitute themes' in clauses in which their referent is delayed to the end, *eg: they're good these peaches*. (iii) As a special case of the last, *it* is very frequently used in this way where the subject of the clause is a nominalization, as in *it's true that he works very hard*. This is in fact the unmarked or typical form in such cases; the alternative, *that he works very hard is true*, is possible but restricted. All such cataphoric reference is structurally determined and makes no direct contribution to the texture.

There is one cataphoric use of *it* that is cohesive, illustrated by [2:27]:

[2:27]   I would never have believed it. They've accepted the whole scheme.

This happens only where *it* is text-referring (see 2.3.3 above); again, like its anaphoric equivalent, it has more in common with demonstrative reference than with personal reference.

Thus, to sum up, not all occurrences of personal forms are anaphoric, nor is the mere presence of a personal reference item by itself an indication of a cohesive tie. In the first place, the reference may be exophoric, interpretable by recourse to the context of situation: either in the generalized exophoric sense of *we, you, they* or *it*, or in the special exophoric sense of the speech roles expressed by *you* and *I*. Exophoric reference does not constitute a cohesive tie. In the second place, it may be cataphoric; it will then be cohesive only in the case of the special use of *it* exemplified by [2:27] above. This does constitute a tie, linking up with what follows. All other instances are anaphoric, including most occurrences of third person forms and some occurrences of first and second person forms (those in a context of quotation). Usually there is no great difficulty in recognizing an anaphoric personal form; and we are all sensitized to the presence of one which seems to be anaphoric but for which no clear reference is available. Perhaps this is one of the reasons why children used to be discouraged from using them. The other reason is one of manners: 'It's rude to point', and exophoric reference is, after all, just pointing with words.

2.4 Demonstrative reference

Demonstrative reference is essentially a form of verbal pointing. The speaker identifies the referent by locating it on a scale of proximity. The system is as follows:

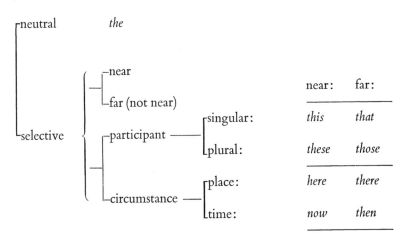

The circumstantial (adverbial) demonstratives *here, there, now* and *then* refer to the location of a process in space or time, and they normally do so directly, not via the location of some person or object that is participating in the process; hence they typically function as Adjuncts in the clause, not as elements within the nominal group. They have a secondary function as Qualifier, as in *that man there*. The remaining (nominal) demonstratives *this, these, that, those*, and *the* refer to the location of some thing, typically some entity – person or object – that is participating in the process; they therefore occur as elements within the nominal group. They belong to the class of determiners, and have the experiential function of Deictic; in the logical structure they function either as Modifier or as Head, with the exception of *the* which is a Modifier only. In this respect the nominal demonstratives resemble the possessives, which can also function either as Modifier or as Head, although, unlike the possessives, the demonstratives have only one form – there is no distinction between demonstrative determiner and demonstrative pronoun corresponding to that between possessive determiner (*eg: your*) and possessive pronoun (*eg: yours*):

	as Modifier	as Head
demonstrative	that garden seems bigger	that is a big garden
possessive	your garden seems bigger	yours is a big garden

In the case of the demonstratives, however, there are certain differences in meaning between the functions of Modifier and Head; a demonstrative functioning as Head is more like a personal pronoun. Historically, in fact, both *it* and *the* are reduced forms of *that*; and, although *it* now operates in the system of personals, both can be explained as being the 'neutral' or non-selective type of the nominal demonstrative – as essentially one and the same element, which takes the form *it* when functioning as Head and *the* when functioning as Deictic (see further 2.4.2 below).

Like personals, the demonstratives regularly refer exophorically to something within the context of situation. This is the primary form of verbal pointing; and it may be accompanied by demonstrative action, in the form of a gesture indicating the object referred to. Examples are obvious enough:

[2:28] Pick these up!
[2:29] How would you like a cruise in that yacht?

Similarly with the demonstrative adverbs:

[2:30] Leave that there and come here!

In general *this, these* and *here* imply proximity to the speaker; *that, those* and *there* imply distance from the speaker, which may or may not involve proximity to the addressee – the meaning is 'near you, or not near either of us, but at any rate not near me'. Many languages, for example Japanese, have a set of three demonstratives in which the meanings 'near you' and 'not near either of us' are kept distinct; this system is found in one or two dialects of English, which have *this, here* 'near me', *that, there* 'near you' and *yon, yonder* 'not near either of us'. In such languages there is a close parallelism between the demonstrative and the personal systems, with 'this' corresponding to 'I' (speaker), 'that' to 'you' (addressee), and 'yon' to 'he, she, it' (other location or role).* In languages like Standard English, with only the two terms, 'this' is more specific than 'that', since 'this' has the speaker as its point of reference while 'that' has no particular reference point – it is simply interpreted as 'not this'. This explains why the neutral forms *the* and *it* derived from *that* and not from *this*.

We are not concerned here with exophoric reference, for the reasons already given: it is not textually cohesive. But the uses of *this* and *that* in endophoric reference are explainable by reference to their exophoric meanings; so it is important to start from the general concept of proximity as this is interpreted situationally. The same applies to the definite article: *the* is also used exophorically, where the situation makes it clear what referent is intended, as in

[2:31] Look at the flowers!
[2:32] Don't go; the train's coming.

This is the meaning of *the* here: namely that the referent is fully specified by the context and no further specification is needed. The anaphoric and cataphoric uses of *the* are likewise more readily interpretable if we relate them to its meaning as an exophoric deictic.

Demonstrative reference is discussed in more detail in the next three sections: 2.4.1, the selective nominal demonstratives; 2.4.2, *the*; 2.4.3, the adverbial demonstratives.

2.4.1 *The selective nominal demonstratives:* this, these, that, those

These demonstratives occur extensively with anaphoric function in all

---

* The third term 'yon' is sometimes explained as 'in the proximity of some third person', but that is a misinterpretation, based on the assumption that demonstratives are DERIVED FROM personals. Rather we should say that the third demonstrative, where it is found, shares with the third person the common meaning 'other', *ie* neither of the two specific possibilities. So 'he, she, it' is 'neither speaker nor addressee, but some other entity'; 'yon' is 'neither near speaker nor near addressee, but some other location'.

varieties of English. In principle, they embody within themselves three systematic distinctions:

(1) between 'near' (*this, these*) and 'not near' (*that, those*)
(2) between 'singular' (*this, that*) and 'plural' (*these, those*)
(3) between Modifier (*this*, etc, plus noun, *eg: this tree is an oak*) and Head (*this*, etc, without noun, *eg: this is an oak*).

All these distinctions have some relevance to cohesion, in that they partially determine the use of these items in endophoric (textual) reference. They are discussed in the next three subsections.

2.4.1.1 NEAR AND NOT NEAR: *this/these* VERSUS *that/those*

Both *this* and *that* regularly refer anaphorically to something that has been said before. In dialogue there is some tendency for the speaker to use *this* to refer to something he himself has said and *that* to refer to something said by his interlocutor; compare [2:33] and [2:34]:

[2:33] a. There seems to have been a great deal of sheer carelessness. This is what I can't understand.
b. There seems to have been a great deal of sheer carelessness. – Yes, that's what I can't understand.

This distinction is clearly related to that of 'near (the speaker)' versus 'not near'; 'what I have just mentioned' is, textually speaking, 'near me' whereas 'what you have just mentioned' is not. The tendency seems to be further reinforced if the referent is also in some way ASSOCIATED WITH the speaker; for example,

[2:34] I like the lions, and I like the polar bears. These are my favourites. – Those are my favourites too.

Here there are as it were two kinds of proximity: the lions and the polar bears have not only been mentioned by the speaker but also explicitly linked to his personal feelings, so that he naturally refers to them as *these*.

Co-existing with this tendency is another one whereby proximity is interpreted in terms of time; in this case *that* tends to be associated with a past-time referent and *this* for one in the present or future. For example,

[2:35] a. We went to the opera last night. That was our first outing for months.
b. We're going to the opera tonight. This'll be our first outing for months.

Compare this with the exophoric use of *this* to refer to current periods of time: *this morning, this year* and so on; and also *in those days, in these* days.

Neither of these tendencies is fully dominant. If in a given instance both are working in the same direction, the choice is likely to follow the expected pattern; for example

[2:36] 'I couldn't afford to learn it,' said the Mock Turtle with a sigh.
'I only took the regular course.'
'What was that?' inquired Alice.

Here Alice could hardly have said *What was this?* Similarly with [2:37]:

[2:37] a. What about this exhibition?
b. What about that exhibition?

If we hear [2:37a] we are likely to supply something like 'that I told you is on now; shall we go and see it?'; whereas with [2:37b] the presupposition is more likely to be 'that you told me was on earlier; did you go and see it?' – at least, it could not be the other way round. But the criteria may conflict, precisely because the notion of proximity has various interpretations; and in such cases there is no very clearly felt distinction between *this* and *that*. In [2:38] we could easily substitute *that:*

[2:38] But then, Mr. Dubois reflected gloomily, women never had any prudence. Though he had profited by this lack many a time, it annoyed him now.

In any case there are marked differences among different styles and varieties of English as regards their patterns of anaphoric usage of *this* and *that*, the study of which goes beyond our present scope. For example, in narrative of a traditional kind, such as children's stories and ballads, we often find *that* where, in conversational narrative, a speaker would tend to use *this*, conveying a sense of immediacy and also of solidarity with the hearer, of shared interest and attention. So the ballad of the three little pigs has

[2:39] And after a time those little pigs died.

whereas if we were recounting the incident we should probably say *these little pigs*. It is this assumption of shared interest and attention which lies behind the use of the 'near' forms, *this* and *these*, in conversational narrative where they are not strictly 'phoric' at all: *There was this man . . .*, where 'this man' is present neither in the text nor in the situation but only in the speaker's mind. The context is one of highly coded, in-group speech, and the effect is to emphasize common experience and a common interest.

2.4.1.2 SINGULAR AND PLURAL: *this/that* VERSUS *these/those*

In general this distinction follows the expected pattern: *this/that* refer to count singular or mass nouns, *these/those* to count plural. The most important difference is that which separates the SINGULAR FORMS USED AS HEAD (*ie: this* and *that* without following noun) from the rest; this will be discussed in 2.4.1.3 below.

Otherwise, we may note simply that the plural forms may refer anaphorically not merely to a preceding plural noun, as in [2:39], but also to sets that are plural in meaning, for example

[2:40] 'Where do you come from?' said the Red Queen. 'And where are you going? Look up, speak nicely, and don't twiddle your fingers all the time.'
Alice attended to all these directions, and explained, as well as she could, that she had lost her way.

Conversely the singular demonstrative may refer to a whole list irrespective of whether or not it contains items that are themselves plural:

[2:41] I've ordered two turkeys, a leg of lamb, some cooked ham and tongue, and two pounds of minced beef. –
Whatever are you going to do with all that food?

But these uses follow from the general nature of anaphoric reference items, that they refer to the meanings and not to the forms that have gone before.

2.4.1.3 HEAD AND MODIFIER: *this*, ETC, AS PRONOUN VERSUS *this*, ETC, PLUS
           FOLLOWING NOUN

A demonstrative as Modifier ('demonstrative adjective') may refer without restriction to any class of noun. A demonstrative as Head ('demonstrative pronoun'), on the other hand, while it can refer freely to non-humans, is highly restricted in its reference to human nouns; it cannot refer to a human referent except in the special environment of an equative clause. For example, in

[2:42] 'Now the cleverest thing I ever did,' the Knight went on after a pause, 'was inventing a new pudding during the meat-course.
. . . I don't believe that pudding ever was cooked.'

it would be perfectly possible to omit the second *pudding* and say *I don't believe that ever was cooked* (*cf* [2:40] and [2:41]). On the other hand, in

[2:43] I must introduce you to the surgeon who looked after me when I

was in hospital. That surgeon really did a fine job, and nothing
was too much trouble for him.

we could not replace *that surgeon* by *that*. The only instance where demonstratives can refer pronominally to human referents, whether anaphorically or exophorically, is in relational clauses of the equative type where
one element is supplying the identification of the others, for example

[2:44] a. Do you want to know the woman who designed it? That was
        Mary Smith.
    b. Who are those colourful characters? – Those must be the
        presidential guards.

Compare the exophoric *Who's that?*, *this is John* (when introducing him),
those are the people I was telling you about; but never *let's ask this, I don't know
what that's laughing about*. The principle is that the demonstrative pronoun
corresponds to *it* and not to *he* or *she*. The fact that the plural form *they* is
the same for both human and non-human referents may explain why the
demonstrative is slightly less unacceptable with a human referent when it
is in the plural; we might perhaps accept *let's ask these, I don't know what
those are laughing about*.

There is one other important characteristic of demonstrative reference
that is specifically a feature of demonstratives functioning as Head. This
concerns the level of generality of the referent.

If the demonstrative is used with a noun, then the meaning is always
identical with that of the presupposed item. Examples are [2:39], [2:42]
and [2:43]. This normally holds true even if the noun following the
demonstrative is not identical with the presupposed item; it may be some
kind of a synonym, like *food* in [2:41], which is a SUPERORDINATE (*ie* a
more general term), or like *directions* in [2:40]. There is still identity of
reference in such instances; it is 'that particular food', 'those particular
directions'. These are in fact different types of lexical cohesion, and are
discussed further in Chapter 6. To invent one further example, in [2:45] it
does not matter whether we have *cat* or *animal* or *trickster* in the second
sentence; the reference is still to the original *cat*:

[2:45] There's a cat trying to get in, shall I open the window? –
        Oh, that cat / that animal / that trickster's always coming here
        cadging.

Suppose however that we use the demonstrative alone, without a following noun. The reference may still be identical; but it may be broader,

referring to the general class denoted by the noun, including but not limited to the particular member or members of that class being referred to in the presupposed item. If for example the first sentence in [2:45] had begun *There are two cats trying to get in*, then the answer *those cats* would still have referred only to the original *two cats;* but the answer *those, eg: Those have to be kept out*, could refer not just to the two cats mentioned but to cats in general. Compare:

[2:46] There's been another big industrial merger. It seems that nothing can be done about this.

where the meaning is not 'this particular merger' but 'mergers in general', as we can see by substituting *this merger*, or *this one*, for *this*. A related instance is provided by [2:47]:

[2:47] His hand groped for the knife. If he could only reach that he would be safe.

Here we could, in fact, substitute *that knife*, but not *that one*; the meaning is not 'that particular knife' but 'that particular object, namely the knife'. This affords a very good illustration of the difference between reference and substitution, as summarized at the beginning of Chapter 3 below. In the plural, the distinction is less clearcut, and there is the possibility of ambiguity:

[2:48] How did you like the recitations? I find those boring.

If it had been *I found*, the meaning would have been 'those particular recitations' and we could have substituted *those recitations* or *those ones.** I *find*, however, suggests '(those particular things, namely) recitations in general'; here we could certainly not substitute *those ones*, but it would perhaps be possible to substitute *those recitations* and still interpret it in this sense. In a comparable way, given *there are two cats trying to get in*, the answer *those creatures have to be kept out* is ambiguous as between 'those particular cats' and 'those particular creatures, namely cats in general'.

The general principle behind this is simply that demonstratives, since

* In most varieties of written English, and with some speakers, *these ones* and *those ones* do not occur; but there is a growing tendency to use these forms in speech precisely in order to make this distinction in meaning; to give another example, *Do you like my hydrangeas? – Yes, I like those* ('hydrangeas in general') contrasted with *Yes, I like those ones* ('those particular hydrangeas'). The form with *one(s)* is very often used exophorically, though not exclusively so. We are now beginning to hear *my one(s)*, *your one(s)* etc in place of *mine*, *yours*, etc, although here the distinction is unnecessary because the latter occur only in the second, particularized sense. See 3.2 below.

(like other reference items) they identify semantically and not grammatically, when they are anaphoric require the explicit repetition of the noun, or some form of synonym, if they are to signal exact identity of specific reference; that is, to refer unambiguously to the presupposed item at the identical degree of particularization. A demonstrative without a following noun may refer to some more general class that includes the presupposed items; and this also applies under certain conditions to a demonstrative with a following noun – namely if the context is such that the noun can be INTERPRETED more generally. It is not easy to specify exactly what these conditions are, but they are more likely to obtain with plural or mass nouns because these are general unless specified. In spoken English there is a one-way phonological distinction: the demonstratives have a weakened form that is used ONLY when they are NOT specifying and the meaning is one of generalized reference; for example

[2:49] How did you manage with the new drugs I gave you?
    (i) ‖ those / new / drugs up/set me ‖
    (ii) ‖∧ those / new / drugs up/set me ‖

Here (i) is ambiguous: it might mean either ‘the particular ones you gave me’ or ‘new drugs in general’; whereas (ii) can mean only ‘new drugs in general’. The generalized type is typically associated with expressions of attitude, for example *I don't trust these lawyers* (‘lawyers in general’), *those French are so touchy* (note that in the particularized sense it would have to be *those French people*); and also *that Bach had genius*, meaning not ‘J.S. as opposed to the rest of the family’ but ‘Bach, that we all know’. All these are simply equivalent to non-specific forms (*new drugs, lawyers, the French* and *Bach*) to which a demonstrative has been added, often for anaphoric purposes but without carrying over any specificity there may have been in the item that is presupposed.

The distinction between the particular use of a demonstrative, having exact identity of reference with the presupposed item, and the generalized use is related to that between defining and non-defining modifiers. In *that Bach, that* is non-defining; but if we change to it *that fellow Bach* it becomes defining. Similarly if we interpret *that* in [2.47] as ‘that knife’ it is non-defining, but if we interpret, it as ‘that thing’ it is defining. Compare *this* in

[2.50] They wept like anything to see
    Such quantities of sand.
  ‘If this were only swept away,’
    They said, ‘it would be grand’

– 'this sand', or 'this stuff'. The distinction does not, however, affect the textual function of demonstratives, since both uses are equally associated with anaphoric reference, and hence contribute to cohesion within the text.

2.4.1.4 EXTENDED REFERENCE AND REFERENCE TO 'FACT': *this* AND *that*

Related to the last, generalized type of demonstrative reference, but at the same time quite distinct from it, is the use of demonstratives to refer to extended text, including text as 'fact' (*cf: it* in 2.3.3.1 above). This applies only to the singular forms *this* and *that* used without a following noun. For example:

> [2:51] They broke a Chinese vase.
>   (i) That was valuable.
>   (ii) That was careless.

In (i) *that* refers to the object *vase*; we could have *that vase* instead. In (ii) *that* refers to the total event, 'their breaking of the vase'. If there had been more than one breakage we could have had *those were valuable* but not *those were careless:*

> [2:52] They broke a Chinese vase and damaged two chandeliers.
>   (i) Those were all very valuable.
>   (ii) That was all very careless.*

Extended reference probably accounts for the majority of all instances of demonstratives in all except a few specialized varieties of English. For example, in the last two chapters of *Alice's Adventures in Wonderland* there are 51 demonstratives, made up of 22 *this*, 24 *that*, 3 *these* and 2 *those*. Of the total, 31 are used in extended reference. Of the remaining 20, 3 refer to time, which is another form of extended reference, (*eg* [2:53a]), 10 are exophoric in the dialogue (*eg* [2:53b]), and 5 are anaphoric to preceding nominals (*eg* [2:53c]):

* A demonstrative functioning pronominally, *ie* without a following noun, is sometimes regarded as an instance of ellipsis; *eg* in [2:51i] we might be inclined to consider *that* as 'elliptical for' *that vase*. But in many instances we cannot, in fact, 'fill out' with a 'missing' noun because, as we have seen, there is no appropriate noun available: either because the reference is compound, as in [2:52i], or generalized, as in [2:46]; or because it is to an extended passage of text, as in [2:52ii]. Moreover reference is different in meaning from ellipsis (see Chapters 4 and 7 below); and all demonstratives, whether functioning as Modifier or as Head, satisfy the semantic conditions of reference, whereas they do not satisfy those of ellipsis.

[2:53] a. Just at this moment Alice felt a very curious sensation.
   b. 'Treacle,' said a sleepy voice behind her. 'Collar that Dormouse,' the Queen shrieked out.
   c. One of the jurors had a pencil that squeaked. This, of course, Alice could *not* stand . . .

Two instances are unclassifiable (*before she had this fit*, in the verses read out by the White Rabbit and repeated by the King). Examples of extended reference are:

[2:54] a. 'Give your evidence,' said the King; 'and don't be nervous, or I'll have you executed on the spot.'
   This did not seem to encourage the witness at all.
   b. 'But what did the Dormouse say?' one of the jury asked. 'That I can't remember,' said the Hatter.
   c. '"I gave her one, they gave him two" – why, that must be what he did with the tarts, you know.'

It is not always easy to say whether the referent of a demonstrative in a given instance is a particular nominal item in the text or should be taken to include something more; the *this* in [2:53c] could be supposed to refer to the whole of the preceding sentence. The distinction is not a sharp one, and it is usually irrelevant; in either case the effect is cohesive. But in many instances the referent clearly is an extended passage of text, and this, together with the related use of *it*, is one of the major cohesive devices of the English language.

Perhaps the most frequent form taken by such extended reference is in equative clauses where the demonstrative provides the 'given' element in the message and this then serves to identify some other element that is 'new', by simply being equated with it. [2:54c] is one example; here are some others:

[2:55] a. [following the White Rabbit's reading of the verses] 'That's the most important piece of evidence we've heard yet,' said the King, rubbing his hands.
   b. I come from Wolverhampton. – That's where I come from too.
   c. No one will take it seriously. This is the frightening thing.

Spoken English is typically held together by internal cross-referencing of this kind, which combines powerful structure with great flexibility and freedom of movement.

2.4.1.5 ANAPHORIC AND CATAPHORIC DEMONSTRATIVES

There is differentiation between *this* and *that* in extended text reference, which relates to their differentiation in terms of proximity. Whereas *that* is always anaphoric, *this* may be either anaphoric or cataphoric. Some Shakespearean examples:

[2:56] a. Viola: I am all the daughters of my father's house
          And all the brothers too, -- and yet I know not. --
          Sir, shall I to this lady?
      Duke: Ay, that's the theme.

    b. Hamlet: Do not look upon me
          Lest with this piteous action you convert
          My stern effects: then what I have to do
          Will want true colour; tears perchance for blood.
      Queen: To whom do you speak this?
      Hamlet: Do you see nothing there?
      Queen: Nothing at all; yet all that is I see.
      Hamlet: Nor did you nothing hear?
      Queen: No, nothing but ourselves.
      Hamlet: Why, look you there! look, how it steals away!
          My father, in his habit as he liv'd!
          Look, where he goes, even now, out of the portal!
      Queen: This is the very coinage of your brain.

    c. Cassius: That you have wronged me doth appear in this:
          You have condemn'd and noted Lucius Pella
          For taking bribes here of the Sardians;
          Wherein my letters, praying on his side,
          Because I knew the man, were slighted off.

[2:56a] has anaphoric *that*, (b) three instances of anaphoric *this*, and (c) cataphoric *this*.

This use of *this*, together with the parallel use of *here* (see 2.4.3 below), is the only significant instance of cataphoric cohesion in English. We have distinguished this, in the previous discussion, from structural cataphora as in *he who hesitates*; structural cataphora is very common, especially with the definite article (see 2.4.2 below), but it is simply a realization of a grammatical relationship within the nominal group and has no cohesive, text-forming function. Textual cataphora, by contrast, is true reference forward in the text; it therefore is cohesive, not by picking up what has preceded but by anticipating what is to follow. From *Alice*:

[2:57] These were the verses the White Rabbit read: – [followed by the verses]

In writing, sentences which are related cataphorically are often joined by a colon; but there is no structural relation between the two – this is a purely orthographic convention, serving precisely to signal the presence of cataphoric cohesion.

A final point to note is that in spoken English *this* and *that* in extended reference often carry the tonic (primary stress). In this they are unlike all other cohesive items in the language. Since, in the most general terms, tonicity is associated with information that is new, it is not surprising to find that anaphoric items, which by definition are not 'new', because they are referring to what has gone before, do not normally carry the tonic. (The position is quite different with reference items used exophorically; these are often tonic – again, not surprisingly, since in this case the referent has not been mentioned before.) We can be quite precise about anaphoric items: they are tonic when and only when they are contrastive, and this is part of the same story. The semantic category of 'new' means 'information being treated by the speaker as non-recoverable to the hearer'; it may be non-recoverable either because it has not been previously mentioned or because it has been previously mentioned but is unexpected and hence contrastive in the particular context. For example, in [2:58] *these* is 'new' in this second, contrastive sense:

[2:58]   The first row of cottages looked empty and decrepit. But behind them stood another row, well kept and with small bright gardens. Whoever lived in these cottages lived well enough.

A demonstrative with textual reference, however, is very frequently tonic; and this arises in two ways, both of which are simply extensions of the principle mentioned above, that tonicity signals what is new. In the first place there are very many instances in which the reference, while anaphoric, is in fact contrastive, this being the whole point of the utterance; for example

[2:59]   Where are you going?
         – To feed the fish.
         – THAT's what I was trying to remember to do just now.

In the second place, the reference may be cataphoric, in which case the referent has not been mentioned before; a cataphoric demonstrative is therefore regularly tonic. Contrast [2:60a], where *this* is anaphoric, meaning 'what I've just said', with [2:60b] where it is cataphoric, and means 'what I'm just going to say':

> [2:60] a. I can't get any reliable INFORMATION. This is what WORRIES me.
>   b. THIS is what worries me: I can't get any reliable INFORMATION.

(In [2:60a] *this* could be replaced by *that*, whereas in [2:60b] it could not.) As a corollary of its carrying the tonic, the cataphoric *this* could equally come at the end: in (b) we might well have *What worries me is this:*, whereas in (a) such a reversal is highly improbable.

2.4.2 *The*

The definite article *the* has usually been set apart, in grammars of English, as a unique member of a class, its only relative being the indefinite article *a*. There is some justification for this; no other item in English behaves exactly like *the*. On the other hand, it has important similarities with a whole group of other items, so that we need not hesitate to classify it with the determiners; and, more particularly, with the specific determiners, the class which includes the demonstratives and the possessives. (Likewise the indefinite article is a member of the wider class of non-specific determiners.) The full set of specific determiners is as follows:

	Demonstrative	Possessive
Referential	Selective $\begin{cases} this\ that \\ these\ those \end{cases}$	Speech roles *my, your, our*
	Non-selective *the*	Other roles $\begin{cases} his,\ her,\ their \\ its \\ one's \end{cases}$
Interrogative	*which*	*whose*

Hence *the* in many ways resembles the demonstratives, from one form of which it is derived. It is originally a reduced form of *that*, functioning only as a modifier, in the same way that *a* is a reduced form of *one* likewise restricted to the modifier function. And this is reflected in its meaning. Essentially *the*, like the demonstratives, is a specifying agent, serving to identify a particular individual or subclass within the class designated by the noun; but it does this only through dependence on something else – it contains no specifying element of its own.

This can be explained as follows. All other specific determiners are semantically selective; they contain within themselves some referential element in terms of which the item in question is to be identified. With the possessives, it is person: the item is identified as belonging to, or associated with, a recognizable participant – speaker, addressee or some person or object in the environment. With the demonstratives, it is proximity: the item is identified as present in the environment and more, or less, remote. In both these instances the environment, as we have seen, may be situational or textual; and when it is textual, this form of specification by reference becomes cohesive.

The definite article has no content. It merely indicates that the item in question IS specific and identifiable; that somewhere the information necessary for identifying it is recoverable. Where is this information to be sought? Again, either in the situation or in the text. The reference is either exophoric or endophoric. If it is exophoric, the item is identifiable in one of two ways. (1) A particular individual or subclass is being referred to, and that individual or subclass is identifiable in the specific situation. An example was [2:32] *Don't go; the train's coming*, where *the train* is interpreted as 'the train we're both expecting' – contrasted with *Don't go; a train's coming* which would perhaps be a warning to avoid being run over. All immediate situational instances of *the* are exophoric in this way: *mind the step; pass me the towel; the children are enjoying themselves; the snow's too deep; the journey's nearly over*, and so on. (2) The referent is identifiable on extralinguistic grounds no matter what the situation. This has something in common with the generalized exophoric use of the personal forms, and it occurs under two conditions. It may arise, first, because there exists only one member of the class of objects referred to, for example *the sun*; or, at least, one member which will be assumed in the absence of specific indication to the contrary, for example *the baby* ('our baby'), *the government* ('of our country'), *the time* ('now'). Secondly, it may arise because the reference is the whole class, *eg: the stars*; or the individual considered as a representative of the whole class, like *the child* in *As the child grows, he learns to be independent*, or *the snail* in *The snail is considered a great delicacy in this region*. This type of exophoric reference, which does not depend on the specific situation, has been called HOMOPHORIC to distinguish it from the situationally specific type.

Alternatively, the source of identification may lie in the text: what we are calling *endophoric* reference. In this case there are again two possibilities: reference forward, and reference backward. (3) Cataphoric or forward reference, with *the*, is limited to the structural type. Unlike the selective demonstratives (*this*, *these* and *here*), *the* can never refer forward cohesively. It can only refer to a modifying element within the same nominal group as itself. Here are some examples:

[2:61] a. The ascent of Mount Everest
b. The party in power
c. The people who predicted a dry summer
d. The longest stretch
e. The best way to achieve stability

What is the significance of *the* in such instances? It is, as always, a signal of identity; or rather, of identifiability, showing that criteria for identifying WHICH *ascent*, WHICH *party* etc is intended are recoverable – in this instance, they are recoverable from the nominal group in which the *the* occurs. In other words *the* is a signal that the modifying elements are to be taken as defining: we are to understand only such members of the general class named by the Head noun as are specified in the Modifier. The defining elements are *of Mount Everest, in power, who predicted a dry summer, longest,* and, in (e), the discontinuous Modifier *best . . . to achieve stability.*

(4) Finally there is anaphoric reference, the only one of the four conditions in which *the* is cohesive. The clearest instances of this are those in which the item is actually repeated, *eg: hall* in

[2:62] She found herself in a long, low hall which was lit up by a row of lamps hanging from the roof. There were doors all round the hall, but they were all locked.

Often the reference is to a synonym or near-synonym, or to some other item which by its connotations provides a target for the anaphora; in [2:63], *the eyes* are clearly those of the Cat (and note the lexical cohesion between *eyes* and *mouth*):

[2:63] 'How are you getting on?' said the Cat, as soon as there was mouth enough for it to speak with. Alice waited till the eyes appeared, and then nodded.

This shades into the sort of extended reference and text reference that we have found with *it*, *this* and *that;* for example *the prospect* in

[2:64] 'A nice mess we're all in. Pictures in the papers and reporters coming round.' She paused, obviously visualizing the future in a series of crude, highly-coloured pictures. He thought that the prospect was still not wholly unpleasing.*

Once again, *the* signals identifiability; but here the information about WHICH *hall*, WHICH *eyes* and WHICH *prospect* is to be recovered from the preceding text. This is what provides the 'texture'.

There is a commonly held belief that the typical function of *the* is the anaphoric one: that it invariably specifies by reference back in the text. Indeed it has sometimes been referred to as the 'second mention article'. It should be stressed, therefore, that anaphoric reference is only one means whereby *the* achieves specificity (and even when it is anaphoric, more often than not there is no 'second mention' of the same noun). It is probably true that purely anaphoric reference never accounts for a majority of instances: in pragmatic speech *the* is primarily exophoric, and in most other varieties of spoken and written English its predominant function is cataphoric. What must be recognized, however, is that these various types of reference are not mutually exclusive. A given occurrence of *the* might have any two or even three functions at the same time.

Consider for example:

[2:65] Last year we went to Devon for a holiday. The holiday we had there was the best we've ever had.

Here *the* is both cataphoric, pointing forward to *we had there*, and also anaphoric, referring the second occurrence of *holiday* back to that in the preceding sentence; and it would be meaningless to argue that it must be just the one or the other. Now suppose the same example continues:

[2:65] (cont'd) The people we stayed with had four children. The eldest girl was about nine.

The first *the* is cataphoric only, since there is no lexical relation between *people* and anything in the preceding passage. The second is again both cataphoric and anaphoric: cataphoric, showing that *eldest* defines *girl*, and anaphoric because *girl* is related to *children*. We might even construct an example with all three types of reference:

[2:66] Look at the moon! The daytime moon always seems so sad.

Here the second occurrence of *the* is cataphoric to *daytime*, anaphoric to the earlier *moon*, and exophoric both in the 'homophoric' sense, since there is

---

* Agatha Christie, *Pocketful of Rye*, Fontana Books.

only one moon, and also in the situational sense since it is specifically an object of attention. Such instances of fourfold reference are presumably fairly rare.

The function of the definite article can be summed up by saying that it is an unmarked or non-selective referential deictic. Its meaning is that the noun it modifies has a specific referent, and that the information required for identifying this referent is available. It does not contain that information in itself; it is the 'definite article' in the sense that its function is to signal definiteness, without itself contributing to the definition. Nor does it say where the information is to be located. It will be found somewhere in the environment, provided we interpret 'environment' in the broadest sense: to include the structure, the text, the situation and the culture. Whenever the information is contained in the text, the presence of *the* creates a link between the sentence in which it itself occurs and that containing the referential information; in other words, it is cohesive.

2.4.3 Demonstrative adverbs

There are four of these, *here*, *there*, *now* and *then*, although *now* is very rarely cohesive. Three of them need to be distinguished from their homographs – other words written the same way but, now at least, having different functions in the language. (1) Demonstrative *there* is to be distinguished from pronoun *there* as in *there's a man at the door*. (2) Demonstrative *now* is to be distinguished from conjunction *now* as in *now what we're going to do is this*. (3) Demonstrative *then* is to be distinguished from conjunction *then* as in *then you've quite made up your mind?* As a general rule the non-demonstrative forms are phonologically reduced, whereas the demonstratives are not reduced, though there may be no phonological difference in the case of *then*. It is the demonstratives only with which we are concerned here.

As reference items, *here* and *there* closely parallel *this* and *that*, respectively. For example

[2:67] 'Do you play croquet with the Queen today?'
    'I should like it very much,' said Alice, 'but I haven't been invited.'
    'You'll see me there,' said the Cat, and vanished.

The meaning of *there* is anaphoric and locative; it refers to 'playing croquet with the Queen'. Both *here* and *there* regularly refer to extended text, and then often with a meaning that is not one of place but of 'respect': 'in this respect', 'in that respect'. For example

[2:68] 'Of course it would be all the better,' said Alice:
'but it wouldn't be all the better his being punished.'
'You're wrong *there*, at any rate,' said the Queen.

In such contexts *here*, like *this*, may be cataphoric; in example [2:33] *this* could be replaced by *here* and *that* could be replaced by *there*. The demonstratives *this*, *these* and *here* provide, in fact, almost the only sources of cataphoric cohesion: they are the only items in English which regularly refer forward TEXTUALLY, to something to which they are not linked by a structural relationship.★ (An example of the cataphoric use of comparatives, which is much rarer, will be found in the next section.)

The temporal demonstratives *then* and *now* are much more restricted in their cohesive function. The cohesive use of demonstrative *then* is that embodying anaphoric reference to time; the meaning is 'at the time just referred to':

[2:69] In my young days we took these things more seriously.
We had different ideas then.

The use of *now* is confined to those instances in which the meaning is 'this state of affairs having come about', for example [2:70a]; [2:70b] shows a comparable use of *then*:

[2:70] a. The plane touched down at last. Now we could breathe freely again.
b. Why not tell your parents? Then we can stop pretending.

This is already approaching the use of *then* as a conjunctive; see 5.7 below.

2.4.4 A final note on demonstratives

There are very many expressions containing a demonstrative that occur as adjuncts, typically at the beginning of a clause; in general they come within the category often known as 'discourse adjuncts'. Examples are *in that case, that being so, after that, at this moment, under these circumstances.*

In the present analysis, we are treating these as conjunctives, not as

---

★ They do also occur in a form of structural cataphora, exemplified by *here in London, there on the opposite page;* compare *this* and *that* in *this mania for washing cars, that turkey we had for Christmas,* and also the special use of *those* in *those who*, meaning 'the people who', as in *those who predicted an earthquake.* Like other forms of structural cataphora, these make no contribution to cohesion.

demonstratives; see Chapter 5 below. This is on semantic grounds: the principle is that any semantic relation which is itself conjunctive is treated as conjunctive in all its realizations, whether or not there is a demonstrative or other reference item present in its expression. This also avoids making an awkward and artificial distinction between pairs of items such as *as a result* and *as a result of this;* both of these are interpreted in the same way, as conjunctives.

In fact, there is overlap between conjunction and reference at this point, and there would be no need in principle to force a classification in terms of just one or the other. But one of the purposes of the present study is to make it easy to analyse and compare texts in respect of their cohesive properties; and for this reason, in all instances of indeterminacy we have taken a decision one way or the other. As far as possible the decision has followed the line of semantic consistency, at the same time with an eye to applicability in practice.

2.5 Comparative reference

The table of comparative reference items was given in 2.2 above (Table 4). The system is as follows:

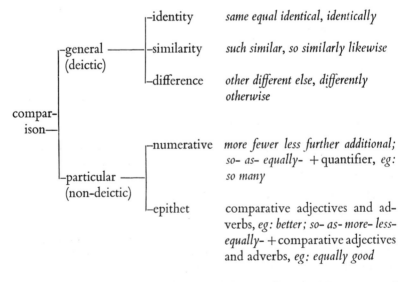

By 'general comparison' is meant comparison that is simply in terms of likeness and unlikeness, without respect to any particular property: two things may be the same, similar or different (where 'different' includes both 'not the same' and 'not similar'). General comparison is expressed by a certain class of adjectives and adverbs (separated from each other by a comma in the above lists). The adjectives function in the nominal group either as Deictic (*eg: identical* in *the identical two cards*) or as Epithet (*eg: identical* in *two identical cards*); it will be seen that these have different meanings (see 2.5.1 below). The adverbs function in the clause, as Adjunct (*eg: identically* in *the others performed identically*). These are called ADJECTIVES OF COMPARISON, ADVERBS OF COMPARISON, to distinguish them from COMPARATIVE ADJECTIVES and COMPARATIVE ADVERBS, which are the comparative forms of ordinary adjectives and adverbs, *eg: bigger, better, faster, more quickly.*

'Particular comparison' means comparison that is in respect of quantity or quality. It is also expressed by means of adjectives or adverbs; not of a special class, but ordinary adjectives and adverbs in some comparative form. The adjectives function, as always, within the nominal group, but not as Deictic; they function either as Numerative (*eg: more* in *more cards*) or as Epithet (*eg: better* in *better cards*). The adverbs function in either of two ways: either as Adjunct in the clause (*eg: better* in *the others performed better*) or as Submodifier, in which case they simply occur within an Epithet (*eg: such* in *such good cards, identically* in *an identically designed house*) or a Numerative (*eg: so* in *so many words*), or within an Adjunct (*eg: equally* in *the others performed equally badly*). It makes no difference whether the comparative adjective or adverb is inflected (*eg: slower, slowlier*) or compounded (*eg: more lengthy, more lengthily*); the meaning and function are not affected by this distinction.

The same principles operate with comparison as with other forms of reference: it may be anaphoric, and therefore cohesive, or it may be cataphoric or even exophoric. Only brief illustrations will be given of the non-anaphoric uses.

General comparison is discussed in 2.5.1 and particular comparison in 2.5.2.

2.5.1 General comparison

General comparison expresses likeness between things. The likeness may take the form of identity, where 'two things' are, in fact, the same thing, as in [2:71a]; or of similarity where two things are like each other, as in [2:71b]. Each of these has its negative; there is non-identity, and non-similarity. But these two concepts are conflated, in the semantic system, into a single meaning, that of non-likeness, or difference, as in [2:71c].*

> [2:71] a. It's the same cat as the one we saw yesterday.
>   b. It's a similar cat to the one we saw yesterday.
>   c. It's a different cat from the one we saw yesterday.

Likeness is a referential property. A thing cannot just be 'like'; it must be 'like something'. Hence comparison is a form of reference, alongside personal and demonstrative reference; and it embraces the same set of possibilities. The referent of the comparison may be in the situation, or it may be in the text. If it is in the text, the reference may be backwards or forwards, and it may be structural or non-structural (cohesive). With comparison, however, there is one further possibility: the comparison may be internal – the likeness expressed as *mutual* likeness without a referent appearing as a distinct entity.

All the examples in [2:71] were cataphoric in the structural sense; in each case the referent was *the one we saw yesterday*, and the comparatives *same*, *similar* and *different* were pointing forward to it in just the same way that *those* points forward to *who predicted an earthquake*. Other examples:

> [2:72] a. We have received exactly the same report as was submitted two months ago.
>   b. There are other qualities than conviviality needed for this job.
>   c. Find a number equal to the square of the sum of its digits.

The referents are [*the one that*] *was submitted two months ago*, *conviviality*, and *the square of the sum of its digits*. Such cataphoric reference is fully determined by the structure and therefore, as always, has no cohesive function.

Instances of cohesive cataphora, with comparatives, are not very common, but they do occur:

> [2:73] The other squirrels hunted up and down the nut bushes; but Nutkin gathered robin's pincushions off a briar bush, and stuck them full of pine-needle pins.

---

* There is probably a systematic distinction between the two in certain contexts, for example *someone other than John* 'not identical with', *someone different from John* 'not similar to'. But *different* is used in both senses, and there appears to be no consistent distinction in anaphoric contexts. An interesting example of the resulting semantic confusion occurs in the following dialogue with a three-year-old: Child: Who's Peter's daddy? Mother: Peter's daddy is Uncle Jack. Child: Is my daddy quite different from Peter's daddy? Mother: Oh yes. Child: But he's got eyebrows. (*ie* there is at least something in common between them.)

Here *other* is cataphoric to *Nutkin*; although the two are separated only by a semicolon, the effect is cohesive, as they are not structurally related. Compare:

> [2:74] The blow would have knocked anyone else cold. The champ just leaned to one side, then straightened again.

Examples such as those in [2:75] might be exophoric, the referent being retrievable from the situation:

> [2:75] a. I was expecting someone different.
>   b. Would you prefer the other seats?

the first being interpreted as 'different from you' or 'different from that person there', the second as 'other than those you see here'. Either however might equally be anaphoric, given contexts such as:

> [2:76] a. Jennings is here to see you. – I was expecting someone different.
>   b. They've given us special places in the front row. Would you prefer the other seats?

Another example of anaphoric comparison is [2:77], where *such* refers back to the nominal group qualifier *of mildly but persistently depressive temperament*:

> [2:77] Gerald Middleton was a man of mildly but persistently depressive temperament. Such men are not at their best at breakfast.*

Again, as with other types of reference, the referent may be a passage of any extent, *eg: so* in [2:78a] and *such* in [2:78b]:

> [2:78] a. 'Everybody says "Come in!" here,' thought Alice, as she went slowly after the Gryphon: 'I never was so ordered about in all my life, never!'
>   b. 'I see nobody on the road,' said Alice. 'I only wish I had such eyes,' the King remarked, 'To be able to see nobody – and at that distance too!'

Or it may be text treated as 'fact', when an expression such as *the same questions arise . . .* refers back to the whole of some previous discussion.

All the above patterns of reference are familiar from the personals and the demonstratives. But it should be noted that *same, similar, identical, equal* and *different* do not necessarily imply reference of any kind: the compari-

---

* Angus Wilson, *Anglo-Saxon Attitudes*, Secker & Warburg.

son may be purely internal, two or more things being compared with each other. For example

[2:79] a. Most people have the same breakfast every day.
     b. The candidates gave three similar answers.
     c. All parties showed an identical reaction to the news.

The first means 'the same as every other day', though with the possible ambiguity of 'the same as each other'; the second 'similar to each other', the third 'reacted in the same way as each other'. Here the comparatives are functioning not as Deictic but as Epithet, and therefore in this use they will FOLLOW any numeral that may be present, whereas in Deictic function they precede it: contrast [2:80a], where *different* is Deictic and referential, with [2:80b] where it is Epithet and non-referential:

[2:80] a. They were a different two colours.
     b. They were two different colours.

The first means 'different from the two referred to', the second 'different from each other'. Usage is not totally consistent, however, and one not infrequently comes across the second type used in the first of the two meanings. The words *other*, *additional* and *else* occur only in the referential sense; *equal*, on the other hand, is normally not referential, and can be so only when modifying nouns such as *number*, *amount* and *quantity*.

A brief comment on *other* and *else*. *Else* is distinguished not only by its unique position in relation to what it modifies, following instead of preceding, but also by the fact that it can accompany only the general nouns and adverbs *someone*, *nothing*, *everywhere* etc, or the corresponding interrogatives *who*, *what*, *where* etc. *Other* has two meanings, 'different' and 'additional', leading at times to uncertainty of interpretation:

[2:81] I need some other clothes. – As well, or instead?

2.5.2 *Particular comparison*

Particular comparison expresses comparability between things in respect of a particular property. The property in question may be a matter of quantity or of quality.

(1) If the comparison is in terms of quantity, it is expressed in the Numerative element in the structure of the nominal group; either (a) by a comparative quantifier, *eg: more* in *more mistakes*, or (b) by an adverb of comparison submodifying a quantifier, *eg: as* in *as many mistakes*.

(2) If the comparison is in terms of quality, it is expressed in either of two ways: (i) in the Epithet element in the nominal group, either (a) by a comparative adjective, *eg: easier, more difficult* in *easier tasks, more difficult tasks,* or (b) by an adverb of comparison submodifying an adjective, *eg: so* in *so difficult a task*; (ii) as Adjunct in the clause, either (a) by a comparative adverb, *eg: faster* in *Cambridge rowed faster,* or (b) by an adverb of comparison submodifying an adverb, *eg: as* in *she sang as sweetly.*

Particular comparison, like general comparison, is also referential; there must be a standard of reference by which one thing is said to be superior, equal, or inferior in quality or quantity. An example of the hearer's demand for a referent, when faced with a comparative of this kind, is the well-known passage:

[2:82] 'Take some more tea,' the March Hare said to Alice, very earnestly.
'I've had nothing yet,' Alice replied in an offended tone, 'so I can't take more.'

The standard of reference may be another thing, *eg:* 'this tree is taller than that tree', or a measure, *eg:* 'this tree is taller than ten feet'. The other thing may be implicit, as in the copy-writer's formula *for a tastier meal, use* . . ., where the comparison is presumably with a meal prepared without the product, or perhaps one prepared with 'Brand X'. It may be some generalized situational referent, as in

[2:83] We are demanding higher living standards.

– presumably 'than we have now'. The most generalized comparative is, actually, the superlative: *highest* means, simply, 'higher than any other'. Superlatives are non-referential because they are self-defining; and for this reason they regularly act as defining Modifier, being shown to be defining in the usual way by the presence of the definite article: so in *the highest mountain in Europe, the* shows that *highest . . . in Europe* specifies which mountain (*cf* [2:61e] above). In some languages which, in this region of the grammar, have resources similar to English the superlative is, in fact, the combination of the comparative with the definite article. English keeps comparison and definiteness formally apart, and so has, on the one hand, generalized exophoric comparatives used as defining modifiers, as in *the milder tobacco* ('than any'), and on the other hand non-defining superlatives such as *a latest notion is* . . ., meaning 'one of the latest notions'.

All the usual types of reference are found. For example, the following are cataphoric:

[2:84] a. There were twice as many people there as last time.
    b. He's a better man than I am.
    c. There are more things in heaven and earth, Horatio, than are
       dreamt of in your philosophy.

[2:84a] is comparison of quantity, with a Numerative as comparative, and
[the people who were there] *last time* as referent; (b) is quality, with an
Epithet as the comparative, and *I* – or rather, [the man that] *I am* – as
referent. In (c), the referent is [the things that] *are dreamt of in your philosophy*; the comparison is again quantitative, but the example shows that
more has some of the ambiguity that is present with *other* (see end of 2.5.1
above): we interpret Hamlet as meaning not just a greater quantity of
things but things that are different in kind. All these represent structural
cataphora; the referent is within the nominal group. Also structurally
cataphoric are examples such as [2:85], where the comparative is an
Adjunct in the clause:

[2:85] The little dog barked as noisily as the big one.

Here the referent is not a thing but a process: not *the big one* but *the big one*
[barked]. Examples [2:84] and [2:85] illustrate the point that the referent
of a cataphoric comparative is not necessarily made fully explicit in the
structure. It may be, as in *John is older than Peter*, where the second term in
the comparison presupposes nothing from the first; but in many instances
the common element in the two terms is carried over by presupposition –
this is what is shown in square brackets above. This phenomenon is outside our present scope, since this feature has nothing to do with cohesion;
but it is of considerable interest, and has been described and explained in a
number of detailed studies. Other examples of cataphoric comparatives:

[2:86] a. I have never seen a more brilliant performance than last night/
       last night's.
    b. She has a similarly furnished room to mine.

We do find examples of particular comparison which are cataphoric but
in the cohesive sense, such as the following from *Alice*:

[2:87] She thought that in all her life she had never seen soldiers so un-
       certain on their feet: they were always tripping over something
       or other, and whenever one went down, several more always fell
       over him, . . .

The comparative element is *so uncertain on their feet*; the text then has a
colon as a signal that this is to be interpreted as pointing forward.

It is easy to think of exophoric examples; one is the fisherman's *so big* with the arms held apart to indicate the size of the catch, another the hairdresser's *would you like the water cooler?* This type of exophoric comparative is a very commonly used form of instruction and observation in everyday life: we relate our wishes to the actual state of things, or relate what is there to what was there or what is somewhere else: *not so much noise!*, *go slowlier!*, *I need a sharper one, mine was much prettier* and so on. One of Alice's comments on her experiences took such a comparative form: '*Curiouser and curiouser!*'

As always, it is the anaphoric type that interests us, since this is what brings about cohesion in the text; examples are perhaps obvious enough:

[2:88] a. Cassius: Ye gods, ye gods, must I endure all this?
           Brutus: All this? Ay, more! Fret till your proud heart break.
       b. 'When £8,000 is a minor matter, it must be really large-scale crime that is in question?'
           'Bigger rackets go on.'
       c. Apparently Brown resigned, when his proposal was rejected.
           – I wish he could have acted less precipitately.

The anaphoric comparatives are *more*, *bigger* and *less precipitately*; and their referents are clearly identifiable as *this*, *£8,000* and *resigned*. As usual there is also extended reference to longer and less clearly defined passages of text, for example *so many* in [2:89]:

[2:89] Here the Red Queen began again. 'Can you answer useful questions?' she said. 'How is bread made?'
       'I know *that*!' Alice cried eagerly. 'You take some flour –'
       'Where do you pick the flower?' the White Queen asked. 'In a garden, or in the hedges?'
       'Well, it isn't *picked* at all,' Alice explained: 'it's ground –'
       'How many acres of ground?' said the White Queen. 'You mustn't leave out so many things!'

It is in the nature of comparatives that, of all the reference items, they are the ones that are most typically anaphoric rather than exophoric. This is to be expected. Personals and demonstratives both involve a form of reference that is inherently extralinguistic, though it may be reinterpreted in linguistic terms: reference to speech roles (the roles of the participants in the communication process), and to proximity to the speaker, is essentially reference to the situation, and only the 'third person' personals, whose situational definition is a purely negative one – person or thing

OTHER THAN speaker or addressee –, have the anaphoric function as the clearly predominant one, with exophoric reference being only secondary. With comparison, however, although the relationship is still clearly a referential one (in the sense in which we are using the term), the specific nature of this relationship, that of likeness or comparability between things, makes it more probable that the things which are being related to one another should be at the same level of abstraction; in other words, that both the comparative and its referent should be located at the semantic level (*ie* in the text) rather than the one in the text and the other in the situation. Thus while there certainly is exophoric reference with the comparatives – the sentence following [2:89] provides a nice example of it:

> [2:89] (cont'd) 'Fan her head!' the Red Queen anxiously interrupted. 'She'll be feverish after so much thinking!'

– as a general rule they tend to be text-oriented, and to give the reader or hearer a strong sense of fibres of internal cohesion.

Like general comparison, particular comparison may also be purely internal, and thus not referential at all; in this case it is expressed by sub-modifiers in *-ly*, nearly always *equally:*

> [2:90] They asked me three equally difficult questions.

As it stands, this is ambiguous; it could be anaphoric. But in the sense of 'each as difficult as the others', it is non-referential, like [2:79] above.

2.5.3 A note on so, such and as

Among the words of comparison, these require a brief special mention. In principle they can be regarded as variants of the same word, which takes the form *such* when it is an adjective, *so* when it is a free adverb and *as* when it is a bound adverb. This is something of an oversimplification, but it approximates to the facts; all have the same meaning of 'similar(ly)', and the choice among them is largely a matter of grammatical function.

We find *so* and *such* used simply as intensifiers, meaning 'extremely', although perhaps even here there is a nuance of 'such as you would never have imagined':

> [2:91] a. The war scenes in the film were so terrifying.
> b. Our neighbours are such a nuisance.

These become structurally cataphoric in [2:92]:

[2:92] a. The war scenes in the film were so terrifying that many of the audience left.
　　　 b. Our neighbours are such a nuisance that we may have to move.

Historically [2:93] are also cataphoric, though they are no longer felt to be so:

[2:93] a. He hid in the shed so that no one would find him.
　　　 b. Our fear of her was such that we dared not contradict her.

Both [2:92] and [2:93] are unusual among instances of cataphora in that the referent is not part of the nominal group; in addition, *so*, *such* and *as* all occur in the usual type of cataphora where the referent is a Qualifier, for example:

[2:94] Such an efficient man as John ⎫
　　　 So efficient a man as John 　 ⎬ is unlikely to be mistaken.
　　　 A man so/as efficient as John ⎭

Exophorically we find *such* and *so*; *as* is unusual among reference items in having no exophoric use – this is a corollary of its 'bound'-ness. So if we were watching someone lifting a heavy weight we might say [2:95a], but not [2:95b], which could occur only anaphorically, following something like *I didn't expect John to beat Peter*:

[2:95] a. I never thought he was so strong.
　　　 b. I never thought he was as strong.

Alternatively we could make the *as* in [2:95b] cataphoric by adding *as that* at the end, with the exophoric reference carried by the *that*. Another example of exophoric *so* is the Carpenter's

[2:96] I wish you were not quite so deaf – I've had to ask you twice!

though that is simultaneously cataphoric to the succeeding line. None of these items, however, is as frequently used in exophoric contexts as the demonstratives are; as we have already remarked, comparatives as a whole are more text-oriented than demonstratives, and *so*, *such* and *as* are quite typical in this respect.

We have already cited examples of their anaphoric use, both independently, in general comparison (*eg*: [2:77], [2:78]), and as Submodifiers in particular comparison [2:89]. Three further examples:

[2:97] a. He seemed most upset. – I never knew he cared so.
    b. Let me have men about me that are fat!
       Yon Cassius hath a lean and hungry look.
       Such men are dangerous.
    c. 'Are five nights warmer than one night, then?' Alice ventured to ask.
       'Five times as warm, of course.'

We shall come across *so* and *such* in other cohesive functions, in substitution (Chapter 3) and conjunction (Chapter 5). In particular, *so* has a wide range of uses, partly owing to its functioning freely both as Submodifier and as Adjunct. In this respect, it is resembled by *more* and *less*; to give one more example, they are Adjunct in [2:98a], Submodifier in [2:98b]:

[2:98] a. He seemed most upset.– I never knew he cared so. – He used to care even more.
    b. He comes every week. – I never knew he came so often. – He used to come even more often.

But *more* and *less* are only comparatives, whereas *so* is many other things besides, all of them cohesive in one way or another.

Finally there are a number of expressions which resemble the comparatives in meaning but are themselves constructed in other ways, exemplified in [2:99a–e]:

[2:99] a. 'Oswyn then says that a well-drilled equerry took two steps forward, received the picture from you, and took two steps back. He was accustomed to the whole manoeuvre, that is to say. And then the visit ended. Would you say that's right?' 'Nothing of the kind, my dear fellow.'*
    b. 'If we'd gone on pretending long enough, I believe we might have *been* happy together, sometimes. It often works out like that.'†
    c. Walk right up, and take the box where everyone can see you. That way it won't look as though you're stealing.
    d. Edward ran up and vaulted the fence without effort. John tried to do likewise – with disastrous results.
    e. You don't seem to have got very far with all those jobs I asked you to do. And another thing – what have you done with the scissors?

* Michael Innes, *A Family Affair*, Gollancz.
† J. B. Priestley, *Dangerous Corner* (The Plays of J. B. Priestley, Vol. 1), Heinemann.

Expressions such as *of the kind, like that, that way, do likewise, and another thing* show a semantic likeness to the comparatives which suggests that they might be treated under this heading. But it would not be easy to define or to list the set of expressions that were being included within this category. What is more important, they can all be identified in one way or other with other types of cohesion, either because they contain a demonstrative (*the, this, that*) or a substitute (*do*), or because they fall within one of the conjunctive categories (*eg:* the discourse adjuncts *in addition, and another thing, similarly, in other words, so far*); and it is this that determines how they are used. It seems more satisfactory therefore to interpret them not as comparatives but as falling under those other headings, always bearing in mind that the different forms of cohesion are nowhere sharply set apart one from another.

Chapter 3

Substitution

3.1 Substitution and ellipsis

In this and the next chapter we shall be discussing another type of cohesive relation, which takes two different forms: substitution, and ellipsis. These can be thought of in simplest terms as processes within the text: substitution as the replacement of one item by another, and ellipsis as the omission of an item. Essentially the two are the same process; ellipsis can be interpreted as that form of substitution in which the item is replaced by nothing. But the mechanisms involved in the two are rather different, and also, at least in the case of ellipsis, fairly complex; so we shall devote a chapter to each.

3.1.1 Substitution and reference

The distinction between substitution and reference is that substitution is a relation in the wording rather than in the meaning. It has been emphasized already that the classification of cohesive relations into different types should not be seen as implying a rigid division into watertight compartments. There are many instances of cohesive forms which lie on the borderline between two types and could be interpreted as one or the other. The situation is a familiar one in many fields, and when one is attempting to explain phenomena as complex as those of human language it would be surprising to find things otherwise; this is particularly so when we are concerned with phenomena which are both semantic and grammatical, since it frequently happens that semantic criteria suggest one interpretation while grammatical criteria suggest another, and the description has to account for both, facing both ways at once. The analysis that is adopted here is based on certain general principles, to which particular instances can be more or less unambiguously referred.

The principle distinguishing reference from substitution is reasonably clear. Substitution is a relation between linguistic items, such as words or phrases; whereas reference is a relation between meanings. In terms of the linguistic system, reference is a relation on the semantic level, whereas substitution is a relation on the lexicogrammatical level, the level of grammar and vocabulary, or linguistic 'form'. Ellipsis, as we have already remarked, is in this respect simply a kind of substitution; it can be defined as substitution by zero. So we have:

Type of cohesive relation:	Linguistic level:
Reference	Semantic
Substitution (including Ellipsis)	Grammatical

The meaning of the reference item *he* is 'some person (male), other than the speaker or addressee, who can be identified by recourse to the environment'. The cohesion lies in the semantic identity; and the fact that in a given instance the relevant environment may be the preceding text, in which, say, *John Smith* has occurred, is incidental. Anaphoric reference, as we have seen, is merely a special case of reference in general, and the text is merely a special case of the environment; the reference may just as well be exophoric, where the relevant environment is the situation. Anaphoric and exophoric reference are both derived from the general underlying notion of recoverability of meanings from the environment.

Substitution, on the other hand, is a relation within the text. A substitute is a sort of counter which is used in place of the repetition of a particular item. For example, in

[3:1] a. My axe is too blunt. I must get a sharper one.
       b. You think Joan already knows? – I think everybody does.

one and *does* are both substitutes: *one* substitutes for *axe*, and *does* for *knows*. And whereas in reference there is no implication that the presupposed item could itself have figured in the text, and in many instances we know it could not have done, this is implied in the case of substitution. Thus, in [3:1 a and b] it would be entirely possible to 'replace' *one* by *axe* and *does* by *knows*.

It follows that, as a general rule, the substitute item has the same structural function as that for which it substitutes. In the above example, *one* and *axe* are both Head in the nominal group; and *does* and *knows* are both Head in the verbal group. The identity is less obvious in [3:2]:

[3:2] Has Barbara left? – I think so.

where the substitute *so* stands for (*that*) *Barbara has left*. But here too the *so* has the same function in relation to *I think* as has a clause of reported speech. Again, we have seen that reference is different; there is no such restriction there, and the grammatical function of a reference item may be quite different from that of its referent (example [2:21] and [2:22]).

From the point of view of textual cohesion, of course, substitution resembles reference in being potentially anaphoric, and hence constituting a link between parts of a text. But here too there is a difference, following from the different nature of the two types of relation. Because reference is basically a non-verbal relation, a reference item may point in any direction, and pointing to the preceding text is only one among the set of possibilities. Substitution, on the other hand, being a verbal relation, is essentially confined to the text. Exophoric substitution is fairly rare; and it has the effect of implying that something HAS been said before. If the fisherman sees me admiring his catch, he may say, without my having uttered a word:

[3:3] Ah! but you should have seen the one that got away.

In doing so, however, he 'puts into my mouth' some such observation as *That's a good-sized trout you've got there*. I myself might even have said *That's a good-sized one you've got there*, using exophoric substitution, in the first place; even here, however, there would be a shared assumption that the fish in front of us was already the topic of conversation. The vast majority of all instances of substitution are endophoric; and of these again, the vast majority are anaphoric, although we shall come across the possibility of cataphoric substitution under certain circumstances. Nearly every occurrence of a substitute, in other words, is a source of cohesion with what has gone before.

3.1.2 Types of substitution

Since substitution is a grammatical relation, a relation in the wording rather than in the meaning, the different types of substitution are defined grammatically rather than semantically. The criterion is the grammatical function of the substitute item. In English, the substitute may function as a noun, as a verb, or as a clause. To these correspond the three types of substitution: nominal, verbal, and clausal.

These will be discussed in turn: nominal substitution in 3.2, verbal substitution in 3.3 and clausal substitution in 3.4. The following is a list of the items that occur as substitutes; the list is very short:

Nominal: *one, ones; same*
Verbal: *do*
Clausal: *so, not*

There are a few expressions in which there is some indeterminacy among the three types, for example, *do so, do the same*; these will come up for discussion where they seem most appropriate. In addition, there is a borderline where substitution shades into lexical cohesion, involving the use of GENERAL WORDS such as *thing* in a cohesive function. For the discussion of these see the chapter on lexical cohesion (Chapter 6).

3.2 Nominal substitution

The substitute *one/ones* always functions as Head of a nominal group, and can substitute only for an item which is itself Head of a nominal group. For example:

[3:4]   I shoot the hippopotamus
       With bullets made of platinum
   Because if I use leaden ones
       His hide is sure to flatten 'em.★

Here *bullets* is Head of the nominal group *bullets made of platinum* and *ones* is Head of the nominal group *leaden ones*.

The two nominal groups need not themselves have the same function in the clause; either may have any function that is open to a nominal group. Sometimes, as with reference, the presupposed item is buried deep inside a complex structure: the hearer generally has no difficulty in recovering it (*cf* [2:23] above);

[3:5]   If only I could remember where it was that I saw someone putting away the box with those candles in I could finish the decorations now. – You mean the little coloured ones?

The substitute may differ from the presupposed item in number; in the following the presupposed item is the singular *cherry*, whereas the substitute is plural:

[3:6]   Cherry ripe, cherry ripe, ripe I cry.
   Full and fair ones – come and buy.

★ H. Belloc, 'The Hippopotamus' in *The Bad Child's Book of Beasts*, Duckworth.

But the noun that is presupposed is always a count noun; there is no substitute form for mass nouns. Contrast [3:7a and b]:

[3:7] a. These biscuits are stale. – Get some fresh ones.
       b. This bread's stale. – Get some fresh.

In (b) the only possible form of substitution is substitution by zero, which is what we call ellipsis (Chapter 4). Semantically, ellipsis and substitution are very close; we have said that ellipsis can be interpreted as substitution without a substitute. Grammatically, however, the two are fairly distinct.

Some further examples of *one/ones* as substitute:

[3:8] a. So she wandered on, talking to herself as she went, till on turning a sharp corner, she came upon two fat little men, so suddenly that she could not help starting back, but in another moment she recovered herself, feeling sure that they must be –
       TWEEDLEDUM AND TWEEDLEDEE . . .
       They stood so still that she quite forgot they were alive, and she was just looking around to see if the word 'TWEEDLE' was written on the back of each collar, when she was startled by a voice coming from the one marked 'DUM'.
       b. I've heard some strange stories in my time. But this one was perhaps the strangest one of all.
       c. Which kind of engines do you want? Ones with whistles, or ones without?
       d. My dear, I really must get a thinner pencil. I can't manage this one a bit; it writes all manner of things that I don't intend.

3.2.1 *The meaning of substitute* one/ones

The substitute *one/ones* presupposes some noun that is to function as Head in the nominal group. It is a substitution counter put in to fill the 'Head' slot. The meaning is 'the noun to fill this slot will be found in the preceding text (occasionally elsewhere)'.

In the typical instance the substitute 'carries over' only the Head itself; it does not carry over any modifying elements by which this may have been accompanied. So for example in [3:4] the use of *ones* as substitute specifically excludes the defining Modifier *made of platinum*; *ones* replaces *bullets* and that is all. Furthermore, however, in place of the original modifying elements the substitute regularly brings with it its own defining

Modifier, in this case *leaden*. The effect is differential: *leaden ones* is specifically differentiated from (ones that are) *made of platinum*.

It is this differentiation which is characteristic of the use of substitutes in general. A substitute is a carrier of some information which differentiates the instance in which it occurs from the other instance to which it relates by cohesion. In the case of a nominal substitute, this means that it is the carrier of some modifying element which has this differential function: so, *ones* is a 'carrier' for *leaden* which has the function of differentiating the bullets mentioned in this instance from the ones mentioned earlier, those *made of platinum*.

It follows therefore that the nominal substitute *one/ones* is always accompanied by some modifying element which functions as DEFINING in the particular context. This element is not necessarily the same in its structural function in the nominal group as that which it repudiates; in our example [3:4], the repudiated element *made of platinum* is a Qualifier, whereas the one accompanying the substitute, *leaden*, is a Classifier. (There is a similar example in the sentence just written, where the same thing happens in reverse; here the substitute is accompanied by a Qualifier, namely *accompanying the substitute*, and what it repudiates is a Classifier, namely *repudiated*.) Another example:

[3:9] I thought I'd finished with the toughest assignments. They didn't tell me about this one.

where the Epithet *toughest* is repudiated by the Deictic *this*. In all such instances the modifying element in the anaphoric nominal group, namely *leaden, accompanying the substitute*, and *this*, is acting as a defining Modifier.

We have used the term REPUDIATION, and this concept provides a key to the understanding of substitution (including ellipsis), distinguishing it at the same time rather clearly from reference. The notion of repudiation is explained as follows. In any anaphoric context, something is carried over from a previous instance. What is carried over may be the whole of what there was, or it may be only a part of it; and if it is only a part of it, then the remainder, that which is not carried over, has to be REPUDIATED. For example, in

[3:10] We have no coal fires; only wood ones.

fires is carried over anaphorically, but *coal* is repudiated.

Semantically this means that, given the set of things designated in the original instance, what is now being designated is in some sense a new subset. It may be a different subset from that specified previously, as in

[3:10]; or a subset now specified where none had been specified before, as in [3:11].

[3:11] Did you light fires? – Only wood ones.

It may merely be a new aspect of or angle on what was there before, as in

[3:12] Do you remember that thunderstorm we had the last time we were here? That was a terrifying one!

It may even be THE SAME subset or aspect, where the sameness is itself unexpected or contrastive. This, interestingly, is the only class of instances in which the substitute *one/ones* carries the tonic nucleus:

[3:13] Would you like me to change the pictures in your room? – No, I think we'd like to keep the same ONES.

Whereas in [3:10] there is repudiation of an explicit subset, the class of 'coal fires', in examples such as [3:11–3:13] what is repudiated is implicit: 'fires other than wood ones', 'thunderstorms other than terrifying ones' (or 'thunderstorms in their non-terrifying aspects'), and 'pictures other than the same ones' (*ie* all those that would result from the process of changing). But what is common to all is that in one way or another there is a redefinition of the 'thing' that is represented by the Head noun, involving some form of repudiation of the definition in the original instance.

This does not necessarily mean that EVERYTHING in the original definition must be repudiated. In [3:8a], for example, the presupposed instance is *two fat little men*; the presupposing one is *the one marked 'DUM'*. Now Tweedledum is just as fat and little as Tweedledee is; the only element that is repudiated here is the *two*. Compare:

[3:14] That new cloth-backed Ordnance Survey one-inch tourist map you sold me was ideal – but I gave it away. Have you got another one?

where everything is carried over except the *that*. In instances like this where the Head noun that is presupposed is accompanied by a string of modifying elements, the context will usually make it clear how much is carried over, working backwards, as it were, from the Head. Exactly the same phenomenon arises in ellipsis, and it will be illustrated further in the next chapter.

We said at the beginning of 3.2.1 that the substitute *one/ones* is a substitution counter filling the Head function in the nominal group, and that it normally carries over only the Head itself. We can now put this more precisely. The use of the substitute always involves some new modifying element that is, therefore, defining: *this one, another one, the biggest one, the one that got away* and so on. This does not imply that none of the modifying elements can be carried over from the presupposed item. It means merely that there is always some point of contrast; the meaning of the nominal group containing the substitute is never exactly identical with that of the nominal group that is presupposed.

This is the essential difference between personal or demonstrative reference and nominal substitution. In reference there is a total referential identity between the reference item and that which it presupposes; nothing is to be added to the definition. In substitution there is always some redefinition. Substitution is used precisely where the reference is not identical, or there is at least some new specification to be added. This requires a device that is essentially grammatical rather than semantic; the presupposition is at the grammatical level. The substitute *one/ones* is the marker of a grammatical relation; it presupposes a particular noun, typically one that is to be found in the preceding text, and is itself merely a kind of counter for which that noun has been exchanged. Since its role is to signal that there is some form of redefinition, it has to be accompanied by some defining Modifier, and can therefore be thought of as a carrier for such defining elements. The process of defining has the effect of repudiating whatever is not carried over in the presupposition relation: the new definition is contrastive with respect to the original one.

For this reason, *one* can never substitute for a proper name: a proper name is already fully defined as unique, and there is no way of adding to or altering the definition. (Oddities like *Have you seen John? – Well, I saw the tall one just now*, where there is more than one *John*, are exceptions not to the use of *one* but to the general definition of proper names. In this instance *John* is being treated by the respondent as a class name.)

3.2.2 *Conditions of use of the nominal substitute*

As illustration of the use of the nominal substitute *one/ones*, let us first consider the following forms:

[3:15]	(i)	(ii)	(iii)
	a. this one	this new one	this one with wheels
	b. the one	the new one	the one with wheels
	c. one	a new one	one with wheels

Those in row (a) might occur in some such text as *Mummy, will you buy me a bus? I want* . . . All occur quite freely since each one contains a modifying element (*this, this new, this . . . with wheels*) to which *one* is attached as Head, and which is interpreted as defining in function (it was pointed out above that substitute *one* always requires to be defined).

Those in row (b) have the definite article which, as we saw in Chapter 2, does not itself carry the necessary specification; it merely indicates that this specification is available in the environment. In (bii) and (biii) the specification is contained in the Modifier (Epithet *new*, Qualifier *with wheels*), to which *the* refers cataphorically. But (bi) is odd; it has no defining Modifier, and can therefore occur only in a highly restricted context where the meaning is fully specified anaphorically, and so the sense is 'the one you mean', as in *I know the one, that's the one, these are the ones*. In other contexts only some expanded form such as *the one you mean* can occur.

Those in row (c) have the indefinite article. This is obvious in (cii), since both *a* and *one* appear. In (ciii) the indefinite article and the substitute are fused, so that 'a one' is represented simply as *one*; it is in fact not impossible, though it is still relatively rare, to keep them apart and say *a one with wheels*. What about (ci)? This might at first sight also seem to be a fusion of substitute *one* with the indefinite article; but this interpretation will not really stand. For one thing, it is semantically undefined; there is no explicit form to which it can be related, as *the one* relates to *the one you mean* -- naturally, since if there was it would have the definite article and not the indefinite. For another thing, it has no plural *ones*, whereas the substitute *one* always participates in the singular/plural system realized as *one/ones*, eg: *I know the ones* (*you mean*). In fact, its plural is *some* (*I want one/I want some*), and this provides the clue to its interpretation: it is simply the indefinite article in the form which it takes as Head of the nominal group. Thus *I want one* is simply the realization that takes the place of *I want a;* the *one* is anaphoric, but by ellipsis (not replacement) of the noun functioning as 'Thing'. The relation between substitute *one* and determiner (indefinite article) *one* is discussed further in 3.2.3.3 below.

Leaving aside (ci), then, on the grounds that it does not contain the substitute *one*, we can say that in all the other examples under [3:15] the substitute *one* is obligatory; as we expressed it earlier, it is a carrier of the specifying element *this, new* etc. Even in (ai) it cannot be omitted without changing the meaning. *I want this* is perfectly grammatical but means 'I want this thing', not 'I want this bus' (or whatever the *one* in *I want this one* is substituting for). There are environments, however, in which the substitute *one* is optional, giving a choice between substitution and ellipsis:

[3:16]	(i)	(ii)	(iii)
a.	these ones	these new ones	these (ones) with wheels
b.	which (one)	which new one	which one with wheels
c.	hers (?her one)	her new one	hers (her one) with wheels
d.	Paul's (one)	Paul's new one	Paul's one with wheels
e.	each (one)	each new one	each one with wheels
f.	the last (one)	the last new one	the last one with wheels
g.	two (?ones)	two new ones	two (ones) with wheels

Column (i) is tending to be filled out; one hears not only *her one*, *his one*, and others such as *what one*, but also, especially in children's speech, *two ones*. In column (ii) the substitute is obligatory, since the nominal group cannot normally end with an Epithet. Column (iii) is very variable, and in some instances an alternative of the form *that one of hers with wheels*, *two of the ones with wheels* would tend to be preferred. Note that although *this* does not mean the same as *this one* (ie cannot be interpreted as ellipsis), *these* can mean the same as *these ones* (ie it is ambiguous in contexts where it could be interpreted elliptically): *I want these* means either 'I want these (ones, *eg*) buses' or 'I want these things'.

As mentioned earlier, the plural of the substitute *one* is *ones*. With the exception of [3:15ci], the plural *ones* could occur in all positions in [3:15] and [3:16], showing that these are indeed all instances of substitution. The nominal substitute can in fact substitute for any count noun (any noun participating in the number system), either non-human or human; in this it differs from the 'pro-noun', the only other form of *one* which has plural *ones* (see 3.2.3.4 below).

Aside from the doubtful cases of determiner plus substitute, such as *my one*, *two ones* cited above, the one structural environment in the nominal group in which the substitute cannot occur is within a nominal compound: thus we do not normally find examples such as

[3:17] a. Lend me a pen. – I've only got a fountain one.
   b. Let's go and see the bears. The polar ones are over on that rock.
   c. Is that a tennis racket? – No it's a squash one.
   d. Are you planting trees here? – I thought of planting some apple ones.

This restriction can be stated roughly by reference to tonic accent: a word FOLLOWING the accented word in a nominal expression cannot be substituted; and since tonic accent is itself a realization of a compound noun structure, this is equivalent to saying that there can be no substitution within a compound noun. However the restriction also extends, under conditions which are not clear, to certain instances which on the criterion of tonicity would not be compounds but structures of Classifier plus Thing, *eg*

[3:18] a. He's an idiot. – The village one?
b. We sat by a lovely little stream. It was cool and clear, like all mountain ones.

The tonic structure of *village idiot, mountain stream*, shows that they are Classifier-Noun structures, not compound nouns; and yet it is scarcely possible to substitute the Head noun in such cases.

3.2.3 *The word* one *other than as substitute*

We have noted that not all occurrences of *one* are instances of substitution, and it is useful to distinguish the substitute *one* from the various other words *one*, the other items which are forms of the same etymon. These are the personal pronoun *one*, cardinal numeral *one*, determiner *one* (alternative form of the indefinite article) and a fourth *one* which is related to the category of general nouns (see 6.1 below) and which we might refer to as a 'pro-noun', using a hyphen.

3.2.3.1 PERSONAL PRONOUN *one*

This is the personal form with generalized reference, sometimes called 'generic person', discussed in Chapter 2 (2.3.1, examples [2:8], [2:9]). Another example of it is:

[3:19] One never knows what might happen.

This *one* has no cohesive force; it is never used anaphorically, but only exophorically, not unlike *you* and *we* in their generalized exophoric sense. It is rather easily distinguishable from the substitute *one*, since it always occurs alone as the sole element in a nominal group, an environment that is impossible for the substitute, which is always modified (*cf* 3.2.2 above).

3.2.3.2 CARDINAL NUMERAL *one*

This is exemplified in:

[3:20] a. He made one very good point.
b. Ten set out, but only one came back.

Again it is clear from inspection that neither of these occurrences of *one* is a substitute. That in (a) is functioning as (Numerative) Modifier in the nominal group *one very good point*, whereas the substitute *one* functions only as Head; that in (b) is functioning as Head, but it is unmodified, whereas the substitute is always modified. The *one* in (b) looks at first sight like a substitute because it is clearly anaphoric: there must be some word such as *man* presupposed for interpretation to be possible. Actually however it is the cardinal numeral *one* with ellipsis. In ellipsis, the pre-supposed item, if it is to be made explicit, is ADDED TO the presupposing one: it does not replace it; so *ten men set out, but only one man came back* (not *but only man came back*). In substitution, on the other hand, the pre-supposed item, if it is to be made explicit, REPLACES the presupposing one: it cannot be added to it; so in

[3:21] Mummy will you buy me a bus? I want that red one.

the non-presupposing form would be *that red bus*, not *that red one bus*. In any case once such a nominal group is filled out the distinction becomes obvious, since the numeral always precedes any Epithet that is present, whereas the substitute, since it functions as Head, always follows it.

Cardinal numeral *one* and substitute *one* are quite distinct in meaning. The former contrasts (1) as a Numerative, with the other numerals *two, three*, etc; (2) as a Deictic, with *some, other, both*, etc as in:

[3:22] a. The one friend who never let her down was Enid.
       b. Can I have those peaches? – You can have one; leave me the other.

where again (b) is cohesive by ellipsis, like [3:20b] above.

The substitute *one* enters into no systemic contrasts; on the other hand it may be either singular or plural, whereas the cardinal *one* is naturally always singular (except in the expression *in ones and twos*). The two mean-ings are compatible with each other, so we regularly find examples such as

[3:23] You've already got one red one.

where the first *one* is a numeral and the second a substitute: as long as there is an Epithet or Classifier present, both will occur, since the numeral must precede and the substitute follow. If there is no Epithet or Classifier, then the word *one* can occur only once; the language has not yet admitted sentences like *you've already got one one*, though this will probably occur in the speech of the next generation of children. Meanwhile a form such as *you've already got* ONE might be seen as a fusion of numeral *one* and substitute *one*, since the meanings are compatible. However, this interpretation will not really stand, for the same reasons as were given for rejecting the interpretation of [3:15ci] as a fusion of the substitute with the indefinite article. In an example such as *you've already got one*, there are just two interpretations, the two forms being identical in writing but distinct in speech: either the *one* is phonologically salient, in which case it is the cardinal numeral, or it is phonologically weak, in which case it is the indefinite article (see next section). Neither involves substitution, but both are elliptical.

There are other factors differentiating the numeral from the substitute. The numeral accepts submodification, *eg: just one, only one, not one*, which the substitute does not; on the other hand the substitute is regularly modified by a Deictic, *eg: this one, your one*, which is rare with the numeral functioning as Head. Even where the numeral is preceded by a Deictic, there is no ambiguity in speech, for the reason already given: the numeral is salient, the substitute weak. Hence

[3:24] Have you any envelopes? I need another one.

is ambiguous only in writing; in speech, if *one* is a numeral, so that the 'filled out' form is *another one envelope*, the tonic will fall on *one*, whereas if *one* is a substitute, the filled out form being *another envelope*, the tonic will fall on *another*.

3.2.3.3 INDEFINITE ARTICLE *one*

The normal form of the indefinite article is *a/an*; etymologically this is a weakened form of the numeral *one*. The term 'article' is somewhat unnecessary, as it suggests that the articles form a separate word class, whereas both *a* and *the* are simply members of the more general class of determiner. Within the determiner, *a* belongs to the non-specific class (including *any, either, no* etc). The two major types of determiner, specific and non-specific, embody different number systems. The specific determiners distinguish singular/plural, with 'mass' grouped with the singular, as it is in the noun; so *this house, this sugar* (singular), *these houses* (plural). The non-specific determiners distinguish (count) singular/non-singular, with 'mass' being grouped with the plural; so the form corresponding to *a*, namely *some*, is used with mass and plural nouns: *a house* (count singular), *some sugar, some houses* (non-singular). This *some* is also a phonologically weakened form.

Like many other determiners, the indefinite article can occur elliptically, as Head in the nominal group; for example

[3:25] a. Are there lions in those hills? – Yes, we saw some on the way over.
   b. I'd like some coffee. – Then make some.

The filled out forms are *we saw some lions, make some coffee*. What is the equivalent form of the indefinite article when presupposing a count singular noun?

[3:26] a. Are there lions in those hills? – Yes, we saw one on the way over.
   b. I'd like a cup of coffee. – Then pour yourself one.

Here the filled out forms are *a lion, a cup of coffee* (not *one lion, one cup of coffee*); *one* is the form taken by the indefinite article when it is functioning as Head of an elliptical nominal group (*cf: Have one of mine!*). That this is not the substitute *one* is shown by the fact that it has the non-singular *some*, and not *ones*; *cf: Have some of mine!* and [3:25a], where we could not say *we saw ones on the way over*. Moreover the substitute *one* does not occur without a Modifier (*cf* [3:21] above). That these forms are elliptical determiners, not substitutes, is further borne out by the fact that in negative and interrogative they are replaced by *any*, exactly as the indefinite article is: *we didn't see any on the way over*. (Likewise, the instances where *one* is retained in a negative environment are also those where *a* would be retained in the filled out equivalent, *ie* where the meaning is specifically singular, *eg*

[3:27] 'I vote the young lady tells us a story.' 'I'm afraid I don't know one,' said Alice.

– filled form *I don't know a story;* contrasting with *I'm afraid I don't know any (stories)*.)

This form of the indefinite article is phonologically simply a non-salient form of the numeral *one*. There is therefore an interesting parallelism between the definite and the indefinite articles in the way they have evolved in English.

Selective form [salient] as Modifier or Head	Article [non-salient] as Modifier [reduced]	as Head [weak]
(demonstrative) that	the	it
(numeral) one; some	a/an; [səm]	one; some

Note the proportionality in the following pairs of examples:

[3:28] a. They need that CHAIR. They need THAT. They need the
CHAIR. They NEED it.
    b. They need one CHAIR. They need ONE. They need a CHAIR.
They NEED one.

There is thus ambiguity in the written language between *one* as numeral
and *one* as indefinite article, when functioning as Head of an elliptical
nominal group. This is not usually so in speech, because of the difference
in salience: the numeral is always salient, and may carry tonic prominence,
whereas the article is normally not salient – under certain conditions it
can be, but it can never be tonic. There is typically a contrast between
[3:29a and b]:

[3:29] a. I've lost my coat. – // ∧ I / saw / one in the / HALL / yesterday //
    (= one coat (numeral); non-singular would be . . . / saw
    / some . . .)
    b. I've lost my coat. – // ∧ I / saw one in the / HALL / yesterday //
    (= a coat (article); non-singular would be . . . / saw some . . .)

As far as the substitute *one* is concerned, however, it is distinct from both,
by virtue of its occurring only as Head WITH a Modifier present (the one
environment that is impossible for numeral or article). Thus in [3:15]
above, all occurrences of *one* are instances of the substitute except (ci),
which is the indefinite article. That the substitute and the indefinite article
are now quite distinct in meaning is shown by the fact that they readily
co-occur, as in [3:15cii] *a red one, another one*. Where there is no intervening element, the normal form of realization is a fusion of the two into a
single element *one*, as in (ciii) *one with wheels*; but even here they may be
kept discrete, as in *I need a one with a sharp point, there's a one I hadn't
seen before.*

3.2.3.4 'PRO-NOUN' *one*
There is one further meaning of *one*, in which it is restricted to human
referents; this is not a substitute form, in the sense that it has no cohesive
force, but it is not always easy to distinguish it from the substitute *one*
in texts. Examples:

[3:30] a. If such a one be fit to govern, speak.
    b. The ones she really loves are her grandparents.

Here *one* means 'person' and *ones* means 'people'; but they are not anaphoric – there is no presupposition of an earlier occurrence of the WORD *person* or *people* or any similar noun.

The only other word that functions exactly in this way in English is *thing*. These words *one* and *thing* are special items that we might refer to as 'pro-nouns'; they are in a sense intermediate between the substitute *one* and the class of general noun discussed in Chapter 6 below (6.1). It is this *one* and *thing* that are found as components in the words *something*, *nothing*, *anything*, *everything*, *someone*, *no one* etc. Strictly speaking these items *one* and *thing* are members of a class of 'pro-forms' which are the equivalent of the interrogative words *what*, *who* and so on; the class of 'pro-nouns' thus also includes *time*, *place*, *way* and perhaps *reason*. Of the two words *one* and *thing*, *thing* corresponds to *what* and *one* corresponds to *who;* hence *thing* refers to non-human nouns and indefinite nouns, while *one* refers to definite human nouns. So for example:

[3:31] a. What does he need? The thing he needs (What he needs) is a passport.
b. What does he need? The thing he needs is his passport.
c. What does he need? The thing he needs is a lawyer.
d. Who does he need? The one he needs is his lawyer.

Here *the thing* can be replaced by *what; the one* cannot, however, be replaced by *who*, at least not in modern English.

Like the substitute, but unlike all the other forms of *one*, the pro-noun *one* has plural *ones;* for example (*cf* [3:30b] above)

[3:32] Now, my dearest ones; gather round.

Since it also functions as Head in the nominal group, and is normally accompanied by some modifying element, it is easily confused with the substitute (and is generally regarded by grammarians as the same item). However, for the purpose of the study of cohesion it is important to keep the two apart, since the substitute is cohesive whereas the pro-noun is not. Moreover there can be ambiguity between them; consider the example

[3:33] The children seemed to enjoy the outing. The one who didn't was George.

Is George one of the children, or is he the teacher? If *one* is a substitute, it presupposes *child* and means 'the child who didn't . . .'; if it is a pro-noun, it does not presuppose anything and means 'the person who didn't . . .'. Given the further fact that the substitute is not limited to human referents, while the pro-form is, it seems desirable to recognize them as two distinct items.

The principal use of the pro-form *one* in modern English is that exemplified in [3:31d] (and [3:33] in its second interpretation): that is, in clauses displaying 'theme identification'.* A clause such as *the one he needs is his lawyer* is related to *he needs his lawyer* in a systematic way; its meaning is that the message consists of two parts, a theme 'his need' and a rheme 'his lawyer', with an equals sign between the two. Compare

> [3:34] I know nothing about this scheme. The one you should ask is Dr Rawlinson.

meaning 'there is someone you should ask, namely . . .'. In earlier English it was more widely used in the general sense of 'someone', *ie* 'one of the ones who . . .', as in Cassius'

> [3:35] Hated by one he loves, brav'd by his brother.

Such uses have by no means disappeared from the language; but they are more common in written styles than in speech.

3.2.4 Summary of uses of one

Here are some further examples to relate the nominal substitute *one* to the various other items that have been discussed, and to distinguish it from other, non-cohesive forms of the word *one*. They are constructed for brevity, which explains (even if it does not excuse) their uninspiring style.

> [3:36] a. I'm fed up with this watch. (1) The thing never works.
> (2) My old one worked all right, but this one's hopeless.
> (3) The thing I want now is a solid state microchronometer.
> (4) Perhaps I'll get one.
> b. I like the new manager. (1) The man's really efficient.
> (2) The previous ones were hopeless, but this one knows his job. (3) The thing we need now is some new technicians.
> (4) Perhaps he'll appoint some.

In each example, (1) contains a 'general noun', *thing* and *man*, cohesive (see Chapter 6); (2) contains two substitutes, *one(s)*, also cohesive; (3) con-

---

* See M. A. K. Halliday, 'Notes on transitivity and theme in English', *Journal of Linguistics* 3, 1967, especially Part II, Section 6 (*pp* 223–236).

tains a 'pro-noun', *thing*, not cohesive; (4) contains an indefinite article, *one* and *some*, cohesive by ellipsis (see Chapter 4).

The full list of the elements discussed above is given in Table 5. Of those listed, only (1) is a substitute; it is therefore the only one that is properly the subject of the present discussion. (2) is the generic personal pronoun, and is never cohesive. (3) and (4), the cardinal numeral, and (5) and (6), the 'indefinite article', may occur in a cohesive context, functioning as Head of the nominal group; in that case the form of cohesion is through ellipsis (see Chapter 4). (7), the 'pro-noun', resembles the substitute in having the plural form *ones*, but it is never cohesive. (8) is the class of 'general noun', the members of which regularly enter into cohesive relations; these are treated below, in Chapter 6.

In the great majority of instances, the substitute *one* is anaphoric in orientation. Cataphoric instances are less common; an example would be

[3:37] She picked out the loveliest ones of all the roses in the garden and gave them to me.

where *ones* points forward to *roses*. Such instances are however within the structural confines of the sentence, and contribute nothing to cohesion. Finally, we noted earlier that, although substitution is essentially a textual relation, occasional exophoric instances will be found; see the discussion in 3.1.1, and example [3:3].

3.2.5 *Nominal substitute* same

We saw in Chapter 2 that the item *same* occurs as a cohesive element of the comparative type (2.3.1, examples [2:21-2]). In such instances, *same* is a reference item, not a substitute. There is another cohesive use of *same*, this time as a nominal substitute, typically accompanied by *the*. Unlike *one*, which presupposes only the noun Head, *the same* presupposes an entire nominal group including any modifying elements, except such as are explicitly repudiated. For example

[3:38] A: I'll have two poached eggs on toast, please.
       B: I'll have the same.

Not, of course, *the same eggs*, which would be reference, not substitution. No regular modifying element may occur with *the same*; but it is possible to add a reservation to it, and this takes the form of a Qualifier, which is normally introduced by *but* and often starts with the word *with* (adding a modification) or *without* (deleting a modification, ie repudiating it),

Table 5: The forms of *one*, and related items

Item	Class	Function	Phonological status	Section	Examples
1 *one, ones*	nominal substitute	Head (always modified)	salient or weak	3.2, 3.2.1	3:8–15
2 *one (they, you, we)*	personal pronoun	Head (never modified)	weak	3.2.3.1	3:19
3 *one (two, three . . .)*	cardinal numeral	Numerative; Modifier or Head	salient	3.2.3.2	3:20
4 *one, some (both, other)*	cardinal numeral	Deictic; Modifier or Head	salient	3.2.3.2	3:22
5 *a/an, some (any)*	determiner ('indefinite article')	Deictic; Modifier	reduced	3.2.3.3	
6 *one/some (any)*	determiner ('indefinite article')	Deictic; Head (never modified)	weak	3.2.3.3	3:25–7
7 *one, ones (thing)*	pro-noun	Head	salient	3.2.3.4	3:30–1
8 *thing, person, creature, etc*	general noun	Head (usually with *the*)	weak (when anaphoric)	6.1	6:1–5

eg: the same but fried, the same (but) without the toast. The presupposed item is almost always non-human, and it cannot be a proper name. It can, however, be an Attribute: that is, an adjective occurring (in the usual Epithet function) as Head of a nominal group in a clause of ascription:

> [3:39] A: John sounded rather regretful.
> B: Yes, Mary sounded the same.

Since an adjective is a kind of noun, and *rather regretful* is a nominal group, this is still a form of nominal substitution, and so the use of *the same* in such instances is entirely to be expected (*cf* 3.5.2.3 below).

There was an earlier use of *the same* as a pronominal reference item, replaceable – as the substitute is not – by *him, her, it,* or *them; eg*

> [3:40] This is Othello's ancient, as I take it.
> – The same indeed; a very valiant fellow.

This is sometimes imitated in contemporary usage, especially in the form *the very same*. Otherwise, this pattern is largely confined today to legal and commercial registers, where the reference is again always non-human and *the* may be omitted. Note that in this use *same* can never carry the tonic:

> [3:41] We have today dispatched the first consignment of your order. Kindly arrange to accept delivery of same.

In Shakespeare's language this pronominal usage with non-human reference is more general:

> [3:42]   I am bound to you
> That you on my behalf would pluck a flower.
> – In your behalf still will I wear the same.

3.2.5.1 SAY THE SAME

In the environment of a process in which a 'fact' is involved, *the same* can often substitute for the fact: for example

> [3:43] John thought it was impossible. – Yes, I thought the same.

More often than not one element in the presupposed clause, usually a nominal, remains outside the domain of the substitution:

> [3:44] a. We can trust Smith. I wish I could say the same of his partner.
> b. Winter is always so damp. – The same is often true of summer.

In (a) *the same* substitutes for 'that we can trust ...', 'Smith' being repudiated by the following *of his partner*. Similarly in (b) *the same* substitutes for 'is always so damp', with *winter* being repudiated by *summer*. One form of this usage which is especially common in dialogue is *the same applies (to), ... goes for*, as in

[3:45] A: His speech didn't say anything new, did it?
        B: The same applies to most political speeches.

All these are devices for making it explicit that *the same* has the status of a fact.

3.2.5.2 DO THE SAME

Secondly, the nominal substitute *the same* is often combined with the verb *do* as a substitute for the process in certain types of clause. An alternative form is *do likewise*. For example

[3:46] a. They all started shouting. So I did the same.
        b. My bank manager bought shares in the canal company. Why don't you do likewise?
        c. That noise really unnerves me. – Yes it does the same to me too.

What is being substituted here is the process plus any subsequent element that is not repudiated.

This form of substitution is slightly odd, in that what is being substituted is essentially the verbal element in the clause, and yet the structural means is that of nominal and not verbal substitution (for which see the next section). The verb *do* here is not, in fact, the verbal substitute *do* but the 'general verb' *do*, that which occurs in *What are you doing? Don't do that!*, *I've got nothing to do* and so on; it is the parallel, in the verb class, to the 'general nouns' *thing*, *person* etc (see 6.1). It is distinct from the verbal substitute *do* in a number of respects. Phonologically, the substitute *do* is weak while the general verb *do* is salient. Moreover the substitute *do* substitutes for all verbs except *be* and (in British English generally) *have*; whereas the general verb *do* is restricted to clauses of ACTION as opposed to SUPERVENTION – essentially, those where the meaning is 'someone did something' rather than 'something happened to someone'. So we can have

[3:47] a. I liked the second movement more than I had done the first.
        b. That sign means they're busy – it usually does, anyway.

in both of which *do* is a verbal substitute; but we could not have, following (a), *Yes I did the same*, or, following (b), *Is that what it does?* (in both of which *do* is the general verb), because *like* and *mean* are not action-type processes. In some instances there is an equivalent form of nominal substitution for 'happening'-type clauses, with *the same (thing) happens,* eg

> [3:48] I lost my way in the galleries. – The same thing happened to me.

meaning 'I also lost my way in the galleries'.

Hence *the same*, although itself a form of nominal substitute, is used as a means of substituting a nominal or other element in the process as a whole, including the process itself. A form such as *do the same* reflects the general tendency of English to express a process in a nominalized form, by means of an 'empty' verb plus its object: *do a run-through, do a left turn* for 'run [it] through', 'turn left'; *cf: have a fight, give a glance, make a fuss.* The presupposing form *the same* can thus occur as a substitute not only for nominals expressing things, as in [3:38], but also for facts, as in *say the same*, and for elements that are not strictly nominal at all. Whereas *one* substitutes just the noun (Head), in the environment of a nominal group having other elements that are contrastive, *the same* substitutes a nominal group (or something else) in the environment of a clause, so that it is other elements in the clause that provide the contrastive context.

3.2.5.3 BE THE SAME

As already pointed out, the form *the same* occurs as Attribute in clauses of ascription, where it may substitute either a noun or an adjective – that is, a nominal group having either noun or adjective as Head, for example (and *cf* [3:39] above)

> [3:49] Charles is now an actor. Given half a chance I would have been the same.

Note the potential ambiguity between substitution and reference in such contexts. In [3:50], if *the same* is a substitute the meaning is '(and) they also taste more bitter than the last ones', whereas if it is a reference item the meaning is '(but) they taste the same as the last ones did':

> [3:50] These grapefruit smell more bitter than the last ones we had. – They taste the same.

(In the third possible interpretation, 'they taste like each other', which is improbable here, *the same* is also a reference item, but functioning as Epithet and therefore non-cohesively; *cf* 2.5.1 above, examples [2:79] and [2:80].) For the use of *so* in such instances see the next section.

3.2.6 *Difference between* the same *and* one(s) *as nominal substitutes*

Apart from the type of example illustrated in [3:40 – 3:42] above, *the same* as substitute is always phonologically salient. It contains an accent, and therefore carries the tonic under typical or 'unmarked' conditions: that is to say, if occurring finally it is tonic unless rejected for contrastive reasons. For example,

> [3:51] A: I'll have two poached eggs on toast please.
> B: I'll have the SAME.
> C: I'd LIKE to have the same, but ...

B's utterance has unmarked information focus. In C's the information structure is marked, with contrastive focus on *like*.

This gives the clue to the role of *the same* in nominal substitution. The substitute *one* is a grammatical item which contains no accent; it is always 'given' in meaning, and serves as a peg on which to hang the new information. In this respect it resembles *do* (3.3) and *so* (3.4). The substitute *the same*, however, functions like a lexical item; it can carry the information focus, and typically does so when in final position. The meaning is 'the information conveyed by this item in this context is new, but the item itself has occurred before'. So for example

> [3:52] The neighbours grow yellow chrysanthemums. {
> a. I could grow RED ones
> b. I could grow the SAME
> c. I could grow some (TOO)
> d. I could grow some of the SAME

In (a) the substitute *ones* is used so that the Epithet *red* can carry the UNMARKED tonicity: that is, so that the focus of information falls on *red* WITHOUT this becoming contrastive. In (b) the 'yellow' is included in the presupposition, and the substitute *the same* carries the focus: the information as a whole is encoded as new, with the meaning 'yellow chrysanthemums' shown to have been present earlier. (Once again it is substitution that is appropriate and not reference. They will not be referentially 'the same chrysanthemums'; and hence the form *I could grow them* would be odd here, with *them* 'referring' as it were at the lexicogrammatical instead of the semantic level.) In (c) the indefinite article *some* is used as non-specific Deictic, and the form is elliptical; this focuses information on the *I* and encodes the whole of the remainder as explicitly given. Finally (d) is like (b), with the addition of the indefinite article as Deictic as in (c). Note that there is no form *I could grow red same*, since here the unmarked tonic would be on *same* where it should be on *red*; instead the form is *I could grow the same but red*, which puts the tonic where it is required while still leaving it unmarked.

Essentially the same relation obtains between *the same* and substitute *so* as between *the same* and *one(s)*. The patterns discussed in 3.2.5.1–3 (*say the same, do the same, be the same*) are the contexts in which the non-salient substitute alternating with *the same* would in fact be *so* and not *one(s)*. In general *so* substitutes for a clause, and is dealt with in 3.4 below. However there is no very clear line between nominal and clausal substitution, and these examples are in a way intermediate between the two. In the following the weak form of the substitute is *so:*

[3:53] (1) John felt it was
disappointing.
- (i)
  - a. He SAID so (TOO)
  - b. He said the SAME
- (ii)
  - a. MARY felt so (TOO)
  - b. Mary felt the SAME

(2) John left before the end.
- a. I did so (TOO)
- b. I did the SAME

(3) John sounded regretful
- (i)
  - a. He LOOKED so (TOO)
  - b. He looked the SAME
- (ii)
  - a. MARY sounded so (TOO)
  - b. Mary sounded the SAME

In type (3) it would be possible to interpret *so* following *look, sound, seem*, etc as substituting for a clause: *Mary sounded as if she was regretful too*. Compare

[3:54] '. . . being so many different sizes in a day is very confusing.'
'It isn't,' said the Caterpillar.
'Well, perhaps you haven't found it so yet,' said Alice; . . .

where *so* in the last line substitutes for *very confusing* but could also be filled out as *to be very confusing*. On the other hand the presupposed item need not be of this form, as the examples in [3:53] show; and in [3:55] neither the presupposed nor the presupposing item could be expanded into a clause:

[3:55] John has become depressed. – Has he ever been so before?

These are in fact instances in which *so* is substituting for an Attribute: corresponding to *he seems intelligent, he seems to be intelligent, he seems as if he is intelligent* we have *he seems so, he seems to be so, he seems as if he is so*. If on the other hand the Attribute is represented by a noun, this must always be a count noun and the weak form is *one(s)*; so we should have *they taste so (too)* in [3:50] above but *I would have been one (too)* in [3:49].

In general, therefore, although it takes a nominal form, *the same* functions as the accented form of the substitute in all types of substitution, clausal and verbal as well as nominal:

	Non-accented	Accented form (*same* salient)
Nominal:		
count noun	*one(s)*	*the same*
attribute	*so*	*(be) the same*
Verbal	*do*	*do the same*
Clausal (reported)	*so*	*(say) the same*

It may also be accompanied by a pro-noun *thing* (*way* when substituting for an Attribute), as in *said the same thing, tastes the same way*; these are constructed like reference items but have come to be used as substitutes in the same way as the items *same* and *so* themselves.

3.3 Verbal substitution

The verbal substitute in English is *do*. This operates as Head of a verbal group, in the place that is occupied by the lexical verb; and its position is always final in the group. Here are two examples from *Alice*; in both, the substitute is the word that has the form *do* (not *did* or *don't*):

> [3:56] a. . . . the words did not come the same as they used to do.
>   b. 'I don't know the meaning of half those long words, and, what's more, I don't believe you do either!'

The first *do*, in (a), substitutes for *come*; that in (b) substitutes for *know the meaning of half those long words*.

In [3:56] the presupposed items are in the same sentence, and so the substitution is not by itself cohesive. But verbal substitution regularly extends across sentence boundaries, as in

[3:57] He never really succeeded in his ambitions. He might have done, one felt, had it not been for the restlessness of his nature.

Here *done* substitutes for *succeeded in his ambitions*, and so serves to link the two sentences by anaphora, exactly in the same way as the nominal substitute *one*. In the three succeeding subsections we shall discuss the meaning of verbal substitution, the conditions of use of the verbal substitute, and other uses of the verb *do* which are distinct from its use as a substitute (and from which its use as a substitute is derived).

3.3.1 The meaning of the verbal substitute do

In many ways the verbal substitute *do* is parallel to the nominal substitute *one*, and it is likely that its evolution in Modern English has followed the analogy of *one* rather closely.

There are striking parallels between the structure of the verbal group and the nominal group in Modern English, although superficially they are very different from each other. Like the nominal group, whose structure was discussed in section 2.1 above, the verbal group has a logical structure consisting of Head and Modifier, and an experiential structure in which the lexical verb expresses the 'Thing'. In the case of the nominal group the 'Thing' is typically a person, creature, object, institution or abstraction of some kind, whereas in the verbal group it is typically an action, event or relation; but these are simply different subcategories of experiential phenomena, and in any case there is considerable overlap and interchange between the two.

In both nominal group and verbal group, the lexical 'Thing' is substitutable by an empty substitution counter that always functions as Head. The substitution form in the nominal group, as we have seen, is *one(s)*. In the verbal group it is *do*, with the usual morphological scatter *do, does, did, doing, done*.

There is a difference between *one* and *do* in their potential domains, the extent of the items that they can presuppose. Whereas *one* always substitutes for a noun, *do* may substitute either for a verb, as in [3:56a], or for a verb plus certain other elements in the clause, as in [3:56b] and [3:57].

At first sight it might seem as if *do* substituted for the whole of what is called the 'predicate' in a Subject-Predicate analysis – the predicator (the verbal group itself), minus its auxiliaries, together with any complements and adjuncts that are present. But any of these may be repudiated, as the following examples show:

> [3:58] a. Does Granny look after you every day? – She can't do at weekends, because she has to go to her own house.
> b. Have they removed their furniture? – They have done the desks, but that's all so far.

In (a) *do* substitutes for *look after me* but *every day* is repudiated by *at weekends*. In (b) *done* substitutes only for *removed*; *their furniture* is repudiated by *the desks*.

As was pointed out in the discussion of *one*, substitution and ellipsis are different manifestations of the same underlying relation, that of presupposition at the lexicogrammatical level. The use of elliptical forms of the verbal group is very common, and there is very little difference in meaning between a verbal group having substitution by *do* and one having ellipsis (*ie* substitution by zero). For example

> [3:59] Inspector (taking back the photograph): You recognize her?
> Mrs Birling: No. Why should I?
> Inspector: Of course she might have changed lately. But I can't believe she could have changed so much.
> Mrs Birling: I don't understand you, Inspector.
> Inspector: You mean you don't choose to do, Mrs Birling.*

Both elliptical and substitute forms of the verbal group are illustrated here. *Why should I?* is elliptical, presupposing *Why should I recognize her?*; and *you don't choose to do* is a substitute form, presupposing *you don't choose to understand me*. There is very little difference; *do* could be added in the first and deleted in the second with hardly any change of meaning. Unlike the nominal group, however, in which under many conditions (*eg* following an Epithet) ellipsis is generally impossible, and substitution by *one* is therefore obligatory as the expression of cohesion, in the verbal group there are very few contexts in which the substitute *do* MUST be used (for these see 3.3.2 below). In general, substitute *do* alternates with zero as a cohesive device, and the meaning is the same in both: the specific process – event, action, relation, etc – that is being referred to must be recovered from the preceding text. If the substitute *do* is used, its function is to act explicitly as a place-holder, marking out the point at which presupposition is involved. It is possible to construct examples in

---

* J. B. Priestley, *An Inspector Calls* (The Plays of J. B. Priestley, Vol 3), Heinemann.

which its presence appears to resolve what would otherwise be an ambiguity, *eg*

[3:60] What are you doing here? – We're mycologists, and we're looking for edible mushrooms. – Yes, we are doing too.

where the last sentence without the substitute *doing* would be interpreted as 'we are also mycologists'.

Like the nominal substitute *one*, the verbal substitute *do* is typically associated with contrast. It occurs in the context of some other item which contrasts with an element in the presupposed clause. This is well illustrated by instances in which the two clauses, presupposing and presupposed, are related by comparison, *eg*

[3:61] John is smoking more now than
{
a. Mary is doing.
b. he should be doing.
c. he used to do.
d. he was doing before.
}

In (a), *Mary* contrasts with *John;* in (b), *should be* contrasts with *is;* in (c), *used to* contrasts with *is . . . ing;* in (d), *was . . . before* contrasts with *is . . . now.* Similarly *do* is frequent in the second of two clauses related by *before, after, if, when,* etc, as in *you will finish well before I have done.* Since in these cases the two clauses are structurally related, the presence of *do,* while it reinforces this relationship, is not needed as the cohesive factor; but the principle appears clearly, that substitution is a means of representing given information in the environment of new. Exactly the same principle operates where there is no structural relationship between the two clauses, as in examples [3:57–60] above; and here the use of the substitute is precisely what provides the cohesion.

Since the substitute is by definition 'given', in that it is a signal that information is to be recovered from elsewhere, it is phonologically unaccented, or non-prominent. It is usually weak (non-salient) in all positions except when it is the initial, and therefore the only, item in the verbal group; in the latter context it is salient, but still non-tonic. For example:

[3:62] a. Has anybody fed the cat? – // SOMEbody / must have done //
b. Did anybody feed the cat? – // SOMEbody / did //

Related to this is the fact that a finite verbal operator preceding substitute *do* in the verbal group can never be in the reduced form, since this would force prominence on to the *do*: hence forms such as *he'll do, he's doing, he's done* cannot occur as substitutes, at least across a sentence boundary.

However, we saw that with the nominal substitute *one* there are circumstances under which it is accented, and so can carry the tonic, namely when the 'given-ness' of the information it conveys is precisely what is new about it; this is the typical pattern following *the same (the same* ONES). Likewise with *do* there is one condition in which it is accented, and as far as the meaning is concerned this is essentially the same condition that we had found with *one*, although the form of expression is different: it is when *do* is followed by *so* (DO *so*). The expression *do so* conveys essentially the same meaning: the action, event or relation in question has been referred to before, but it is precisely here that the new information lies. So for example

> [3:63] a. 'Yes, I think you'd better leave off,' said the Gryphon: and Alice was only too glad to do so.
>
> b. Just finish off watering those plants. And let me know when you've done so.

The expression *do so* derives from pro-verb *do* (see 3.3.3.3 below) followed by anaphoric *so*. The *do* is accented; it is therefore typically salient, with the potentiality of carrying the tonic. The difference in the rhythmic patterns of the two forms of the verbal substitute, *do* and *do so*, can be seen in the following example:

> [3:64] Shall I make an ⎰a. //∧ you / can do / NOW //
> announcement? ⎱b. //∧ you can / do so / NOW //

In many instances either *do* or *do so* can occur, with only a slight difference in meaning: the form with *so* combines anaphora with prominence, so that it has the effect of explicitness, of specifying that it is precisely the verbal element mentioned earlier that is the point of information here. But for this very reason there are certain instances where *so* is obligatory. They are those where *do* is REQUIRED to be the point of information because there is no element of contrast present, as in [3:63b] above. Elsewhere *so* is optional; and there are two conditions under which it cannot occur. The first of these is in a comparative clause with *than* or *as*, such as [3:56] and [3:61] above. In fact the form with *so* is less frequent in all cases where the presupposing clause is structurally related to the presupposed one; so

[3:65] I want to read this document. You can sign it after I've done so.

is likely to mean 'after I've read it' (with the tonic on *done*) rather than 'after I've signed it' (with the tonic on *I've*); the latter meaning would more probably be expressed as *after I have done*. The second condition where *so* cannot occur is if the goal is repudiated, as in [3:58b]. With the provisos mentioned here, the verbal substitute may take either form, and the choice between *do* and *do so* is often made at the phonological level, on purely rhythmic grounds: because the one form fits into the rhythm of the sentence more smoothly and effectively than the other.

3.3.2 Conditions of use of the verbal substitute

There is considerable variation in the use of the substitute *do* in contemporary English. It appears to have evolved by analogy with the nominal substitute *one*, but to be lagging somewhat behind *one* in range of uses, perhaps because ellipsis is almost always an acceptable alternative. In Shakespearean English, the verbal substitute *do* was much less clearly distinct from the finite verbal operator *do* (see 3.3.3.4 below) because of the more general use of the latter in a positive declarative verbal group, *eg: as I do live* (Modern English *as I live*). Clear instances of the verbal substitute in Shakespeare almost always have the form *do so*. In the following examples, the *do* would be a substitute in Modern English; but here it was probably in fact an operator:

[3:66] a. Never a woman in Windsor knows more of Anne's mind
than I do.
b. Thou makest a testament as worldlings do.

As a very broad generalization, the verbal substitute is used more in speech than in writing, and more in British than American English. Within each of the varieties there are wide dialectal and individual differences. In British English it can substitute for any verb except *be*, and (in most dialects) except *have* in the sense of 'possess'; those verbs substitute for themselves:

[3:67] a. I've been very remiss about this. – I think we all have been,
at times.
b. I've had serious doubts about this. – I think we all have had,
at times.
c. I had serious doubts about this. – I think we all had, at times.

In (c), American and some British speakers would substitute *had* by *did*; but probably no speakers of English would substitute *been* by *done* in (a). In American English, on the other hand, *do* does not generally substitute for verbs of the *seem* class; in British English it does, provided the following Attribute is within the domain of the substitution and is not repudiated:

[3:68] Paula looks very happy.
{
a. She always used to do, I remember.
b. She seems happier now than she did last time we met.
}

Many, possibly all, American speakers would find *do* in (a) and *did* in (b) both impossible; they would prefer the elliptical form *used to* in (a) and the repetition of *seemed* in (b).

There is another factor leading to a considerable differentiation between British and American speakers in their use of the verbal substitute, one which is present in [3:68a] and, in fact, in most of the examples of *do* that have been cited up to now. This relates to the structure of the verbal group in the presupposing clause. If this consists of one word only (simple past or present tense in positive declarative mood), then both American and British speakers regularly use the substitute; *eg: does* in

[3:69] Does Jean sing? – No, but Mary does.

(Because such examples are easily confused with the finite verbal operator *do* we have been avoiding them up to now. The difference will be discussed in 3.3.3.4 below.) If it consists of more than one word, so that the substitute would appear following one or more auxiliaries (in the form *do, doing,* or *done*), American speakers prefer the elliptical form in which the lexical verb is not substituted but simply omitted. In [3:57], for example, the preferred form in American English is *he might have*; and in [3:61a–d] elliptical forms would be expected throughout, and likewise in [3:67a and b].

If the presupposing verbal group is non-finite, ellipsis is under most circumstances impossible. The rule is that an imperfective non-finite verbal group (those in the 'participial' form -*ing, eg: going, having gone*) cannot be elliptical; a perfective one (those in the 'infinitive' form with *to, eg: to go, to have gone*) can be elliptical only if negative, or if following another verb (*eg: want to go*) or cataphoric *it*. For example, in [3:70], (d), (e) and (f) could be elliptical, whereas (a), (b) and (c) could not:

> [3:70] I finally called on him.
> a. Having done so I feel better.
> b. I felt bad at not having done (so) before.
> c. To do so seemed only courteous.
> d. Not to (do (so)) would have been discourteous.
> e. I have wanted to (do (so)) for a long time.
> f. It seemed only courteous to (do so).

In (a)–(c) both American and British English would use the substitute, with American preferring the form *do so* if there is any choice. In (d)–(f) American English tends to use the elliptical form, or else the substitute with *so*, whereas British speakers select among all three, at least in (d) and (e), with perhaps some preference for the one with *do* alone. (In (a), (c) and (f) the substitute *do* cannot occur without *so*, for the reasons given earlier: there is no contrasting element present. In (b), (d) and (e) the contrast is provided by *not* and by *wanted*.) There are thus minor but still interesting differences between different varieties of English revolving around the nature and potential of verbal substitution.

The domain of verbal substitution, as remarked in 3.3.1 above, is the lexical verb together with such other elements in the clause as are not repudiated by some contrasting item. In principle any element can be repudiated in this way, although certain patterns, particularly those in which a Complement is repudiated, sound a little awkward, and ellipsis, where it is possible, seems to fit them better than substitution; this is illustrated by the examples in [3:71] (and *cf* [3:58] above):

> [3:71] a. Can lions climb trees? – No, but leopards can (do).
> b. Can lions kill elephants? – No, but they can (do) giraffes.
> c. Have they given the lions their meat? – No, but they have (done) the cheetahs.
> d. Can lions kill with their tails? – No, but they can (do) with their paws.

In (a) it is the Subject that is repudiated, in (b) and (c) a Complement ('direct object' and 'indirect object'), and in (d) an Adjunct. The only element in the clause that cannot be repudiated is the Attribute; [3:72] is impossible, and cohesion could be achieved here only lexically, by repetition of the verb *seemed*:

> [3:72] Did the lions seem hungry? – No, but they did restless.

There are certain contexts, however, in which irrespective of its function in the modal structure a particular element in the clause cannot be repudiated, so that it is not possible to presuppose the verb without this other element also falling within the domain of the presupposition. In [3:73] the clause containing a verbal substitute is not acceptable following (i) in each instance, although it is acceptable following (ii):

[3:73] a. (i) She's never lived in England. ⎫
          (ii) She's never sung in England. ⎬ She has done in France.
       b. (i) You mustn't put them on the table. ⎱ You can do on the
          (ii) You mustn't cut them on the table. ⎰ bench.
       c. (i) The door was shutting.   ⎱ The windows were do-
          (ii) The door was falling to pieces. ⎰ ing too.
       d. (i) We can't shut the door.   ⎱ We might do the win-
          (ii) We can't smash in the door. ⎰ dows.

The reason is that in (i) there is a strong expectancy binding the repudiated element to the one that is presupposed by the substitute. For example, *live* expects a locative; hence it cannot be substituted without at the same time carrying over any item having a 'Location' function that is structurally associated with it. This does not apply to *sing*, which has no such expectancy. Nor does it apply to *live* in company with other types of Adjunct; there is no difficulty about

[3:74] You can't live on what they would pay you. You could do on twice as much, maybe.

The same principle lies behind the other examples; *put* also presupposes a locative and so cannot be substituted without entailing the 'Location' Adjunct, whereas *cut* shows no such restriction. In (c) and (d) there is a collocational expectancy between *door* and *shut*, so we cannot substitute *shut* without also presupposing *door*; notice that it makes no difference whether the *door* is Subject or Complement – the relevant role is that of Medium, which is common to both instances. The restriction does not apply to *smash in* or *fall to pieces*, which can be substituted on their own while still allowing *the door* to be repudiated. All these are instances of patterns of expectancy between (i) the Process – action, event, etc – and (ii) a particular role that is related to it in the structure, such as Location or Medium, or a particular item or class of items that functions in that role, *eg*: *door* as Medium in relation to the Process *shut*. An item standing in this relation to the process cannot be excluded from the domain of a verbal substitution.

It is the repudiation of other elements in the structure which provides the contrastive environment within which the substitution takes place. In [3:71], for example, each pair of clauses represents a particular distribution of elements into the presupposed, which are within the domain of the substitution, and the contrasted, which are repudiated from this domain:

	Presupposed	Contrasted
[3:71] a.	can climb trees	lions: leopards
b.	lions can kill	elephants: giraffes
c.	they have given meat	to lions: to cheetahs
d.	lions can kill	with tails: with paws

We have illustrated this by reference to elements in the structure of the clause, but the same principle operates within the verbal group: the contrast may occur within the systems associated with the verb itself, such as tense, polarity and modality. So for example:

[3:75] Have you called the doctor? – I haven't done yet, but I will do. – I think you should do.

Here the lexical verb *call* is presupposed throughout, but there is repudiation first of the polarity (negative *haven't* contrasting with positive *have*), then of the tense (future *will* contrasting with past in present *have . . . -ed*), and finally of the modality (modalized *should* contrasting with non-modalized). The one system that is subject to restriction here is that of voice, for the reason that substitution is not possible in the passive. Normally therefore there is no change of voice between the presupposed and the presupposing clause; both are active. It is possible however for a passive verbal group to be substituted in the active, for example

[3:76] Has the doctor been called by anyone? – I don't know. I haven't done. Maybe someone else has done.

There is a tendency in the history of English for active forms of the verb, which evolve first, to be matched by corresponding passive forms after an interval; this has happened consistently with the tense system, and it may be that we are just beginning to see verbal substitution introduced in the passive. In general, however, while ellipsis occurs in the passive in the normal way, subject to exactly the same principles as in the active, substitution does not.

In other respects, all the preceding discussion applies to ellipsis as much as it does to substitution, and many speakers would tend to prefer elliptical forms in many of the examples cited. (It is safe to assert, however, that many people who reject the substitute when their attention is drawn to it actually make frequent use of it in their own speech, including in those very contexts in which they claim not to do.) We have stressed all along that ellipsis and substitution are essentially the same relation, so that it is not surprising to find both as alternative forms of cohesion in broadly the same range of contexts. In the next chapter we shall bring up various other contexts in which there is no explicit substitution but only ellipsis.

With respect to the use of the substitute, the proviso made in the previous section concerning *do* and *do so* applies equally where the contrast is within the verbal group. Wherever the focus of information is required to fall on the Head of the verbal group – the lexical verb itself, as opposed to an auxiliary – the substitute takes the form *do so*. This is sometimes determined by the context, but sometimes appears as an independent choice, as in

[3:77] Why do you smile? $\begin{cases} \text{a. } /\!/\wedge I \,/ \text{ didn't } / \text{ know I } / \text{ WAS doing } /\!/ \\ \text{b. } /\!/\wedge I \,/ \text{ didn't } / \text{ know I was } / \text{ DOING so } /\!/ \end{cases}$

where the answer (a) treats the polarity-tense complex (present in past, positive) as the focus of information, and hence treats *smile* as simply given, while (b) focuses on *smile* as precisely the element in which the information resides. There is one other condition which tends to impose prominence on the lexical verb and thus to demand *do so* as the substitute form: this is when the mood of the presupposing clause is other than declarative, *ie* when it is interrogative or imperative. The reason is that if the verb in an interrogative or imperative clause is anaphoric, the contrast normally resides in the mood itself, and hence is located within the verbal group:

[3:78] Shall I call the doctor? $\begin{cases} \text{a. Haven't you done so?} \\ \text{b. When will you do so?} \\ \text{c. Please do so, as soon as possible.} \end{cases}$

The various conditions on the use of the verbal substitute, leaving aside variations between different forms, such as *do so* and *do*, or zero, and between different dialects or individual speakers, resolve themselves into what are essentially manifestations of the same underlying principle: that of continuity in the environment of contrast. The continuity, obviously, is provided by substitution as a cohesive agency: the replacement of the verb by a substitution counter signalling that the relevant item is to be recovered from elsewhere. But, as in nominal substitution, the significance of this continuity lies in the fact that its context is one of non-continuity or contrast: some entity or circumstance associated with the process expressed by the verb, or some internal condition of time, mood, polarity or the like, is not as it was in the previous instance. (This is the major distinction between the meanings of substitution and reference as cohesive devices; see Chapter 7 below.)

It follows that, if there are certain elements so closely bonded with the Process that they cannot be varied while the latter is kept constant, they cannot provide a contrasting environment, and hence cannot be repudiated under conditions of substitution. We referred to these above. It should follow also that the continuity that is being expressed, since it is in the environment of contrast, is not mere reference back but positive confirmation, a marking of the fact that the lexical verb still holds good. This can be seen to be the case, if we consider one further set of examples.

[3:79] a. Smith isn't playing tiddlywinks for his health. He is (doing) for money.

b. Were you talking to me? – No, I was (doing) to myself.

By any normal interpretation these are wrong. Instead of substitution, some form of reference should have been used: *he's doing it* or *he's playing* in (a), *I was talking to myself* in (b). Why? Because the substitute form of (a) means 'Yes he is playing, but it's for money'; its information structure is that of *What Smith is doing = playing tiddlywinks, and for money*. This applies to both the elliptical form and that with the verbal substitute *doing*. The required meaning however is 'No, he's playing only for money', with the information structure of *What Smith is playing tiddlywinks for = money*. In other words, the process *playing tiddlywinks* is not part of the information content of the message; it is not marked out for confirmation, but merely used as a peg on which to hang the information contained in *for money*. Similarly in (b) the information structure is not *What I was doing = talking, but to myself*, which is what substitution implies, but *The one I was talking to = myself*. This demonstrates the principle on which substitution is based, and explains the types of limitation that there are on its use.

Like the nominal substitute *one*, the verbal substitute *do* is one of a number of related items: lexical verb, 'pro-verb' and so on. A summary account of these is given in the next section.

3.3.3 *The word* do *other than as substitute*

In addition to functioning as the verbal substitute, the verb *do* occurs in

Modern English as lexical verb, general verb, 'pro-verb' and verbal operator. These are all related to each other and form a continuum, or at least a cluster, of meanings that shade into one another at the edges, yielding various indeterminate instances. But the distinctions are significant for the construction of text, so we will discuss each of these forms briefly in turn (3.3.3.1–3.3.3.4).

3.3.3.1 LEXICAL VERB *do*

This is an ordinary verb of the English language, found in examples such as *he has done the job, I have work to do, let's do the accounts.* Other than in two special meanings, (i) as in *do well, do badly,* (ii) as in *that will do, will it do?, it will never do to let them know,* it is always transitive: it has an inherent Goal. In an active clause this Goal functions as a Complement of the 'direct object' type; and since under normal circumstances in English the Goal-Complement cannot be omitted if the Head verb is expressed (*eg* we cannot say *Have you mended the garage door yet? – Yes, I've mended.*), this helps in distinguishing lexical *do* from substitute *do.* The *doing* in [3:80] must be the verbal substitute.

[3:80] He ought to be doing his homework. – He IS doing.

If it had been lexical *do* the form would have been *He's doing it.* This would have been recognizable as not being the substitute because of the tonic prominence in *doing,* the reduced form of *is,* and the presence of the non-contrastive Complement *it* – as we have seen, only contrasting items can occur in the environment of the substitute *do* (except as Subject, since English normally requires the Subject to be made explicit in indicative clauses whether linked by presupposition or not). Likewise if the answer had been in the passive, *eg: it's being done now,* this could only be lexical *do.* It is perhaps worth remarking here on the fact that substitute *do* can substitute for lexical *do* in the same way as it can for other verbs.

Ambiguity may arise where a Complement is present as in

[3:81] I don't think he likes his new employer much. – No, but he does his job.

where *does* could either be a substitute for *likes* ('he likes his job') or lexical do in the expression *do the job.*

Lexical *do* has in itself no cohesive significance, other than through repetition (Chapter 6).

3.3.3.2 GENERAL VERB *do*

This is a member of a small class of verbs, equivalent to the class of general nouns referred to in 3.2 (and discussed in 6.1 below). They are lexical items with generalized meanings. This form *do* occurs in expressions such as *they did a dance*, meaning simply 'they danced', *they do lunches* 'they provide lunches', *it does no harm*. Other verbs in the class include *make*, as in *make a mistake* 'err', *have* as in *have a bath* 'bathe', *take* in *take exception to*. An example from *Alice*:

[3:82] 'A little kindness – and putting her hair in papers – would do wonders with her.'

3.3.3.3 PRO-VERB do

Again, this class corresponds to an equivalent nominal class, that of pro-nouns (3.2.3.4 above). The only members of the class of 'pro-verb' are *do* and *happen*. These stand for any unidentified or unspecified process, *do* for actions and *happen* for events (or for actions encoded receptively, in some kind of passive form). Their occurrence does not necessarily involve an anaphoric or cataphoric reference; there is nothing cohesive about their use in the following examples:

[3:83] a. What was she doing? – She wasn't doing anything.
b. What's happening? – Nothing's happening.
c. 'What *am* I to do?' exclaimed Alice, looking about her in great perplexity.

However, pro-verb *do* is often used endophorically, in that it functions as a carrier for anaphoric items, especially *it* and *that*. The expressions *do that*, *do it* in fact function as reference items; there are no 'reference verbs' in the language, so we say *he did it* because we cannot say *he itted*, and *he does that* because we cannot say *he thats*. Examples:

[3:84] a. 'She's tired, poor thing!' said the Red Queen. 'Smooth her hair – lend her your nightcap – and sing her a soothing lullaby.'
'I haven't got a nightcap with me,' said Alice, as she tried to obey the first direction: 'and I don't know any soothing lullabies.'
'I must do it myself, then,' said the Red Queen.
b. Her chin was pressed so closely against her foot, that there was hardly room to open her mouth; but she did it at last, . . .
c. 'They lived on treacle,' said the Dormouse, after thinking a minute or two.

'They couldn't have done that, you know,' Alice gently remarked: 'they'd have been ill.'
'So they were,' said the Dormouse; 'very ill.'
d. Whenever the horse stopped (which it did, very often), he fell off in front.

The mechanism of cohesion, in such instances, is through the use of the reference items *it* and *that*; but it is really the verbal group as a whole that refers back, so that we could regard *do it* and *do that* as compound reference verbs. An occurrence of *do that* constitutes a single cohesive tie, not two.

It is the pro-verb *do* that occurs in the expressions *do the same* (3.2.5.2) and *do so* (3.3.1). It combines with the pro-noun *thing* in the expressions *do something, – anything, – nothing, – a* (. . .) *thing* and (semantically the same element) *what . . . do?* Here it often occurs in cataphoric contexts, for example:

[3:85] 'The first thing I've got to do,' said Alice to herself . . . 'is to grow to my right size again.'

The pro-verb *do* occurs regularly in the passive, for example

[3:86] I told someone to feed the cat. Has it been done?

the active equivalent being *Has someone done it?* Here *it* refers anaphorically to 'the feeding of the cat'; this is the *it* with extended reference (*cf* 2.3.3.1 above, [2:18]), and it is perhaps worth pointing out the distinction between a pro-verb *do* with this type of *it* and a general verb *do* with *it* in a simple pronominal context. In example [3:87]

[3:87] I want to make a paper chain. But it can't be done in a hurry.

the second clause is ambiguous; it is either (i) *it* ('the making of a paper chain') *can't be done* (pro-verb) *in a hurry*, or (ii) *it* ('a paper chain') *can't be done* (general verb, 'made') *in a hurry*. The distinction is clear in the plural:

[3:88] I want to make some { (i) But it can't be done in a hurry.
paper chains.   { (ii) But they can't be done in a hurry.

The pro-verb *do* in combination with a reference item *it, this* or *that* may be anaphoric to any process of the action type. The general verb *do* is anaphoric only by lexical cohesion, in that it stands as a synonym for a set of more specific verbs, as in *do sums, do an essay, do the vegetables*, or combines with them in their nominalized forms, as in *do the cooking, do the writing*, and therefore coheres with such items if they have occurred in the preceding text. All such anaphoric instances of general verb or pro-verb *do* are instances of reference, not of substitution.

3.3.3.4 VERBAL OPERATOR *do*

The last of the words having the form *do* is the finite verbal operator or 'auxiliary'. This is in principle totally distinct from all the others, in that it is a purely grammatical element whose function is to express simple present or past tense in specific contexts: when interrogative (*do you know?*), negative (*you don't know*) or marked positive (*you do know*); for example

[3:89] Does she sing? – She doesn't sing. – She does sing.

This *do* is always finite, and always occurs as first word in the verbal group; it can never represent the lexical element in the process (the 'Thing').

It would therefore be totally distinct from substitute *do* were it not for the fact of ellipsis. [3:89] might be rewritten as

[3:90] Does she sing? – No, she doesn't. – Yes, she does.

where *she doesn't* and *she does* are elliptical forms having the operator *do* as Head. The distinction between this and substitution appears in:

[3:91] Does she sing? { a. Yes, she does.
                       { b. No, but Mary does.

[3:91a] is elliptical; *does* is the operator and, since it is elliptical, *sing* or the substitute *do* could be added after it: *she does sing, she does do.* [3:91b] is a substitute form; *sing* could not be added after *does*, but it could replace it: *No, but Mary sings.* In speech the two types are more distinct than in writing, because the substitute *do* is weak whereas the operator *do* is salient if it is final in the verbal group (*ie*, if elliptical in the declarative). An elliptical interrogative form, such as *Does Mary?*, is quite unambiguous because the substitute could never occur in this form: the interrogative of *Mary does*, with *does* as substitute, is *does Mary do?* (consisting of operator + *Mary* + substitute as Head).

The auxiliary *do* is not itself in any sense a cohesive agent. But the type of elliptical verbal group in which the operator occurs alone is extremely frequent, and this of course is cohesive by virtue of being elliptical. This is discussed in 4.3.

3.3.4. *Summary of uses of* do

The set of related words *do* can be illustrated in the following passage:

> [3:92] What's John doing these days? (1) John's doing a full-time job at the works. (2) That'll do him good. (3) I'm glad he's doing something. (4) Does he like it there? (5) He likes it more than I would ever do.

Here (1) contains the lexical verb *do*, (2) the general verb, (3) the pro-verb, which is also present in the original question, (4) the operator and (5) the substitute.

Table 6 gives a summary of the items discussed in this section. Of those listed, (1) and (2) are substitutes, and are the subject of this chapter; they are normally cohesive (see below). (3) and (4) are lexical items and are cohesive only in the special context of lexical cohesion; see Chapter 6. (5), the 'pro-verb', is not in itself cohesive; but it regularly combines with reference items, particularly *it* and *that*, to form what is in effect a verb of reference which is typically anaphoric and cohesive. (6), the verbal operator, likewise has no cohesive force; but it figures prominently in elliptical forms of the verbal group which are themselves cohesive by virtue of the ellipsis; see Chapter 4.

The substitute *do* is almost always anaphoric; it may presuppose an element within the same sentence as itself, so that there is already a structural relation linking the presupposed to the presupposing clauses; but it frequently substitutes for an element in a preceding sentence, and therefore it is, like the nominal substitute, a primary source of cohesion within a text. Only occasionally is it cataphoric, and then only within the sentence, and so making no contribution to cohesion; an example is

> [3:93] Since I have done, will you join too?

It occurs exophorically under appropriate conditions, for example a warning to someone who has been caught doing something forbidden:

> [3:94] I shouldn't do, if I was you.

Here the speaker is simulating a textual relation in order to suggest that the action in question is already under discussion. But its primary function is anaphoric, and it is a rich source of continuity in everyday linguistic interaction.

There is one further type of substitution, that of a clause, which is discussed in the next section (3.4).

Table 6: The forms of *do*

Item	Class	Function in verbal group	Phonological status	Section	Examples
1 *do*	verbal substitute	Head	weak	3.3.1–2	
2 *do so*	verbal substitute	Head	salient	3.3.1	
3 *do*	lexical verb	Head	salient	3.3.3.1	[3:80–1]
4 *do* (*make, take,* etc)	general verb	Head	salient or weak	3.3.3.2	[3:82]
5 *do* (*happen*)	pro-verb	Head	salient or weak	3.3.3.3	[3:83–6]
6 *do*	verbal operator (auxiliary)	Finiteness: Modifier (Head if elliptical)	salient or weak	3.3.3.6	[3:89–90]

3.4 Clausal substitution

There is one further type of substitution in which what is presupposed is not an element within the clause but an entire clause. The words used as substitutes are *so* and *not*. (For *yes* and *no* see 3.4.3.1 and 4.4.3 below.)

3.4.1. Difference between clausal and other types of substitution

We pointed out at the beginning of the chapter that, since substitution is a formal relation, contrasting in this respect with reference which is a semantic one, a substitute typically has the same structural function as that for which it is substituting. So, for example, *one* functions as Head of a nominal group and substitutes for a noun which was Head of a nominal group. In the same way *do* functions as Head of a verbal group and substitutes for a verb which was Head of a verbal group.

In the case of *do*, however, the substitution may extend over other elements in the clause: any complements or adjuncts that are not repudiated fall within the domain of the substitute *do*. The verb *do* thus comes close to functioning as a substitute for an entire clause, but for the rule of English grammar which requires the Subject to be made explicit. In an example such as

[3:95] The children work very hard in the garden. – They must do.

the children falls within what is presupposed in the second sentence as clearly as the other elements do, but it has to be expressed by the personal pronoun *they*.

However, *do* is not a clausal substitute. This is not because of the requirement of a Subject, but for another, more significant reason: namely that with *do* the contrastive element which provides the context for the substitution is located within the same clause. It may be within or outside the verbal group, but it is always in the clause itself. This was illustrated in [3:58] above. Although other elements may fall within its domain, *do* is a verbal not a clausal substitute.

In clausal substitution the entire clause is presupposed, and the contrasting element is outside the clause. For example,

[3:96] Is there going to be an earthquake? – It says so.

Here the *so* presupposes the whole of the clause *there's going to be an earthquake*, and the contrastive environment is provided by the *says* which is outside it.

There are three environments in which clausal substitution takes place: report, condition and modality. In each of these environments it may take either of two forms, positive or negative; the positive is expressed by *so*, the negative by *not*. We shall consider each of these in turn.

3.4.1.1 SUBSTITUTION OF REPORTED CLAUSES
Here are three examples from *Alice*:

[3:97] a. '. . . if you've seen them so often, of course you know what they're like'.
'I believe so,' Alice replied thoughtfully.
b. 'How am I to get in?' asked Alice again, in a louder tone. '*Are* you to get in at all?' said the Footman. 'That's the first question, you know.'
It was, no doubt: only Alice did not like to be told so.
c. 'The trial cannot proceed,' said the King in a very grave voice, 'until all the jurymen are back in their proper places – *all*,' he repeated with great emphasis, looking hard at Alice as he said so.

In (a), *so* substitutes for (*that*) *I know what they're like*; in (b), for *that was the first question*; and in (c) for '*all*'. As example (c) shows, the presupposed element may be in the quoted form ('direct speech').

The reported clause that is substituted by *so* or *not* is always declarative, whatever the mood of the presupposed clause. There is no substitution for interrogative or imperative (indirect questions or commands), and therefore the clause substitutes do not occur following verbs such as *wonder, order* or *ask*.

The essential distinction to be made here is that between reports and facts. This is a complex distinction, but it is fundamental to language and is reflected in the linguistic system in very many ways. Broadly speaking, facts and reports are those elements in a linguistic structure which represent not the phenomena of experience themselves – persons, objects, actions, events, etc – like 'children', 'throw' and 'stones' in *the children were throwing stones*, but such phenomena already encoded in language, for example 'the fact that the children were throwing stones' as in (*the fact*) *that the children were throwing stones displeased their parents*. These encodings then participate in linguistic structures in the normal way, as this example illustrates, although there are clear restrictions on the types of clause into which they can enter.

What matters here is that these encodings are of two kinds: facts, and reports. The two are rather different, though they are not always easy to tell apart. Facts are phenomena that are encoded at the semantic level, as meanings; reports are phenomena encoded at the lexicogrammatical level, as wordings. Report corresponds more or less to the concept of 'speech' in 'direct speech' and 'indirect speech'. Here are some examples of both; those in column (i) are reports, those in column (ii) are facts:

[3:98]
(i) Report   (ii) Fact

a. Mary said: 'John's late.'
b. Mary's assertion: 'John is late.'
c. Mary said that John was late.   Mary resented that John was late.
d. Mary's assertion that John was   Mary's resentment that John was
   late.   late.
e.   Mary resented John's lateness.
f.   It was that John was late that
                                        Mary resented.
g. Mary was afraid that John was late. Mary was angry that John was late.
h. Mary's fear that John was late.
j.   That John was late angered Mary.

It will be seen that, although the typical form of expression for facts and reports is the same, as illustrated in (c), (d) and (g), there are other realizations which are restricted to one or the other. The restrictions are not as totally clearcut as they have been made to appear here, because other factors are involved as well; but they are valid in general, and they follow from the general distinction between fact as meaning and report as wording.

This last formulation should not be taken to imply that a report always follows the exact wording of what was said, or that there necessarily was an act of speaking corresponding to it. Reports are associated with thinking as well as with saying. It merely means that facts are semantic structures while reports are lexicogrammatical structures. And this enables us to predict, what is actually the case, that reports can be substituted whereas facts cannot – since, as we have seen, substitution is a lexicogrammatical relation.

Hence, corresponding to (c) and (g), we can have *Mary said so*, *Mary was afraid so* in column (i); but we cannot have *Mary resented so* or *Mary was angry so* in column (ii). (The fact that *so* could not appear in (b) and

(h) is a purely structural limitation; we cannot say *Mary's fear so* because here *so* would be a Qualifier within the nominal group, which is not a possible structural function for it.) The pattern appears clearly with words that are used to introduce both facts and reports, *eg: regret*, which means either 'be sorry about the fact that' or 'be sorry to say that'; the substitute can be used only in the latter sense. Facts can be presupposed by reference, but not by substitution:

[3:99] a. They've failed, then? – I regret so.
    b. They've failed. – I regret it. – Everyone regrets it.

The negative form of the clausal substitute is *not*, as in

[3:100] Has everyone gone home? – I hope not.

However with some verbs negation tends to be transferred into the reporting clause so that, for example, the normal pattern of *think* plus negative substitute is *don't think so* rather than *think not*; *cf* also *I don't believe/suppose/imagine so*. The word *not* can be interpreted as the 'portmanteau' realization of the substitute and negative polarity.

All such expressions, positive and negative, are particularly frequent in first person singular, where their meaning comes very close to that of expressions of modality (*cf* 3.4.1.3 below). Another example:

[3:101] 'Of course you agree to have a battle?' Tweedledum said in a calmer tone.
    'I suppose so,' the other sulkily replied, as he crawled out of the umbrella.

There is some restriction on the use of the substitute in the context of expressions of certainty; we say *I'm afraid so* but not *I'm sure so, you think not* or *you don't think so* but not *you know not* or *you don't know so*. The same restriction turns up with modality, though only in the positive; we say *perhaps so* but not *certainly so*, although here *certainly not* is regular and frequent. This is perhaps correlated with the distinction between facts and reports: a report that has certainty ascribed to it strongly resembles a fact – unless the certainty lies in its negation. But the pattern is by no means a consistent one.

One type of report in which substitution is especially frequent is the impersonal type, *eg: they say so/not, it says so/not, it seems/appears so/not*; including, rather more restrictedly, those in the passive form: *it was reported so, it is said not*. For example,

[3:102] Ought we to declare our winnings? – It says not.

There is a possibility of overlap between this structure and that in which *so* is substituting for an Attribute in a clause of ascription; for example, in

[3 : 103] Is this mango ripe? – It seems so.

the answer is strictly speaking ambiguous: it may be 'this mango seems ripe', with personal reference item *it* and *so* as nominal substitute, or 'it seems that this mango is ripe' with impersonal (non-anaphoric) *it* and *so* as clausal substitute. The distinction becomes clear in the plural: *Are these mangoes ripe? – (i) They seem so. (ii) It seems so.* The difference in meaning is slight, but it is easily perceived. Note that the negative is *not* in both instances, (i) *They seem not.* (ii) *It seems not*; showing that both are in fact substitution forms.

Finally, *so* as a report substitute occurs in initial position in expressions such as *so it seems, so he said, so I believe, so we were led to understand*. This has the effect of making the *so* thematic in the clause. Since negation when not combined with other meanings is rarely thematic in modern English, there is no equivalent negative form.

3.4.1.2 SUBSTITUTION OF CONDITIONAL CLAUSES

A second context for clausal substitution is that of conditional structure. Conditional clauses are frequently substituted by *so* and *not*, especially following *if* but also in other forms such as *assuming so, suppose not*:

[3 : 104] a. Everyone seems to think he's guilty. If so, no doubt he'll offer to resign.
  b. We should recognize the place when we come to it.– Yes, but supposing not: then what do we do?

Here *so* in (a) substitutes for *he is guilty*, *not* in (b) for *we don't recognize the place when we come to it*.

3.4.1.3 SUBSTITUTION OF MODALIZED CLAUSES

Finally, *so* and *not* occur as substitutes for clauses expressing modality, *eg*

[3 : 105] a. 'Oh, I beg your pardon!' cried Alice hastily, afraid that she had hurt the poor animal's feelings. 'I quite forgot you didn't like cats.'
  'Not like cats!' cried the Mouse, in a shrill, passionate voice. 'Would *you* like cats if you were me?'
  'Well, perhaps not,' said Alice in a soothing tone: . . .

b. 'May I give you a slice?' she said, taking up the knife and fork, and looking from one Queen to the other.
'Certainly not,' the Red Queen said, very decidedly: 'it isn't etiquette to cut anyone you've been introduced to. Remove the joint!'

Modality is the speaker's assessment of the probabilities inherent in the situation, as in (a); or, in a derived sense, of the rights and duties, as in (b). These may be expressed either by modal forms of the verb (*will, would, can, could, may, might, must, should, is to,* and *ought to*), or by modal adverbs such as *perhaps, possibly, probably, certainly, surely*; the latter are frequently followed by a clausal substitute, with the proviso already noted, that those expressing certainty do not accept substitution in the positive, though they do in the negative.

3.4.2 Similarity among the types of clausal substitution

We have distinguished the three types or contexts of clausal substitution: report, condition, and modality. It is important to emphasize, however, what they have in common.

To start from modality: there is considerable similarity in meaning between a modalized clause, on the one hand, and a reported clause dependent on a first person singular verb of cognition on the other; for example between *probably he's right* and *I suppose he's right* – and hence between *probably so* and *I suppose so*. But *I suppose* is merely a special instance of 'someone supposes'; and supposing is merely one way of 'cognizing' a report, among a set of possible ways including thinking, assuming, believing, knowing and so on. The unmarked context for a report, however, is one not of cognizing but of verbalizing: not of thinking, but of saying. Hence there is a semantic continuity, a 'cline', all the way from *probably he's right*, through *I think he's right* and *they think he's right* to (impersonal) *they say he's right* and *Mary says he's right*. All of these can be substituted by *so* and, in the negative, by *not*.

Looked at from another angle, however, a conditional clause is also semantically related both to a reported one and to a modalized one. The form *if he's right* means 'let us suppose he's right; then . . .'; the condition may be expressed by non-finite (dependent) forms of verbs of cognition, such as *supposing, assuming* (and in many languages by verbs of saying, equivalent to 'let it be said that . . .: then . . .'). Likewise, we can interpret

if he's right as a modality, similar to 'possibly he's right; in that case . . .';
and again there is a modalized form for the expression of a conditional:
should he be right, . . .

All three types have the property of being at one remove from (statements of) reality; they are hypothetical. Modalizing, reporting and
conditionalizing are all ways of assigning dependent status to the clause
in question. This is reflected in the structure; reported and conditional
clauses are both HYPOTACTIC but not 'embedded' (*ie* not RANKSHIFTED;
it is this that is the relevant concept, since 'embedding' has not been
clearly distinguished from hypotaxis in much recent grammatical analysis). That is to say, such a clause is DEPENDENT ON another clause but
not structurally integrated into it; it is not A CONSTITUENT OF it. Since
modality is normally expressed within the clause, by a modal Adjunct
such as *possibly*, or by a modal operator in the verbal group such as *may*,
there is no hypotaxis involved; but where modality is expressed by a
separate clause, then the modalized clause is likewise hypotactically related
to it, as in *it may be that he's right.*

This then is the general environment for clausal substitution. It occurs
in the context of hypotaxis: a clause that is hypotactically related to
another clause may be substituted by *so* or *not*. Semantically this hypotactic structure is the expression of dependent or hypothetical status, in the
form of report, condition or modality; and the possibility of substitution
therefore also extends to the other realization of this relation, namely a
modalized clause in which the modality is expressed simply by insertion
of a modal Adjunct.

As with nominal and verbal substitution, the key concept is one of
continuity in the environment of contrast. It is not possible to substitute
a clause which is functioning independently, just because it is being
repeated; in such instances it must be presupposed by reference, typically
by *it, this* or *that*. Substitution is used in order to display the clause as a
repetition but in a contrastive context, one in which it is dependent on
something else – a report, a condition, an opinion. As always, what we are
calling 'contrast' is not necessarily a negation of the context that was
there before; there may have been no such context, and even if there was,
the presupposing context may be simply a reaffirmation of it. But there
is always some redefinition of the environment of the presupposed
clause; the speaker or writer is encoding the clause as itself recoverable
but in a context which is non-recoverable. This is the underlying meaning
of clausal substitution, and it relates it clearly to substitution in the other
contexts, nominal and verbal.

3.4.3. *Some related patterns*

There are various patterns either related to or in some way resembling clausal substitution which may be brought together for a brief mention here. These fall under two headings: forms of response, and other uses of *so* and *not*.

3.4.3.1 RESPONSE FORMS

The following examples illustrate forms of response which could be interpreted as substitution:

	(i)	(ii)
[3:106] a. Hens lay eggs.	So they do!	So do turkeys.
b. Hens don't fly.	So they don't!	Nor/Neither do turkeys.

Those in column (ii) are responses which add a new Subject; the meaning is 'and + (Subject) + do so'. Since they have alternative forms *turkeys do (so) too, turkeys don't (do so) either*, they can reasonably be interpreted as forms of verbal substitution of the *do so* type (3.3.2 above), with the additional meaning of 'and, too'. This meaning is always present in the negative form *nor* 'and not'; in this structure it is present also as a component in the *so*, by virtue of its initial position (*cf* the discussion of 'and' in Chapter 5 below).

The examples in column (i) are exclamatory responses, acknowledging new information and expressing agreement with it: 'now that you mention it, I see you're right'.

There is no meaning of 'and' here, but some speakers have an alternative form of the negative, namely *nor/neither they do!*; and what may be a subset of the same speakers have *too* in the positive, *they do too!*, (more used in contexts of contradiction) – perhaps this pattern has evolved through influence from the column (ii) forms. The column (i) expression as a whole is undoubtedly cohesive; but it seems that the cohesion here is rather a matter of ellipsis, and that the *so* is being used in the non-cohesive sense of 'true' (see next section). Note that there is a superficially identical structure in which *so* is a reference item, meaning 'like that', 'as previously stated', *eg* (*cf* the last sentence of example [3:84c] above):

[3:107] It can't have helped very much, all that shouting. –
So it didn't. It only made things worse.

The other response forms that need to be mentioned are *yes* and *no*. These could be thought of as clause substitutes; but they are really more readily interpretable as elliptical forms. (See Chapter 4, section 4.4.3, for discussion of *yes* and *no*.) They express just the polarity option in the clause, positive or negative, leaving the remainder to be presupposed. It is important to make this clear: what is expressed by *yes* and *no* is the polarity of the presupposing clause, irrespective of the polarity of what it pre- supposes – they do not, as their dictionary equivalents in some languages do, express agreement or disagreement with what has gone before. Consequently the response *yes* means 'I am tired' no matter what the polarity and mood of the presupposed clause:

[3:108] a. You're tired.
         b. Are you tired?
         c. You're not tired? } Yes. (I am tired.)
         d. Aren't you tired?
             etc

The substitutes *so* and *not* are exactly parallel to *yes* and *no* in this respect; so for example

[3:109] a. Is he going to pass the exam?   I hope so. (I hope he is.)
         b. Isn't he going to pass the   I'm afraid not. (I'm afraid
            exam?   he isn't.)

3.4.3.2 OTHER USES OF *so* AND *not*

In Chapter 2 we discussed the use of *so* as a reference item, meaning 'like this' or 'to this extent'. There is no such thing as negative reference, so the form *not* does not appear under this heading.

In Chapter 5 we shall deal with *so* as a conjunction, meaning 'conse- quently'. Here too there is no related negative form.

In this chapter we have treated *so* as a substitute, in nominal, verbal and clausal substitution, in which it stands for the whole or part of another (typically a preceding) clause. Clausal substitution is the only context in which *so* has a corresponding negative, namely *not*. It is also the only context in which *not* is a cohesive element; elsewhere it is simply the expression of negative polarity.

In all these instances, *so* is cohesive. There remains one further use of the word, in which it is not cohesive, but simply has the meaning 'true'. (This has already been mentioned in the last section, as the interpretation of *so* in *So they do!*)

It is this meaning of *so* that is found in the expressions *that is so*, *this being so*, *is that so?*, and so on. Here the meaning is 'that is true', 'that is the case'. That this is not the substitute *so* is shown among other things by the negative; the negative of *that is so* is never *that is not*, but only *that is not so, that isn't so* (in substitution both forms would be expected to occur). The cohesiveness of expressions of this kind derives not from the *so* but from the anaphoric reference item *that* or *it*.

In this sense *so* almost always follows the verb *be*. It might be possible to interpret *it seems so* in this way; but here there is the corresponding negative *it seems not* as alternative to *it doesn't seem so*. Moreover the *so* in *it seems so* is typically non-tonic, which suggests the unaccented, substitute form; whereas the *so* following the verb *be* is typically tonic, *eg: that is so, it's not so*. The difference between the two is shown by the fact that, by itself, *it is so* is not a possible response; [3:110] is unacceptable:

[3:110] Everyone's leaving. – It is so.

whereas *it seems so* would be quite acceptable. Perhaps in a sequence such as

[3:111] Everyone's leaving. – It seems so. – It is so!

where the context sets the tonic on *is* and not on *so*, we have a true substitute *so* following *be*; but this is clearly a special case, and can be felt to be somewhat odd.

3.4.4 *Summary of uses of* so

The meanings of *so* are summarized in Table 7. Of the items listed, (1–6) are all cohesive; only (7) is not. (1) and (2) are reference items (Chapter 2, sections 2.5.1 and 2.5.2). (3) refers to the only use of *so* as a nominal substitute, as Attribute in ascriptive clauses such as *they seem so*. In (4), *so* is the verbal substitute *do so*, discussed in 3.3; for the form *so do I*, see 3.4.3.1. (5) is *so* as the clausal substitute, in contexts of report, condition and modality; this was treated in 3.4.2. In (6) *so* is a conjunction (Chapter 5, especially 5.6). In (7), *so* has the meaning of 'true'; it is not cohesive, and so not discussed in detail, but the forms *it is so* and *so they do!* were mentioned briefly in sections 3.4.3.1 and 3.4.3.2.

As a clausal substitute, *so* is almost always anaphoric, exactly as are all substitutes. Like the others, it may presuppose an element to which it is already structurally related; but since it itself substitutes for a clause, the only conditions under which this can occur are those of structural relations between clauses, paratactic as in [3:112a], or hypotactic as in [3:112b]:

[3:112] a. He may come, but he didn't say so.
        b. He'll come if he said so.

Table 7: The forms of *so*

Item	Cohesive type	Class	Function	Phonological status	Section	Examples
1 *so*	reference	adverb	Submodifier in nominal group	weak	2.5.1-2	[2:87]
2 *so*	reference	adverb	Adjunct	salient	2.5.1-2	[2:78a]; [3:84c]; [3:107]
3 *so*	substitution (nominal)	adverb	Attribute	weak	3.2.6	[3:54]; [3:103]
4 *so* (in *do so*)	substitution (verbal, part of)	adverb	(part of) Head of verbal group	weak	3.3; 3.4.3.1	[3:77-8]; [3:106(ii)]
5 *so*	substitution (clausal)	adverb	Adjunct	salient	3.4.1-2	[3:95-105]
6 *so*	conjunction	conjunctive adverb	Adjunct	weak	5.6	[5:43-6]
7 *so*	—	adverb	Attribute	salient	3.4.3.2	[3:106(i)]

where *so* substitutes for *he would come* in each case. (Note that in (a) *may* is the realization of 'possibly + future'; the substitute presupposes the 'future' but not the modality.) Such instances derive their cohesion internally from the structure. Even more frequently than the other substitutes, however, *so* presupposes across the sentence boundary, and hence functions as the primary means of textual cohesion. Cataphoric instances are infrequent but by no means impossible:

[3:113] If he said so, he'll come.

But it is difficult to construct exophoric examples, because of the particular nature of the contrastive contexts – report, condition and modality – in which clausal substitution occurs. As was mentioned at the beginning of this chapter, substitution is fundamentally a textual relation; the primary meaning is anaphoric, and a substitute is used exophorically only when the speaker wants to simulate the textual relation in order to create an effect of something having already been mentioned. This rarely happens where the presupposition extends over the meaning of an entire clause.

Substitution forms are summarized in Table 8.

Table 8: Summary of substitution forms

		Non-prominent (given)	Prominent (new)
Nominal	Thing (count noun)	one(s)	the SAME
	Process (nominalized) Attribute Fact }	so	do be } the SAME say
Verbal	Process (+...)	do	DO SO
Clausal (β): report, condition, modality	positive	so	so
	negative	not	NOT

Chapter 4

Ellipsis

4.1 Ellipsis, substitution and reference

In one sense, the break between Chapters 3 and 4 is an unnatural one, because substitution and ellipsis are very similar to each other. As we expressed it earlier, ellipsis is simply 'substitution by zero'.

For practical purposes, however, it is more helpful to treat the two separately. Although substitution and ellipsis embody the same fundamental relation between parts of a text (a relation between words or groups or clauses – as distinct from reference, which is a relation between meanings), they are two different kinds of structural mechanism, and hence show rather different patterns.

The starting point of the discussion of ellipsis can be the familiar notion that it is 'something left unsaid'. There is no implication here that what is unsaid is not understood; on the contrary, 'unsaid' implies 'but understood nevertheless', and another way of referring to ellipsis is in fact as SOMETHING UNDERSTOOD, where *understood* is used in the special sense of 'going without saying' (compare *it is understood that we are to be consulted before any agreement is reached*).

There is no mystery in the fact that much can be 'understood' in this way. As we have stressed all along, language does not function in isolation; it functions as TEXT, in actual situations of use. There is always a great deal more evidence available to the hearer for interpreting a sentence than is contained in the sentence itself. However, it is important here to distinguish between two different kinds of evidence from which we may (to use another familiar term) 'supply' what is left unsaid. Only one of these is associated with ellipsis: that where there is some presupposition, in the structure, of what is to be supplied.

Consider an example such as

[4:1] Hardly anyone left the country before the war.

In order to interpret this, we should probably want to know whether *country* meant 'rural areas' (hence 'hardly anyone moved into the towns') or 'national unit'; if the latter, which country was being referred to, and whether *left* meant 'emigrated' or 'went abroad on holiday'; which war; whether *hardly anyone* referred to the whole population, or a given social or family group; and so on. All this is relevant information if we want to understand this sentence. But there is nothing in the structure of the sentence to suggest that it has been left out. There are two occurrences of the reference item *the*, both of them probably generalized exophoric; but there is nothing to make us feel that we must have missed some vital previous clause or sentence. The structure is not such as to presuppose any preceding text.

When we talk of ellipsis, we are not referring to any and every instance in which there is some information that the speaker has to supply from his own evidence. That would apply to practically every sentence that is ever spoken or written, and would be of no help in explaining the nature of a text. We are referring specifically to sentences, clauses, etc whose structure is such as to presuppose some preceding item, which then serves as the source of the missing information. An elliptical item is one which, as it were, leaves specific structural slots to be filled from elsewhere. This is exactly the same as presupposition by substitution, except that in substitution an explicit 'counter' is used, *eg: one* or *do*, as a place-marker for what is presupposed, whereas in ellipsis nothing is inserted into the slot. That is why we say that ellipsis can be regarded as substitution by zero.

For example,

[4:2] Joan brought some carnations, and Catherine some sweet peas.

The structure of the second clause is Subject and Complement. This structure normally appears only in clauses in which at least one element, the Predicator, is presupposed, to be supplied from the preceding clause. Note that there is no possible alternative interpretation here; the second clause can be interpreted only as *Catherine brought some sweet peas*.

There the two clauses are structurally related; the second is BRANCHED. Now consider

[4:3] Would you like to hear another verse? I know twelve more.

Here there is no structural relationship between the two parts. The second sentence contains a nominal group *twelve more*, consisting of a Numerative only, for which we have to supply a Head noun *verses* presupposed from the first sentence. Again, a nominal group having a Numerative but no

Head will normally be found only in contexts of presupposition. To give a slightly more complex example:

[4:4] 'And how many hours a day did you do lessons?' said Alice, in a hurry to change the subject.
'Ten hours the first day,' said the Mock Turtle: 'nine the next, and so on.'

The nominal group *nine* is presupposing, meaning *nine hours*, and so is *the next*, meaning *the next day*. The two clauses *nine the next* and *ten hours the first day* are also both presupposing, representing *we did lessons ten hours the first day*, etc. In all these examples the clauses and the nominal groups display structures that clearly show them to be presupposing.

Where there is ellipsis, there is a presupposition, in the structure, that something is to be supplied, or 'understood'. This is not quite the same thing as saying that we can tell from the structure of an item whether it is elliptical or not. For practical purposes we often can; but it is not in fact the structure which makes it elliptical. An item is elliptical if its structure does not express all the features that have gone into its make-up – all the meaningful choices that are embodied in it.

In other words, we can take as a general guide the notion that ellipsis occurs when something that is structurally necessary is left unsaid; there is a sense of incompleteness associated with it. But it is useful to recognize that this is an over-simplification, and that the essential characteristic of ellipsis is that something which is present in the selection of underlying ('systemic') options is omitted in the structure – whether or not the resulting structure is in itself 'incomplete'.

Like substitution, ellipsis is a relation within the text, and in the great majority of instances the presupposed item is present in the preceding text. That is to say, ellipsis is normally an anaphoric relation. Occasionally the presupposition in an elliptical structure may be exophoric – we noted in Chapter 3 that this could also happen with substitution. If a housewife on seeing the milkman approach calls out *Two please!* she is using exophoric ellipsis; it is the context of situation that provides the information needed to interpret this. But exophoric ellipsis has no place in cohesion, so we shall not explore it any further here.

Let us summarize here the general features of reference, substitution and ellipsis, harking back to what was said in the final paragraph of Chapter 3. All three are forms of presupposition, devices for identifying something by referring it to something that is already there – known to, or at least recoverable by, the hearer. Since this 'something' that is presupposed may be an element in a preceding sentence, these devices have a cohesive effect; they contribute very largely to cohesion within the text.

Reference is presupposition at the semantic level. A reference item signals that the meaning is recoverable, though not necessarily in the form of the actual word or words required. For this reason a reference item cannot necessarily be replaced by what it presupposes; even if the presupposed item is present in the text, the reference to it may require an item of a different function in structure. At its simplest, reference is a form of situational (exophoric) presupposition; but it is regularly used in textual (endophoric) presupposition, pointing backwards (anaphoric) or sometimes forward (cataphoric). In many styles of discourse, including almost all written language, reference is always textual rather than situational.

Substitution, and here we include ellipsis as a special case of substitution, is presupposition at the level of words and structures. When a substitute is used, it signals that the actual item required, the particular word or group or clause, is recoverable from the environment; and the substitute preserves the class of the presupposed item, which may therefore be replaced in the 'slot' created by it. The difference between substitution and ellipsis is that in the former a substitution counter occurs in the slot, and this must therefore be deleted if the presupposed item is replaced, whereas in the latter the slot is empty – there has been substitution by zero. Unlike reference, substitution is essentially a textual relation; it exists primarily as an anaphoric (or occasionally cataphoric) device, and in its rare exophoric use it tends to give an effect of 'putting the words in the other person's mouth'.

In tabular form:

	Reference	Substitution and ellipsis
Level of abstraction	semantic	lexicogrammatical
Primary source of presupposition	situation	text
What is presupposed?	meanings	items (ie words, groups, clauses)
Is class preserved?	not necessarily	yes
Is replacement possible?	not necessarily	yes
Use as a cohesive device	yes; anaphoric and cataphoric	yes; anaphoric (occasionally cataphoric)

Examples:

[4:5] a. This is a fine hall you have here. I'm proud to be lecturing in it.

b. This is a fine hall you have here. I've never lectured in a finer one.

c. This is a fine hall you have here. I've never lectured in a finer.

Example [4:5a] is reference. It would be possible to replace *it* by some expression containing the word *hall*; but it would have to be altered from the original (*eg: in this fine hall*), and it still sounds somewhat awkward. Examples (b) and (c) are substitution and ellipsis, and it would be quite natural to add *hall* after *finer* (deleting *one* in (b)).

In what follows, we shall discuss ellipsis under three headings:

Nominal ellipsis (4.2)
Verbal ellipsis (4.3)
Clausal ellipsis (4.4)

There is one further general point to be made first. We noted above, in Chapters 2 and 3, that a reference item, or a substitute, may relate to something in the same sentence, such that the presupposition takes place within the confines of a single structure. This is no different in principle from any other instance of reference or substitution, though it may have certain special features, such as the cataphoric reference of *the* to a qualifier in the nominal group in example [2:61]. But in the analysis of texts, relations within the sentence are fairly adequately expressed already in structural terms, so that there is no need to involve the additional notion of cohesion to account for how the parts of a sentence hang together.

Between sentences, however, there are no structural relations, and this is where the study of cohesion becomes important. For this reason in both these chapters we concentrated on reference and substitution as relations between sentences, largely ignoring intra-sentence presupposition.

We shall do the same here. Ellipsis, or something closely related to it, also occurs within sentences, as in [4:2] above; and there are certain special structural possibilities, types of BRANCHING structure, which do not occur when the presupposition is between sentences. In general we shall not be concerned with ellipsis within the sentence, for the same reason as already given; it can be explained in terms of sentence structure and does not constitute an independent agency of cohesion in the text. What we are interested in is ellipsis as a form of relation between sentences, where it is an aspect of the essential texture. The relevance of ellipsis in the present context is its role in grammatical cohesion.

4.2 Nominal ellipsis

4.2.1 Ellipsis within the nominal group

By NOMINAL ELLIPSIS we mean ellipsis within the nominal group. The structure of the nominal group was outlined in 2.1. On the logical dimension the structure is that of a Head with optional modification; the modifying elements include some which precede the Head and some which follow it, referred to here as Premodifier and Postmodifier respectively. Thus in *those two fast electric trains with pantographs* the Head is *trains*, the Premodifier is formed by *those two fast electric* and the Postmodifier by *with pantographs*.

The Modifier is combined with another structure, on the experiential dimension, which consists of the elements Deictic (d), Numerative (n), Epithet (e), Classifier (c), and Qualifier (q), represented here by *those, two, fast, electric* and *with pantographs* respectively. The Deictic is normally a determiner, the Numerative a numeral or other quantifier, the Epithet an adjective and the Classifier a noun; but these correspondences are by no means exact. There may be Submodifiers at various places; these are usually adverbs like *so, very* and *too*. The Qualifier is normally a relative clause or prepositional phrase. The noun in this structure has the function referred to as the Thing. Most elements may occur more than once, and the tendency for this to happen increases as one moves towards the later elements of the structure.

The function of Head, which is always filled, is normally served by the common noun, proper noun or pronoun expressing the Thing. Personal pronouns are reference items and were described in Chapter 2; they will not be discussed further. Proper nouns designate individuals, and are therefore not capable of further specification; they may sometimes be accompanied by descriptive modifiers, but these are not subject to ellipsis. Common nouns, on the other hand, designate classes; they are often further specified, and this is the function of the elements Deictic, Numerative, Epithet and Classifier. Now under certain circumstances the common noun may be omitted and the function of Head taken on by one of these other elements. This is what is meant by nominal ellipsis.

In a non-elliptical nominal group, the Head is the Thing, the noun designating the individual or class referred to. This may be a phenomenon of any kind: person, animate or inanimate object, abstraction, institution, process, quality, state or relation. In an elliptical nominal group, this element is not expressed, and one of the other elements (Deictic, Numerative, Epithet or Classifier) functions as Head. This is very frequently a Deictic or Numerative, much less frequently an Epithet. It is very rarely a Classifier; since the Classifier is usually a noun, if it functioned as Head it would be liable itself to be interpreted as the Thing (so, for example, we cannot replace *a tall brick chimney* by *a tall brick; see* 4.2.3 below).

In general, with exceptions to be noted below (4.2.3 and 4.2.3.5), any nominal group having the function of Head filled by a word that normally functions within the Modifier is an elliptical one.

Nominal ellipsis therefore involves the upgrading of a word functioning as Deictic, Numerative, Epithet or Classifier from the status of Modifier to the status of Head. For example,

[4:6]   Four other Oysters followed them,
        and yet another four.

In the second line *four*, which is a Numerative and therefore normally acts as Modifier, is upgraded to function as Head. Similarly in

[4:7]   Which last longer, the curved rods or the straight rods? – The straight are less likely to break.

straight is an Epithet, functioning as Modifier in the question but as Head in the response. Both *another four* and *the straight* are elliptical nominal groups.

An elliptical nominal group clearly requires that there should be available from some source or other the information necessary for filling it out. Faced with *another four*, we need to know 'another four what?' Normally, the source of information is a preceding nominal group. A nominal group that is elliptical presupposes a previous one that is not, and it is therefore cohesive.

If we want to fill out an elliptical nominal group, for text analysis purposes, there are two ways of doing so. One way is simply to 'push down' the element functioning as Head, making it a Modifier, and add the 'missing' Head in its place. (The question whether any other 'missing' elements would have to be supplied is discussed in 4.2.3 below.) By this process *another four* in [4:6] would become *another four oysters*. The other way of doing it is to keep the elliptical group as it is and add a partitive Qualifier; this would give *another four of the oysters*. The partitive is possible only under certain conditions: generally, when the elliptical group designates some aggregate – a subset, fraction, quantity or collective – that is different from that designated by the presupposed group. Hence in [4:7] the partitive form is not possible. The head noun in the partitive expression will be singular or non-singular (plural or mass) according to the type of aggregate: singular if the elliptical group is partitive in the narrower sense (*ie* designating a fraction), and non-singular otherwise. The former type are less readily elliptical (but see 4.2.3.4 below on indefinite quantifiers):

[4:8] a. How did you enjoy the exhibition? – A lot (of the exhibition) was very good, though not all.

　　　b. How did you enjoy the paintings? – A lot (of the paintings) were very good, though not all.

So an elliptical nominal group may always be replaced by its full, non-elliptical equivalent, either in simple form or in expanded, partitive form. In either case, the presupposed items are restored. The two possibilities arise because the partitive type is in any case a regular form of the English nominal group, obligatory in some instances, such as where there is quantification within the deixis as in [4:9a], and optional in certain others such as [4:9b]:

[4:9] a. Two of my rosebushes were uprooted.

　　　b. That was his most popular film/the most popular of his films.

The partitive Qualifier may itself contain an elliptical nominal group, as in *one of the three, any of Fred's*. We may now modify the earlier statement that a nominal group having Deictic, Numerative, Epithet or Classifier as Head is always elliptical. If it contains a partitive Qualifier, it is not elliptical – unless the partitive Qualifier is itself elliptical.

Some further examples:

[4:10] Which hat will you wear? This is
{
a. the best.
b. the best hat.
c. the best of the hats.
d. the best of the three.
e. the best you have.
}

In all cases *the* is Deictic, *three* is Numerative, *best* is Epithet and *hat* is the common noun representing the Thing. Then:

(a) is elliptical; *the* is Modifier, *best* is Head.

(b) is non-elliptical; *the best* is Modifier, *hat* is Head.

(c) is non-elliptical; *the* is Modifier, *best* is Head, *of the hats* is partitive Qualifier, non-elliptical.

(d) is elliptical; structure as (c), except that the partitive Qualifier *of the three* is itself elliptical.

(e) is elliptical; structure as (c), except that the Qualifier *you have* is not partitive.

4.2.2 *Presupposition of nominal elements*

An elliptical nominal group is cohesive; it points anaphorically to another nominal group which is presupposed by it. But how much of the presupposed group is in fact included within the presupposition? So far we have merely indicated that the Thing designated by the common noun is presupposed. But there may be other elements in the presupposed group which likewise do not occur in the elliptical one; for example

[4:11] Here are my two white silk scarves. I can lend you one if you like.

Here *one* presumably presupposes not only *scarves* but also the garnishings *white* and *silk*; it could be filled out as *one white silk scarf*, or *one of my white silk scarves*. This makes it possible to state what CAN be presupposed, by reference to the structure of the nominal group in terms of the elements Deictic, Numerative, Epithet and Classifier; note that these elements occur in the order stated, followed by the Thing. In ellipsis, the Thing is always presupposed. (We have already pointed out that in ellipsis the Thing is always a common noun, since proper nouns and pronouns do not take defining Modifiers.) In addition, any element following the one that is upgraded in the elliptical nominal group may be presupposed. Thus

If Head is filled by	This must be presupposed:	These may be presupposed:
Deictic	Thing	Numerative, Epithet, Classifier
Numerative	Thing	Epithet, Classifier
Epithet	Thing	Classifier
Classifier	Thing	–

As already noted above, it is rare for the Classifier to occur as Head. These patterns are exemplified in [4:12]. In [4:12a], *yours* (Deictic) is Head, and the presupposed elements include not only *scarves* (Thing) but also *silk* (Classifier), *white* (Epithet) and possibly *two* (Numerative):

[4:12] Here are my two white silk scarves.
    a. Where are yours?
    b. I used to have three.
    c. Can you see any black?
    d. Or would you prefer the cotton?

[4:12b] is like [4:11]; *three* presupposes *scarf, silk* and *white*. In (c) the elliptical group is *any black*; this presupposes *scarf* and *silk*, but there may be any number and they may not be mine. Finally, in (d) only *scarf* is presupposed.

In general, then, the range of possible presuppositions is dependent on the structure of the nominal group. It extends only over that part of the presupposed group which could follow the element acting as Head in the elliptical group. Those parts which would precede or be concurrent with it are excluded from the presupposition; and this restriction apparently applies even to subcategories within the Deictic and Numerative (see 4.2.4.1–4 below), for example:

[4:13] a. They haven't got my usual morning paper. Can I borrow yours?
 b. The first three buds all fell off. We'll have to watch the next.

where *yours* excludes *usual* (even though *your usual* could occur) because both *your* and *usual* are Deictic elements, and *next* excludes *three* (even though *next three* could occur) because both are Numerative elements. But there is considerable indeterminacy at this point.

What can be presupposed, therefore, is anything having a function in the series d – n – e – c that is LATER than that occupied by the Head of the elliptical group. Whatever has the same or a preceding function is repudiated. To exemplify once more, if the presupposed group is *those two tall brick chimneys*, the following table shows what is repudiated and what is not repudiated (and therefore may be taken over by presupposition) by the various elliptical groups; note that x stands for the function of Thing:

If elliptical group is:	These are repudiated:	These are not repudiated:
which? (d)	d	n e c x = two tall brick chimneys
three (n)	d n	e c x = tall brick chimneys
two not so tall (n e)	d n e	c x = brick chimneys
some stone (d c)	d n e c	x = chimneys

The further 'to the right' the final element of the presupposing group, the more usual it is to presuppose by substitution rather than by ellipsis. We would expect *some stone ones* rather than *some stone* (*stone* = Classifier); and perhaps also *two not so tall ones* (*tall* = Epithet).

However, it is not necessarily the case that everything that could be presupposed actually is presupposed. We can take it as a general guiding principle that it will be, but this will certainly need to be modified to some extent. Consider an example such as

[4:14] Don't you like those three little white eighteenth-century stone cottages? – I prefer mine.

My three little white eighteenth-century stone cottages? Or just my cottage? The answer is possible even if 'mine' is one large red Elizabethan brick and timbered one. We would accept any interpretation that made sense and was consistent with what we already knew. It is worth noting, at the same time, that a form such as *mine* in this context is in the strict sense of the term ambiguous: it could stand as the realization of a number of different selections.

We do find a rough scale of probability, extending from right to left in the nominal group. Of the elements that MAY be presupposed in any given instance, namely those that follow the element that is explicitly repudiated in the elliptical group, we have seen that the Thing, that which is designated by the Head in a non-elliptical structure, always is presupposed. Going 'from right to left', the Classifier, if present, is very likely to be: the Epithet somewhat less likely, and the Numerative less likely still. The Deictic, being the first element, normally cannot be presupposed, by the principle illustrated in [4:12] and [4:13] above. And there is an overriding principle that the presupposed items must be continuous: it would not be possible for *mine* in [4:14] to presuppose *three little white* but not *eighteenth-century stone*.

It is slightly odd, therefore, to find all the elements in a long nominal group, including the Classifier, repudiated in an instance where structurally they could be presupposed. [4:15] is only doubtfully acceptable:

[4:15] I think I'll get one of those gorgeous big red china dogs. Mine barks too much.

In spoken English, there is often a phonological indication of the extent of presupposition. It is characteristic of an elliptical nominal group that its Head carries tonic prominence in the tone group. This is natural, since tonic prominence is the realization of new or contrastive information, and an elliptical nominal group (like one with substitution) is inherently new, in the sense that it differs in some respect from the one it presupposes; not necessarily having a different referent (it could refer contrastively to the same thing), but the function of an elliptical item is to start afresh, taking the presupposed item as a reference point. Thus the occurrence of an elliptical nominal such as *mine* allows us to predict that somewhere in the environment is an item expressing a Thing, such as *hat*, which either was not 'mine' or, if it was, demanded some explicit reaffirmation of the fact, as it would for example in answer to the question *Whose is this hat? – It's mine.* In this sense an elliptical group always embodies some new information.

Now it often happens that the presupposed nominal group signals a particular point of repudiation – an element with which the presupposing elliptical group is specifically in contrast – by the device of tonic prominence. For example, if *your hat* is to be followed by *mine*, the tonic will fall on *your*. This is especially likely to happen in a question–answer sequence, or if the two nominal groups are part of an utterance by the same speaker, who may have planned the information structure as a whole: *That's not* YOUR *hat. It's* MINE. A MARKED tonic (tonic prominence falling on some element other than the last) signals contrastive information; *eg*

[4:16] The two WHITE silk scarves were beautifully made.

Here the word *white* is tonic, and this gives an expectation that if an elliptical (or substitute) nominal group follows it will be one that repudiates *white*, such as *why did you buy the pink (one)?*

4.2.3 Types of nominal ellipsis

We now consider in more detail some examples of the most frequently occurring types of nominal ellipsis, with comments on the words or word classes that function as Head in the elliptical group.

We have already noted that the Classifier is very rarely left to function as Head. In [4:17a–d] we have four examples in which the presupposing group contains a Classifier; they are given in a substitute form, with *one(s)* as Head, and only in the last of the four would it be possible to delete the substitute leaving an elliptical group ending in a Classifier:

[4:17] a. Don't you like babies? – Yes, but I can't stand crying ones.
       b. I've never tried Mrs Sugden's cherry cake, but I like her ginger one.
       c. Borrow my copy. The library one is out on loan.
       d. Did you win a first prize? – No, I only got a third one.

The principle behind this restriction is very clear. The Classifier is typically, though not always, realized by a word that could also realize the

Thing: usually a noun, as in (b) and (c), or the *-ing* form of a verb as in (a). Hence a nominal group having such an item as its Head would normally be interpreted as non-elliptical (so *I can't stand crying* would be interpreted not as 'crying ones; *ie* crying babies' but simply as 'the phenomenon of anyone crying'). There are some instances where a Classifier CAN function as Head, usually those where the elliptical interpretation of the resulting nominal group is in some way the most natural one: for example if the Classifier is not a noun, as in [4:17d], or if the presupposing status of the nominal group is signalled by an anaphoric *the* as in [4:12d] above. These, however, are a minority.

But, as suggested in the previous section, we really have a gradation or 'cline' here, rather than a sharp distinction between the classifier and the rest. The structural formula Deictic – Numerative – Epithet – Classifier represents a gradual move, in the process of specifying the class of 'things' that is expressed by the Head, from one type of specification to another: beginning, in the Deictic, with a kind of specification that is temporary, and related to the actual speech situation, and moving on to one that is increasingly permanent and inherent. Specification of the first kind is achieved by items in closed systems, such as *this/that*, or the pronominal possessives; that of the second kind by lexical items, which form 'open' classes. Hence as one moves along this scale, the actual words used are more and more noun-like; they are words which themselves have the potential of expressing a class of 'things' such as is typically expressed by a noun functioning as Head, and so they are liable to be interpreted as Head. This being the case, such words are LESS likely to function as Head when they are expressing something else. This does not mean that a nominal group having an Epithet or Classifier in it CANNOT be anaphoric and cohesive; but it will tend to achieve this status by substitution rather than by ellipsis.

The most characteristic instances of ellipsis, therefore, are those with Deictic or Numerative as Head. Here the situation is the other way round: substitution is much less common, and in some cases excluded altogether. So we have for example

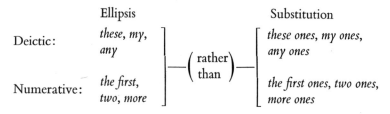

	Ellipsis		Substitution
Deictic:	*these, my, any*	— (rather than) —	*these ones, my ones, any ones*
Numerative:	*the first, two, more*		*the first ones, two ones, more ones*

In principle any Deictic or Numerative element can function as Head in nominal ellipsis, with some minor exceptions which will be noted.

For the remainder of 4.2, therefore, we shall be concerned mainly with deictic and numerative elements, with a relatively short section on epithet ellipsis at the end. Deictics are considered first.

4.2.3.1 SPECIFIC DEICTICS

Following on from the earlier account of deixis in the nominal group, we recognize a division of the Deictic element into two parts, one forming the Deictic properly so called and one which has been referred to as POST-DEICTIC. The words functioning as Deictic are mostly of the class of determiner; with the demonstrative, possessive and indefinite determiners forming a network of systemically related categories – one that includes the articles, which are thus shown to be part of a wider system. Those functioning as Post-deictic are adjectives. In

[4:18] Here the other guinea-pig cheered, and was suppressed.

the is Deictic and *other* is Post-deictic. Post-deictics are discussed in 4.2.3.3 below.

Within the Deictic proper, the major distinction, and that which is most relevant to ellipsis, is into specific deictics (possessives, demonstratives and *the*) and non-specific (*each, every, all, both, any, either, no, neither, some,* and *a*). Non-specific and specific deictics may be combined only through the use of a partitive qualifier, eg: *each of my children, any of the answers, some of that pudding.* The exceptions are *all* and *both*, which can be joined directly to another determiner, in what is sometimes therefore referred to as PRE-DEICTIC position, as in *all our yesterdays, both these gates.*

The words *all* and *both* very frequently function elliptically. They may refer back to a single nominal group; if so it will be plural, having the sense of 'two' if presupposed by *both* and more than two if presupposed by *all*. There is no equivalent singular form; and curiously *all* is NOT used elliptically to refer to a mass noun, even though in non-elliptical nominal groups it is regularly 'mass', as in *all the milk was sour.* For example:

[4:19] a. The men got back at midnight. Both were tired out.
b. The men got back at midnight. All were tired out.
c. The milk couldn't be used. All was sour.

Of these, (c) is impossible; there is in fact no elliptical form here, just as there is no form of substitution with mass nouns. At the same time, however, the item presupposed by *all* or *both* may consist of separate nominal groups; so we would have to say rather that these words presuppose a certain number of entities, which may have been expressed either in the form of one plural noun or as different nouns, singular or plural. Furthermore these 'entities' are themselves sets of any extent.

We can summarize this by saying that *both* refers to two sets and *all* to three or more sets. These sets may be combined in one nominal group, as in [4:19a and b] above, and in [4:20a] where the presupposed item is *the parents*, ie '(i) the father and (ii) the mother'. Or each one may be a separate nominal group, not always in the same sentence but usually with some indication that they belong together, such as parallelism of structure; an example is [4:20b] where *both* presupposes (i) *the parents* and (ii) *the children*. And in this case any one set may itself be complex and consist of a further coordination, as in [4:20c], which has (i) *parents and other responsible adults* and (ii) *children*.

> [4:20] a. The parents could not be traced. Apparently both were abroad.
>
> b. The parents may enjoy it, but the children will be bored. You cannot please both.
>
> c. If parents and other responsible adults make no concessions, children will rebel. And both will be certain they are right.

In the last type, there must be explicit linkage between the items that are being treated as a single set (*parents and other responsible adults*). We cannot have *both* presupposing (i) *the boy's parents* and *his teachers*, and (ii) *the boy*, in [4:21], because there is nothing to show that *the boy's parents* and *his teachers* belong together:

> [4:21] The boy's parents had no time for him. At school, his teachers could make little contact. Yet the boy had a lot of ability, if he'd tried. I suppose both were at fault, really.

Sometimes it is not clear which items are being grouped together, and ambiguity results, as in

> [4:22] The father and the mother were so busy making money that the two children were left to their own devices. Naturally both were resentful.

In addition to *all* and *both*, other Deictic elements regularly function as Head of an elliptical nominal group. The specific deictics are (i) demonstratives and *the*, and (ii) possessives. The demonstratives (*this, that, these, those,* and *which?*) all occur elliptically, with very great frequency. Since they are themselves reference items (see 2.4 and 2.4.1), they are often anaphoric anyway; but wherever the nominal group could be 'filled out' with a noun Head, or by the substitute *one(s)*, a demonstrative functioning as Head is in fact an example of ellipsis. One example will suffice; *those* is elliptical for *those pills:*

> [4:23] Take these pills three times daily. And you'd better have some
> more of those too.

The word *the* does not operate elliptically; since its function is to signal that the 'thing' designated is fully defined, but by something other than *the* itself, it normally requires another item with it, as in *the two, the small (one), the one that got away*. Where it could have occurred elliptically it is replaced by its non-reduced cognate form *that*.

Possessives include both nominals (*Smith's, my father's*, etc) and pronominals (*my, your*, etc). The latter have a special form when functioning as Head: *mine, ours, yours, his, hers, theirs, whose*, and (rarely) *its*. Whenever a possessive occurs as Head it is elliptical, and in the case of the third person pronominals this means, as noted in Chapter 2 above (see 2.3.4, [2:24]), that there is a double cohesive tie. An item such as *hers* presupposes both a person as possessor and a thing possessed, the former by reference (*her*), the latter by ellipsis (the possessive):

> [4:24] Just ask Janet how to polish the brassware. Hers sparkles.

4.2.3.2 NON-SPECIFIC DEICTICS

The non-specific Deictics are *each, every, any, either, no, neither, a*, and *some*, as well as *all* and *both* which have already been discussed. Of these, all occur as Head of an elliptical nominal except *every*, but *a* and *no* have to be represented by the forms *one* and *none* respectively. Some examples:

> [4:25] a. I hope no bones are broken? – None to speak of.
>   b. I won't be introduced to the pudding, please. May I give you
>   some?
>   c. Have some wine. – I don't see any wine. – There isn't any.
>   d. Write an essay on the Stuart kings. Two pages about each will
>   do.
>   e. His sons went into business. Neither succeeded.

Of these, *either* and *neither* are like *both* in presupposing two sets; and *each* presupposes two or more. Again, these may be expressed either as one plural nominal group or separately; and if they are separate, any one set may itself be a coordination, as in [4:26a and b]. Hence ambiguity may arise in the same way as with *all* and *both*; for example if [4:26b] had *three bedrooms*, the *each* might presuppose just these:

> [4:26] a. Smith and Jones are on holiday. I wonder if either has left an
>   address.
>   b. The flat has a sitting-room, a dining-room and one bedroom.
>   Each has a window overlooking the park.

The non-dual equivalents of *either* and *neither* are *any* and *no*; they are like *all*, except that they can occur elliptically with singular and mass nouns, as in [4:25a and c]. The two pairs are proportional: *no* is to *any* as *neither* is to *either*. *No* and *neither* are of course negative, but are usually restricted to clauses of declarative mood where the verb is positive; while *any* and *either* occur in clauses which are interrogative or hypothetical, OR where the verb is negative, or is positive and the sense is 'it doesn't matter which'. In the latter type *any*, when used elliptically, repudiates any cardinal numeral in the presupposed group and is usually singular (= 'any one') unless some numeral occurs with it, such as *any three*. Hence

> [4:27] Here are thirteen cards. Take any. Now give me any three.

In its interrogative, hypothetical or negative use (*has he any? if he has any; he hasn't any*), the difference between singular and plural is neutralized. In non-elliptical groups, the plural form is usually used (*has he any friends?*), as it tends to be also with *no* (*he has no friends*); but when *any* is Head of an elliptical group this may be filled out with either a singular or a plural noun Head irrespective of the number of the presupposed group, and likewise if *any* is Subject it may occur with either singular or plural verbs:

> [4:28] a. I want a map of the Lake District.   ⎫
>   I want some maps of the Lake District. ⎬ Have you got any?
>   ⎭
>   b. I'm expecting a letter.   ⎫ ⎧ Has any come?
>   I'm expecting some letters. ⎬ ⎨ Have any come?
>   ⎭ ⎩

In the same way the singular/plural distinction is neutralized with the negative *no*. Its elliptical form *none* (= *no* + *one*) shows that it was originally treated as singular, but usage is no longer consistent:

> [4:29] I've checked all the files. None were/was missing.

The elliptical *some* was mentioned in Chapter 3 (3.2.3.3, [3:25] and

Table 5). This is the non-singular (mass or plural) form of the indefinite article, and when functioning elliptically, as Head, it is always in its non-reduced form, *ie* [sʌm] not [sm̩]. The nominal group presupposed by it may be singular or plural, and any numeral is repudiated:

[4:30] a. These apples are delicious. Let's buy some.
b. I had a dozen tennis balls; where are they? – I've got some; you can borrow mine.

In (b), *some* does not mean 'some of the dozen'; *cf: I haven't got any*.

Parallel to *some* in its non-reduced form is *one*, which is the non-reduced form of the singular indefinite article *a*. It is this from which is derived the nominal substitute *one* discussed in Chapter 3 (3.2 and 3.2.1). As pointed out there (3.3.3.3, [3:15ci]), it is difficult to distinguish elliptical *one* from one of the uses of the substitute *one*; but the difference appears in the plural, since the plural of the substitute *one* is *ones* whereas the plural of the determiner (indefinite article) *one* is *some*. In [4:31] the *one* is an elliptical indefinite article (*cf* [3:27]):

[4:31] But you make no remark? – I didn't know I had to make one, just then.

The elliptical use of deictic elements is a major source of cohesion in English texts. The Deictic is the element in the nominal group that relates to the HERE AND NOW, linking the thing referred to to its verbal and situational context. It is natural, therefore, that it should be typically used as a means of harking back to a thing that has already been mentioned, while at the same time recontextualizing it by anaphoric or exophoric reference.

4.2.3.3 POST-DEICTICS

The words functioning as Post-deictic element in the nominal group are not determiners but adjectives. There are some thirty or forty adjectives used commonly in Deictic function, and a number of others used occasionally in this way; the frequent ones include *other, same, different, identical, usual, regular, certain, odd, famous, well-known, typical, obvious*. They combine with *the, a* or other determiner (the combination *a+other* being written and pronounced as one word *another*); and they may be FOLLOWED BY a Numerative, unlike adjectives in their normal function as Epithet which must FOLLOW any numerative element. The distinction of meaning between Deictic and Epithet (and *cf* 2.5.1 [2:80] above) can be seen in

Deictic	Epithet
the identical three questions	three identical questions
the usual two comments	two usual comments
a different three people	three different people
the odd few ideas	a few odd ideas
the obvious first place to stop	the first obvious place to stop

Of the adjectives used in deictic function the ones which regularly occur elliptically are *same* and *other*. The elliptical use of *the same* was treated as substitution (3.2.5), since it has been extended to very general use including clause substitution, as in *do the same*; actually an example such as [3:51] above (*I'll have the same*) is simply an elliptical nominal group with *same* as Head. The Post-deictic *other* combines either with specific Deictic (*the other, that other*, etc) or with non-specific (*any other, another*, etc), and when it is used as Head it has a special plural form *others*. The nominal group which it presupposes need not be of the same number, and any numeral in it is repudiated, as with *any*.
Example:

[4:32] I've used up these three yellow folders you gave me. Can I use the other?

which does not mean 'the other three'. With a specific Deictic, *other(s)* refers to the last remaining member(s) of a set, and therefore it presupposes that all others must have been specified. This explains the frequency with which it is preceded by another nominal group, often also anaphoric (*eg: one, some of them, the first*, etc) which is both presupposed and presupposing: presupposed by *other*, but itself also relating back to the ultimately presupposed item. For example

[4:33] A group of well-dressed young men suddenly appeared on the stage. One of them bowed to the audience; the others stood motionless.

The original item must be semantically plural – it must refer to more than one set, as described in 4.2.3.1 above; and the elliptical *other(s)* presupposes just as much of it as does the intermediate item. Here *one of them* and *the others* both presuppose *well-dressed young men*.
The elliptical use of *other* illustrates very well the indeterminacy which may arise in the extent of presupposition. If we had just the example

[4:34] I see you've sold those two large red china dogs. Have you any others?

in the absence of further evidence we could not tell whether to fill this out as *china dogs*, *red china dogs* or *large red china dogs*. Similarly in [4:32]: *the other yellow ones* or just *the other one*? As we pointed out earlier, the extent of the presupposition may be signalled in the spoken language by the location of the tonic nucleus. So if in [4:34] the tonic falls on *red*, *others* means 'of another colour'; if on *large*, it means 'any small ones', and so on.

Finally we may note that elliptical nominal groups with Deictic as Head may also be exophoric, either in the generalized sense or specifically to the context of situation:

[4:35] a. Some say one thing, others say another.
     b. All is lost.
     c. All go into the other room.
     d. Have you been to Mary's recently?
     e. I'll have the usual, please.

4.2.3.4 NUMERATIVES

Of the elements occurring after the Deictic in the nominal group, only the Numerative and certain types of Epithet function at all regularly as the Head in ellipsis.

The Numerative element in the nominal group is expressed by numerals or other quantifying words, which form three subcategories: ordinals, cardinals, and indefinite quantifiers. The ordinals are *first*, *next*, *last*, *second*, *third*, *fourth*, etc; they are often used elliptically, generally with *the* or a possessive as Deictic:

[4:36] Have another chocolate. – No thanks; that was my third.

Like the superlative form of an adjective, which in many ways it resembles (ordinals are in a sense 'superlative numerals'), an ordinal is itself likely to be presupposing even if the nominal group in which it occurs is not elliptical; thus *the second question* presupposes that there was a first question, and *the first question* that there is likely to be a next. Again like superlatives, ordinals are often cataphoric to a Qualifier which indicates the domain of the ordering, supplying the information 'first, etc, in what respect?'; for example, *to leave* in

[4:37] Smith was the first person to leave. I was the second.

Cardinal numerals are also frequent in ellipsis, and may be preceded by any Deictic that is appropriate in number, *eg*: *the three*, *these three*, *any three*, *all three*, and also by post-deictic adjectives as in *the usual three*, *the same three*.

[4:38] a. Have another chocolate. – No thanks; I've had my three.
       b. 'The other messenger's called Hatta. I must have two, you
          know. One to come, and one to go.'

With both ordinals and cardinals the presupposed noun may be either
singular or plural, but it cannot be a mass noun unless there is also some
measure word present or presupposed – naturally, since 'mass' = 'uncount-
able'. For example if in [4:36] and [4:38a] we had *Have some more tea*, the
answer would still be possible in each case, but only because it could be
interpreted as presupposing 'cup(s)'.

The indefinite quantifiers are items such as *much, many, more, most, few,
several, a little, lots, a bit, hundreds,* etc; they include numerous transient and
more or less slang expressions especially used by children. Like other items
with a numerative function, they are very frequently used in ellipsis; being
indefinite, they are usually not accompanied by a Deictic, except where *a*
is demanded as in *a lot,* although the comparative forms *more, fewer* and
less may be preceded by *no* or *any.* Some of them are specific to either count
or mass nouns.
Examples:

[4:39] a. Can all cats climb trees? – They all can; and most do.
       b. 'You ought to have a wooden horse on wheels, that you
          ought!' – 'I'll get one,' the Knight said thoughtfully to him-
          self. 'One or two – several.'

Many of the indefinite quantifiers derive from measure nouns; for
example *lot, amount,* and the larger numbers such as *hundred* and *thousand.*
Since these still require partitive Qualifiers (*a lot of* . . .), they are not very
clearly distinguished from the general class of measure noun, which includes quantitatives (*eg: half, piece, dozen*), partitives (*eg: part, side, end*) and
collectives (*eg: group, set, pack*). For the purposes of cohesion, these also can
be regarded as requiring to be 'filled out' by a partitive Qualifier, and
therefore as elliptical if functioning as Head. Hence Alice's predicament in

[4:40] 'One side will make you grow taller, and the other side will
       make you grow shorter.' 'One side of *what*? The other side of
       what?' thought Alice to herself. 'Of the mushroom,' said the
       Caterpillar, just as if she had asked it aloud.

Some combinations of quantifiers are possible, namely ordinal numeral
plus cardinal or, in a few cases, ordinal numeral plus indefinite; usually in
the order stated. The combination of cardinal plus indefinite occurs only

if the indefinite is comparative, as in *three more*. Such combinations are regularly elliptical, *eg: the last three, the next few*.

Whereas the specific Deictics – the demonstratives and possessives – tend to occur alone, being themselves reference items, the Numeratives, like the non-specific Deictics, tend to be filled out precisely by a reference item in the form of a partitive Qualifier with third person pronoun. So we often find *any of them, the first of them, three of them* and so on. These are of course still cohesive, but the presupposition is of the reference type rather than ellipsis.

Like the Deictics, Numeratives in elliptical use may be exophoric; *eg* in [4:37] we might have had *Smith was the first to leave*, with *person* understood. The presupposed item will be assumed to be some general category of which the item referred to, here *Smith*, is a member. This can be demonstrated by

[4:41] Her money will be the first to leave her. Her husband will be the next.

which puts *her money* and *her husband* into the same general category by presupposition. Note the special exophoric use of a possessive Deictic plus cardinal numeral to mean 'children', as in the proud mother's remark

[4:42] My three are absolute terrors.

Indefinite quantifiers occur exophorically in expressions like

[4:43] He expects a lot. But you can't do much to help him.

4.2.3.5 EPITHETS

The function of Epithet is typically fulfilled by an adjective. It is not common to find adjectives occurring as Head in ellipsis – colour adjectives are perhaps the most usual – except in their comparative and, especially, superlative forms. This reflects the fact that superlative and comparative adjectives are really functioning in a way that is more like a Numerative; possibly instead of the function Numerative in the nominal group we should recognize a more general function Ordinative, which would include superlative and perhaps also comparative adjectives, as well as the classes of word that function as Numeratives proper (numerals and indefinite quantifiers).

The superlative adjective precedes other Epithets and, like ordinal numerals (*cf* 4.2.3.4 above), is usually accompanied by *the* or a possessive Deictic. Note in this connection the difference between (a) and (b) in [4:44]:

[4:44] a. Apples are the cheapest in autumn.
   b. Apples are cheapest in autumn.

In (a) we may fairly ask 'the cheapest what?'; *the cheapest* is an elliptical group presupposing some item such as *fruit*. Example (b) is however not elliptical; it is like *apples are cheap*, and the domain of the superlative is provided by the time element within the clause, *ie* 'cheaper in autumn than at other times'.

Even where the superlative is elliptical, the presupposed group may still be within the clause. This happens only in equative clauses of the identifying type (those which are reversible, *eg: apples are the cheapest, the cheapest are apples*), which are probably the most frequent environment for elliptical superlatives. So in [4:45a and b] we get two quite different notions of the qualities of the clown:

[4:45] a. That clown is the finest I've ever seen.
   b. They are fine actors. That clown is the finest I've ever seen.

In [4:45a] we assume that the presupposed item is *clown*, so although *the finest* is elliptical the presupposition is within the clause. In [4:45b], on the other hand, *the finest* presupposes *actor* from the preceding sentence.

More accurately, [4:45b] is ambiguous; it may mean 'the finest actor' or just 'the finest clown'. Like an ordinal, a superlative presupposes some item that is semantically plural (more than one set, which as usual may be expressed in one nominal group or by a coordination); with the difference that, in the case of the superlative, this may also take the form of a mass noun, with the interpretation 'the . . . -est kind of', as in

[4:46] 'I told you butter wouldn't suit the works.' – 'It was the *best* butter.'

As long as the clause is equative and the Subject is a common noun, an elliptical superlative as Complement will always be ambiguous in this way. Otherwise, there is no ambiguity. If it is not equative, the superlative must refer to a preceding clause, as in [4:47a]; and likewise if the Subject is a proper noun, as in [4:47b] which cannot be interpreted as 'the finest Smith':

[4:47] a. They are fine actors. Jones always gets hold of the finest.
   b. They are fine actors. Smith is the finest I've ever seen.

As would be expected, a superlative repudiates all Numeratives, including cardinals, in the presupposed group. It may itself be singular or plural, and if plural may be preceded by its own cardinal as in *the three youngest*.

Comparatives are rather different from superlatives. Comparative adjectives are inherently presupposing by reference; this has been discussed above in 2.5. There must be a standard of comparison: anything that is bigger is bigger 'than' something else (which may be than itself under other circumstances). There are two specified sets involved, whereas with the superlative there is only one. This presupposition is not, however, an instance of ellipsis.

One use of the comparative FORM of the adjective, always with deictic *the*, is actually semantically superlative: this is that in which the sense is 'the . . . -est of two'. An equative clause having this type of comparative in complement position, such as *Smith is the better actor*, is of the IDENTIFYING type; and if the comparative functions as Head, as it does in [4:48a], then it is elliptical, just as a superlative would be (*cf* [4:44a]). The true comparative, however, does not take *the*, and an equative clause such as [4:48b] is not identifying but attributive.

[4:48] a. Mary is the cleverer.
       b. Mary is cleverer.

[4:48b] is not an elliptical clause. It presupposes by reference, but not by ellipsis; it cannot be 'filled out' by a noun Head or a noun substitute. The structure, in fact, is that of [4:44b]. In other words, the three clauses *apples are cheap*, *apples are cheaper* ('than pears') and *apples are cheapest* ('in autumn') are all attributive clauses, and the nominal groups which function as Attribute, those consisting just of an adjective (*cheap, cheaper, cheapest*), are not elliptical forms. This function – that of Attribute in the clause – is the only one in which an Epithet occurring as Head is not elliptical.

A nominal group with a true comparative as Head is, however, elliptical under all other conditions; for example

[4:49] I'll buy you some prettier.

These are less common than elliptical superlatives, but more common than elliptical uses of the adjective in a non-compared form (see below). The presupposed nominal group may be count singular, count plural or mass.

There is one use of the true comparative which is confusing because it is preceded by *the* and looks like a superlative. This is as in

[4:50] The smaller the dog, the louder the bark.

Here *the* is not a Deictic but a Submodifier with the sense of 'by how much', 'by that much' – originally not the definite article but the instrumental case of *that*. There may be ambiguity between this type and [4:48a], as in

[4:51] Mrs Jones always uses Bliss. Her clothes are the whiter.

– 'the whiter for it', or 'the whiter of the two'?

We have exemplified superlatives and comparatives only in the inflected forms -*est* and -*er*, but they may also of course be expressed by *more* ... and *most*.... Everything that has been said applies to those forms also. Notice that they differ from *more* and *most* as indefinite quantifiers (4.2.3.4); ambiguity may arise between the two, but only in the full form of the nominal group, not when they are elliptical.

Superlatives and, less often, comparatives may presuppose exophorically, as in *you take the biggest* ('of the things in front of you'). Examples of idiomatic uses are *the latest*, in the special sense of 'news' or 'fashion', and *survival of the fittest*. With comparatives we find mostly the superlative type with *the*, in the sense of 'those who are ... -er than other people', *eg: the weaker*.

Finally, other items functioning as Epithet – that is, adjectives that are neither superlative nor comparative – do not very often occur as Head in ellipsis, although colour words, which are anomalous in various ways, form something of an exception. Of the following, only [4:52a] is elliptical; in [4:52b] *green* is a noun:

[4:52] a. The green suits you very well.
       b. Green suits you very well.

So in (a) we could have *the green one*, with substitution instead of ellipsis.

In fact, this is the more usual pattern; substitution tends to be preferred to ellipsis wherever the presupposing nominal group contains an Epithet or Classifier. Ellipsis occurs in an example such as

[4:53] I like strong tea. I suppose weak is better for you.

But, as already noted, where the Epithet is functioning as an Attribute in the clause, it always appears as Head of the nominal group; in *apples are cheap*, *cheap* is not elliptical. Items like *the rich*, *the long and the short of it*, on the other hand, are elliptical, but they are exophoric, and so do not contribute to cohesion. In its cohesive function, nominal ellipsis is largely confined to instances where the presupposing element is a Deictic or Numerative; in other words, where it is one of the closed system elements in the nominal group. Lexical elements usually require to be accompanied by the substitute *one(s)*.

4.3 Verbal ellipsis

4.3.1 Ellipsis within the verbal group

By VERBAL ELLIPSIS we mean ellipsis within the verbal group. For example in

[4:54] a. Have you been swimming? – Yes, I have.
      b. What have you been doing? – Swimming.

the two verbal groups in the answers, *have* (in *yes I have*) in (a) and *swimming* in (b), are both instances of verbal ellipsis. Both can be said to 'stand for' *have been swimming*, and there is no possibility of 'filling out' with any other items. So, for example, *swimming* in (b) could not be interpreted as *I will be swimming* or *they are swimming*. It could be interpreted only as *I have been swimming*; and it could, furthermore, be REPLACED BY *I have been swimming*, since as in all types of ellipsis, the full form and the elliptical one are both possible.

An elliptical verbal group presupposes one or more words from a previous verbal group. Technically, it is defined as a verbal group whose structure does not fully express its systemic features – all the choices that are being made within the verbal group systems. The elliptical form *swimming* in [4:54b] has the features POSITIVE (as opposed to negative), FINITE (as opposed to non-finite) and ACTIVE (as opposed to passive), as well as those of a particular tense, PRESENT IN PAST IN PRESENT; but none of these selections is shown in its own structure. They have to be recovered by presupposition. A verbal group whose structure fully represents all its systemic features is not elliptical.

This definition shows how verbal ellipsis differs from nominal ellipsis. In the verbal group, there is only one lexical element, and that is the verb itself: *swim* in [4:54] above. The whole of the rest of the verbal group expresses systemic selections, choices of an either-or type (though not always restricted to two possibilities) which must be made whenever a verbal group is used. The principal systems are:

(1) Finiteness: finite or non-finite
        if finite: indicative or imperative
        if indicative: modal or non-modal
(2) Polarity: positive or negative, and marked or unmarked
(3) Voice: active or passive
(4) Tense: past or present or future (recursively)

These selections are obligatory for all verbal groups. There is one other system, that of 'Contrast: contrastive or non-contrastive', which appears in spoken English only, since it is expressed by intonation. It is sometimes given partial expression in the written language by means of italics or other forms of typographical prominence, eg: You WOULD do that! We shall not deal separately with it as a verbal system; but some reference is made to cohesion by intonation in 5.9.

Taken all together, the words that go to make up any non-elliptical verbal group, such as *have been swimming*, express all the features that have been selected. In this instance it is finite, indicative, non-modal, positive, active, and 'present in past in present'. But there is no direct correspondence between the words and the features. We cannot pick out one word expressing voice, another for tense and so on. The selections are expressed as a whole by the words that are used and by their arrangement in a particular structure.

Ellipsis in the nominal group was not described in this way, because the nominal group is not made up, to anything like the same extent, of grammatical systems. It contains many more open choice (lexical) items. Actually there is no difference in principle; the same theoretical definition of ellipsis is valid for the nominal group also. But it would be much more complex to describe nominal ellipsis in terms of systems; so it was presented in structural terms instead. For the verbal group, on the other hand, it is the system that provides the simplest way of explaining the facts of ellipsis, and so the systems listed above have been used as the basis for organizing the present section.

Being able to give a theoretical definition in these terms does not mean, however, that for every instance of a verbal group we can always recognize whether it is elliptical or not just by looking at it. This is because, as we have already pointed out, the structure of the verbal group does not represent its meaning in a direct and obvious way. In the first place, although all verbal groups express tense, voice, etc, we cannot identify each of these with a particular word or other element in the structure of the verbal group. Consider for example the verbal group *has been seen*. This is finite, indicative, non-modal, positive, passive, past in present. The features 'finite: indicative' are expressed by the fact that the first word *have* is in the finite form *has*; 'non-modal' by the absence of a modal element; 'positive' by the absence of a negative element; 'passive' by the word *be* in next to last place plus the fact that the verb *see* is in the passive participle form *seen*; 'past in . . .' by the word *have* plus the fact that the next word *be* is in the past participle form *been*; and '. . . in present' by the fact that the first word *have* is in the present tense form *has*. The whole thing is quite straightforward, although the details appear complex.

In the second place, however, the forms themselves are often multi-valent and even the whole verbal group may be ambiguous. Thus *has* is always finite and present; but *have* may be EITHER finite present OR non-finite, and so *have been seen* is ambiguous – it might be a non-finite verbal group. The form *saw* (past finite) is distinct from *seen* (past or passive participle); but in most verbs these are the same, *eg: heard, made*, and all regular weak verbs. And *have, be*, and *do* occur BOTH as realizations of the grammatical features of tense, voice, etc, AND as lexical verbs in their own right; in [4:55], *has, is* and *does* are grammatical in (1) and lexical in (2):

[4:55] (1)   (2)
    a. John has caught a cold.   a. John has a cold.
    b. Mary is looking pretty.   b. Mary is pretty.
    c. Does John work well?   c. John does his work well.

So although the verbal group in English is extremely regular it is also fairly complex. It embodies a large number of systemic choices, especially those of tense, and it expresses these in ways which are not readily accessible to any kind of automatic recognition procedure. In general, we cannot say just by looking at a verbal group whether it is elliptical or not, as we usually can with a nominal group; it is often necessary to consult the 'co-text' in order to find out. For example, each of the forms *taking, has been* and *may have* might be elliptical, or they might not. In [4:56], they are non-elliptical in (1) but elliptical in (2) (with non-elliptical equivalents in square brackets):

[4:56] (1)   (2)
    a. Taking photographs is   a. What is he doing? Taking
       a waste of time.   photographs. [is taking]
    b. Jane was secretary once,   b. Jane should have been told, but
       but I don't think Mary   I don't think she has been. [has
       ever has been.   been told]
    c. Has he a car? He may   c. Has he seen it? He may have.
       have.   [may have seen]

But this is merely another aspect of what we have been stressing all along: cohesion is a feature of texts, and the question whether a particular instance is a cohesive form or not can often be settled only by reference to its textual environment.★

★ The description of the verbal group on which this section is based will be found in M. A. K. Halliday, *The English verbal group* (1965, mimeographed). An account of it can be found in Geoffrey J. Turner and Bernard A. Mohan, *A linguistic description and computer program for children's speech*, London, Routledge & Kegan Paul, 1970 (Chapter 6).

4.3.2 Lexical ellipsis

Nevertheless it may be helpful to approach the discussion of verbal ellipsis through a consideration of those instances where we CAN recognize that a particular verbal group is elliptical simply by inspecting its form. If we hear only the following sentence in a conversation

[4:57] It may or it may not.

we know that the verbal items *may* and *may not* must be elliptical. At least one word must be added following either of them in order to 'fill out' the verbal group. The word *may* is a VERBAL OPERATOR expressing 'finite: indicative: modal'. It has no other functions, and cannot be a LEXICAL VERB. Hence *may* and *may not* have no lexical verb in them, and this is sufficient evidence to show that they are elliptical.

Any verbal group not containing a lexical verb is elliptical. (Note that the term 'lexical verb' includes the verbal substitute *do* discussed in 3.3 above.) This enables us to identify one of the two types of verbal ellipsis, the one which we shall refer to as LEXICAL ELLIPSIS. It is the type of ellipsis in which the lexical verb is missing from the verbal group. The other type is OPERATOR ELLIPSIS, described below in 4.3.3.

All the modal operators *can, could, will, would, shall, should, may, might, must, ought to*, and *is to* are alike in that none of them can function as a lexical verb. (Here *is to* stands for all the forms *am to, is to, are to, was to, were to*; since this is a modal operator, it has no non-finite forms and no further variation in tense. There are two other modal operators, *need* and *dare*; but they can also be used as lexical verbs. We ignore the special case of *will*='bring about by willpower', as in *to will one's own destruction* – as well as, of course, *will* in *to will one's fortune* and *can* in *to can fruit!*) So any verbal group consisting of a modal operator only can immediately be recognized as elliptical. Examples:

[4:58] Is John going to come? – He might. He was to, but he may not.
   – He should, if he wants his name to be considered.

Here *might, was to, may not* and *should* are all elliptical verbal groups consisting of modal operator only; each one of them could be filled out by the lexical verb *come*, or by the verbal substitute *do*.

The modal operators are always finite, and hence always occur in first position in the verbal group. There are other verbal operators, expressing not modality but tense, which may be finite or non-finite; any verbal group which ends in one of these is also elliptical, but here the situation is less clear because some of the items functioning as temporal operators can be lexical verbs as well.

The finite temporal forms *will, would, shall, should* (all these are temporal as well as modal) and *used to* are ambiguous, like the modals; and so are the non-finite equivalents of *will*, namely *(be) going to* and *(be) about to*. All these are operators; a verbal group which ends in any one of them lacks a lexical verb and is therefore elliptical. But *be* and *have*, which occur as temporal operators in all their forms, both finite and non-finite, function ALSO as lexical verbs; so no simple rule can be given to say that a verbal group ending in a form of *be* or *have* is elliptical – it may or may not be. The same applies to the one remaining verbal operator (finite only) *do*, which is the carrier of negative and marked positive polarity in simple present and past tense; in *does see, did see*, etc, *do* is an operator, but *do* can also be a lexical verb (see above, 3.3.3.1) as well as being the verbal substitute.

To give some further examples, the verbal groups *may be, are going to have* and *did* (cf 3.3.3.6, [3:89–91]) are non-elliptical in [4:59 (1)] but elliptical in [4:59 (2)]:

[4:59] (1) (non-elliptical):
   a. He seems quite intelligent. – He may be, I agree.

   b. I've decided to leave. – I hope you're going to have second thoughts.

   c. Did Jane know? – No, but Mary did.

(2) (elliptical):
   a. Is he complaining? – He may be; I don't care.

   b. I haven't finished it yet. – I hope you're going to have by tomorrow.

   c. Did Jane know? – Yes, she did.

Here the distinction between elliptical and non-elliptical forms has to be recovered from the presupposed clause. The lexical verbs *be* and *have* always require a Complement. With all other verbs, there is a general rule whereby if a Complement is omitted (by clausal ellipsis) then the lexical verb must also be either omitted or substituted. But this does not apply to *be* and *have*; these verbs may occur with ellipsis of the Complement, as in [4:59 (1a)] and [4:56 (1b and c)], the verbal groups themselves being non-elliptical. Hence all that can be said is that if there is no Complement following *be* or *have* there must be SOME ellipsis; but it may be EITHER verbal ellipsis, with *be, have* as operator, OR clausal ellipsis (cf 4.4 below), with *be, have* as lexical verb, and in order to determine which, it is necessary to refer to the presupposed clause. If there is a Complement, and the verbal group ends in *be* or *have*, then there may be EITHER verbal ellipsis, with *be*, *have* as operator, OR no ellipsis at all, and *be*, *have* as lexical verb; the clause in question is often ambiguous by itself, *eg: he has some of the paintings* in [4:60a] and *she is the doctor* in [4:60b]:

[4:60] (1) (non-elliptical):
a. Has he all these items in his own collection? – He has some of the paintings; I'm not sure about the rest.

b. She ought to know what to do. She is the doctor.

(2) (elliptical):
a. Has he sold his collection yet? – He has some of the paintings; I'm not sure about the rest.

b. Is she suing the hospital? – She is the doctor.

As far as *do* is concerned, the lexical verb *do* also usually requires a Complement, except in the special sense of 'be satisfactory', *eg: will it do?* The substitute *do*, however, does not; and a verbal group such as *did* in [4:59c] may be non-elliptical, with substitute *do*, as in (1), or elliptical, with operator *do*, as in (2). The difference is shown by the fact that the non-presupposing form of (1) would be *Mary knew*, with *did* REPLACED by *knew*, whereas that of (2) would be *she did know*, with the elliptical form *did* FILLED OUT by the lexical verb *know*. But since the verbal operator *do* occurs as a finite form only, and hence comes first in the verbal group, whereas the substitute *do* is a substitute for the lexical verb, and hence comes last, such instances of overlap can occur only with a verbal group consisting of just the one word, *do*, *does*, or *did*.

With *do* the negative forms are unambiguous, since only the operator *do* has *don't*, *doesn't* and *didn't* as its negative forms. This is because the operator *do* is in fact simply a 'carrier' of the expression of polarity: negative (*eg: didn't see*) and marked positive (*eg: did see*), the latter being the form used in interrogative clauses (*did you see John?*, not *saw you John?*). So any verbal group consisting only of *don't*, *doesn't* or *didn't* must be elliptical, and likewise any group consisting solely of *do*, *does* or *did* preceding the subject in an interrogative clause, *eg: did you?*

The lexical verb *do* forms its negative like other lexical verbs: so we say *he doesn't do his work properly*, not *he doesn't his work properly*. Lexical *be* and *have*, on the other hand, form their negatives like verbal operators; hence *he isn't, is he?*, *he hasn't, has he?* may be either elliptical (operator only) or non-elliptical (lexical verb). There is a rider to this; there are actually two distinct lexical items *have*, one meaning 'possess' and expandable into *have got*, the other meaning 'take' and not expandable. Only the former has the negative *hasn't* (*eg: he hasn't any money*), and that not in all dialects; the latter forms its negative like other lexical verbs, by means of the operator *do*, as in *he doesn't have breakfast*. Apart from this exception the negative forms *isn't*, *hasn't*, etc may be either operator or lexical verbs, and hence one cannot say that a verbal group consisting of one of these forms alone is definitely elliptical: in [4:55] they could occur in either column (1) or column (2).

Finally there is the form *to*. We have seen that this occurs as part of the operators *going to*, *about to*, *used to*, *is to* and *ought to*; and a verbal group in which *to* occurs finally, not followed by a lexical item, is bound to be elliptical (*cf* 3.3.2, [3:70]). This applies also to a verbal group consisting only of the word *to*, as a marker of the infinitive (that is, of the perfective form of the non-finite verb, *to see*, *to have seen*, etc); for example

[4:61] I'd better see him. I don't really want to.

In what we are calling LEXICAL ELLIPSIS, it is the lexical verb that is always omitted. Other words in the verbal group may also be omitted, with the exception of whatever word is in first position – the finite operator if finite, and *to* or an *-ing* form if non-finite. So we may have, in answer to *John should have been coming every day*:

[4:62]	(1) *non-elliptical*	(2) *elliptical*
a. *finite*:		
I don't think he . . .	has been coming	has been
		has
b. *non-finite, perfective*:		
At least I under-	to have been coming	to have been
stand him . . .		to have
		to
c. *non-finite, imperfective*:		
I think he rather	having been coming	having been
regrets . . .		having

Lexical ellipsis is ellipsis 'from the right': it always involves omission of the last word, which is the lexical verb, and may extend 'leftward', to leave only the first word intact. So for *has been coming* we may find *has been* or simply *has*. With a very long verbal group there would be more possibilities: *could have been going to be consulted* might be reduced, by lexical ellipsis, to *could have been going to be*, *could have been going to*, *could have been, could have* or simply *could.* Usually the 'outer' forms are preferred: that which is minimally elliptical with ONLY the lexical verb omitted, or that with everything omitted that can be presupposed from the context. So following *wasn't John going to be consulted?* we would most probably find either *he could have been going to be* or *he could have been.* But intermediate forms also occur. Note that the extent of the presupposition is not affected by these variations. Thus in [4:62] the elliptical forms presuppose all the tense selections as well as the lexical verb: the form *has,* in (2a), stands for *has been coming* and not *has come.* In general, any selections that are not explicitly repudiated are automatically presupposed.

A very clear example of lexical ellipsis is provided by question tags. All question tags have maximum lexical ellipsis and presuppose all the features of the relevant verbal group; so

[4:63] a. John couldn't have been going to be consulted, could he?
        b. Mary didn't know, did she?
        c. They'll have been working on it all night, won't they?

The presupposition of particular systemic features is discussed in more detail in 4.3.4.1–4 below.

4.3.3 *Operator ellipsis*

There is another type of verbal ellipsis, which is ellipsis 'from the left'. We shall refer to this as 'OPERATOR ELLIPSIS', since it involves only the omission of operators: the lexical verb always remains intact. Example [4:54] showed the difference between the two: [4:54a] is lexical ellipsis, [4:54b] is operator ellipsis. In operator ellipsis the Subject also is always omitted from the clause; it must therefore be presupposed.

One type of operator ellipsis, which is very frequent, will not concern us here, since it does not contribute to cohesion: this is operator ellipsis within the sentence, in the context of coordination. In this type it is possible to introduce a new Subject, as in [4:64c]. So for example in

[4:64] a. They must have been both watching and being watched.
        b. After we've brought them out so far and made them trot so quick.
        c. Some were laughing and others crying.

the verbal forms *must have been* (*both watching and being watched*), *have* (*brought . . . out . . . and made . . .*) and *were* (*laughing and . . . crying*) are 'branched': the operators are structurally related to both halves of the coordination, as indicated by the bracketing. Note that this also happens in lexical ellipsis, with one lexical verb being related to two or more co-ordinate operators; the most usual form of this is the coordination of positive and negative operator with *or*, as in

[4:65] They might or might not have objected.

Verbal coordination of this type, however, accounts for a relatively small proportion of the total incidence of lexical ellipsis, which is more often BETWEEN sentences (and therefore cohesive in our sense).

Operator ellipsis, when it occurs across sentences, is found mainly in very closely bonded sequences such as question and answer, in which the lexical verb either supplies the answer to 'do what?', as in [4:54b], or repudiates the verb in the question, as in

[4:66] Has she been crying? – No, laughing.

In most instances of operator ellipsis, everything is presupposed but the lexical verb – that is, the entire selection within the systems of tense, voice, polarity and so on; and all words except the last are omitted. Occasionally it is the voice, the choice of active or passive, that is being repudiated, in which case if the elliptical group is passive the *be* immediately preceding the lexical verb must also be present, since it is part of the realization of the selection of passive; for example

[4:67] What have you been doing? – Being chased by a bull.

Operator ellipsis is fairly easy to recognize, with the provisos made in 4.3.1 above, since there is no finite element in the elliptical group. There are two sources of uncertainty, and these have to be resolved by reference to the surrounding text. One is that in most verbs the past tense and the past or passive participle have the same form, so that an item like *made* in [4:64 b] taken on its own could be a simple past tense instead of being elliptical for *have made*. The other problem is that a FINITE verbal group WITH operator ellipsis is identical with a NON-FINITE verbal group that is NOT elliptical, *eg: being watched, made, singing, being chased*, so that one has to ask whether the context demands a verbal group that is non-finite or one that is finite. But this is not usually much of a problem, and it is further simplified by the fact that the perfective form of the non-finite verbal group nearly always has *to* at the beginning. The only point to note is that a non-finite verbal group may itself have operator ellipsis, either by simple omission of *to* or, if it is marked for tense, by omission of the tense opera-tor (or operators), *eg*

[4:68]   (1) non-elliptical: (2) elliptical:
    a. What do you want to do? – To   Go out to the pictures.
        go out to the pictures.
    b. Why was he so angry when the
        game was stopped? Because of
        having been losing? –
        No; having been winning!   No; winning!

As a final example, in

[4:69] What must I do next? – Play your highest card.

it is not very clear whether *play* is an elliptical indicative, for *you must play*, or a non-elliptical imperative; nor does it seem to matter very much. It is probably the former: the tag would be *shouldn't you?*, and we would probably find the same form following *he*, where it could not be imperative: *What must he do next? – Play his highest card*. But the difference in meaning is so slight that it is difficult to sense the ambiguity between the two.

4.3.4 *Presupposition of verbal group systems*

We will consider in turn the various systems of the verbal group, asking whether, and under what circumstances, they are liable to presupposition in cases of ellipsis: whether, that is, the meaning is carried over when no selection from the system is expressed in the structure. We shall refer to polarity, finiteness, modality, voice, and tense; with a very brief mention of the system of contrastiveness that is found only in the spoken language.

4.3.4.1 POLARITY

Polarity is normally expressed at the beginning of the verbal group. A negative verbal group, if it is finite, has *n't* or *not* attached to the first word, *eg: didn't know, did not know*. If it is non-finite, it has *not*, usually as the first word, *eg: not having known, not to have known*, although the *not* may sometimes follow the first verbal operator, *eg: having not known, to have not known*. Other negative adverbs such as *never, hardly, hardly ever*, may occur in place of *not*. The category of negative is not very sharply defined, but it is revealed by the choice of tag. There is a semantic parallel between *he's here, isn't he?* and *he isn't here, is he?*; and the fact that the corresponding form with *hardly ever* is *he's hardly ever here, is he?*, with positive tag, shows that *hardly ever* is really a negative form.

In lexical ellipsis, whatever else is omitted the first operator is always present. This means that the polarity will always in fact be expressed, and the question of what happens if it is omitted does not arise. This is a result of the structure, although it is not simply a grammatical accident. The characteristic function of ellipsis is that of cohesion by presupposition, and there is a large class of cohesive sequences in which the one thing that cannot be presupposed is polarity: namely those where the response (*eg:* to a yes/no question) serves precisely to SUPPLY the polarity, all else being taken for granted. For example

[4:70] a. Were you laughing? –
        No, I wasn't.
     b. Cats like cheese. – They don't, do they? –
        Yes, they do. – Well, some do and some don't.

This makes it easy to understand the general principle whereby, whatever else may be presupposed in verbal (lexical) ellipsis, the polarity has to be made explicit. The principle applies to both finite and non-finite verbal groups; and in the non-finite (perfective) there is a special elliptical form of the negative, namely *not to*, as in *I'd hate not to, not to would be silly*, which expresses simply the non-finiteness and the polarity, and nothing else. There is an equivalent positive form *to* which is, however, much more restricted: we say *I'd love to* but we do not say *to would be silly* (*cf* 3.3.2, [3:70c, d and e]).

We should distinguish here the special type of negation in which the negative is attached specifically to some other element in the verbal group as in

[4:71] a. I've kept on telephoning, but they've simply been not answering.
     b. He says he's been not being informed about these developments.

Here the verbal group itself is positive, and certain items or features in it are explicitly negated: the lexical verb *answer* in (a), the lexical verb *inform* and the passive voice selection in (b). In such instances there is uncertainty about whether the polarity is presupposed with lexical ellipsis. Conceivably the response *He has* to [4:71b] might be used to express agreement, *ie* 'he has been not being informed'. But there is a strong tendency in English for the polarity of the verbal group itself – that is, as expressed in first position – to determine the polarity of the whole, so that even here the negative is unlikely to be presupposed: one would expect rather (*Quite right.*) *He hasn't* in the sense of 'I agree' and (*Oh yes.*) *He has*, with contrastive intonation, in the sense of 'I disagree'.

Turning now to operator ellipsis, we might expect that here, where among the items omitted is always the one which carries polarity, the polarity would naturally be presupposed by the elliptical verbal group. In fact as a rule it is not, although the reasons are different. As we have seen, operator ellipsis is characteristic of responses which are closely tied to a preceding question or statement, and which have the specific function of supplying, confirming or repudiating a lexical verb. The following is a typical sequence, illustrating how the polarity is restated each time:

[4:72]	A:	What are you doing?	(positive)
	B:	Thinking.	(positive; 'I'm . . .')
	A:	Not day dreaming?	(negative; 'aren't you . . .?')
	B:	No, thinking.	(positive; 'I'm . . .')

If there is a change in polarity, this may go in either direction, from positive to negative or from negative to positive; note that the final occurrence of *thinking* in [4:72] does not take over the selection of negative from the presupposed group.

One typical context for a verbal group with operator ellipsis is as a response to a WH-question with the interrogative on the verb, such as *What are you doing?* This is a demand for a lexical verb, and the normal response is simply to supply the verb, everything else being omitted. Here it might be said that the polarity is presupposed. But there is really no way of testing this statement, since the verbal group in the question is bound to be positive; one does not ask *What aren't you doing?* (except in the special instance of an echo question, where the polarity clearly IS presupposed in the response, as in *Smith isn't cooperating. – What isn't he doing? – Cooperating*). The other most usual context is that of a yes/no question, and this is precisely a demand for the polarity to be supplied; the polarity cannot therefore be presupposed. The words *yes* and *no* are purely indicators of polarity, and they are regularly elliptical for the whole of the presupposed clause (see below, 4.4.3). But the speaker may repeat the lexical verb, in order to deny it or explicitly to affirm it; in this case the polarity is always restated and, interestingly, operator ellipsis is possible only if the polarity is explicitly expressed – that is, if the answer is negative (since the negative requires to be stated by *not*, with or without a preceding *no*) or, if it is positive, provided it is introduced by *yes*:

[4:73] (1) Weren't you complaining? – (No,) Not complaining.
       (2) Were you complaining? – Yes, complaining.

In (2) the answer could not be simply *Complaining*. If however the answer is a contradiction, involving a change of polarity, the elliptical form is much less likely: (b) would be preferred to (a) in both [4:73 (3) and (4)]:

[4:73] (3)	Weren't you com-	a. Yes, complaining.
	plaining ? –	b. (Yes,) I was complaining.
(4)	Were you com-	a. (No,) Not complaining.
	plaining ? –	b. (No,) I wasn't complaining.

Occasionally a yes/no question may be answered (or, more accurately, responded to; such a response is not an answer) with a different lexical verb, and here, predictably, no ellipsis is possible:

[4:74] A: Were you thinking?
        B: I wasn't daydreaming, if that's what you mean.

B's response could not take the form *Not daydreaming*.

Hence in verbal ellipsis of any kind the elliptical verbal group makes a new selection in the system of polarity: polarity is not included in what is presupposed. In lexical ellipsis, this is because the one element that must be present, whatever else is omitted, is the initial element, and this is the one that carries the expression of polarity. In the case of operator ellipsis, the reason is semantic rather than grammatical; the expression of polarity is not required by the structure, but operator ellipsis is largely restricted to responses in which either the polarity can only be positive (and the question of presupposition does not arise) or else it is precisely the information 'yes or no?' that is being asked for, in which case it cannot possibly be presupposed in the answer.

A consideration of marked polarity (*cf* 4.3.1 above) would take us into too much detail, but it needs a brief mention to conclude this section. What is meant by MARKED POLARITY is the assignment of special prominence to the selection of positive or negative in order to draw attention to it. In the finite verbal group this is realized by the use of non-reduced forms of the finite operator or (where relevant) the negative: *is, had, was, can, shall, should*, etc instead of the reduced forms *'s, 'd, 'll*, [wəz] for *was*, [ʃd] for *should* (not distinct in writing), etc, *not* instead of *n't*, and also *does see, did see* instead of *sees, saw*. (Note that the non-reduced forms are NOT necessarily TONIC ('primary stress'), though they must be SALIENT ('secondary stress').) In a verbal group with operator ellipsis, therefore, it is impossible to express marked polarity; even if the presupposed item has it, as in [4:75], where *doing* is tonic and *is* is salient, it tends merely to express the questioner's attitude, impatience or something of the sort:

[4:75] What is he DOING all this time? – Reading, probably. (//1 what /
is he / DOING / all this / time //)

– in any case it cannot be carried over. A verbal group with lexical ellipsis,
on the other hand, must have the polarity marked; so the finite operator
cannot be reduced:

[4:76] a. Who'll put down five pounds? – I will. (*not* I'll)
b. John's arrived, has he? – Not yet; but Mary has. (*not* Mary's)

This applies to all positive forms. The negative may or may not be reduced; we could have *I won't* in [4:76a], and *Mary hasn't* in [4:76b] – this
is no doubt because the negative is itself a kind of marked polarity. The
preference for marked forms of polarity in this type of verbal ellipsis is
probably to be explained by the fact that so often in sequences of this kind
it is the expression of polarity that is the whole point of the response.

4.3.4.2 FINITENESS AND MODALITY

The systems of FINITENESS and MODALITY are also closely associated
with first position in the verbal group, and this largely determines the
possibilities of their presupposition by means of ellipsis.

A verbal group which is finite always expresses its finiteness in the first
word. Either the group consists just of a finite form of the lexical verb,
present or past (*walk, walks; walked*), or it begins with a finite verbal
operator; the latter is either a tense operator:

(1) am, is, are; was, were [*ie* finite forms of *be*]
(2) have, has; had [*ie* finite forms of *have*]
(3) do, does; did
(4) shall, will
(5) used (to)

or a modal operator:

(6) shall, will, should, would, can, could, may, might, must, ought (to)
(7) am to, is to, are to; was to, were to [*ie* finite forms of *be*, plus *to*]
(8) need, dare (in one use)

Any verbal group which does not have a finite form as its first word is
automatically non-finite. A verbal group consisting just of the base form
of the verb, *eg: walk*, is therefore ambiguous: it may be finite (present
tense, *eg: I walk*), or non-finite (perfective, *eg: made me walk*). But the distinction is always clear in the context; moreover the non-finite perfective

nearly always has *to* before it (*eg: wanted me to walk*). The imperative form *walk* has something of the finite and something of the non-finite about it, but is best treated as a finite verbal form.

Verbal groups with operators are never ambiguous as to finiteness. It is true that *have* and *do* are ambiguous by themselves; but *do* occurs as operator ONLY in finite verbal groups, while *have* in a non-finite group is ALWAYS preceded by *to*.

In lexical ellipsis, as we have seen, the ellipsis is 'from the right' and the one element that is never omitted is the finite operator. So, as with polarity, there is no question of what happens if the finiteness is not expressed; it always is. A verbal group that is lexically elliptical is always explicitly either finite or non-finite. It cannot simply take over the selection made by the verbal group which it presupposes.

There is no restriction of the presupposition of a finite verbal group by a non-finite or vice versa. We may have all possible sequences:

[4:77] a. [finite presupposed by finite]
   The picture wasn't finished. If it had been, I would have brought it.
   b. [finite presupposed by non-finite]
   He's always being teased about it. I don't think he likes being.
   c. [non-finite presupposed by finite]
   What was the point of having invited all those people? – I didn't; they just came.
   d. [non-finite followed by non-finite]
   It was hard work parcelling all those books. – I'm sure it was; and I'd much prefer you not to have.

With operator ellipsis, the situation is exactly reversed; here the first word MUST be omitted, whatever else is or is not present, and so the elliptical verbal group cannot express the choice between finite and non-finite. As is to be expected, therefore, it takes over the selection from the presupposed group:

[4:78] a. [finite: 'they are finishing']
   What are they doing now? – Finishing their essays.
   b. [non-finite: 'to be finishing']
   What would you like them to be doing while you're away? – Finishing their essays.

All that has been said with regard to finiteness applies equally to modality. Modality (*ie* the choice between modal and non-modal, and, if modal, among the various modal categories) is a subcategory of 'finite', and is expressed by the presence or absence of a modal operator. In a verbal group with lexical ellipsis, therefore, the modality is always explicit, and there is no restriction on what may be presupposed by what:

[4:79] a. [modal presupposed by non-modal]
I could help them. – Why don't you?
b. [non-modal presupposed by modal]
Are you going to tell her? – I ought to.
c. [modal presupposed by same modal]
He must have destroyed them. – Someone must have, certainly.
d. [modal presupposed by different modal]
He must have destroyed them. – He may have, I suppose.

In a verbal group with operator ellipsis, the modality is never explicit and, like the finiteness, is always carried over from the presupposed group:

[4:80] a. [non-modal: [4:78a] 'they are finishing']
What are they doing now? – Finishing their essays.
b. [modal: 'they will be finishing']
What will they be doing now, do you think? – Finishing their essays, probably.

4.3.4.3 VOICE

When we come to the system of VOICE (the choice between active and passive) the position is somewhat different. Voice is expressed towards the end of the verbal group, by the presence (passive) or absence (active) of some form of *be* or *get* just before a lexical verb, with the lexical verb in the passive participle form. Any verbal group displaying both these features is passive, *eg: was stolen, has been robbed, being taken, get arrested*; all others are active. Therefore it does not follow automatically that an elliptical verbal group either will or will not contain an overt expression of voice.

Nevertheless in lexical ellipsis the rule is quite clear; the voice selection is always presupposed. So although the examples in [4:81] make perfectly good sense, they are impossible, because the elliptical form here repudiates the voice of the presupposed verbal group.

[4:81] a. [active followed by passive: 'if it had been finished']
They haven't finished the picture. If it had been. I would have brought it.

   b. [passive followed by active: 'if she does beat him']
      Johnny hates being beaten at any game by his sister. If she does,
      he sulks.
   c. [active followed by passive: 'she has never been loved']
      Mary could love very deeply. Unfortunately she never has
      been.
   d. [passive followed by active: 'she has forgiven them']
      She is forgiven, apparently. But I don't think she has them.

No doubt the reason these are unacceptable is that the second sentence in each case involves a change in the alignment of structural functions. Either the Subject changes, the Actor/Goal relationship remaining the same, as in (a) and (b); or the Actor/Goal relationship changes, the Subject remaining the same, as in (c) and (d). In either instance, and even if one element is an unexpressed 'someone' as in (c), we feel the proposition should be restated in full. The voice selection, in other words, cannot be repudiated by an elliptical structure; and the mere fact that the lexical verb needing to be supplied is already in the right form, as in (a) *finished* and (d) *forgiven*, is not enough to override the rule that voice must be carried over. Presumably we feel little in common between *has forgiven* and *is forgiven*, even though the participle is formally the same.

In operator ellipsis, as we saw earlier, the Subject is always omitted; it must therefore be carried over by presupposition. This means that we cannot have a change of Subject for the elliptical group; so in an example such as

[4:82] Were Australia leading England at the time, then? – No, Eng-
       land were winning.

we cannot replace the second sentence by the elliptical form *No, England winning*. In other words, here, as in lexical ellipsis, the voice selection must be presupposed if the presupposing group is elliptical; it cannot be repudiated. But there is one condition under which the voice can be repudiated in operator ellipsis: namely if the Actor/Goal relationship changes, leaving the Subject unaltered. One example of this was given in [4:67] above; others would be

[4:83] a. Will you be interviewing today? – No; being interviewed.
     b. John has loved Mary for a long time. – Or at least been loved
        by her.

TENSE			Non-finite, and finite modal, tenses (12): read as far as β		Finite non-modal tenses (36): read as far as α		
ϵ	δ	γ	β		α		
			(none)	I		past	1
						present	2
						future	3
			past	II	in	past	4
						present	5
						future	6
			present	III	in	past	7
						present	8
						future	9
			future	IV	in	past	10
						present	11
						future	12
		past	in future	V	in	past	13
						present	14
						future	15
		present	in past	VI	in	past	16
						present	17
						future	18
		present	in future	VII	in	past	19
						present	20
						future	21
		future	in past	VIII	in	past	22
						present	23
						future	24

Finite non-modal tense		Non-finite, and finite modal tenses: (perfective, imperfective; modal)
1 took / did take 2 take(s) / do(es) take 3 will take	I	to take, taking; can take
4 had taken 5 has taken 6 will have taken	II	to have, having; can have + taken
7 was taking 8 is taking 9 will be taking	III	to be, being; can be + taking
10 was going to take 11 is going to take 12 will be going to take	IV	to be, being; can be + going/about to take
13 was going to have taken 14 is going to have taken 15 will be going to have taken	V	to be, being; can be + going to have taken
16 had been taking 17 has been taking 18 will have been taking	VI	to have, having; can have + been taking
19 was going to be taking 20 is going to be taking 21 will be going to be taking	VII	to be, being; can be + going to be taking
22 had been going to take 23 has been going to take 24 will have been going to take	VIII	to have, having; can have + been going to take

past	in future	in past	IX	in {	past 25
					present 26
					future 27
present	in past	in future	X	in {	past 28
					present 29
					future 30
present	in future	in past	XI	in {	past 31
					present 32
					future 33
present	in past	in future	in past	XII in {	past 34
					present 35
					future 36

4.3.4.4 TENSE

The English tense system is complex, though its complexity is more apparent than real. It is based on two very simple principles: (1) that there is a choice of past, present and future, and (2) that this choice may be made repeatedly (within limits), each new choice taking the previous one as its point of departure. Both these principles apply whenever a verb is used, unless that verb is in the imperative, which has no choice of tense.

So, for example, I may choose a future tense: *I will play*. But having thus shifted my standpoint into the future I may then take this as a base for a further point, say past; I then get the tense 'past in future', which is *I will have played*. Supposing once again I take this as a base line and select, say, present: the tense is then 'present in past in future', *I will have been*

25 had been going to have taken		
26 has been going to have taken	IX	to have, having; can have+been going to have taken
27 will have been going to have taken		

28 was going to have been taking		
29 is going to have been taking	X	to be, being; can be+going to have been taking
30 will be going to have been taking		

31 had been going to be taking		
32 has been going to be taking	XI	to have, having; can have+been going to be taking
33 will have been going to be taking		

34 had been going to have been taking		
35 has been going to have been taking	XII	to have, having; can have+been going to have been taking
36 will have been going to have been taking		

playing. This can happen up to five times, subject to increasing restrictions which end up by precluding a sixth choice altogether. The most complex tense form in English is one like *had been going to have been playing*, which is 'present in past in future in past in past'. It may be helpful here to list the full set of finite and corresponding non-finite tenses of the English verb. The column headed α is the PRIMARY TENSE (FIRST ORDER TENSE); it is always expressed by a finite form, and a verbal group with primary tense is always finite. The other columns represent the SECONDARY TENSES (SECOND ORDER, THIRD ORDER and so on); the LAST ORDER TENSE is always the one that appears earliest in the NAME of the tense. Thus 'present in past in future' has primary (first order) tense future, and secondary tenses past and present, of which the last order tense is present.

It will be seen that the non-finite forms, which are also those of the finite verbal group if it is modalized, are equal to the finite (non-modal) forms minus the 'alpha–' or primary tense choice. So, for example, non-finite *having taken* corresponds to all three of the finite tenses *took, has taken* and *had taken*.

A tense form embodying only one choice is a SIMPLE tense; hence '(simple) past' *I took*, '(simple) present' *I take*, '(simple) future' *I will take*. All other tenses are COMPOUND.

Like the tense system itself, the principles of the presupposition of tense selections in verbal ellipsis look rather complex at first sight; but actually they are fairly simple.

Let us consider the following instances of lexical ellipsis:

[4:84] a. I protest. – Do you?
　　　　b. He usually talks all the time. He didn't, yesterday.
　　　　c. It doesn't turn. – It will if you press it in first.
　　　　d. She won't agree. – She did last time.
　　　　e. Is he arguing? – Yes, he always does.
　　　　f. Was he going to apologize? He won't now.
　　　　g. Has she heard about it yet? – No, but she soon will.
　　　　h. You have been forgetting every morning. Today you did again.

The choice of tenses in these examples is as follows:

	Presupposed group	Elliptical group
(a)	present	present
(b)	present	past
(c)	present	future
(d)	future	past
(e)	present in present	present
(f)	future in past	future
(g)	past in present	future
(h)	present in past in present	past

In each case the elliptical verbal group makes a simple tense choice, which is fully explicit in the operator (*did, does, will*); hence the only presupposition is of the lexical verb, which is to be supplied in its base form. No tense selection is carried over from the presupposed group.

Now consider the case where the second verbal group, the one that is elliptical, is making a compound tense selection. Here are some acceptable examples:

[4:85] a. At least Stan has tried. I don't think Bob has.
   b. I'm going home this weekend. I shall be every weekend now.
   c. Are you dieting? – I have been for some time.
   d. He was going to build it himself. He isn't any longer.
   e. She really has been working hard. – And she's going to be again before long.

Presupposed group	Elliptical group
(a) past in present	past in present
(b) present in present	present in future
(c) present in present	present in past in present
(d) future in past	future in present
(e) present in past in present	present in future in present

The following however are much less acceptable:

[4:86] a. Have you discussed it yet? – No, we are now.
   b. You've been forgetting every morning. Today you have again.
   c. He was going to tell us. But he still hadn't, yesterday.

Presupposed group	Elliptical group
(a) past in present	present in present
(b) present in past in present	past in present
(c) future in past	past in past

For these to become acceptable, the second verbal group would have to be filled out by the lexical verb or verbal substitute:

(a) *discussing it/doing* (b) *forgotten/done* (c) *told us/done*

The principle seems clear. In compound tenses, the tense selection is not made clear by the finite verbal operator alone; other elements are needed, and the form of the lexical verb itself may change. If the tense in the elliptical verbal group is a compound one, then it must be such that the lexical verb can be carried over IN THE SAME FORM. So in [4:85] the elliptical verbal group could in fact be filled out by the lexical verb with its form unchanged: (a) *tried*, (b) *going*, (c) *dieting*, (d) *(going to) build*, (e) *working*. This means that the last-order tense, the one that is EXPRESSED last in the verbal group (though it appears first in the NAME of the tense), is carried over from the presupposed group. If this changes, then the form of the lexical verb changes, and the lexical verb must be repeated (or substituted), as in [4:86].

To summarize: a verbal group with lexical ellipsis must have either a tense that is fully explicit even in the elliptical form, or one in which the lexical verb can be carried over unchanged from the presupposed group. In other words, either it has simple past, present or future; or, if the tense is compound, it has the same last-order tense as the presupposed group. So, for example, if the presupposed group has 'future in present', *he was going to leave*, there can be lexical ellipsis in a following verbal group provided that that verbal group has any simple tense, *eg* past *but he didn't* (*cf* [4:84f]), or a compound tense which is also 'future in . . .', *eg* future in present *but he isn't now* (*cf* [4:85d]). It is not that all other instances are totally unacceptable; we might accept *but he hasn't* in this instance, and the following also:

[4:87] a. I'm staying at home this weekend. I haven't for some time.
b. It was going to snow, they said. Why isn't it?

where (a) has past in present presupposing present in present, and (b) has present in present presupposing future in past. But these are all a little awkward, and a more natural form is that with substitute *do: I haven't done for some time, why isn't it doing?*

We have illustrated tense in verbal ellipsis by reference to finite verbal groups; but the same principles apply to those which are non-finite, including instances where, of the two verbal groups involved in the presupposition, one is finite and the other non-finite. Here are some varied examples:

[4:88] a. He shows no sign of having been studying. – He hadn't/hasn't/ wasn't.
b. She intends to come. – She won't.
c. Will he give in to them? – He doesn't seem to be going to.
d. We seem to be being followed. – I remember having been when we were here before.

Presupposed group	Elliptical group
(a) non-finite: present in past (corresponding to all three:)	finite: present in past in past finite: present in past in present finite: present in past
(b) non-finite: tenseless	finite: future
(c) finite: future	non-finite: future
(d) non-finite (perfective): present	non-finite (imperfective): past

Verb forms which include the selection of 'future' at any point will normally be longer, in terms of words, than the corresponding forms with present or past; in the simple tense, past and present consist of one word only (*took, takes*), future of two (*will take*). The 'marked positive' forms (see 4.3.4 above) of past and present are *did take, does take;* and the paradigm of simple tenses in spoken English is actually quite symmetrical:

	positive		negative	
	unmarked	marked	unmarked	marked
past	he took	he did take	he didn't take	he did not take
present	he takes	he does take	he doesn't take	he does not take
future	he'll take	he will take	he won't take	he will not take

Hence as we have already seen the elliptical forms of the simple tenses are all forms consisting of one word: *he did, he does, he will.* But the non-finite form of the future is *be going to* or *be about to;* this is the form in which it occurs anywhere other than as primary tense. This does not affect the principles stated above, but it makes it simpler to state them by reference to the tense SYSTEMS: that is, in terms of the selection of tenses in the verbal group, rather than in terms of the words that are used to express the tense selections.

With operator ellipsis, which as we saw earlier is characteristically associated with question–answer sequences where the question centres around the lexical verb, the elliptical group normally takes over the total tense selection of the group which is presupposed. So:

[4:89] a. What is he going to do with all that paraphernalia? – Catch fish. [= He's going to catch fish]
b. Have you been digging? – No, weeding. [= I've been weeding]
c. What should she have done? – Told the police. [= She should have told the police]

This type of ellipsis is very frequent, and the result looks like an ordinary non-finite verbal group. If the question is a simple present or past tense, there is no possibility of verbal ellipsis in the response, as the verbal group consists of only one word.

It is possible for a verbal group in such contexts to repudiate some or all of the tense selection of the presupposed group, but this has to be done explicitly – anything that is omitted through ellipsis will be carried over. So we understand the response in [4:90]

[4:90] He must have mended it. – Or been going to mend it, rather.

as *he must have been going to mend it*. It is possible to construct ambiguous examples if one tries hard enough, *eg* [4:91]

[4:91] He could have been going to mend it – or be mending it.

where the response might be either *he could have been going to be mending it* (at some particular time later, *eg* just when you arrived), or *he could be mending it* (now). But the general principle is the usual one that whatever is not specifically repudiated is presupposed by the elliptical form.

4.3.5 Summary of verbal ellipsis

We can now give a brief summary of lexical and operator ellipsis in the verbal group. Lexical ellipsis, it will be remembered, is ellipsis 'from the right': the final element in the verbal group, the lexical verb, is omitted, and preceding elements may be omitted, all except the initial operator. Operator ellipsis is ellipsis 'from the left': the initial element in the verbal group (finite verbal operator, if finite; otherwise first non-finite operator) is omitted, and following elements may be omitted, all except the lexical verb.

An elliptical verbal group carries over certain systemic selections from the group that it presupposes. The general principles regarding this presupposition are as follows:

	Lexical ellipsis	Operator ellipsis
Polarity	inapplicable (always expressed)	not presupposed
Finiteness and modality	inapplicable (always expressed)	presupposed
Voice	presupposed	presupposed (can be repudiated under certain conditions)
Tense	not presupposed (except last order selection in compound tense)	presupposed unless repudiated
Lexical verb	presupposed	inapplicable (always expressed)

This pattern is relatable to the different contexts of the two types of ellipsis. Operator ellipsis involves omission of the MODAL BLOCK – the Subject and finite verbal operator (see 4.3.6 and 4.4.1 below) – in the clause; this is the element that expresses mood. Operator ellipsis is therefore characteristic of those contexts in which the mood is taken over from the previous clause. Typically this happens within the sentence, but we are not considering presupposition relations within the sentence because they do not form part of the total picture of cohesion, which is an intersentence relation. Between sentences, the typical context in which there is presupposition of mood is that of question and response; hence, as we have seen, we find operator ellipsis in answers to questions, particularly those where what is asked for is the identity or confirmation of the lexical verb, *eg: what are you doing?, are you thinking (or . . .)?* So in operator ellipsis the finiteness is always presupposed, whereas the polarity never is. Tense and voice may or may not be; that is, they are presupposed unless repudiated.

Lexical ellipsis, on the other hand, leaves out nothing of the modal block, so that the mood of the clause is fully explicit: in a verbal group with lexical ellipsis the finiteness is always expressed, so the question of its presupposition from an earlier verbal group does not arise. Lexical ellipsis occurs in those contexts where the lexical verb is not in question; the lexical verb itself is therefore always presupposed, and so is the voice, since the lexical verb carries with it the implications of its transitivity – if the *love* from *John loves Mary* is taken over by presupposition into the next clause, then naturally this presupposition extends also to the fact that it was *loves* and not *is loved by*. If we want to override this and talk about Mary loving John, we must restate it as a new proposition, in full.

Polarity however is not presupposed. In fact it is impossible not to restate the polarity, because it is tied structurally to the initial operator, which is always present in lexical ellipsis. But behind this is a more important reason, namely that the polarity may be precisely the question at issue, as in sequences like *Did John come? – No, he didn't. – Didn't he?*; as also in question tags, which are not treated in detail here because they are within the sentence and therefore not cohesive. Similarly, tense is not carried over; the primary tense choice has to be restated, being embodied in the initial operator, and tense also may be up for consideration, as in *John came, didn't he? – No, but he will.*

Thus the pattern of presupposition reflects the different functions of the two types of verbal ellipsis in bringing about cohesion within a text. We have illustrated mainly with question–answer sequences, because these allow us to display the cohesive relations more clearly in a short space. But verbal ellipsis is characteristic of all texts, spoken and written, and provides an extremely subtle and flexible means of creating varied and intricate discourse.

4.3.6 Verbal ellipsis and the clause

This final subsection is designed to provide a link between the present section and the next. We have seen that verbal ellipsis often entails the omission of other elements in the clause besides verbal ones. Specifically, operator ellipsis involves ellipsis of the whole MODAL element in the clause, and lexical ellipsis involves ellipsis of the whole of the residue, the PROPOSITIONAL element in the clause. So, for example, the clause *the cat won't catch mice in winter* has as its structure (on the interpersonal dimension of meaning):

the cat	won't	catch	mice	in winter
Modal		Propositional		
Subject	Predicator		Complement	Adjunct
nominal group	verbal group		nominal group	prepositional group

If this is followed by *Or chase birds*, with operator ellipsis, then the Subject *the cat* is omitted as well as the verbal operator *won't*. If it is followed by *won't it?*, with lexical ellipsis, then the remainder of the propositional element, consisting of the Complement *mice* and the Adjunct *in winter*, is omitted along with the lexical verb *catch*.

Verbal ellipsis is always accompanied by the omission of the related clause elements, those that are in the same part of the clause as the relevant portion of the verbal group. So in operator ellipsis, where there is omission of the finite part of the verbal group, the Subject is also omitted; in lexical ellipsis, where there is omission of the non-finite part of the verbal group, all Complements and Adjuncts are also omitted. These elements are omitted, that is to say, unless they are explicitly repudiated. It is important to note that they can be repudiated; we might have, with lexical ellipsis.

[4:92] The cat won't catch mice in winter.
- a. [operator ellipsis; Subject repudiated: 'nor will the dog chase rabbits in winter']
  – Nor the dog chase rabbits.
- b. [lexical ellipsis; Complement repudiated: 'it will catch birds in winter']
  – It will birds.
- c. [lexical ellipsis; Adjunct repudiated: 'it will catch mice in summer']
  – It will in summer.

But if there is verbal ellipsis, then any structurally-related element in the clause that is not contrastive with that in the presupposed clause must be omitted also. You cannot say, following [4:92] above:
- d. – Nor the cat chase birds (repeating *the cat*)
- e. – It will birds in winter (repeating *in winter*)
- f. – It will mice in summer (repeating *mice*)

nor is it possible to use a reference item in this context, *eg* (d) *Nor it chase birds*. Such elements can be repeated or referred to only provided there is no verbal ellipsis: *nor will the cat/it chase birds, it will chase birds in winter/ then, it will chase mice/them in summer*. Hence in an example such as

[4:93] Have you checked this page? – I have (done) THIS page.

the answer is possible only with *this* in a contrastive sense, meaning either a different page, or this page in contrast to others.

The principle here is that which is common to all forms of ellipsis: namely, that although the structural elements themselves are not present in the elliptical item, the features that are realized by these elements ARE present. So a clause in which there is operator ellipsis of the verbal group has no Subject; but if the clause presupposed by it is indicative (indicative being the feature realized by the presence of a Subject), then it also is indicative even though it has no Subject. Similarly a clause in which there is lexical ellipsis of the verbal group has no Complement or Adjunct, but it takes over any of the features realized by these elements (type of transitivity; time, place, manner, etc) that are present in the presupposed clause. Therefore if the elliptical clause is making a DIFFERENT selection within these features – referring to a different time, a different goal, different location, etc – this MUST be expressed overtly, in order to repudiate the previous selection; and on the other hand if it is making the same selection – *ie* if there is no contrast between the two clauses with respect to a given selection – this CANNOT be expressed overtly. Anything else would conflict with the basic function of ellipsis, which is to create cohesion by leaving out, under definite rules, what can be taken over from the preceding discourse, making explicit only what contrasts with it.

Finally, we should mention the limits of cohesion through verbal ellipsis, in terms of the function of the clause in question. An elliptical verbal group cannot in general presuppose a verbal group in an embedded clause (one that is embedded in the narrower sense of the word, *ie* RANK-SHIFTED; *cf* 3.4.2 above). Consider for example:

[4:94] a. The policeman paid no attention to the girl who was driving the car. – Was she?
b. The policeman paid no attention to Mrs Jones, who was driving the car.
– Was she?

[4:94a] is impossible; here *who was driving the car* is genuinely embedded (rankshifted), so that it becomes part of the nominal group *the girl who was driving the car*. In [4:94b], however, where *who was driving the car* is not rankshifted, but is related to the other clause by hypotaxis, the response is quite acceptable. A clause which is rankshifted loses its functional identity as a clause: it does not operate as an element of the sentence. But a hypotactic clause does not lose its identity; it is still an element of sentence structure, and so readily serves as the target of presupposition from another sentence. This is the basis of the distinction between hypotaxis and rankshift, which tends to be obscured in the use of the term 'embedding'; and cohesion provides evidence of the importance of this distinction. Similarly:

[4:95] a. I shall stay in the city when I retire this year. – Do you?
b. I shall stay in the city, even though I retire this year. – Do you?

Here again, the clause *when I retire this year* in (a) is rankshifted and therefore cannot be presupposed; so [4:95a] is unacceptable. But the clause *even though I retire this year* in (b) is hypotactic; this, therefore, is accessible by presupposition, and [4:95b] is a perfectly good example of cohesion by verbal ellipsis.

4.4 Clausal ellipsis

4.4.1 Modal and propositional

We have included under verbal ellipsis all instances of ellipsis in the verbal group. However, both types of verbal ellipsis, both operator ellipsis and lexical ellipsis, also involve ellipsis that is external to the verb itself, affecting other elements in the structure of the clause.

We can therefore look at these two types of ellipsis from another angle, taking the clause as the point of departure. The clause in English, considered as the expression of the various speech functions, such as statement, question, response and so on, has a two-part structure consisting of MODAL ELEMENT plus PROPOSITIONAL ELEMENT (*cf* 4.3.6 above), for example

[4:96] (1) The Duke was │ going to plant a row of poplars in the park
            (Modal element) │ (Propositional element)

The MODAL element, which embodies the speech function of the clause, consists in turn of the Subject plus the finite element in the verbal group. Strictly, the part of the verbal group that goes in the modal block is simply the finiteness, which may not be realized in a separate element: it may be fused with the remainder of the verb, as in simple past and present tenses *planted, plant(s)*. The PROPOSITIONAL ELEMENT consists of the residue: the remainder of the verbal group, and any Complements or Adjuncts that may be present. The difference between a Complement and an Adjunct is, briefly, that the Complement could become a Subject if the clause was turned round in some way, *eg: a row of poplars was going to be planted by the late Duke;* whereas the Adjunct could not.

In the favourite clause type the Modal element precedes the Propositional, though it need not do; we may have

[4:96] (2) In the park │ the Duke was │ going to plant a row of poplars.
            Proposi- │ Modal element │ -tional element

or [4:96] (3) A row of poplars │ the Duke was │ going to plant in the park.
               Proposi- │ Modal element │ -tional element

The two types of verbal ellipsis are derivable from these two major divisions of the clause. Under certain conditions there is ellipsis of the Modal element: thus

[4:97] What was the Duke going to do? – Plant a row of poplars in the park.

In the answer, the Modal element is omitted: the Subject and, within the verbal group, the finite operator *was*. Hence there is operator ellipsis in the verbal group. In other circumstances there may be ellipsis of the Propositional element:

[4:98] Who was going to plant a row of poplars in the park? – The Duke was.

Here there is omission of the Complement and the Adjunct, and, within the verbal group, of the lexical verb *plant*: so we have lexical ellipsis in the verbal group. The verbal element *going to*, which is neither finite operator nor lexical verb – it is a non-finite tense operator – is omitted in both examples here: this is one of the features of verbal ellipsis which cannot be accounted for simply by reference to the clause (it was dealt with in a preceding section, 4.3.4.4).

There is no need to repeat here the details of what from the clause standpoint are modal ellipsis and propositional ellipsis, since those have already been discussed in connection with operator ellipsis and lexical ellipsis in the verbal group. In brief, modal ellipsis is associated with a context where there is no choice of mood in the clause – mood, the choice of declarative, interrogative, imperative and their subcategories, is the realization of speech function, and is expressed by the Modal element. Likewise, in modal ellipsis the polarity is determined, and the Subject can be presupposed from what has gone before. Typically, in other words, modal ellipsis occurs in response to a WH- question asking 'what (did, does, etc) ... do?' (*cf* [4:97] above):

[4:99] What were they doing? – Holding hands.

The usual type of non-finite dependent clause is, in fact, simply a clause with modal ellipsis; but it is one which presupposes another clause within the same sentence, this being what is meant by 'dependent', and so it does not enter into cohesion; an example would be

[4:100] Holding hands they stole quietly out of the house.

Propositional ellipsis, on the other hand, is associated with those instances where the mood and the polarity are the principal components of the message: typically, responses to statements and yes/no questions, where the subject is presupposed by a reference item, as in

[4:101] a. The plane has landed. – Has it?
b. Has the plane landed? – Yes, it has.

It is also found in response to WH- questions where the unknown element happens to be the Subject (*cf* [4:98] above):

[4:102] Who taught you to spell? – Grandfather did.

In general, in a finite clause with either of these two types of ellipsis the verbal group will also be elliptical:

	Clause	Verbal group
(1)	modal ellipsis	operator ellipsis
(2)	propositional ellipsis	lexical ellipsis

But there are certain circumstances under which this does not hold.

(1) Modal/operator ellipsis. If the verb is in simple past or present tense, modal ellipsis may not involve operator ellipsis; moreover it is not always possible to say whether it does or not:

[4:103] a. What did he do? – Ran away. (Run away.)
            (but note: *What did he do, run away?*)
         b. What do they do? – Run away.
         c. What does he do? – Runs away. (Run away.)

It would be possible to have *run away* in (c) and also in (a); they would then be, appropriately, instances of operator ellipsis, since the full forms would be *He runs* (=*does*+*run*) *away*, *He ran* (=*did*+*run*) *away*. There is some uneasiness about *run away* in these contexts, perhaps because it APPEARS to be finite (and therefore wrong, either in number or in tense); on the other hand the non-elliptical forms also seem wrong, because they are clearly finite and yet lack a Subject, which is contrary to normal patterns. So the preferred form is often that with pronoun Subject added: *he ran away, he runs away*. With [4:103b] the problem does not arise, since the non-finite *run* would in this case also be the appropriate finite form.

(2) Propositional/lexical ellipsis. There are two occasions when propositional ellipsis does not involve lexical ellipsis. One is very general: the speaker may use the substitute *do* rather than the elliptical form of the verbal group (see above, Chapter 3, especially 3.3.2). Here 'speaker', as always, includes 'writer'; but in fact substitution is more common in spoken than in written English, ellipsis being often preferred in writing. Moreover, as already noted, there is considerable variation among different dialects; and there are individual differences also. But with some speakers, at least, the substitute form of the verbal group may be used in all instances of propositional ellipsis except those where the verb is passive, which do not substitute at all, and those where the verb is *be* or *have*, which

'substitute' for themselves (the verb *do* does in fact substitute by *do*, though the result does not show). But substitution is less usual in question-answer sequences, which have marked polarity and therefore are more often elliptical. Some examples:

[4:104]

Presupposed clause	Elliptical form	Substitute form	Full form
(a) Has the plane landed?	Yes it has.	Yes it has done.	Yes it has landed.
(b) Keep out of sight till the plane lands.	It has.	It has done.	It has landed.
(c) Who was playing the piano?	Peter was.	Peter was doing.	Peter was playing the piano.
(d) Was John playing the piano?	No. Peter was though.	No. Peter was doing, though.	No. Peter was playing the piano, though.
(e) Are the rest finished?	Yes, they are.	–	Yes, they are finished.
(f) Does Jane sing?	Yes, she does.	Yes, she does do.	Yes, she does sing.
(g) Does Jane sing?	–	No, but Mary does.	No, but Mary sings.
(h) Has May done her homework?	Yes, she has.	Yes, she has done.	Yes, she has done her homework.
(j) Has the weather been cold?	Yes, it has.	(Yes it has been.)	Yes, it has been cold.
(k) I hear Smith is having an operation?	He has.	(He has had.)	He has had an operation.

Strictly speaking in [4:104g] there is no elliptical form (*cf* [3:91] in 3.3.3.3), although effectively the distinction between ellipsis and substitution is neutralized here. This is, in fact, the second of the two occasions where propositional ellipsis does not lead to lexical ellipsis, and it is not very interesting; namely, in simple past or present tense with unmarked positive polarity, where there simply is no distinct elliptical form. Hence the difference between (f) and (g) above: whereas in [4:104f] there IS a distinct form with lexical ellipsis, because the verb has marked polarity (the full form is *does sing*), in [4:104g] there is not – the polarity is unmarked and the full form is simply *sings*. And since the verbs *be* and *have* (*ie* the *have* meaning 'possess', which is replaceable by *have got*, as in *he had a yacht*; not that meaning 'take', 'undergo', etc as in *he had an operation, he had breakfast*) do not take the verbal operator *do* – their 'marked positive' form is simply the non-reduced *is*, *has*, by contrast with reduced *'s*, etc – these verbs NEVER have an elliptical form in simple past and present tense. So

[4:104] (cont'd.)

Presupposed clause	Elliptical form	Substitute form	Full form
(f) Does Jane sing?	Yes, she does.	Yes, she does do.	Yes, she does sing.
(g) Does Jane sing?	No, but Mary does.		No, but Mary sings.
(l) Is he suspicious?	Yes, he is.		Yes, he is suspicious.
(m) Is he suspicious?	No, but John is.		No, but John's suspicious.
(n) Has he (got) a prejudice against it?	Yes, he has.		Yes, he has (got) a prejudice against it.
(o) Has he (got) a prejudice against it?	No, but John has.		No, but John has (John's got) a prejudice against it.

Some varieties of English treat this *have* like the majority of other verbs and use the operator *do* with it; for speakers of such varieties, examples (n) and (o) would not be valid.

To summarize the circumstances under which clausal ellipsis, modal or propositional, may be found unaccompanied by ellipsis in the verbal group: operator ellipsis may be avoided in simple past and present tense; and substitution may be used in most instances instead of lexical ellipsis, the two being indistinguishable from each other in simple past and present (unmarked positive form), and indistinguishable also from the full form in the case of the verbs *be* and *have* (= 'possess'). Otherwise, verbal ellipsis and clausal ellipsis go together.

The next section (4.4.2) deals with some instances of the omission of single elements in the clause. After that we go on to consider clausal ellipsis in its typical context of question–response and other types of rejoinder, first in direct speech (4.4.3) and then in indirect speech (4.4.4). A final section refers to ellipsis in clause complexes (4.4.5).

4.4.2 No ellipsis of single elements

It is not possible in English to say

[4:105] Has she taken her medicine? – She has taken.

Either we must reply with a full, non-elliptical clause *she has taken her medicine* (or *she has taken it*, using reference to presuppose *her medicine*); or we must omit BOTH *her medicine* AND the lexical verb *take* and say *she has* (or *she has done*, using the substitute *do* in its place). Let us tabulate these, from the point of view of ellipsis:

[4:106] a. Has she taken her medicine? –

    (i) No ellipsis:

        (1) no presupposition   She has taken her medicine.

        (2) presupposition of Complement by reference   She has taken it.

    (ii) Clausal ellipsis:

        (1) with verbal ellipsis   She has.

        (2) with verbal substitution   She has done.

It may be helpful to give equivalent sets for *do, have* and *be*:

[4:106] b. Has she done her homework?	c. Has she had her breakfast?	d. Has she been unhappy?
(i) (1) She has done her homework.	She has had her breakfast.	She has been unhappy.
(2) She has done it.	She has had it.	–
(ii) (1) She has.	She has.	She has.
(2) She has done.	She has had.	She has been.

(We cannot say *she has been it*, at least not in answer to *has she been unhappy?*, although this would have been acceptable if the Complement had been a noun, *eg: Isn't it time she was secretary? – Oh no, she's been it already.*)

The notion that *do, have* (all senses) and *be* 'substitute for themselves' is useful in explaining the forms given under (ii2). If these were not sub-stitute forms, they would be impossible in the same way that *She has taken* is impossible: it is not possible to leave out the Complement but retain the Predicator (verbal group) intact.

This in turn is part of a very general restriction on ellipsis, whereby it is not possible to omit single elements from the structure of the clause. If a single element of clause structure is to be presupposed, for purposes of co-hesion, it must be expressed by a reference item; so (to vary example [4:96])

[4:107] The Duke has planted poplars in the park.
　　　　Presupposing:　　we have:
　　　　(a) The Duke　　He has planted poplars in the park.
　　　　(b) poplars　　　The Duke has planted them in the park.
　　　　(c) in the park　　The Duke has planted poplars there.

We cannot omit *he* in (a) or *them* in (b); and although we could omit *there* in (c), in the sense that it would still leave an acceptable clause struc-ture, there would be no presupposition and therefore no feature of 'place' in the clause. There is no type of clausal ellipsis which takes the form of the omission of single elements of clause structure.

It should be stressed once again that we are confining our definition of ELLIPSIS to its non-structural, cohesive sense; that is, as a form of pre-supposition between sentences. Within the sentence, we find internal BRANCHING which may involve the omission of single elements of clause structure (as well as structures of any other rank), for example:

[4:108] a. John loves Mary but is loved by Jane.
　　　　　　b. Either Peter will play his cello or Sally her guitar.
　　　　　　c. Anne cut out and Sarah sewed a dress for every doll.

Similarly for combinations of two elements:

[4:108] d. Sybil takes coffee very strong but Joan rather weak.
　　　　　　e. We climbed Great Gable on Tuesday and Sca Fell two days later.

But here in all instances the two parts are structurally related, by coordina-tion, and the patterns of occurrence are quite different. The same explana-tion holds for

[4:108] f. The cat catches mice in summer. – And the dog rabbits.
　　　　　　g. The cat won't catch mice in winter. – Nor the dog rabbits.

Even though these are written as separate sentences, they are in fact linked by coordination; this pattern would not be possible with *but*, *so* or other conjunctive elements (see Chapter 5).

Aside from this structural 'branching', there remains one other phenomenon which is to be distinguished clearly from ellipsis; this is not in fact an instance of omission, and involves no presupposition of any kind, but it is sometimes referred to, rather confusingly, as if it was a form of ellipsis in the clause. Examples would be:

[4:109] a. Simon's playing. Let's not interrupt.
     b. Sandra cleans for me when I'm out.
     c. Run!

These are sometimes described as elliptical forms of, *eg, Simon's playing the piano, Sandra cleans the flat, You run!* Actually however they are systematic variants in which nothing is omitted, any more than an expression of time or place can be said to be 'omitted' from a clause which does not contain one. They have no systemic features which are not expressed in their structure. It is misleading to call them 'elliptical' because this suggests they have some cohesive function similar to that of the elliptical forms we are discussing here, whereas in fact they have none. If there was ellipsis of the Complement, they would presuppose the Complement, which they do not. They do not presuppose any preceding item; in general, they cannot occur in contexts where there is presupposition, for example

[4:110] a. Does Sandra clean the windows? – She cleans for me when I'm out.
     b. They asked Simon to play some Chopin. When he started playing, it was Liszt.

In (a) the one thing the response could *not* mean is 'she cleans the windows for me', which would make it like [4:105] above. This is borne out by [4:110b], where the response is quite acceptable and *started playing* clearly does NOT presuppose *Chopin*.

We have emphasized at various points in the discussion that the distinctions we are drawing, while they are useful and important for explaining the patterns that lie behind the construction of text, are not to be taken too rigidly. When we say that there is no type of clausal ellipsis consisting in the omission of individual elements of structure of the clause, we are stating a generalization, one which explains why certain theoretically possible clause types cannot occur independently – though they may occur in branching structures. This does not mean that a single element of clause structure can never be presupposed under any circumstances. We can have sequences like

[4:111] a. We went on the river yesterday. We had dinner out too.
   b. Can you read the print without your glasses? – No, but I can look at the pictures.

where the second sentence in (a) also refers to 'yesterday' and the response in (b) refers to 'without my glasses'. But these are not elliptical sentences. They merely imply, in the particular context in which they occur, the particular time, manner, etc referred to in the preceding sentence. So in [4:111b] the response implies 'I can look at the pictures without my glasses', but it does not itself embody a feature of manner, nor is *without my glasses* in any sense omitted from it.

   At the same time, the line between what is elliptical and what is not elliptical is not a completely sharp one. Most instances are clear; there is no doubt that the omission of modal and propositional elements in the clause, as in [4:97] and [4:98], is to be explained as elliptical, whereas the types represented in [4:109–111] are not. But there are some doubtful instances. For example it might reasonably be suggested that in [4:112] the second sentence is actually benefactive, the Beneficiary *him* being omitted by ellipsis:

[4:112] Are you sending Jack anything for his birthday? – I thought of sending a book token.

However, there appear to be no examples of the omission of just one element from the structure of a clause WHERE THAT ELEMENT IS OTHERWISE OBLIGATORY – of the Subject, for example, or a Complement following a verb which must have a Complement (*cf* [4:105] above). Hence instances which on other grounds could be interpreted either as elliptical or as non-elliptical, but which if regarded as elliptical would take the form of the omission of a single element of clause structure, should perhaps for that very reason be excluded from the category of ellipsis. This is a theoretical decision, and one which would allow us to formulate a very general principle about cohesion in the clause.

   This principle is as follows. Other than in a question–answer environment (to be discussed in the remainder of this chapter), the basis of both ellipsis and substitution – and these, as explained earlier, are essentially the same phenomenon – is the two-part structure 'Modal plus Propositional'. One or other of these elements may be presupposed, as a whole; but the smaller elements which make them up – Subject, Complement, Predicator, Adjunct – may not be presupposed in isolation. The facts on which this principle is based are often indeterminate, as the facts of language always are; we do not force them into a mould, but in the uncertain instances we choose that interpretation which brings more of them within the scope of a single generalization – provided it is one which makes good sense. Here it does. It is the Modal-Propositional structure which expresses the function of the clause in the discourse, so it is natural that this structure should provide the means for integrating any clause into a coherent text together with what has gone before.

4.4.3 Ellipsis in question–answer and other rejoinder sequences

Not all questions have an answer; but no less significant is the fact that not all answers have a question. The 'question and answer' sequence is a standard pattern in language, and not surprisingly the special type of cohesive relation that subsists between an answer and its question has its own characteristic grammatical properties. At the same time there are other sequences involving rejoinders of one kind and another.

Let us first make some terminological distinctions. Any observation by one speaker, whether it is a question or not, may be followed by an observation by another speaker that is related to it by some cohesive tie. We shall refer to this very general category of sequel as a REJOINDER. A rejoinder is any utterance which immediately follows an utterance by a different speaker and is cohesively related to it.

A rejoinder that follows a question will be called a RESPONSE. Within the category of responses there is a further distinction between DIRECT RESPONSES and INDIRECT RESPONSES. A direct response is one which answers the question; it is either a form of 'yes' or 'no', if the question is of the yes/no type, or a specification of the information asked for by the WH- element, if the question is of the WH- type. An indirect response is either one which comments on the question (COMMENTARY), or one which denies its relevance (DISCLAIMER), or one which gives supplementary information implying but not actually expressing an answer (SUPPLEMENTARY RESPONSE).

A direct response will also be referred to as an ANSWER. But note that the category of answer, which is the supplying of the particular information that is called for by the question, is not limited to responses, because one can answer one's own questions.

Other rejoinders, not following a question, include ASSENT and CONTRADICTION, following a statement; CONSENT and REFUSAL, following

Table 9: Types of rejoinder

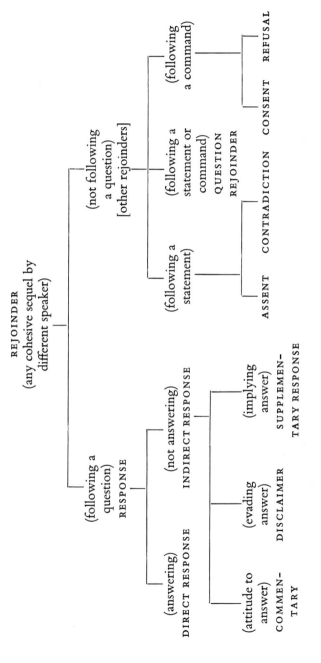

a command; and yes/no or WH- question following either a statement or a command.

Some examples of all these types:

[4:113] a. It's going to rain. – (i) It might. (ii) It isn't. (iii) Is it?
          b. Leave me alone. – (i) I won't. (ii) All right, I will. (iii) Why?

The sequel sentences are rejoinders, since they are cohesive utterances by another speaker; but they are not responses, because the presupposed items are not questions. [4:113a] is a statement, to which the rejoinder is (i) an assent, (ii) a contradiction, (iii) a yes/no question; (b) is a command, to which the rejoinder is (i) a refusal, (ii) a consent, (iii) a WH- question.

[4:113] c. Has John arrived? – Yes, he has.
          d. When did John arrive? – Yesterday.

Here the two sequels are rejoinders of the 'response' type, and both are direct responses, or answers; they give the information that is being sought.

[4:113] e. How did they break in? – I'll show you how.
          f. Why didn't you tell John? – I did.

Here the sequels are still responses, but indirect; the first is a commentary, the second a disclaimer.

[4:113] g. Did you tell John? – He wasn't there.

In (g) the response is also indirect, but here the answer is implied ('... so I couldn't'); these we shall call supplementary responses. Finally

[4:113] h. Did I lock the door? Yes of course I did.

Here there is only one speaker, so the sequel is not a response; but it is an answer, since it gives the information required.

4.4.3.1 DIRECT RESPONSES (I): YES/NO QUESTIONS

Answers to yes/no questions, or POLAR QUESTIONS as they have been called, are very simply dealt with, as the instruction 'Answer yes or no!' suggests: the appropriate answer is *yes* or *no*. The words *yes* and *no* express simply a feature of polarity. They do not mean (as do their dictionary equivalents in some other languages) 'you are right' and 'you are wrong'; they mean 'the answer is positive' and 'the answer is negative'. Hence their meaning is unaffected by the polarity of the question; contrast the forms of the positive in French:

[4:114]

(1) Question	(2) Answer, positive	(3) Answer, negative
a. Are you coming? –	Yes ('I am') [oui]	No ('I'm not') [non]
b. Aren't you coming? –	Yes ('I am') [si]	No ('I'm not') [non]

In this connection it is interesting to note that both *yes* and *no* occur more often as rejoinders to statements than they do as answers to questions; here both of them signal 'I agree', 'I understand', 'I'm listening' – keeping the channel of communication open – and the choice of one or the other simply follows the polarity of the preceding statement:

[4:115] a. The soloist wasn't very inspiring. – No, he seemed rather tired.

b. The car's running very well. – Yes, I had it serviced recently.

It is possible to consider *yes* and *no* as clause substitutes. But they are not really substitutes; for one thing, they can be accompanied by part or even the whole of the clause for which they would be said to be substituting, and that is precluded from substitution as usually defined. For example in [4:114a] the answer (2) could be *yes*, *yes I am*, or *yes I am coming*. They are realizations of a single clause feature, that of polarity, which is being expressed on its own instead of in association with the verbal group; and the fact that it is expressed on its own means that the whole of the remainder of the clause is presupposed; hence their cohesive effect.

The words *yes* and *no* express simple polarity. There are also complex expressions, some meaning 'either yes or no', *eg: maybe, perhaps*, and some meaning 'both yes and no', *eg: sometimes, usually*. The former are often combined with some modality, the speaker's assessment of the relative probabilities of 'yes' and 'no', *eg: probably, possibly*. All these are appropriate answers to yes/no questions; and they are also cohesive, since they presuppose all the remaining features of the clause other than the polarity.

If the answer *yes*, or other expression of polarity, is accompanied by just a part of the clause, this will be the Modal element: *yes I am, no I'm not, sometimes he does, perhaps she has, possibly they might* and so on. The Modal element is itself sufficient as an answer, since it also carries the polarity (and presupposes the Propositional element of the clause); so [4:114a] could be answered simply by *I am, I'm not*. If both occur, as in *yes I am*, they function jointly as the realization of a direct answer; as distinct from

[4:116] Did you see anyone? – Yes, Shirley.

where the second part of the answer, *Shirley*, is an indirect response, giving supplementary information (see 4.4.3.3 below).

4.4.3.2 DIRECT RESPONSES (2): WH- QUESTIONS

At first sight the answer to a WH- question, or NON-POLAR QUESTION, seems very different from the answer to a yes/no question, since the information that is being sought by the two types of question is very different. A WH- question requires the specification of a particular item which is as it were missing from the clause. The respondent knows what the function of this item is in the clause structure, since this has been supplied by the questioner; he knows the total structure of the clause, in fact, and also the actual items that occur in all the other functions. He merely has to fill in the blank. The WH- expression itself indicates whether the missing item is participant or circumstance, and various other things about it: if it is a circumstance, whether it is time, place, cause, manner, etc (*when, where, why, how,* and an open-ended set of forms such as *what time, what with, like what, which way, for whose sake*); if it is a participant, whether it is from a limited set (*which*) or not, whether human (*who, which/what person,* etc, or possessive *whose,* etc) or non-human (*what, which/what thing,* etc), and whether the question is one of degree (*how much/many, how long,* etc) or of kind (*what kind, like what,* etc).

The simplest form of answer, therefore, is one which does merely fill in the blank: which supplies the appropriate nominal, adverbial or prepositional group to act as Subject or Complement or Adjunct, and as Actor or Goal or Beneficiary or Temporal or Locative or whatever function is required. So for example:

[4:117] a. What did I hit? – A root. (Complement; Goal)
b. Who killed Cock Robin? – The sparrow. (Subject; Actor)
c. How much does it cost? – Five pounds. (Complement; Range)
d. How's the patient? – Comfortable. (Complement; Attribute)
e. Till what time are you staying? – Half past three. (Adjunct; Temporal)
f. What did you draw it with? – A pencil. (Adjunct; Instrument)
g. Whose gloves are these? – Sally's. (Complement; Identifier)

The principle underlying these answers is, however, exactly the same as that which governs the answers yes and no to a question of the yes/no type.

In each case, when giving a direct response in its simplest form the speaker makes explicit just one thing, the information that the question calls for, and leaves all the rest to be presupposed by ellipsis. With a yes/ no question, this information is the polarity, so the answer specifies the polarity and presupposes all else. In a WH- question, the information required is the item occupying a particular function (strictly, a particular complex of functions) in the structure; the answer specifies this and presupposes the remainder of the clause. Hence the principle of clausal ellipsis, in clauses which are answers to questions, is general to all types of question. Any clause functioning as answer, in the sense defined above (see [4:113c and d]), has an elliptical form consisting of just one element. Which element this is is explicit in the form of the question, and all remaining features of the question clause – excepting, of course, its interrogative mood – are presupposed. .

Just as with a yes/no question we may also have longer, partially elliptical (or entirely non-elliptical) forms of answer, so too these may be found with WH- questions. If the WH- item is Subject the answer may, like the answer to a yes/no question, have propositional ellipsis; this is because the Subject falls within the Modal element. So the answer to [4:117b] might be *The sparrow did*. Whether or not the WH- item is Subject, the answer can be filled out with no ellipsis at all; we could have *The sparrow killed Cock Robin* in answer to [4:117b] and *You hit a root* in [4:117a]. If the WH- item does not form a complete nominal or prepositional group by itself (*eg: whose gloves, what . . . with, till what time*), then the simplest answer is one in which there is not only clausal ellipsis but also ellipsis within the group, either nominal (*eg: Sally's* in [4:117g], for 'Sally's gloves'; *cf* 4.2.3.1, [4:24] above) or prepositional. We have not discussed the ellipsis of prepositions in the Adjunct as a separate topic, since it occurs only in this context; it is however illustrated by [4:117e and f], where the prepositions *till* and *with* are presupposed in the answer. In such instances there is an intermediate form of answer in which the group is not elliptical but the clause is; so we could have

[4:117] e'. Till what time are you staying? – Till half past three.
     f'. What did you draw it with? – With a pencil.
     g'. Whose gloves are these? – Sally's gloves.

There is no WH- verb in English; we cannot ask *you're whatting the eggs?* – or rather, since the WH- item comes first in the clause, *whatting are you the eggs?* Instead we have the form *what are you doing to the eggs?* This involves the use of the 'pro-verb' *do*, in the combination *do what?* (*cf*

3.3.3.3). The expression *do what?*, like *do that*, presupposes the whole of the propositional element in the clause other than anything that is repudiated, so that the question *what are you doing?* is appropriately answered by a proposition (*ie* a clause with modal ellipsis) rather than just a lexical verb, although the proposition might CONSIST just of a lexical verb. Thus *relaxing, frying eggs, feeding the ducks in the park* could all answer *do what?* questions. If the *do what?* is not intended to embrace the entire proposition the items that are not being asked for are made explicit, *eg: what were you doing in the park?* Such items however can never occur as nominals; they must take the form of a prepositional group. Following *do what?*, a preposition is required even with an item functioning as Goal in the clause structure, usually *to* or *with*:

[4:118] a. What are you doing with the eggs? – Poaching them.
         b. What have the children done to the wheelbarrow? – Broken it.

This is in accord with the general principle whereby all PARTICIPANTS in the structure of the clause, in English, may be related to the verb either directly as nominals or through the medium of a preposition; the prepositional form is used to make the function explicit where this is necessary – as it is here because we do not know what the verb is.* The answer follows the normal pattern except that if there is a Goal-Complement in the question it is usually presupposed by pronoun reference rather than by ellipsis; so we have *them* and *it* in the answers in [4:118].

4.4.3.3 INDIRECT RESPONSES
There is one kind of response which is not an answer in the defined sense, but is what we called an INDIRECT RESPONSE; this may be a COMMENTARY, a DISCLAIMER or a SUPPLEMENTARY. Any question may be greeted by a COMMENTARY, which is really a statement about the speaker's attitude to the answer: his ignorance of it, for example, or his consent or refusal to give it. These, since they are in fact reports, have the elliptical potentialities of 'reporting-reported' sequences as described in 4.4.4 below. Examples are (and *cf* [4:113e]):

[4:119] a. Is it Tuesday today? – I don't know.
         b. Why are the lights turned off? – I'm not supposed to say why.

---

* *Cf* M. A. K. Halliday, 'Language structure and language function', in John Lyons (ed), *New Horizons in Linguistics* (Harmondsworth: Penguin Books, 1970), especially *p* 164.

Likewise, any question may be followed by a DISCLAIMER, which side-steps the question by disputing its relevance. Typically, a disclaimer involves moving from a yes/no to a WH- context, or vice versa, *eg* (and *cf* [4:113f]):

[4:120] a. When did they cancel the booking? – Did they?
        b. What's your telephone number? – We're not on the phone.
        c. Have you tested the battery? – How?

Some questions are framed so as to be difficult to disclaim, such as the notorious *When did you stop beating your wife?*, to which there is no ELLIPTICAL response meaning unambiguously 'I never have beaten her'. Normally however a response of the disclaimer type is elliptical; either it is declarative, with propositional ellipsis, or it is interrogative, in which case it is of the opposite type to the question, and has response-question ellipsis (see below).

The third type of indirect response is a SUPPLEMENTARY RESPONSE, which gives information other than that which is asked for but answers the question by implication, for example (and *cf* [4:113g]):

[4:121] a. Can you make it stand up? – If you keep still.
        b. Have we a car here? – Not unless you came in yours.
        c. Did you get the application form? – It's on my desk.
        d. Are you coming back today? – This evening.

Characteristically these supplementary responses presuppose the entire question; and they stand in a definite structural relation to it – or rather to the declarative clause which would serve as a direct answer to it, by which they would be 'filled out'. In [4:121a], for example, the full form would be *(Yes) I can make it stand up if you keep still*: that is, the direct answer, with the supplementary response hypotactically related to it, as a condition. The answer is positive unless repudiated by *not*, as in [4:121b]; the supplementary is usually conditional or causal ('yes if . . .', 'yes because . . .'), although it may be simply coordinated as in [4:121c] ('yes and . . .') and [4:121d] ('yes, more specifically . . .') – or even with an adversative implication, the presupposed answer then being negative ('no but . . .') as in

[4:122] Did you collect the subscriptions? – Smith did.

Supplementary responses are typically associated with yes/no questions; it is difficult to answer a WH- question by implication, and the nearest equivalent form of response to a WH- question is really a type of disclaimer, like [4:120b]. But the various types of indirect response are all fairly similar and cannot be kept strictly apart.

4.4.3.4 A NOTE ON ZEUGMA

As a postscript to this discussion of ellipsis in responses, we might add a brief note on zeugma. Zeugma is based on ellipsis, and both the WH- and the yes/no types of question afford excellent opportunities for zeugmatic answers. These involve a transfer from one element of clause structure to another; with a WH- question this can be achieved by a direct resqonse (*ie* an answer), as in [4:123a and b], but with a yes/no question it requires an indirect, supplementary response of the 'no but . . .' type, as in [4:123c and d]:

> [4:123] a. What has he been making ? – A big mistake.
> b. How did you travel ? – In considerable discomfort.
> c. Did she make him a good wife ? – No, a good husband.
> d. Was he shot in the street ? – No, in the shoulder.

In (b), for example, *how* is intended in the question as 'by what means?' but is interpreted in the answer as 'in what condition'. In its classical form as a figure of rhetoric, zeugma is embodied in coordinate structures, where the pattern is one of (structural) branching and not cohesion (*eg: we travelled in buses and great discomfort*). But the principle is the same.

4.4.3.5 OTHER REJOINDERS

We have already mentioned the difference between a response and a rejoinder. A response is one kind of rejoinder, one which presupposes a question, and which therefore has special potentialities for ellipsis, as discussed in 4.4.3.1–2 ('direct responses') and 4.4.3.3 ('indirect responses'). A rejoinder is any utterance by a second speaker which presupposes that of the first speaker whether it was a question or not. (We referred above to the frequent use of *yes* and *no* in rejoinders to statements.) From the point of view of cohesion, there is no distinct category of rejoinder; it is simply an ordinary element in a dialogue, and is covered by what has been said about ellipsis in general. But there remain a few observations to be made about rejoinders that are not responses to a question, but cohesive sequels to a statement or a command.

QUESTION REJOINDERS have the function of querying a preceding statement or command, or eliciting supplementary information about it. (1) One type is that which presupposes the entire preceding clause and seeks confirmation of it as a whole; these are yes/no questions and nearly always have the form of interrogative clauses with propositional ellipsis, like the question tag at the end of a declarative or imperative clause, except that with the rejoinder there is a different speaker and the polarity is never reversed. For example

[4:124] a. Peter's here. – Is he?
b. Open that parcel. – Shall I?
c. 'I can't believe *that!*' said Alice.
'Can't you?' the Queen said in a pitying tone.

(2) In another type the speaker identifies one item as requiring confirmation; the remainder of the clause is omitted but this item is queried explicitly:

[4:125] John's coming to dinner. {
a. John? (To dinner?)
b. Tonight?
c. And Mary? (Not Mary?)
}

These are three typical instances. In (a), an existing element is echoed; in (b) a new element is added; and in (c) an existing element is expanded, here by coordination. But the form of ellipsis is the same in all three; only one element in the clause is present in the structure, the remainder being presupposed by ellipsis.

Finally the speaker may similarly focus on one item in the clause but query it in the form of a WH- question. Corresponding to [4:125a] we have the 'echo question' represented in [4:126a], meaning 'please repeat that' ('I didn't hear', 'I'm surprised', etc); this is the only type of WH-question which must be spoken on a rising tone. Corresponding to [4:125b] is [4:126b], where the WH- item represents a new element and the whole of the clause is presupposed; and to [4:125c], [4:126c] where the WH- item *who else?* asks for expansion of an existing element by coordination.

[4:126] John's coming to dinner. {
a. Who? (tone 2)
b. When?
c. And who else?
}

In some instances the rejoinder asks for more specific information about an item that is already present:

[4:126] d. John's coming to dinner. – John who?
e. Alice heard the Rabbit say, 'A barrowful will do, to begin with.' 'A barrowful of *what*', thought Alice.

Often the item requiring further specification is itself indefinite (*cf* [4:129d] below), *eg: Someone's coming to dinner. – Who?* This type could also perhaps be matched in the yes/no series illustrated in [4:125]: *John's coming to dinner. – John Smith?*; *Someone's coming to dinner. – John?*

The other types of rejoinder to a statement or command usually take the form of an elliptical clause consisting of the Modal constituent only – that is, one with propositional ellipsis – with pronoun Subject, but in the declarative form. In [4:127], (a) is an assent, (b) a contradiction, (c) a consent and (d) a refusal:

[4:127] a. 'Everything's just as it was!'
'Of course it is,' said the Queen.

b. '. . . being so many different sizes in a day is very confusing.'
'It isn't,' said the Caterpillar.

c. 'Our family always *hated* cats: nasty, low, vulgar things! Don't let me hear the name again!'
'I won't indeed!' said Alice, in a great hurry to change the subject of conversation.

d. 'Never mind what they all say, my dear, but take a return-ticket every time the train stops.'
'Indeed I sha'n't!' Alice said rather impatiently.

These forms often combine with *yes* and *no*, as in the following:

[4:127] e. It's none of their business. – Yes it is.

f. 'It *must* come sometimes to "jam today",' Alice objected.
'No, it can't,' said the Queen.

As was remarked earlier, *yes* and *no* also occur alone; they are the forms of expression of positive and negative polarity when everything else in the clause is omitted by ellipsis:

[4:127] g. It's cold. – Yes.

h. We're not late. – No.

These are both instances of assent. In contradiction, the Modal constituent of the clause is usually added, and it must be added if the contradiction is positive; so in (h) we could not have just *yes* as a rejoinder (and *cf* (e) above). The same pattern is found following a command; we may have *yes* or *no* alone, but if *yes* occurs following a negative command, and therefore signals a refusal, it must be accompanied by the Modal element of the clause:

[4:127] j. Don't tell anyone what you saw! – Yes, I will.

k. Don't let's go back! – Yes, let's.

All these rejoinders could be 'filled out' in a non-elliptical form. But the pattern which is most typical of ordinary dialogue is that described here, with just one element made explicit, and the remainder presupposed. This use of ellipsis to express the cohesive relation between a rejoinder and the utterances which preceded it, in sequences which are not structured as question–answer, is a very characteristic aspect of the texture of linguistic interaction.

4.4.4 Ellipsis in 'reporting-reported' sequences

There is one further context for clausal ellipsis, that of reported speech. The type of ellipsis found in this context is closely related to some of the instances that we have already met, particularly the 'commentary' type of indirect response [4:119], and the elliptical WH- question as rejoinder [4:126]. Here therefore we shall not be introducing a new type of elliptical structure, but bringing together various instances already met with which have something in common.

What they have in common is the feature REPORTED, which is present in indirect speech: that is, indirect statements, yes/no questions and WH-questions. These are exemplified in their full form in the second clauses of [4:128a, b and c] respectively:

[4:128] John didn't tell me
- a. (that) he was coming.
- b. if/whether he was coming (or not).
- c. why he was coming.

It is perhaps important to point out that the speech function of the report (statement, yes/no question, WH- question) is a feature of the whole complex, even if the same verb (*eg: tell*) occurs in all types. The reported clause itself makes no independent selection of mood, and examples such as *I asked John why was he late* or *I asked Mary would she enjoy it* are not true interrogatives, as shown by the fact that, in the following, (a1): (a2) and (b1): (b2) are not proportional:

(1)	(2)
(a) you'll enjoy it	will you enjoy it?
(b) I asked Mary if she'd enjoy it.	I asked Mary would she enjoy it.

4.4.4.1 INDIRECT WH- QUESTIONS

If the reported clause is an indirect WH- question, it can be elliptical in the same way as its equivalent direct question, the WH- type interrogative clause. For example:

[4:129] a. Who could have broken those tiles? – I can't think who.
b. I said you would mend it for him. – I hope you didn't say when.
c. The jewels are missing. – I wonder what else.
d. They still have some copies in stock. – Did you ask how many?

The target of presupposition is not, of course, the immediately preceding clause, which would be the reporting one, but the preceding sentence; *eg* in (a) *who* presupposes . . . *could have broken those tiles* and not *I can't think*. This is possible because a reported clause is not embedded; the reporting-reported structure is a hypotactic one (*cf* 3.4.2 above; also 4.3.6, [4:94] and [4:95]), and therefore the reported clause can reach out beyond the bounds of the sentence in which it occurs.

The conditions under which elliptical forms tend to occur in indirect questions are those we have already met with in explaining ellipsis in direct questions (*cf* [4:126] above). The 'echo' type occurs where the presupposed clause was itself a WH- question, as in [4:129a]; here however the elliptical clause does not take a rising tone (tone 2), since it is not itself interrogative. In [4:129b] a new element is added which was absent from the clause that is presupposed. In (c) and (d) an element already present in the presupposed clause is offered for expansion, either by coordination (c) or by further specification (d). Characteristically in the last instance the item in the presupposed clause is a non-specific form, with *some-* (*someone, something,* etc), or the indefinite article or other non-specific deictic (see 4.2.3.2 above).

As in a direct question, all features and elements of the presupposed clause are carried over unless repudiated. The presupposed elements may include part of a nominal or prepositional group where the WH- item is a modifier such as *which, whose, how many*; in an example such as [4:129d], in addition to the clausal ellipsis there is also nominal ellipsis, since *how many* could be filled out as *how many copies*. The mood of the presupposed clause is always repudiated, by the WH- item itself. Other elements also are sometimes repudiated, particularly the finite operator; in such instances, however, the WH- clause normally has to be non-elliptical, unless the WH- element is the Subject (which allows for propositional ellipsis) as in *Who's going to lead the way? – I can't think who could.*

4.4.4.2 INDIRECT YES/NO QUESTIONS
If the reported clause is a yes/no question, the most usual elliptical form of it is simply zero:

[4:130] a. Was that an earthquake? – I don't know.
      b. I wonder whether England won the cup. Have you heard?

All features of the presupposed clause are carried over. (All, that is, except the polarity. Polarity has a special meaning in a yes/no question, different from its meaning elsewhere; it expresses the questioner's attitude to the question, as in *Don't you know?* meaning 'I'm surprised', 'you ought to know'. In an indirect question which is elliptical, the polarity is simply neutralized.)

In these instances the presupposed clause is itself a question, direct or indirect, and we could conclude that this feature is also presupposed in the elliptical clause. It is not necessary for the presupposed clause to be a question, however, in order for the ellipsis to be interpreted in this way. If the verb in the reporting clause is one that introduces a question, such as *ask*, then the elliptical reported clause will be interpreted as a question whatever the mood of the presupposed clause. In [4:131a] the indirect yes/no question *whether he was or not* is entirely omitted by ellipsis even though the presupposed clause is not a question of any kind:

[4:131] a. John was very disappointed by the response. You can ask him.

A more usual type is that in which there is a modality in the presupposed clause:

[4:131] b. She might be better living away from home. I'm not sure.

– and these in turn are related, as was pointed out in the context of the discussion of clausal substitution (3.4.1.1), to elliptical modalized clauses in which everything except the modality is presupposed:

[4:131] c. I wonder if it'll rain on the day of the picnic. – Probably.

4.4.4.3 INDIRECT STATEMENTS
For an indirect statement, there is no equivalent elliptical form containing just the marker of the feature 'statement'. Here the cohesive form of the reported clause is the substitute *so*, or its negative *not*, as in

[4:132] I thought Mary was leaving today. – She hasn't said so.

This has been discussed in 3.4.1.1. The elliptical form is again simply zero, as in

[4:133] a. This mango is ripe. I know from its colour.
      b. England won the cup. – Who told you?

Again the whole of the presupposed clause is carried over, including the polarity; but an elliptical indirect statement of this kind does not necessarily follow immediately after the presupposed clause, and the exact domain of the presupposition is sometimes rather uncertain. Consider for example

[4:134] a. John's new cabinet is beautiful. I've seen it being made. You can tell him.

Does this mean 'you can tell him it's beautiful', or 'you can tell him I've seen it being made', or both? If we expand the second sentence to

[4:134] b. John's new cabinet is beautiful. I've seen it being made; it's nearly finished. You can tell him.

the amount of uncertainty becomes even greater. Even where there is no doubt which clause is presupposed, there may still be some more room for uncertainty, usually centring around the expression of modality; for example

[4:135] a. He hasn't finished. – I should have known.

$$\text{You can go home.} \left\{ \begin{array}{l} \text{b. Didn't you know?} \\ \text{c. No one will know.} \end{array} \right.$$

Here (a) might mean either 'I should have known that he hadn't' or 'I should have known that he wouldn't'. More clearly still, whereas (b) means 'didn't you know that you can?', (c) means 'no one will know that you have gone'. The pattern of determination here is not easy to sort out.

4.4.4.4 AMBIGUITY BETWEEN INDIRECT STATEMENTS AND INDIRECT QUESTIONS

Fundamentally this is the same kind of ambiguity as may arise between a statement and a yes/no question if the reporting verb is one that can introduce either, such as *tell, say, report, know*, and the reported clause is omitted by ellipsis. For example, in

[4:136] a. I think the cheque is still valid. The Bank can tell them.

it is not clear whether the meaning is 'the Bank can tell them that the cheque is still valid' or 'the Bank can tell them whether the cheque is still valid or not'. Again, it is not easy to state exactly what the relevant factors are; but the following examples would presumably not be ambiguous:

[4:136] b. The cheque is still valid. The Bank can tell them. (='that it is')

The cheque may still be valid. $\left\{\begin{array}{l}\text{c. The Bank can tell them.}\\ \quad(=\text{'whether it is'})\\ \text{d. The Bank told me.}\\ \quad(=\text{'that it may be'})\end{array}\right.$

With *say* the 'zero' form of the reported clause nearly always presupposes a question: *he didn't say* is likely to mean 'whether . . .', not 'that . . .'. But with other verbs, and also with some adjectives such as *clear*, the presupposed clause may be either question or statement. There is perhaps a tendency here for a 'zero' reported clause to be interpreted as a question if the reporting clause is negative, as it frequently is with these ambiguous expressions (*it isn't clear, he didn't say* are more likely to occur on their own as reporting-reported structures than *it is clear, he said*); on the other hand, whereas *I don't know* is probably 'whether . . .', *I didn't know* is more likely to be 'that . . .'. As [4:136] shows, various factors both in the reporting clause and in the presupposed clause seem to be relevant to the interpretation.

4.4.4.5 REPORTS AND FACTS IN RELATION TO CLAUSAL ELLIPSIS

We should distinguish here between reported clauses and 'fact' clauses (*cf* above, 3.4.1.1). A REPORT clause, as already noted, is related hypotactically to the clause that contains the reporting verb; a sentence such as *John said Mary was leaving* consists of two clauses, the second dependent on (*ie* hypotactically related to) the first. A FACT clause is embedded, in the strict sense of downgraded in rank, or 'rankshifted'; the sentence *John predicted that Mary was leaving* CONSISTS OF only one clause, which has embedded within it another one that no longer functions as a clause but functions as a nominal. There are various differences between report and fact, which were summarized earlier (3.4.1.1); note that some verbs can occur with either. Because of the structural difference between the two, a reported clause can be expressed cohesively through substitution or ellipsis, whereas a fact clause cannot. We have seen that there is no ellipsis of single elements in the structure of the clause; a fact clause, being embedded, functions as a single element, and hence cannot be omitted on its own. This explains why we cannot say

[4:137] a. The opportunity has now been lost. – I sincerely regret.

A fact clause can on the other hand be expressed cohesively, as all single elements of the clause can, by means of reference; so [4:137b] is quite acceptable:

[4:137] b. The opportunity has now been lost. – I sincerely regret it/the fact.

4.4.5 Clausal ellipsis and clause complexes

Two or more clauses that are directly related in structure (as distinct from being related indirectly through rankshift) are said to form a CLAUSE COMPLEX. A clause complex may be either PARATACTIC or HYPO-TACTIC. In a paratactic clause complex the clauses have equal status. The relevant paratactic relation is that of coordination, ie 'and' and 'or'; there are two others, namely apposition and quotation, but we can ignore them here. In a hypotactic complex the clauses have unequal status. There are three types of hypotactic relation in the clause: CONDITION (expressed by clauses of condition, concession, cause, purpose, etc), ADDITION (expressed by the non-defining relative clause) and REPORT. Paratactic and hypotactic structures may combine freely in a single clause complex.

We conclude this chapter with a few observations on clausal ellipsis in clause complexes. This is a big topic, and we have not attempted to treat it in full. We confine ourselves to types of clausal ellipsis not covered by the discussion on verbal ellipsis; essentially to question–answer, and reporting-reported sequences.

The general principle is clear: an elliptical clause of whatever type may presuppose any clause in a complex, and will then automatically presuppose in addition all clauses that are contingent on it: that is, all that come after it (if paratactic) and all that are dependent on it (if hypotactic). So for example:

[4:138] a. Smith was going to take part, but somebody telephoned and asked to see him urgently so he had to withdraw. – Who?
b. I kept quiet because Mary gets very embarrassed if anyone mentions John's name. I don't know why.

In (a), which is paratactic, *who?* coheres with *somebody*; the presupposed clause is *somebody telephoned*, and the remainder of the sentence also falls within the domain of the presupposition: the meaning is 'who telephoned and asked to see him urgently such that he had to withdraw?'. Likewise in the hypotactic example (b), the meaning is 'I don't know why Mary gets embarrassed if anyone mentions John's name'. The first clause, in each case, is outside the domain of what is presupposed.

However, there are a number of restrictions and limitations on this principle, as well as possible sources of ambiguity within it. Ambiguity may arise because it is uncertain which is the clause that is being presupposed, for example

[4:139] a. So you knew the lawyer was responsible. I hadn't realized.

meaning 'that you knew . . .' or 'that the lawyer was responsible'. Compare

[4:139] b. I finished writing that story and it's going to be published. – When?

meaning 'when did you finish . . .?' or 'when is it going to be published?'. A number of factors come in to determine what is the likely interpretation. Some of them are quite specific; for example, if *I* in [4:139a] is stressed contrastively (tone 4), the second interpretation becomes overwhelmingly probable: 'YOU knew that the lawyer was responsible, but I didn't'. But there are also some general considerations. There is a tendency to presuppose what is nearer; that is, to presuppose an element that occurs later in the clause complex rather than an earlier one, especially if the later one is rather long. (This makes the contrast between a clause complex and a simple clause with embedding (rankshift) in it even greater. Embedded clauses tend to occur in later positions; and since they cannot be presupposed, the target of presupposition in such cases tends to be towards the beginning. Compare [4:94] above; [4:94b] is a hypotactic clause complex, whereas in [4:94a], which is a simple clause with embedding, the appropriate rejoinder would be *Didn't he?*, presupposing *the policeman*.) In particular it is unusual to presuppose a dependent clause that precedes the clause on which it is dependent; an example such as [4:140a] is rather unlikely, although there are instances, such as [4:140b], which seem to pose no problem:

[4:140] a. Seeing that Mary's left something behind I really think we should turn round and go back to the hotel. I'm not sure what.
   b. Unless he gives up one of his bishops he's going to be in trouble. It doesn't matter which.

Often an indefinite form such as *somebody* is such a clear invitation to presupposition that its presence is sufficient to override any limiting tendencies of one kind or another. In a very complex structure there are many clauses which would be potential candidates for presupposition, and for precisely that reason presupposition by ellipsis tends to be avoided, since it would lead to too much ambiguity; moreover the clauses which occur later in the complex, and are therefore more accessible from the point of view of distance, are also, in the case of hypotaxis, at greater depth and therefore from another point of view less accessible – because an elliptical clause which presupposed them could not be filled out. A sentence such as [4:141 a] is intractable in this respect:

[4:141] a. I shall be cross if you break that vase, which was a present from my boy friend. – Which?

– if *Which?* means 'which boy friend?' the 'filled out' form would presumably be *Which boy friend was that vase, if I break which you will be cross, a present from?* Nevertheless, given a clear invitation to presupposition in the presupposed complex, such instances become possible; if, for example, the first sentence of [4:141a] ended *which was a present from someone I love*, the rejoinder *Who?* would cause no difficulty; compare [4:141b and c]:

[4:141] b. I'd like you to look at the painting, which my wife picked up somewhere in the country. – Where?
c. Smith said if he could afford it he was going to buy the next-door house and rent it to someone he knew so as to keep it from being pulled down to make way for a block of flats. – Who?

Presupposition of a paratactic clause complex by clausal ellipsis is possible only if all clauses following the one that is presupposed are within the domain of the presupposition. In practice this usually means that they must be branched; that is, they must share at least one element in common, typically though not necessarily the Subject. So we can accept [4:142a], but hardly [4:142b]:

[4:142] a. I left my books here and somebody came in and either borrowed them or put them back on the shelf but didn't say a word to me. I wish I could find out who.
b. I left my books here and somebody complained and the librarian put them back on the shelf but didn't say a word to me. I wish I could find out who.

However, the conditions which determine acceptability are by no means clear. It does not always turn out as expected, and presupposition can extend over a considerable structural distance. We have often cited examples from *Alice* (and *cf* example [3:40] in this connection), so perhaps the last word should remain with her:

[4:143] 'And who are these?' said the Queen, pointing to the three gardeners who were lying round the rose-tree; for, you see, as they were lying on their faces, and the pattern on their backs was the same as the rest of the pack, she could not tell whether they were gardeners, or soldiers, or courtiers, or three of her own children. 'How should *I* know?' said Alice.

Chapter 5

Conjunction

5.1 Conjunction and other cohesive relations

The fourth and final type of cohesive relation that we find in the grammar is that of conjunction. Conjunction is rather different in nature from the other cohesive relations, from both reference, on the one hand, and substitution and ellipsis on the other. It is not simply an anaphoric relation.

Conjunctive elements are cohesive not in themselves but indirectly, by virtue of their specific meanings; they are not primarily devices for reaching out into the preceding (or following) text, but they express certain meanings which presuppose the presence of other components in the discourse.

Where is conjunction located, within the total framework of text-forming relations? Instances of reference, substitution and ellipsis are, on the whole, rather clearly identifiable, perhaps unusually so for linguistic phenomena; there is some indeterminacy among them, and also between them and other structural relations within a text, but this is relatively slight, and we have rarely been in doubt as to the boundaries of the phenomena being described. This is much less true of conjunction, which is not definable in such clearcut terms. Perhaps the most strictly cohesive relation is that of substitution, including ellipsis. Substitution is a purely textual relation, with no other function than that of cohering one piece of text to another. The substitute, or elliptical structure, signals in effect 'supply the appropriate word or words already available'; it is a grammatical relation, one which holds between the words and structures themselves rather than relating them through their meanings. Next in this order comes reference, which is a semantic relation, one which holds between meanings rather than between linguistic forms; it is not the replacement of some linguistic element by a counter or by a blank, as are substitution and ellipsis, but rather a direction for interpreting an element in terms of its environment – and since the environment includes the text (the linguistic environment), reference takes on a cohesive function. A reference item signals 'supply the appropriate instantial meaning, the referent in this instance, which is already available (or shortly to become available)'; and one source of its availability is the preceding (or following) text. With conjunction, on the other hand, we move into a different type of semantic relation, one which is no longer any kind of a search instruction, but a specification of the way in which what is to follow is systematically connected to what has gone before.

In a sense this is putting it rather too concretely. The conjunctive relations themselves are not tied to any particular sequence in the expression; if two sentences cohere into a text by virtue of some form of conjunction, this does not mean that the relation between them could subsist only if they occur in that particular order. This is true even of a conjunctive relation which is itself intrinsically ordered, such as succession in time; two sentences may be linked by a time relation, but the sentence referring to the event that is earlier in time may itself come later, following the other sentence. When we are considering these sentences specifically from the point of view of cohesion, however, we are inevitably concerned with their actual sequence as expressed, because cohesion is the relation between sentences in a text, and the sentences of a text can only follow one after the other. Hence in describing conjunction as a cohesive device, we are focusing attention not on the semantic relations as such, as realized throughout the grammar of the language, but on one particular aspect of them, namely the function they have of relating to each other linguistic elements that occur in succession but are not related by other, structural means.

5.1.1. Structural equivalents of conjunctive relations

There is a range of different structural guises in which the relations that we are here calling CONJUNCTIVE may appear. These relations constitute a highly generalized component within the semantic system, with reflexes spread throughout the language, taking various forms; and their cohesive potential derives from this source. Because they represent very general relations that may be associated with different threads of meaning at different places in the fabric of language, it follows that when they are expressed on their own, unaccompanied by other explicit connecting factors, they have a highly cohesive effect.

Let us take as an example the relation already mentioned above, that of succession in time. This appears in many different realizations, according to the other semantic patterns with which it is associated. It may, first of all, be embodied in a predication, as in [5:1a]; here the verb *follow* means 'occur subsequently in time'. Note that the same relation can be expressed, still as a predication but with the terms reversed, by making the verb passive, or using a different verb *precede*. Secondly, the relation of succession in time can be expressed as a minor predication; that is, it may be realized prepositionally, as in [5:1b]. Again the relationship could be viewed from either direction, with *before* instead of *after*.

Thirdly, time sequence may be expressed as a relationship between predications, with one clause being shown as dependent on another by means of a conjunction as in [5:1c]; sometimes, but not in all instances, the same words may occur both as conjunction and as preposition. Finally, in [5:1d], we have two separate sentences. Here there is no structural relationship at all; but the two parts are still linked by the same logical relations of succession in time.

[5:1] a. A snowstorm followed the battle. (The battle was followed by a snowstorm.)
b. After the battle, there was a snowstorm.
c. After they had fought a battle, it snowed.
d. They fought a battle. Afterwards, it snowed.

Contrast the following:

[5:1] a'. A snowstorm preceded the battle.
b'. Before the battle, there had been a snowstorm.
c'. Before they fought a battle, it had snowed.
d'. They fought a battle. Previously, it had snowed.

In (d) and (d'), the relation of sequence in time is expressed by an adverb, functioning as Adjunct, and occurring initially in the second sentence. Here the time relation is now the only explicit form of connection between the two events, which in the other examples are linked also by various structural relationships. The time sequence has now become a cohesive agent, and it is this, the semantic relation in its cohesive function, that we are referring to as CONJUNCTION. The Adjunct will be referred to as a CONJUNCTIVE, CONJUNCTIVE ADJUNCT or DISCOURSE ADJUNCT.

It is not always possible to find a complete set of structures on the above model to express each one of the set of relations we are interested in, especially if we take account of all their subcategories. But this example is not untypical, and there will always be some form of alternative realization whereby the relations that figure as conjunctive, in the formation of text, can also be systematically embodied in various types of structure. The significance of this fact is that it allows us to recognize that, although for example in [5:1d] the cohesion is achieved through the conjunctive expression *afterwards*, it is the underlying semantic relation of succession in time that actually has the cohesive power. This explains how it is that we are often prepared to recognize the presence of a relation of this kind even when it is not expressed overtly at all. We are prepared to supply it for ourselves, and thus to assume that there is cohesion even though it has not been explicitly demonstrated.

Here is another example, this time of the relation of ADVERSITY:

[5:2] b. He fell asleep, in spite of his great discomfort.
     c. Although he was very uncomfortable, he fell asleep.
     d. He was very uncomfortable. Nevertheless he fell asleep.

It is not obvious whether there is an example corresponding to [5:1a], but perhaps

[5:2] a. His great discomfort did not prevent him from falling asleep.

might be accepted as equivalent. On the other hand, here we could certainly add others, with the discomfort being expressed in a non-finite clause:

[5:2] e. Despite being very uncomfortable, he fell asleep.
     f. Being very uncomfortable, he still fell asleep.

The semantic relationship remains an adversative one throughout.

Not only does the semantic relation remain the same; so do the elements related by it. In [5:1] the two phenomena that are related by succession in time are both processes, and they remain so throughout, even though both of them, the fighting and the snowing, appear now as verbs and now as nouns. In [5:2], one is a process and the other a state; again they remain constant, though appearing in different grammatical forms. This in turn strengthens still further the cohesive potential of the relation in question. The speaker of the language recognizes that the same phenomenon may appear in different structural shapes and sizes; and he is aware that certain types of phenomena are likely to be linked to one another by certain types of meaning relation.

There is one further form of expression to be considered. We might have

[5:1] g. They fought a battle. After that, it snowed.

[5:2] g. He was very uncomfortable. Despite this, he fell asleep.

Here we have, in each case, two sentences, so the link between them is cohesive, as in (d), and not structural. But the cohesion is provided by the reference items *this* and *that*. The words *after* and *despite*, taken on their own, express the relations of time sequence and adversity, as in [5:1b] and [5:2b]; but it is only through their structural association with *this* and *that* that they serve a cohesive function in the given instance. It is the reference items that relate the second sentence to the preceding one.

5.1.2 *Types of conjunctive expression*

With any of the conjunctive relations in question, provided there is a preposition to express it this preposition can always be made to govern a reference item; the resulting prepositional group will then function as a cohesive Adjunct. It is a moot point whether such instances should be treated as conjunction or as reference. Strictly speaking, they belong with reference, because they depend on the presence of a reference item following the preposition. But since they involve relations which also function cohesively when expressed WITHOUT the accompaniment of reference items, it is simpler to include them within the general heading of conjunction. Besides this, there are a number of what are now conjunctive adverbs which, although not made up of a preposition plus a reference item in the contemporary language, have their origin in this construction at an earlier stage: words like *therefore* and *thereby* (and compare those based on the WH- form like *whereupon, whereat*). We no longer feel that these have a demonstrative in them, and this suggests that even in analytic forms such as *after that* we respond to the cohesive force of the phrase as a whole rather than singling out *that* as an anaphoric element on its own.

Furthermore many conjunctive expressions occur in two more or less synonymous forms, one with and the other without a demonstrative. These are the ones which have the same form both as preposition and as adverb, corresponding to [5:1d and g], respectively; or, more accurately (since many are not adverbs but prepositional phrases, like *as a result*), which occur as Adjunct, either alone or followed by a preposition, usually *of*, plus *this/that*: for example *instead (of that)*, *as a result (of that)*, *in consequence (of that)*. It would seem rather artificial to suggest that *as a result* and *as a result of that* represent two quite different types of cohesion. So we shall assume that both of them are to be included under the heading of conjunction, the criterion being that already adopted, or implied: given a particular semantic relation which CAN operate conjunctively (*ie* which takes on a cohesive function when expressed on its own), then any expression of that relation, with or without a demonstrative or other reference item, will be considered to fall within the category of conjunction.

In general, therefore, conjunctive adjuncts will be of three kinds:

(1) adverbs, including:
    simple adverbs ('coordinating conjunctions'), *eg: but, so, then, next*
    compound adverbs in *-ly*, *eg: accordingly, subsequently, actually*
    compound adverbs in *there-* and *where-*, *eg: therefore, thereupon, whereat*
(2) other compound adverbs, *eg: furthermore, nevertheless, anyway, instead, besides*
    prepositional phrases, *eg: on the contrary, as a result, in addition*
(3) prepositional expressions with *that* or other reference item, the latter being (i) optional, *eg: as a result of that, instead of that, in addition to that,* or (ii) obligatory, *eg: in spite of that, because of that.*

The reference item, in (3), is not necessarily a demonstrative functioning on its own as Head; there may be a nominal group with noun Head, the demonstrative or other reference item functioning as Deictic. In order for the total expression to be conjunctive, any form of reference will serve provided it is anaphoric. In [5:3] the expression *as a result of his enquiries* is not conjunctive, since the reference item *his* is cataphoric to *the Inspector*:

[5:3] Jones had been missing for five weeks. As a result of his enquiries, the Inspector was convinced he had left the country.

All the following examples, however, do exhibit cohesion, the expressions beginning with *as a result* all being conjunctive adjuncts:

[5:4] The captain had steered a course close in to the shore.

    a. As a result,
    b. As a result of this, } they avoided the worst of the
    c. As a result of this move, } storm.
    d. As a result of his caution,

If, on the other hand, the second sentence had been

[5:4] e. They were heartily thankful for his caution.

it would still have been cohesive but not by conjunction. The cohesion would be achieved by reference, through the word *his*: there is no conjunctive element (*for his caution* is specifically dependent on *thankful*, which determines the preposition *for*). The meaning is not 'as a result, they were heartily thankful', but rather 'they applauded his caution'. As always, the line between specific instances will be hard to draw in practice; there will be borderline cases, such as

[5:4] f. For his caution he was highly commended.

In the last resort it does not matter, since the effect is cohesive anyway; but a speaker of English is probably aware here of two rather different kinds of texture, even though in some instances he may recognize that he is faced with a mixture of the two.

If the conjunctive is a prepositional expression, such as *because of this*, it will often be possible to find an adverb that is roughly equivalent in meaning (*eg: therefore*). This is because conjunctions express one or other of a small number of very general relations, and it is the conjunctive relation rather than the particular nominal Complement following the preposition that provides the relevant link to the preceding sentence. This Complement, as we have seen, is frequently a purely anaphoric one, typically a demonstrative, *this* or *that;* or, if it is a noun, it is quite likely to be a general noun (of the type described in 6.1 below; *cf: move* in [5:4c] above), which does no more than make explicit the anaphoric function of the whole phrase.

A conjunctive adjunct normally has first position in the sentence (some exceptions are noted below), and has as its domain the whole of the sentence in which it occurs: that is to say, its meaning extends over the entire sentence, unless it is repudiated. However, as evidenced by the indeterminacy, or perhaps flexibility, of our punctuation system, the sentence itself is a very indeterminate category, and it is very common to find conjunctive adjuncts occurring in written English following a colon or semicolon. In terms of our definition of cohesion, if we take the orthographic sentence strictly as it stands, such instances would not be cohesive, since cohesion is a relation between sentences, not a relation within the sentence. But the conjunction has the effect of repudiating – that is, of setting a limit to the domain of – any other conjunction that has occurred previously in sentence-initial position. So for example in

[5:5] So Alice picked him up very gently, and lifted him across more slowly than she had lifted the Queen, that she mightn't take his breath away: but, before she put him on the table, she thought she might as well dust him a little, he was so covered in ashes.

the *but* following the colon presupposes the first part of the sentence; it therefore cancels out the *so* at the beginning, defining the limit of its domain. It would be equally possible, and with very little difference in meaning, to start a new sentence at *but*.

In considering spoken English, we can define the sentence in such a way that this problem does not arise: if we say that a new sentence starts whenever there is no structural connection with what has gone before, then in all such instances there will be a sentence boundary before the conjunction, and the general principle stated above (that a conjunction occurs in first position and has the whole sentence as its domain) will remain valid. But it would be arbitrary to impose this definition on written English, which has its own conventions, including that whereby the notion of a sentence (as written, *ie* extending from capital letter to full stop) is not bound by structural considerations, but takes in other factors as well – being exploited particularly by many writers to reflect patterns of intonation. Hence we have to recognize that in many instances there will be a conjunctive expression in the middle of a sentence, presupposing a previous clause in the same sentence. We saw earlier that there can be instances of anaphoric reference and substitution where the presupposed item is also to be found within the same sentence as the anaphoric one; here too, although for different reasons, elements that create texture by bringing about cohesion between sentences also reinforce the internal texture that exists within the sentence itself.

5.2 Some common conjunctive elements

5.2.1 The 'and' relation

The simplest form of conjunction is 'and'.

Strictly speaking the two elementary logical relations of 'and' and 'or' are structural rather than conjunctive. That is to say, they are incorporated into linguistic structure, being realized in the form of a particular structural relation, that of COORDINATION. Coordination is a structure of the paratactic type (see 4.4.5 above). The 'and' relation is felt to be structural and not cohesive, at least by mature speakers; this is why we feel a little uncomfortable at finding a sentence in written English beginning with *And*, and why we tend not to consider that a child's composition having *and* as its dominant sentence linker can really be said to form a cohesive whole.

However, it is a fact that the word *and* is used cohesively, to link one sentence to another, and not only by children (*cf* 5.5 below). The 'and' relation has to be included among the semantic relations entering into the general category of conjunction. What distinguishes the two is that, in its elementary logical form, this relation is expressed through the medium of linguistic structure. The word *and* is the marker of this structural relation. It is not an Adjunct; in fact it has no status as a constituent at all. It is merely a structure signal.

The coordination relation which is represented by the word *and* may obtain between pairs (or among sets) of items functioning more or less anywhere in the structure of the language. They may be nouns, or nominal groups; verbs, or verbal groups; adverbs, or adverbial or prepositional groups; or they may be clauses. A pair or a set of items which are joined by coordination functions as a single COMPLEX element of structure: as noun complex, nominal group complex, verbal group complex, clause complex, and so on. They function in the same way as the equivalent SIMPLE elements: that is to say, a nominal group complex, for example, functions in the structure of the clause in exactly the same way as does a nominal group.

Compared with its scope as a structure, the scope of the 'and' relation as a form of conjunction is somewhat modified and extended. We shall refer to the conjunctive 'and' by the more general term ADDITIVE, to suggest something rather looser and less structural than is meant by COORDINATE. Thus the coordinate relation is structural, whereas the additive relation is cohesive. The additive is a generalized semantic relation in the text-forming component of the semantic system, that is based on the logical notion of 'and'; and it is one of a small set of four such relations that we are grouping together under the heading of conjunction.

When the 'and' relation operates conjunctively, between sentences, to give cohesion to a text – or rather to create text, by cohering one sentence to another – it is restricted to just a pair of sentences. This provides an indication of the difference between 'and' as a structural relation (coordinate) and 'and' as a cohesive relation (additive). A coordinate item such as *men and women* functions as a single whole; it constitutes a single element in the structure of a larger unit, for example Subject in a clause. There is no reason why this potentiality should be limited to two items; we may have three, as in *men, women and children*, or even more. And if we have more than two, we may, or may not, structure them further by introducing layering, as in *men and women, and boys and girls*, which is '((men and women) and (boys and girls))'. There is no fixed limit either to the depth or to the extent of coordinate structures.

With 'and' as a conjunctive relation, on the other hand, the situation is quite different. Here the relation is between sentences, and sentences follow one another one at a time as the text unfolds; they cannot be rearranged, as a coordinate structure can, in different sequences and different bracketings, *eg: women and men*, or *men and boys, and women and girls*. So there is no question of linking a whole set of sentences together by a single 'and' relation. Each new sentence either is or is not linked to its predecessor, as an independent fact; and if it is, 'and' (the additive relation) is one way in which it may be so linked. For example,

> [5:6] 'I wonder if all the things move along with us?', thought poor puzzled Alice. And the Queen seemed to guess her thoughts, for she cried 'Faster! Don't try to talk!'

The next sentence, in turn, might also be linked by 'and' type cohesion: but if it is, it will simply be linked on to the second one. The three will not form a single whole. If they had done, it would have been possible to omit the *and* between all but the last pair, as in a coordinate series like *men, women and children*. Sets of sentences of this kind do in fact occur, under certain circumstances: particularly if they are closely parallel in structure and meaning. But in such cases they are not really interpretable as separate sentences. The following example, although punctuated as sentences, is really more like a set of coordinate clauses:

> [5:7] 'At the end of *three* yards I shall repeat them – for fear of your forgetting them. At the end of *four*, I shall say goodbye. And at the end of *five*, I shall go!'

5.2.2 *Coordinate* and *and conjunctive* and

The typical context for a conjunctive *and* is one in which there is a total, or almost total, shift in the participants from one sentence to the next, and yet the two sentences are very definitely part of a text. For example

> [5:8] He heaved the rock aside with all his strength. And there in the recesses of a deep hollow lay a glittering heap of treasure.

In narrative fiction such a shift occurs characteristically at the boundary of dialogue and narrative:

> [5:9] 'While you're refreshing yourself,' said the Queen, 'I'll just take the measurements.' And she took a ribbon out of her pocket, marked in inches . . .

A slightly different use, and one in which the cohesive *and* comes perhaps closest to the structural function it has in coordination, is that which indicates 'next in a series (of things to be said)'. This is the INTERNAL sense described in 5.3 below. Here it very often links a series of questions, meaning 'the next thing I want to know is . . .'. There is an excellent example of this in Alice's interrogation of Humpty Dumpty concerning the meaning of Jabberwocky; it is too long to quote in full, but the following extract will show the pattern:

[5:10] 'I see it now,' Alice remarked thoughtfully: 'and what are "*toves*"?'
'Well, "*toves*" are something like badgers – they're something like lizards – and they're something like corkscrews.'
'They must be very curious creatures.'
'They are that,' said Humpty Dumpty: 'also they make their nests under sun-dials – also they live on cheese.'
'And what's to "*gyre*" and to "*gimble*"?'
'To "*gyre*" is to go round and round like a gyroscope. To "*gimble*" is to make holes like a gimlet.'
'And "*the wabe*" is the grass plot round a sun-dial, I suppose?' said Alice, surprised at her own ingenuity.

Or it links a series of points all contributing to one general argument. In this function 'and' perhaps carries over some of the RETROSPECTIVE effect that it has as a coordinator, as in *men, women and children*.

This retrospective function is in fact rather significant. (Perhaps 'retrojective' might be a better word for it, suggesting the appropriate sense of 'projecting backwards'.) In a series such as *men, women and children*, or *Tom, Dick and Harry*, the meaning of *and* is projected backwards so that we interpret as 'men and women and children', 'Tom and Dick and Harry'. (Since much use is being made in this section of the distinction between italics and quotation marks, it may be helpful to give a reminder: a word, or longer piece, that is in italics indicates a 'wording', an item of the language; one in quotation marks indicates a meaning.) This phenomenon of projecting backwards occurs only with the two elementary logical relations of 'and' and 'or', which are the only ones expressed in the form of coordination; parallel to *Tom, Dick and Harry* we have *Tom, Dick or Harry* where the 'or' is also projected backwards, giving the meaning 'Tom or Dick or Harry'. The phenomenon is not limited to strings of words, but is common to all coordinate structures, for example a series such as the following:

[5:11] The balls were live hedgehogs, the mallets live flamingoes, and the soldiers had to double themselves up and to stand upon their hands and feet, to make the arches.

Summarizing, the logical 'and' and 'or' relations differ from the wider set of textual relations that enter into cohesion, in the following ways:

(1) They are expressed structurally, in the form of coordination.
(2) They are retrospective, in the sense just explained.
(3) They have correlative forms *both . . . and*, and *either . . . or*.
(4) They have a negative form *nor* (= 'and not'), together with its correlative *neither . . . nor* (= 'both not . . . and not').

5.2.3 *Other conjunctive elements:* but, yet, so *and* then

The retrospective power of *and* provides a useful insight into the meaning of certain other words, especially *but*. The word *but* expresses a relation which is not additive but ADVERSATIVE. However, in addition to the meaning 'adversative', *but* contains within itself also the logical meaning of 'and'; it is a sort of portmanteau, or shorthand form, of *and however*. The evidence for this is the fact that *but* is also retrospective – but the meaning which it projects in this way is not 'but' but 'and'. Consider the example

[5:12] The eldest son worked on the farm, the second son worked in the blacksmith's shop, but the youngest son left home to seek his fortune.

This has to be interpreted as 'the eldest son worked on the farm and the second . . .'. The fact that *but* contains 'and' is the reason why we cannot say *and but*, although we can say *and yet, and so, and then*, etc. It also explains why the construction *Although . . ., but . . .*, so frequently used by non-native speakers of English, is wrong: a structure cannot be both hypotactic and coordinate (paratactic) at the same time.

The words *yet*, *so* and *then* do not normally project backwards in this way, although they can do in rare instances. In general they do not include any component of 'and'; instead they frequently COMBINE with *and*, as mentioned above. In fact, when the word *and* occurs at the beginning of a new sentence it is very often accompanied by another conjunctive word or phrase, the two together functioning as a single element. The second conjunction may be one expressing a different textual relation from the *and* (such as the adversative *yet*), or it may itself also be additive; so we find not only *and yet, and so, and then, and anyway*, but also *and also, and furthermore, and in addition*.

The different types of conjunctive relation that enter into cohesion are listed in the next section. They are not the same as the elementary logical relations that are expressed through the structural medium of coordination. Conjunction, in other words, is not simply coordination extended so as to operate between sentences. As we saw in 5.1 (examples [5:1] and [5:2]), at least some of the conjunctive relations have equivalents in very different types of structure, such as predication within the clause and hypotaxis between clauses; these are quite unrelated to coordination. There are other conjunctive relations which are closer to coordination; in particular the ADDITIVE, to which the closest parallel among the structural relations is the coordinate 'and'. But this is still not the same thing; the additive relation is a complex one including components of emphasis which are absent from the elementary 'and' relation. The same holds for the coordinate relation 'or'; there is a cohesive category related to 'or', expressed by conjunctions such as *instead*, but it is also a mixture, with other elements present in it. The conjunctive relations are not logical but textual; they represent the generalized types of connection that we recognize as holding between sentences. What these connections are depends in the last resort on the meanings that sentences express, and essentially these are of two kinds: experiential, representing the linguistic interpretation of experience, and interpersonal, representing participation in the speech situation. In the remaining sections of this chapter we attempt to outline the various types of conjunction, with some typical examples of each.

5.3 Types of conjunction

Various suggestions could be taken up for classifying the phenomena which we are grouping together under the heading of CONJUNCTION. There is no single, uniquely correct inventory of the types of conjunctive relation; different classifications are possible, each of which would highlight different aspects of the facts.

We shall adopt a scheme of just four categories: additive, adversative, causal, and temporal. Here is an example of each:

[5:13] For the whole day he climbed up the steep mountainside, almost without stopping.
    a. And in all this time he met no one.   (additive)

    b. Yet he was hardly aware of being tired.   (adversative)
    c. So by night time the valley was far below
       him.   (causal)
    d. Then, as dusk fell, he sat down to rest.   (temporal)

The words *and, yet, so* and *then* can be taken as typifying these four very general conjunctive relations, which they express in their simplest form.

Naturally if we reduce the many very varied kinds of conjunction to this small number of basic types, there is scope for a considerable amount of subclassifying within them. A very simple overall framework like this does not ELIMINATE the complexity of the facts; it relegates it to a later, or more 'delicate', stage of the analysis. Our reason for preferring this framework is just that: it seems to have the right priorities, making it possible to handle a text without unnecessary complication. A detailed systematization of all the possible subclasses would be more complex than is needed for the understanding and analysis of cohesion; moreover, they are quite indeterminate, so that it would be difficult to select one version in preference to another. We shall introduce some subclassification under each of the four headings, but not of any very rigid kind.

There is one very general distinction, common to all four types, which it will be helpful to make at the start. Consider the following pair of examples:

[5:14] a. Next he inserted the key into the lock.
        b. Next, he was incapable of inserting the key into the lock.

Each of these sentences can be seen, by virtue of the word *next*, to pre-suppose some preceding sentence, some textual environment. Moreover in each case there is a relation of temporal sequence between the pre-supposed sentence and this one; both [5:14a and b] express a relation that is in some sense 'next in time'. We shall in fact classify them both as TEMPORAL. But the 'nextness' is really rather different in the two in-stances. In (a), it is a relation between events: the preceding sentence might be *First he switched on the light* – first one thing happens, then another. The time sequence, in other words, is in the THESIS, in the content of what is being said. In (b), on the other hand, the preceding sentence might be *First he was unable to stand upright*; here there are no events; or rather, there are only LINGUISTIC events, and the time sequence is in the speaker's organization of his discourse. We could say the time sequence is in the ARGUMENT, provided 'argument' is understood in its everyday rhetorical sense and not in its technical sense in logic (contrasting with 'operator'). The two sentences are related as steps in an argument, and the meaning is rather 'first one move in the speech game is enacted, then another'.

It would be possible to describe the nature of the temporal relation in [5:14b] in terms of speech acts, the time sequence being a performative sequence 'first I say one thing, then another'. This is quite adequate for the particular example, but is too concrete for this type of conjunction as a whole. As later examples will show, what we are concerned with here is not so much a relationship between speech acts (though it may take this form, especially in the temporal setting) as a relationship between different stages in the unfolding of the speaker's COMMUNICATION ROLE – the meanings he allots to himself as a participant in the total situation. The distinction between (a) and (b) really relates to the basic functional components in the organization of language. In [5:14a] the cohesion has to be interpreted in terms of the EXPERIENTIAL function of language; it is a relation between meanings in the sense of representations of 'contents', (our experience of) external reality. In [5:14b] the cohesion has to be interpreted in terms of the INTERPERSONAL function of language; it is a relation between meanings in the sense of representations of the speaker's own 'stamp' on the situation – his choice of speech role and rhetorical channel, his attitudes, his judgments and the like.

The essential fact here is that communication is itself a process, albeit a process of a special kind; and that the salient event in this process is the text. It is this that makes it possible for there to be two closely analogous sets of conjunctive relations: those which exist as relations between external phenomena, and those which are as it were internal to the communication situation. The clearest instance is to be found in the relation of temporal sequence, as just illustrated: it is fairly obvious that temporal sequence is a property both of the processes that are encoded in language and of the process of linguistic interaction itself. At the same time, the two time sequences are also clearly on different planes of reality, which explains why it is that certain apparently contradictory elements can combine with each other; we may have an example like

[5:15] Next, previously to this he had already offered to resign.

meaning 'and after this (in "internal" or situation time) I shall tell you what happened before this (in "external" or thesis time)'. The analogy in the other types of conjunctive relation, additive, adversative and causal, is somewhat less exact; but it is still exact enough for many of the same conjunctive expressions to be used in both meanings, for example:

[5:16] a. She was never really happy here. So she's leaving.
   b. She'll be better off in a new place. – So she's leaving?

In (a) there is a causal relation between two events – or two phenomena, let us say, since the first is a state rather than an event. The meaning is 'because she was not happy, she's leaving'. In (b) there is also a causal relation, but it is within the communication process; the meaning is 'because you refer to her being about to be in a new place, I conclude she's leaving'. This is a very typical example of the sort of parallelism we find between the two planes of conjunctive relations, the external and the internal.

No pair of terms seems quite right for referring to this distinction in a way that is succinct yet still transparent. We might use 'objective' and 'subjective'; but these are misleading, because the logical relations within the speech situation are no more subjective than those within the thesis or content of what is being said – the communication process itself is as objective as any of the processes that are being talked about. Most appropriate would be a pair of terms relating to the functional components of meaning (experiential and interpersonal; cf Hymes' 'referential' and 'socio-expressive', Lyons' 'cognitive' and 'social'), since the distinction in fact derives from the functional organization of the linguistic system; but these become cumbersome and require a constant effort of interpretation. For want of better, we shall use EXTERNAL and INTERNAL; they are somewhat vague, but preferable to more specific terms which might be suitable, say, in the setting of a temporal relation but not in a causal or adversative one. This is exactly the emphasis we want to avoid. The value of the distinction we are drawing is precisely that it is general to all the different relations that enter into conjunction. When we use conjunction as a means of creating text, we may exploit either the relations that are inherent in the phenomena that language is used to talk about, or those that are inherent in the communication process, in the forms of interaction between speaker and hearer; and these two possibilities are the same whatever the type of conjunctive relation, whether additive, adversative, temporal or causal. In fact we usually exploit both kinds. The line between the two is by no means always clearcut; but it is there, and forms an essential part of the total picture.

Each of the remaining subcategories that we shall set up for the present discussion is specific to one or other of the four types of relation, and will be brought up in the appropriate section. In the following table we set out the four headings, ADDITIVE, ADVERSATIVE, CAUSAL and

Summary Table of Conjunctive Relations

	External/internal	Internal (unless otherwise specified)		
Additive (Addition)	Additive, simple: *and, and also* Additive Negative *nor, and . . . not* Alternative *or, or else*	Complex, emphatic: Additive *furthermore, in addition, besides* Alternative *alternatively* Complex, de-emphatic: Afterthought *incidentally, by the way*	Apposition: Expository *that is, I mean, in other words* Exemplificatory *for instance, thus*	Comparison: Similar *likewise, similarly, in the same way* Dissimilar *on the other hand, by contrast*
Adversative (opposition)	Adversative 'proper': Simple *yet, though, only* Containing 'and' *but* Emphatic *however, nevertheless, despite this*	Contrastive: Avowal *in fact, actually, as a matter of fact* Contrastive (external): Simple *but, and* Emphatic *however, on the other hand, at the same time*	Correction: Of meaning *instead, rather, on the contrary* Of wording *at least, rather, I mean*	Dismissal: Closed *in any case, in either case, whichever way it is* Open-ended *in any case, anyhow, at any rate, however it is*

	External/internal	Internal (unless otherwise specified)		
Causal	Causal, general: Simple — so, then, hence, therefore Emphatic — consequently, because of this Causal, specific: Reason — for this reason, on account of this Result — as a result, in consequence Purpose — for this purpose, with this in mind	Reversed causal: Simple — for, because Causal, specific: Reason — it follows, on this basis Result — arising out of this Purpose — to this end	Conditional (also external): Simple — then Emphatic — in that case, in such an event, that being so Generalized — under the circumstances Reversed polarity — otherwise, under other circumstances	Respective: Direct — in this respect, in this regard, with reference to this Reversed polarity — otherwise, in other respects, aside from this
Temporal (Time)	Temporal, simple (external only): Sequential — then, next, after that Simultaneous — just then, at the same time Preceding — previously, before that Conclusive: Simple — finally, at last Correlative forms: Sequential — first ... then Conclusive — at first ... in the end	Complex (external only): Immediate — at once, thereupon Interrupted — soon, after a time Repetitive — next time, on another occasion Specific — next day, an hour later Durative — meanwhile Terminal — until then Punctiliar — at this moment	Internal temporal: Sequential — then, next, secondly Conclusive — finally, in conclusion Correlative forms: Sequential — first ... next Conclusive — ... finally	'Here and now': Past — up to now, hitherto Present — at this point, here Future — from now on, henceforward Summary: Summarizing — to sum up, in short, briefly Resumptive — to resume, to return to the point

TEMPORAL, and list examples of the words and phrases that express these meanings. The distinction between external and internal, in the sense above, is also built into the table; it will be noted that many though not all of the conjunctions occur in both types of relation, like *next* and *so* in [5:14] and [5:16]. In one or two instances the same word occurs in more than one conjunctive type; *eg: then* is both temporal and causal. Some labels are given to the subcategories, where it is felt that these would be helpful; and the classification of each type is repeated in the form of a list at the end of the section in which it is discussed.

5.4 Additive

We have already discussed (in 5.2) the 'and' relation as it is embodied in the form of coordination, and suggested that the cohesive relation expressed by *And* at the beginning of a new sentence – the ADDITIVE relation – is somewhat different from coordination proper, although it is no doubt derivable from it.

It is not being claimed, of course, that every time a writer puts a full stop before *and* he is thereby at once using the word in a different sense. The distinction is neither as clearcut nor as consistent as this; and in any case the claim would be meaningless for spoken English, for which it would be necessary to adopt and adhere to a particular explicit definition of the sentence. But equally the notion of sentence, vague though it is, is not invalid; we can define the sentence for spoken English if we want to. Probably the simplest definition is that a sentence equals a clause complex: that is, any set of clauses that are hypotactically and/or paratactically related, with the simple clause as the limiting case. Moreover there is a difference in principle between structural relations, which hold within a sentence, and cohesive relations, which hold (within or) between sentences.

When we are considering cohesive relations, we can group together under the heading of additive both of the two types that appear structurally in the form of coordination, the 'and' type and the 'or' type. The distinction between these two is not of primary significance for purposes of textual cohesion; and in any case it is not the same distinction as that which is found between them in coordination. The words *and, or* and *nor* are all used cohesively, as conjunctions; and all of them are classified here as additive. The correlative pairs *both . . . and, either . . . or* and *neither . . . nor* do not in general occur with cohesive function; they are restricted to structural coordination within the sentence. This is because a coordinate pair functions as a single unit, in some higher structure, and so can be delineated as a constituent; whereas a cohesive 'pair' is not a pair at all, but a succession of two independent elements the second of which happens to be tied on to the first (*cf* the discussion on example [5:6] above).

All three, *and, or* and *nor*, may express either the EXTERNAL or the INTERNAL type of conjunctive relation (as these were described in 5.3 above). In the additive context, in fact, there may be no very clear difference between the two; but when *and* is used alone as a cohesive item, as distinct from *and then*, etc, it often seems to have the sense of 'there is something more to be said', which is clearly internal in our terms, a kind of seam in the discourse. For example in [5:17a and b] the *and* has this sense:

[5:17] a. '... I was very nearly opening the window, and putting you out into the snow ! And you'd have deserved it ...'.
b. 'I said you looked like an egg, sir,' Alice gently explained. 'And some eggs are very pretty, you know,' she added ...

Much of the discussion of *and* in 5.2 above illustrates the same point; examples [5:8–10] show different kinds of internal *and* – linking a series of questions, like [5:18]:

[5:18] Was she in a shop ? And was that really – was it really a *sheep* that was sitting on the other side of the counter ?

or linking dialogue and narrative, like [5:19]:

[5:19] '... Who in the world am I ? Ah, that's the great puzzle !' And she began thinking over all the children she knew that were of the same age as herself, to see if she could have been changed for any of them.

Example [5:8] is perhaps on the borderline; here *and* does link two different facts, which makes it external, but at the same time it may serve to convey the speaker's intention that they should be regarded as connected in some way.

The NEGATIVE form of the additive relation is expressed simply as *nor*, as in *Nor can I*. Besides *nor* there are various other composite expressions with more or less the same meaning (*cf: or else* as expansion of *or*, as in [5:24] below): *and ... not, not ... either, and ... not ... either*; and the forms *neither, and ... neither*. Here is an example with a clearly external sense, the form being *and ... not ... either*:

[5:20] I couldn't send all the horses, you know, because two of them are wanted in the game. And I haven't sent the two Messengers either.

It is likely that the expanded forms with *either* have an additional element of explicitness in them, a sense of 'and what is more'. This, in our terms, would be an element of internal meaning, since it is an expression of the speaker's attitude to or evaluation of what he is saying. Example [5:20] would in this sense perhaps be a combination of both external and internal conjunction. There are parallel forms of the positive 'and' relation, namely *and also, and . . . too:*

[5:21] 'To be able to see Nobody! And at that distance, too!'

There are specifically EMPHATIC forms of the 'and' relation occurring only in an internal sense, that of 'there is yet another point to be taken in conjunction with the previous one'. This in fact is essentially the meaning that is taken on by the 'and' relation when it is a form of internal conjunction. There are a large number of conjunctive expressions which have just this meaning, *eg: further, furthermore, again, also, moreover, what is more, besides, additionally, in addition, in addition to this, not only that but.* These give a definite rhetorical flavour, as in

[5:22] My client says he does not know this witness. Further, he denies ever having seen her or spoken to her.

The speaker wants the two sentences to be as it were added together and reacted to in their totality.

With the 'or' relation, the distinction between the external and the internal planes is perhaps more clearcut. The basic meaning of the conjunctive 'or' relation is ALTERNATIVE. In its external sense, the offering of a range of objective alternatives, *or,* together with its expansion *or else,* is largely confined to questions, requests, permissions and predictions (realized in the grammar as interrogative, imperative and modalized clauses). Even here, the alternative could often be regarded as comprising a single sentence, as in

[5:23] 'Shall we try another figure of the Lobster Quadrille?', the Gryphon went on. 'Or would you like the Mock Turtle to sing you a song?'

If it is associated with statements, *or* takes on the internal sense of 'an alternative interpretation', 'another possible opinion, explanation, etc in place of the one just given':

[5:24] Perhaps she missed her train. Or else she's changed her mind and isn't coming.

The form (or) *alternatively* is perhaps an emphatic variant of the 'or' relation, whereby the speaker stresses the alternativeness, in the same way that by using (and) *additionally* he emphasizes the additionalness in the 'and' relation.

Under the heading ADDITIVE we may include a related pattern, that of semantic SIMILARITY, in which the source of cohesion is the comparison of what is being said with what has gone before. Forms such as *similarly, likewise, in the same way* are used by the speaker to assert that a point is being reinforced or a new one added to the same effect; the relevance of the presupposing sentence is its similarity of import to the presupposed one. There may be a likeness in the event; the cohesive use of comparison does not exclude the presence of an external component, as in [5:25a]. But essentially it is the similarity in the context of the communication process that is being used with cohesive effect. [5:25b] brings out this internal aspect.

[5:25] a. Treating people as responsible citizens brings out the best in them; they behave as such. In the same way if you treat them as criminals they will soon begin to act like criminals.

b. Your directors are planning for steady growth over a considerable period of time. Similarly our intentions in adopting this new investment policy are focused on the long-term prospects of the company.

Corresponding to 'similarly' is the negative comparison where the meaning is DISSIMILARITY: 'in contradistinction'. This is frequently expressed by the phrase *on the other hand*; there are other forms such as *by contrast, as opposed to this*, and so on.

[5:26] Our garden didn't do very well this year. By contrast, the orchard is looking very healthy.

The phrase *on the other hand* is unusual among conjunctions in having a correlative form, *on the one hand*; note however that when the two are used together the sense of 'dissimilarity' tends to be weakened, and the effect is little more than a simple additive:

[5:27] Why aren't you going in for a swim? – On the one hand, the air's too cold; I like to be warm when I come out. On the other hand, the current's too strong; I like to be sure I SHALL come out.

Note the similarity between comparison as a conjunctive relation especially in its external sense, expressed by conjunctive Adjuncts of one kind and another, and comparison as a form of reference, expressed by Deictics, Epithets and Submodifiers (see 2.2 and 2.5).

With negative comparison, we are approaching the ADVERSATIVE type of conjunctive relation, where it has the sense of 'not . . . but . . .'; that is, where the first term in the comparison is denied in order to make room for the second one. Here we find expressions such as *instead, rather, on the contrary*. These will be brought up in the next section. Meanwhile there are two other types of relation which can be thought of as sub-categories of the additive. Both of these are really relations on the internal plane – though, as always, they may have external implications.

The first is that of EXPOSITION or EXEMPLIFICATION. This corresponds, structurally, not to coordination but to APPOSITION. Among the items which occur frequently in this function are, in the expository sense, *I mean, that is, that is to say, (or) in other words, (or) to put it another way*; in the exemplificatory sense, *for instance, for example, thus*. Note that the word *or* also occurs alone as a marker of structural apposition, the sense being 'by another (alternative) name'. Other items, such as *namely* and the abbreviations *ie, viz, eg*, are likewise usually used as structural markers within the sentence, although they may occasionally be found linking two sentences. Examples:

[5:28] a. I wonder whether that statement can be backed up by adequate evidence. – In other words, you don't believe me.

b. 'What sort of things do *you* remember best?' Alice ventured to ask. 'Oh, things that happened the week after next,' the Queen replied in a careless tone. 'For instance, now,' she went on . . . 'there's the King's Messenger. He's in prison now, being punished: and the trial doesn't even begin till next Wednesday: and of course the crime comes last of all.'

c. In the Index of Railroad Stations the names of many railroads are followed by small numerals. These are time-table numbers indicating the table in which a given station is shown in the railroad's representation. For example, under Danbury, Ct., is shown "N.Y. New Hav. and H., 12." This means Danbury is found on the time-table No. 12 of that railroad.*

Of these, (a) is expository, (b) exemplifying, while (c) contains an example of each: *this means*, and *for example*.

* *Official Guide to the American Railroads*, September 1967.

Finally there is a small set of items such as *incidentally*, *by the way*, which combine the sense of additive with that of AFTERTHOUGHT. They are perhaps on the borderline of cohesion; they may often hardly presuppose any preceding discourse, although in principle one sentence can be incidental only by reference to a previous one.

[5:29] 'You'll see me there,' said the Cat, and vanished . . . While she was looking at the place where it had been, it suddenly appeared again. 'By-the-bye, what became of the baby?' said the Cat, 'I'd nearly forgotten to ask.'

This sort of afterthought is really a kind of DE-EMPHASIS, reducing the weight accorded to the presupposing sentence and to its connection with what went before; it thus contrasts with the emphatic type described earlier, expressed by *furthermore* and similar forms.

The structural analogue of the additive relation – that is, its equivalent in the form of a relation within the sentence – is parataxis, including both coordination and apposition. To the SIMPLE ADDITIVE (including negative and alternative) forms correspond structures using the same words *and*, *or* and *nor*, as well as their correlative pairs *both . . . and*, etc. To the APPOSITIONAL type corresponds structural apposition, which may be expressed by means of markers such as *namely*, *or*, *that is*, or simply by juxtaposition; in spoken English there must also be tonal concord – a pair of items in apposition always have the same intonation pattern. On the other hand, the COMPARATIVE and the various COMPLEX relations that we have grouped under the heading of ADDITIVE have no equivalent as structural relations within the sentence.

Here is a summary of the conjunctive relations of the ADDITIVE type, with examples of each:

Simple additive relations (external and internal)
Additive:	*and; and also, and . . . too*
Negative:	*nor; and . . . not, not . . . either, neither*
Alternative:	*or; or else*

Complex additive relations (internal): emphatic
Additive:	*further(more), moreover, additionally, besides that, add to this, in addition, and another thing*
Alternative:	*alternatively*

Complex additive relations (internal): de-emphatic
Afterthought:	*incidentally, by the way*

Comparative relations (internal)

Similar:	*likewise, similarly, in the same way, in (just) this way*
Dissimilar:	*on the other hand, by contrast, conversely*

Appositive relations (internal)

Expository:	*that is, I mean, in other words, to put it another way*
Exemplificatory:	*for instance, for example, thus*

5.5 Adversative

The basic meaning of the ADVERSATIVE relation is 'contrary to expectation'. The expectation may be derived from the content of what is being said, or from the communication process, the speaker–hearer situation, so that here too, as in the additive, we find cohesion on both the external and the internal planes.

An EXTERNAL adversative relation is expressed in its simple form by the word *yet* occurring initially in the sentence:

> [5:30] All the figures were correct; they'd been checked. Yet the total came out wrong.

Very similar to *yet* in this function are *but, however,* and *though*. It was suggested earlier (5.2) that *but* differs from *yet* in that *but* contains the element 'and' as one of its meaning components, whereas *yet* does not; for this reason, we regularly find sentences beginning *and yet,* but never *and but.*

The word *however* is different again. Unlike *yet* and *but, however* can occur non-initially in the sentence (in which case it can co-occur with initial *and* or *but,* but not with *yet*); and it regularly occurs as a separate tone group – separate, that is, from what follows – and so is associated with intonational prominence, whereas *yet* and *but* are normally spoken as 'reduced' syllables and become tonal only for purposes of contrast. Finally *though* as a conjunctive is always phonologically reduced; it may occur initially (in which case it is indistinguishable in speech from the subordinating *though* (= *although*) and would be treated as cohesive only if occurring in writing after a full stop), but its normal position is as a tailpiece at the end of the clause. Some examples:

> [5:31] a. All this time Tweedledee was trying his best to fold up the umbrella, with himself in it ... But he couldn't quite succeed,

and it ended in his rolling over, bundled up in the umbrella, with only his head out.

b. . . . it swept her straight off the seat, and down among the heap of rushes. However, she wasn't a bit hurt, and was soon up again.

c. 'I like the Walrus best,' said Alice: 'because, you see, he was a *little* sorry for the poor oysters'.

'He ate more than the Carpenter though,' said Tweedledee.

The following set of examples shows the intonation patterns (*cf* 5.9) that are associated with *however*; example (a) is untypical for *however* but corresponds to the typical use of *but*:

[5:32]

Jane felt most disheartened.

a. //4 However she was not going to let herself be BEATEN //

b. //1 HOWEVER //4 she was not going to let herself be BEATEN //

c. //4 She was not going to let herself be BEATEN however //

d. //4 THIS time however //1 she was not going to let herself be BEATEN //

The pattern in (c) and (d) would also be appropriate to *though*.

The adversative sense is expressed by a number of other words and phrases. The word *only* occurs frequently in this sense in spoken English, always in initial position and phonologically reduced, like *however* in [5:32a]; *eg*

[5:33] I'd love to join in. Only I don't know how to play.

Other adversative words such as *nevertheless* and *still*, and prepositional expressions such as *in spite of this*, are on the other hand usually fully accented, and often also tonic, like *however* in [5:32b]; *eg*

[5:34] It certainly was a *very* large Gnat: 'about the size of a chicken,' Alice thought. Still, she couldn't feel nervous with it, after they had been talking together so long.

In some instances the adversative relation between two sentences appears as it were with the sequence reversed, where the second sentence and not the first would correspond to the *although* clause in a hypotactic structure. Here the normal cohesive form is *yet;* we also find *and* in adversative use in this sense:

[5:35] a. The total came out wrong. Yet all the figures were correct; they'd been checked.

(*cf: The total came out wrong, although all the figures were correct.*)

[5:35] b. 'Dear, dear ! How queer everything is today ! And yesterday things went on just as usual.'

At the same time, *but* and *however* occur in a related though somewhat different sense, which we might call CONTRASTIVE. This they share with *on the other hand* (but never in its correlative form *on the one hand . . . on the other hand*, which is comparative; *cf* 5.4 above). Note that *yet* does not occur in this sense, as can be seen by substituting it for *but* and *however* in the following examples:

[5:36] a. She failed. However, she's tried her best.
       b. He's not exactly good-looking. But he's got brains.
       c. 'I see you're admiring my little box,' the Knight said in a friendly tone. '. . . You see I carry it upside-down, so that the rain can't get in.' 'But the things can get out,' Alice gently remarked.

Here the meaning is not 'despite' but 'as against', 'to be set against'; in fact the expression *as against that* is used in this sense, as well as *on the other hand*, *at the same time* and various others.

It can be seen that if *yet* replaces *however* in [5:36a] the meaning is quite different: it means 'in spite of the fact that she'd tried her best, she still failed'. The two meanings 'in spite of' (the adversative proper, so to speak) and 'as against' can be paralleled within the sentence, in the *although* ('concessive') type of dependent clause. This is normally a true adversative, and it can have ONLY this sense if the *although* clause precedes the main clause (where *although* is accented). But provided the *although* clause follows the main clause, where *although* is normally unaccented, it can express either the meaning 'in spite of' or the meaning 'as against'. Thus we have *she failed, although she'd tried her best*, meaning either 'in spite of the fact that . . .', parallel to [5:35a], or 'as against the fact that . . .', parallel to [5:36c]; or *although she'd tried her best, she failed*, meaning only 'in spite of the fact that . . .', parallel to [5:30]. The latter cannot mean 'as against', which is why *although he's got brains, he's not exactly good-looking* makes no sense.

The adversative relation also has its INTERNAL aspect. Here the underlying meaning is still 'contrary to expectation'; but the source of the expectation is to be found not in what the presupposed sentence is about but in the current speaker-hearer configuration, the point reached in the communication process, as we expressed it earlier. For example:

[5:37] a. '. . . you'll find yourself in the Fourth Square in no time. Well, that square belongs to Tweedledum and Tweedledee – the Fifth is mostly water – the Sixth belongs to Humpty Dumpty – But you make no remark?'

    b. '. . . you might catch a bat, and that's very like a mouse, you know. But do cats eat bats, I wonder?'

In (a) the Red Queen's reasoning is 'I am giving you information, for which you ought to be grateful; and yet you don't show it': that is, contrary to the expectation raised by the communication situation between us. Similarly in (b), Alice recognizes that, although her suggestion is made with the intention of being helpful, it may not in fact be any use.

This is as it were the internal equivalent of the adversative proper; the meaning is not 'in spite of the facts' but it is still 'in spite of' – 'in spite of the roles we are playing, the state of the argument, etc'. There is another form of the adversative relation, also internal, which we may perhaps regard as being the INTERNAL equivalent of the CONTRASTIVE sense identified above, that of 'as against'. This is expressed by a number of very frequent items such as *in fact, as a matter of fact, actually, to tell (you) the truth*. The meaning is something like 'as against what the current state of the communication process would lead us to expect, the fact of the matter is . . .' The conjunction takes the form of an assertion of veracity, an AVOWAL:

[5:38] 'Now the cleverest thing I ever did,' he went on after a pause, 'was inventing a new pudding during the meat-course.'
'In time to have it cooked for the next course?' said Alice. 'well, that *was* quick work, certainly.'
'Well, not the *next* course,' the Knight said in a slow thoughtful tone; 'no, certainly not the next *course*.'
'Then it would have to be the next day. I suppose you wouldn't have two pudding-courses in one dinner.'
'Well, not the *next* day,' the Knight repeated as before: 'not the next *day*. In fact,' he went on, holding his head down, and his voice getting lower and lower, 'I don't believe that pudding ever *was* cooked! In fact, I don't believe that pudding ever *will* be cooked! And yet it was a very clever pudding to invent.'

Related to this 'avowal' type is another form of the adversative which was mentioned above (5.4) as bordering on the sense of negative comparison *eg: by contrast*; *cf* [5:26]. This is the sense of 'not . . . but . . .', which we might refer to as a CORRECTION. The meaning of this cohesive relation itself is again internal – although, as always, the context of its use in any particular instance may be found in the content of the presupposed and presupposing sentences. The general meaning is still 'contrary to expectation', but here the special sense is 'as against what has just been said'; the expectation is there, in other words, simply because it has been put into words. The distinction between this and the 'avowal' type, such as *in fact*, is that the latter is an assertion of 'the facts' in the face of real or imaginary resistance ('as against what you might think'), whereas here one formulation is rejected in favour of another ('as against what you have been told'). Characteristic expressions of this relation are *instead (of that)*, *rather*, *on the contrary*, *at least*, *I mean*. The contrast may be between two alternative phenomena:

[5:39] a. He showed no pleasure at hearing the news. Instead he looked even gloomier.
b. I don't think she minds the cold. It's the damp she objects to, rather.

But it may be between two different formulations of the same phenomenon:

[5:40] 'What a beautiful belt you've got on !' Alice suddenly remarked . . . 'At least,' she corrected herself on second thoughts, 'a beautiful cravat, I should have said – no, a belt, I mean – . . .'.

Finally we bring in here what may be considered a generalized form of the adversative relation, the meaning 'no matter (whether . . . or not; which . . .), still . . .'. This presupposes that some circumstances have been referred to which are then dismissed as irrelevant – either because it does not matter whether they obtain or not, as in [5:41a], or because it does not matter which of the given set of circumstances obtains, as in [5:41b]:

[5:41] a. We may be back tonight; I'm not sure. Either way, just make yourselves at home.
b. Your partner may support you or may change to another suit. In either case you should respond.

DISMISSIVE expressions include *in any/either case/event*, *any/either way*, *whichever happens*, *whether . . . or not*. The same meaning is further generalized to cover an entirely open-ended set of possibilities: 'no matter what', *ie* 'no matter under what circumstances, still . . .'. Taken by itself this seems to have nothing cohesive about it; but it always presupposes that SOMETHING has gone before, remote though it may be. Since whatever it is that has gone before is in any case being dismissed as irrelevant, the meaning 'however that may be' on the internal plane often amounts to nothing more than a change of subject – 'let's leave that aside, and turn to something else' (*cf* 5.8 below). The usual modern sense of the word *however*, as a specific adversative, is in fact derived from the generalized sense which it had earlier; in the same way various other expressions which are essentially of this generalized type, such as *anyhow*, *at any rate*, are now coming to function as adversatives in the more specific sense. Examples of the generalized adversative relation:

[5:42]   a.   'I say, this isn't fair!' cried the Unicorn, as Alice sat with the knife in her hand, very much puzzled how to begin. 'The Monster has given the Lion twice as much as me!'
'She's kept none for herself, anyhow,' said the Lion.

   b.   '. . . the March Hare said – ' 'I didn't!' the March Hare interrupted in a great hurry . . .
'Well, at any rate, the Dormouse said – ' the Hatter went on.

Summary of conjunctive relations of the ADVERSATIVE type:

Adversative relations 'proper' ('in spite of') (external and internal)

Simple:	*yet; though; only*
Containing 'and':	*but*
Emphatic:	*however, nevertheless, despite this, all the same*

Contrastive relations ('as against') (external)

Simple:	*but, and*
Emphatic:	*however, on the other hand, at the same time, as against that*

Contrastive relations ('as against') (internal)

Avowal:	*in fact, as a matter of fact, to tell the truth, actually, in point of fact*

Corrective relations ('not . . . but') (internal)

Correction of meaning:	*instead, rather, on the contrary*
Correction of wording:	*at least, rather, I mean*

Dismissive (generalized adversative) relations ('no matter . . ., still')
(external and internal)

Dismissal, closed:	*in any/either case/event, any/either way, whichever* . . .
Dismissal, open-ended:	*anyhow, at any rate, in any case, however that may be*

5.6 Causal

The simple form of CAUSAL relation is expressed by *so, thus, hence, therefore, consequently, accordingly*, and a number of expressions like *as a result (of that), in consequence (of that), because of that*. All these regularly combine with initial *and*. It is outside our scope here to go into the various positions that can be occupied by these items in the sentence, but the same general types exist as with the adversatives. Thus *so* occurs only initially, unless following *and; thus*, like *yet*, occurs initially or at least in the first part (the Modal element) of the clause; *therefore* has the same potentialities as *however*. Again adverbs such as *consequently* resemble the adversative adverbs like *nevertheless*; and the prepositional expressions such as *as a result (of this)* have on the whole the same potentialities of occurrence as those with an adversative sense.
Examples:

> [5:43] a. . . . . she felt that there was no time to be lost, as she was shrinking rapidly; so she got to work at once to eat some of the other bit.
> b. . . . . she wouldn't have heard it at all, if it hadn't come *quite* close to her ear. The consequence of this was that it tickled her ear very much, and quite took off her thoughts from the unhappiness of the poor little creature.

The causal relation may be reiterated so as to form a cohesive chain, as in the following example from *Alice*:

> [5:44] But they *have* their tails in their mouths; and the reason is . . . that they *would* go with the lobsters to the dance. So they got thrown out to sea. So they had to fall a long way. So they got their tails fast in their mouths. So they couldn't get them out again.

Under the heading of causal relations are included the SPECIFIC ones of RESULT, REASON and PURPOSE. These are not distinguished in the simplest form of expression; *so*, for example, means 'as a result of this', 'for this reason' and 'for this purpose'. When expressed as prepositional phrases, on the other hand, they tend to be distinct.

The distinction between the EXTERNAL and the INTERNAL types of cohesion tends to be a little less clearcut in the context of causal relations than it is in the other contexts, probably because the notion of cause already involves some degree of interpretation by the speaker. Nevertheless the distinction is still recognizable. The simple forms *thus, hence* and *therefore* all occur regularly in an INTERNAL sense, implying some kind of reasoning or argument from a premise; in the same meaning we find expressions like *arising out of this, following from this* (we might include also locutions such as *it follows that, from this it appears that, we may conclude that* and the like):

[5:45] When the breakfast allowed blood sugar to be low during the morning, the increase after lunch rose to the level of cheerfulness and efficiency for only a few minutes; then it fell to a low level which lasted throughout the afternoon. Your selection of food at breakfast, therefore, can prevent or produce fatigue throughout the day.*

The word *so* is not common in this sense, but it occurs frequently in another meaning, also internal, that it shares with *then*; this is as a statement about the speaker's reasoning processes: 'I conclude from what you say (or other evidence)' – compare expressions such as *I gather:*

[5:46] The very first thing she did was to look whether there was a fire in the fireplace, and she was quite pleased to find that there was a real one, and blazing away as brightly as the one she had left behind. 'So I shall be as warm here as I was in the old room,' thought Alice.

The REVERSED form of the causal relation, in which the presupposing sentence expresses the cause, is less usual as a form of cohesion. Within the sentence, it is natural to find the structural expression of cause going in either direction; a structure functions as a whole, and the sequence '*b*, because *a*' is no less acceptable – in fact considerably more frequent – than 'because *a, b*'. With the cohesive relation between sentences, however, in which the text unfolds one sentence after another, the logical precedence of cause over effect is reflected in the typical sequence in

* Adelle Davis, *Let's Eat Right to Keep Fit*, George Allen & Unwin.

which sentences related in this way tend to occur. Nevertheless we do find *the reason was that* and similar expressions; and there is one simple conjunction with this meaning, namely *for*. This is hardly ever heard in spoken English, where its nearest equivalent is the word *because* in phonologically reduced form. Note the examples:

[5:47] a. The next morning she was glad and proud that she had not yielded to a scare. For he was most strangely and obviously better.

b. 'I see somebody now !' she exclaimed at last. 'But he's coming very slowly – and what curious attitudes he goes into !' (For the Messenger kept skipping up and down, and wriggling like an eel, as he came along, with his great hands spread out like fans on each side.)

In [5:47b] the *for* is used in an internal sense, meaning 'this is the reason for what was just said'; compare [5:48] where the conjunction *because* means 'this is why I'm asking':

[5:48] You aren't leaving, are you? Because I've got something to say to you.

One other type of conjunctive relation will be considered here under the general heading of causal: this is the CONDITIONAL type. The two are closely related, linguistically; where the causal means '*a*, therefore *b*' the conditional means 'possibly *a*; if so, then *b*', and although the 'then' and the 'therefore' are not logically equivalent – *a* may entail *b* without being its cause – they are largely interchangeable as cohesive forms.

The simple form of expression of the conditional relation, meaning 'under these circumstances', is the word *then*:

[5:49] a. 'And what does it live on ?'
'Weak tea with cream in it.'
A new difficulty came into Alice's head.
'Supposing it couldn't find any?' she suggested.
'Then it would die, of course.'

b. 'Have some wine,' the March Hare said in an encouraging tone.
Alice looked all round the table, but there was nothing on it but tea. 'I don't see any wine,' she remarked.
'There isn't any,' said the March Hare.
'Then it wasn't very civil of you to offer it,' said Alice angrily.

Other items include *in that case, that being the case, in such an event*; compare also the substitute form *if so* (3.4.1.2, [3:106]).

[5:49b] illustrates the overlap of causal and conditional; the meaning is 'if, as is the case . . ., then . . .'. Here the equivalent relation in sentence structure could be expressed by either *if* or *since, as, seeing that: if/since there isn't any, (then) it wasn't very civil of you to offer it*. In [5:49a] on the other hand, which is hypothetical, only *if* is possible. As the example shows, both types can be expressed in the form of conjunction. There is some difference in the conjunctive items that are used to express them; *so* and the causal adverbs such as *accordingly* are, at least, possible in the type represented by (b), but not in the hypothetical type, whereas expressions like *in such an event* are more appropriate to the latter. The generalized conditional, *under the circumstances*, may be used in either sense, though it is more often non-hypothetical. But on the whole the two types have the same cohesive forms.

The negative form of the conditional, 'under other circumstances', is expressed cohesively by *otherwise*:

[5:50] a. It's the way I like to go to work. One person and one line of enquiry at a time. Otherwise, there's a muddle.

b. Whenever the horse stopped (which it did very often), he fell off in front; and whenever it went on again (which it generally did rather suddenly), he fell off behind. Otherwise he kept on pretty well . . .

It is actually misleading to refer to this as 'negative'; what it does is to switch the polarity, either from positive to negative (in which case the substitute form *if not* can be used) or from negative to positive, as in [5:51]:

[5:51] I was not informed. Otherwise I should have taken some action.

(*ie* 'if I had been'). There are no other very usual equivalents to *otherwise* as a conjunctive form, although various extended paraphrases might still fall under this heading, *eg* the phrase itself *under other circumstances*, and perhaps *that/such not being the case*.

In the conditional relation, the distinction between the external and internal types of cohesion is not at all obvious. But it is probably under this heading that we should take account of the rather vague RESPECTIVE kind of conjunctive link represented by expressions such as *in that respect, with regard to this, in this connection*. In a sense this is the INTERNAL analogue of the CONDITIONAL relation: the meaning is 'if we have now reached this point in the discourse'. The fact that these are related to conditionals is suggested also by the use of *otherwise* to express the same meaning with polarity reversed; *otherwise* is equivalent not only to *under other circumstances* but also to *in other respects, aside/apart from this*. Here we come to the border of the (internal) temporal relation (see 5.7 below); there is a close similarity between the meaning 'if we leave aside what has just been said' and 'we now pass on to the next point'. Two examples will suffice:

[5:52] a. One factor is the level of taxation of personal incomes. With regard to this question, the impressions current among members of the public are often very far removed from the truth.

b. The musicians themselves were somewhat disappointed at the relative lack of interest displayed in the new works which they presented. Leaving that aside, the whole tour seems to have been remarkably successful.

Here is a summary of relations of the CAUSAL type:

Causal relations, general ('because . . ., so') (external and internal)
Simple: *so, thus, hence, therefore*
Emphatic: *consequently, accordingly, because of this*

Causal relations, specific
Reason: (mainly external) *for this reason, on account of this*
                            (internal) *it follows (from this), on this basis*
Result: (mainly external) *as a result (of this), in consequence (of this)*
                            (internal) *arising out of this*
Purpose: (mainly external) *for this purpose, with this in mind/view, with this intention*
                            (internal) *to this end*

Reversed causal relations, general
Simple: *for; because*

Conditional relations ('if . . ., then') (external and internal)
Simple: *then*

Emphatic:	*in that case, that being the case, in such an event, under those circumstances*
Generalized:	*under the circumstances*
Reversed polarity:	*otherwise, under the circumstances*

Respective relations ('with respect to') (internal)

Direct:	*in this respect/connection, with regard to this; here*
Reversed polarity:	*otherwise, in other respects; aside/apart from this*

5.7 Temporal

The relation between the theses of two successive sentences – that is, their relation in external terms, as content – may be simply one of sequence in time: the one is subsequent to the other. This TEMPORAL relation is expressed in its simplest form by *then:*

> [5:53] (Alice) began by taking the little golden key, and unlocking the door that led into the garden. Then she set to work nibbling at the mushroom . . . till she was about a foot high: then she walked down the little passage: and *then* – she found herself at last in the beautiful garden.

In this SEQUENTIAL sense we have not only *then* and *and then* but also *next, afterwards, after that, subsequently* and a number of other expressions.

> [5:54] a. [continuation of [5:49a]] 'But that must happen very often,' Alice remarked thoughtfully.
> 'It always happens,' said the Gnat.
> After this, Alice was silent for a minute or two, pondering.
> b. . . . she heard a little shriek and a fall, and a crash of broken glass, from which she concluded that it was just possible it had fallen into a cucumber-frame, or something of the sort. Next came an angry voice – the Rabbit's – 'Pat! Pat! Where are you?' And then a voice she had never heard before, . . .

The temporal relation may be made more specific by the presence of an additional component in the meaning, as well as that of succession in time. So, for example, we may have 'then + immediately' (*at once, thereupon, on which*); 'then + after an interval' (*soon, presently, later, after a time*); 'then + repetition' (*next time, on another occasion*); 'then + a specific time interval' (*next day, five minutes later*) and so on. Examples:

[5:55] a. 'Tickets, please !' said the Guard, putting his head in at the window. In a moment everybody was holding out a ticket.
  b. 'You alarm me !' said the King. 'I feel faint – Give me a ham-sandwich !'
  On which the Messenger, to Alice's great amusement, opened a bag that hung round his neck, and handed a sandwich to the King, who devoured it greedily.

In all these instances the external temporal relation is paralleled by the sequence of the sentences themselves: the second sentence refers to a later event. But this is not necessarily the case; the second sentence may be related to the first, still by means of temporal cohesion, through an indication that it is SIMULTANEOUS in time, or even PREVIOUS. In the sense of 'simultaneous' we have (*just*) *then, at the same time, simultaneously*; and here too the simple time relation may be accompanied by some other component, *eg* 'then + in the interval' (*meanwhile, all this time*), 'then + repetition' (*on this occasion, this time*), 'then + moment of time' (*at this point/moment*), 'then + termination' (*by this time*), and so on:

[5:56] a. '. . . That *will* be a queer thing, to be sure ! However, everything is queer today.'
  Just then she heard something splashing about in the pool a little way off . . .
  b. 'You'll get used to it in time,' said the Caterpillar; and it put the hookah into its mouth and began smoking again.
  This time Alice waited patiently until it chose to speak again.

In the sense of 'previous' we have *earlier, before that, previously*, with, again, the possibility of combination with other meanings: 'before + specific time interval' (*five minutes earlier*), 'before + immediately' (*just before*), 'before + termination' (*up till that time, until then*), 'before + repetition' (*on a previous occasion*), and so on:

[5:57] a. The organ . . . developed an ornamental style of its own, which players of other instruments were recommended to imitate in the early sixteenth century. Hitherto, the role of the organ in sacred music had not apparently called for any such virtuoso treatment.*

---

* *The Pelican History of Music*, Penguin Books.

b. The weather cleared just as the party approached the summit. Until then they had seen nothing of the panorama around them.

The presupposing sentence may be temporally cohesive not because it stands in some particular time relation to the presupposed sentence but because it marks the end of some process or series of processes. This CONCLUSIVE sense is expressed by items such as *finally, at last, in the end, eventually*:

[5:58] All this time the Guard was looking at her, first through a telescope, then through a microscope, and then through an opera-glass. At last he said 'You're travelling the wrong way,' and shut up the window and went away.

In one respect temporal conjunction differs from all other types, namely in that it does occur in a CORRELATIVE form, with a cataphoric time expression in one sentence anticipating the anaphoric one that is to follow. The typical cataphoric temporal is *first*; also *at first, first of all, to begin with*, etc. Given any one of these, the expectation is that an item such as *then, next, second* or *finally* will follow:

[5:59] [Obrecht] subjects his *cantus firmus* to the most abstruse manipulations. First, he extracts all the longs from the tune, and strings them together in succession; then he does the same with the breves, and finally with the semibreves. He then reverses this procedure, starting with the shorter values first.*

In temporal cohesion it is fairly easy to identify and interpret the distinction between the EXTERNAL and the INTERNAL type of conjunctive relation. In the INTERNAL type the successivity is not in the events being talked about but in the communication process. The meaning 'next in the course of discussion' is typically expressed by the words *next* or *then*, or by *secondly, thirdly*, etc, and the culmination of the discussion is indicated by expressions such as *finally, as a final point, in conclusion*:

[5:60] a. 'What sort of insects do you rejoice in, where you come 'from?' the Gnat inquired . . .
'Well, there's the Horse-fly,' Alice began, counting off the names on her fingers . . .
'And then there's the Butterfly,' Alice went on.

---

* *Ibid.*

b. Finally we should record that the influence of the humanists contributed a good deal towards the final decay of the plainsong tradition.*

The sense of temporal successivity in the enumeration of points in an argument is clearly shown by the strong tendency to anticipate a sequence of points by the use of the cataphoric conjunctive *first*, or related expressions such as *in the first place*:

[5:61] 'There's no sort of use in knocking,' said the Footman, 'and that for two reasons. First, because I'm on the same side of the door as you are; secondly, because they're making such a noise inside, no one could possibly hear you.'

In this particular instance the two cohering passages are punctuated as a single sentence, but the relation between them is cohesive rather than structural.

One important type of internal temporal conjunction which is linked to the one just discussed is the relating of what is being said to the particular stage which the communication process has reached: to the HERE AND NOW of the discourse, as it were. This may take a past, present or future form. Typical expressions are: past, *up to now, up to this point, hitherto, heretofore;* present, *at this point, here;* future, *from now on, henceforward, hereunder;* etc. Examples:

[5:62] a. The Middle Ages have become the Renaissance, and a new world has come into being: our world. In what way is it 'our world'? At this point we run into some difficulty.*
b. And then we are back in a strange land, the later Middle Ages, where our modern preoccupations can only hinder understanding. So far we have tried to imagine the way an interested but uninstructed listener might react, in general terms, to early Renaissance music. It is now time to go into greater detail.*

We have not cited any equivalent external forms of expression; not because they do not exist but because they are not cohesive, they are deictic. Expressions like *now, up to now, in future* relate what is being said to the present situation, the 'here and now' of reality; they do not therefore presuppose anything in the preceding text. If on the other hand, 'here

* *Ibid.*

and now' means 'here and now in the text', then such forms will have a cohesive effect.

These internal aspects of the temporal relations are 'temporal' in the sense that they refer to the time dimension that is present in the communication process. The communication process is certainly a process in real time; but it is at one remove from the time dimension of the processes of the external world that form the content of communication. Hence this 'time two' is felt to be already in some way a metaphorical extension of the concept of time as in the 'time one' of these external processes; and this makes it fairly easy for it to be extended still further into meanings that are not really temporal at all.

By such an extension, we move from the sense of 'finally, to conclude' to that of 'to round off the point' and hence 'to sum up'. The expressions *finally, in conclusion* are themselves used in this CULMINATIVE sense; it is reasonable to suggest therefore that the meaning of 'to sum up' is basically a form of temporal conjunction even when expressed by other items such as *to sum up, in short, in a word, to put it briefly*:

[5:63] Your nutrition can determine how you look, act and feel; whether you are grouchy or cheerful, homely or beautiful, physiologically and even psychologically young or old; whether you think clearly or are confused, enjoy your work or make it a drudgery, increase your earning power or stay in an economic rut. The foods you eat can make the difference between your day ending with freshness which lets you enjoy a delightful evening or with exhaustion which forces you to bed with the chickens. To a considerable degree, your nutrition can give you a coddled-egg personality or make you a human dynamo. In short, it can determine your zest for life, the good you put into it, and the fulfilment you get from it.*

And finally by a still further extension we may include here the sense of 'to return to the point', where the speaker indicates that he is resuming the main purpose of the communication following a digression of some kind. This RESUMPTIVE relation is also, of course, an internal one, and is expressed by words and phrases such as *anyway, to resume, to come back to the point*:

[5:64] The distinction between reliability and validity made above is an important one. It is perfectly possible for an examination to be reliable but invalid; reliable in the sense that different examiners

---

* Adelle Davis, *Let's Eat Right to Keep Fit*, George Allen & Unwin.

would award the same marks to the same paper. For example, in a country where I used to work it was not uncommon for examinations to include a question in which students were asked to explain the meanings of allegedly 'well-known' English proverbs. They were in fact usually Victorian in character and had long ago dropped out of popular usage, if indeed they had ever been represented in it. The way in which sensible students used to prepare for this question was to buy bazaar cribs which listed and explained proverbs, and to learn the contents by heart. The marking was therefore reasonably reliable, but by no stretch of the imagination could the procedure be called valid. It was not a test of English. To return to the effects of examinations upon teaching; when a teacher does his own testing then there need be no effect on his teaching, for he can test according to his own criteria, whatever they might be.*

The following is a summary of the conjunctive relations of the TEMPORAL type:

Simple temporal relations (external)

Sequential:	(*and*) *then, next, afterwards, after that, subsequently*
Simultaneous:	(*just*) *then, at the same time, simultaneously*
Preceding:	*earlier, before then/that, previously*

Complex temporal relations (external)

Immediate:	*at once, thereupon, on which; just before*
Interrupted:	*soon, presently, later, after a time; some time earlier, formerly*
Repetitive:	*next time, on another occasion; this time, on this occasion; the last time, on a previous occasion*
Specific:	*next day, five minutes later, five minutes earlier*
Durative:	*meanwhile, all this time*
Terminal:	*by this time; up till that time, until then*
Punctiliar:	*next moment; at this point/moment; the previous moment*

Conclusive relations (external)

Simple:	*finally, at last, in the end, eventually*

---

* Brian Harrison, *English as a Second and Foreign Language*. London: Edward Arnold (series: Explorations in Language Study), 1973, *p* 102.

Sequential and conclusive relations (external): correlative forms
Sequential: *first . . . then, first . . . next, first . . . second . . .*
Conclusive: *at first . . . finally, at first . . . in the end*

Temporal relations (internal)
Sequential: *then, next, secondly . . .*
Conclusive: *finally, as a final point, in conclusion*

Temporal relations (internal): correlative forms
Sequential: *first . . . next, first . . . then, first . . . secondly . . . ;
in the first place . . . ; to begin with . . .*
Conclusive: *. . . finally; . . . to conclude with*

'Here and now' relations (internal)
Past: *up to now, up to this point, hitherto, heretofore*
Present: *at this point, here*
Future: *from now on, henceforward*

Summary relations (internal)
Culminative: *to sum up, in short, briefly*
Resumptive: *to resume, to get back to the point, anyway*

5.8 Other conjunctive items (continuatives)

In this final section we bring together a number of individual items which, although they do not express any particular one of the conjunctive relations identified above, are nevertheless used with a cohesive force in the text. If necessary these can be referred to simply as CONTINUATIVES.

In a sense this is a residual category of the usual 'miscellaneous' type. But there is a reason for its existence. We have tried to group together, in each of the four preceding sections, both those items which express a particular EXTERNAL relation, adversative, temporal and so on, and those items which express some INTERNAL relations that are closely linked to it. Since in the majority of instances the same items occur in both senses this seems justifiable. For example, *next* means both 'next in time, of the processes being talked about' and 'next in sequence in the current communication process (*eg* next of the points in an argument)', and one does not immediately think of these as two different meanings. But these internal relations may be regarded as an extension of the underlying patterns of conjunction into the communication situation itself, treating it, and thereby also the text – the linguistic component of the communication process – as having by analogy the same structure as 'reality': that is, as the phenomena that constitute the content, or THESIS, of the text.

But the analogy is imperfect, in the sense that it is not exhaustive. There are some subtle and complex relations within the communication process that cannot be closely modelled on those of external processes. We shall not try to treat these in principle, but shall simply discuss informally one or two very frequent items that do not readily fall into the four conjunctive categories dealt with above. Following this we shall end with a note on the place of intonation as a conjunctive device.

We can in fact insert a brief general statement about the intonation pattern that is associated with the CONTINUATIVE items themselves. In general, when functioning cohesively they are 'reduced' forms (*ie* unaccented and with reduced vowel values) of items which also occur, but not cohesively, in a 'full' (non-reduced) form. Their meaning as conjunctive items is derivable from their meaning as full forms; their phonological reduction is simply a signal that they have in fact a backward-linking function – we have seen throughout all the chapters of this work how cohesive items tend to be entirely non-prominent in intonation and accent, unless they are very definitely contrastive.

Six items will be discussed: *now, of course, well, anyway, surely, after all.*

5.8.1 *Now*

If it is tonic, *now* is deictic and not cohesive (unless it is made to be cohesive by the intonation pattern, contrasting with *before*, etc; see 5.9 below). If it is reduced, it means the opening of a new stage in the communication; this may be a new incident in the story, a new point in the argument, a new role or attitude being taken on by the speaker, and so on. For example, in a transaction situation such as a shop encounter, the transition from phatic communion to transactional relations is often made by *now:* *Now what would you like, dear?* Other examples:

[5:65] a. Are you ready? Now when I tell you to jump, close your eyes and jump.
　　　b. 'A slow sort of country!', said the Queen. 'Now, *here*, you see, it takes all the running *you* can do, to keep in the same place.'
　　　c. 'A loaf of bread,' the Walrus said,
　　　　　'Is what we chiefly need:
　　　　　Pepper and vinegar besides
　　　　　Are very good indeed –
　　　　　Now if you're ready, Oysters dear,
　　　　　We can begin to feed.'

5.8.2 Of course

If tonic, this means 'you should have known that already', as in [5:66a]. If reduced, it means 'I accept the fact'; or, rhetorically, 'you must accept the fact' – it is typically used, therefore, to disarm someone into accepting something the speaker knows he is likely to reject. The second meaning is a kind of subliminal form of the first; it often has a slightly adversative force, of the 'as against that' type, derived from the fact that it suggests that something should have been obvious 'but' was overlooked, as in (b) below:

[5:66] a. 'Everything's just as it was!' 'Of course it is,' said the Queen.
     b. They were going to come to the meeting. Of course they may have changed their minds.
     c. You find these properties expensive? Of course prices have increased lately, you know.

5.8.3 Well

This occurs typically at the beginning of a response in dialogue. (We ignore here its use in the original sense, as the adverbial equivalent of *good*; and also the sense as an attribute meaning 'in good health'.) If tonic, it means 'I acknowledge the question, and will give a considered answer', often therefore amounting to no more than a hesitation noise: 'I'm thinking about it'. More or less the same meaning is expressed by various other items such as *as to that*. If reduced, *well* serves to indicate that what follows IS in fact a response to what has preceded: in other words, it slips in quietly the respondent's claim to be answering the question (sometimes with a show of reluctance) and hence is purely cohesive in function. If it is used in a continuation by the same speaker, it introduces an explanatory comment (*cf* [5:37a] above). See also [5:60a], and the linguistic discussion between Alice and Humpty Dumpty from which example [5:10] is taken – [5:67a] is taken from the same context:

[5:67] a. 'And what does "*outgrabe*" mean?'
     'Well, "*outgribing*" is something between bellowing and whistling, with a kind of sneeze in the middle . . .'
     b. 'Do I look very pale?' said Tweedledum, coming up to have his helmet tied on . . .
     'Well – yes – a little,' Alice replied gently.

5.8.4 *Anyway*

The very frequent use of this word that we are referring to here derives from its meaning as described under the heading of adversative above (5.5). In its tonic form it is what we called DISMISSIVE, meaning 'no matter under which, or what, circumstances'; but it also occurs very frequently in a reduced form, in which case it indicates cohesion with the preceding sentence by simply brushing it aside. The meaning is thus also related to the RESUMPTIVE type exemplified in [5:64] (in 5.7), that is, 'to come back to the point'. But this sense is often hardly felt to be present, so we include *anyway* here as a continuative. One or two other items occur with this same meaning of 'let's get on with the job', *eg: anyhow, at any rate:*

> [5:68] a. They changed over to a most peculiar kind of train which
>   you don't see now. I've forgotten what it was called. Was
>   it called a 'steam coach'? I can't remember. Anyway it was
>   just one coach but it ran by steam and it made a funny noise.
>   b. The last time she saw them, they were trying to put the
>   Dormouse into the teapot. 'At any rate I'll never go *there*
>   again,' said Alice as she picked her way through the wood.

5.8.5 *Surely*

If tonic, this invites the hearer to assent to the proposition being enunciated; it is not cohesive, except in the cataphoric sense that a question is cohesive: it demands an answer. If reduced, it has what is basically the cohesive equivalent of the same meaning; that is, 'am I right in my understanding of what's just been said?', and sometimes specifically 'you can't have meant...?' For example:

> [5:69] They'll think you're serious. – Nobody could be so stupid as
>   to think that, surely.

5.8.6 *After all*

In its tonic form, this means 'after everything relevant has been considered, what remains is . . .'. As usual the tone is either 1 or 4, in their typical senses of 'in addition to . . .' and 'in spite of . . .' (what may have been understood). Compare *taking everything into consideration, when all's said and done*. Again, although not itself cohesive this meaning becomes cohesive in context, so *after all* functions as a continuative especially when phonologically reduced: the sense is 'what I have just said is reasonable, when everything is taken into account'.

[5:70] You needn't apologize. After all nobody could have known what would happen.

5.9 The cohesive function of intonation

Continuatives of the kind just discussed are as it were subdued cohesives; they cohere by stealth. A meaning that is basically not conjunctive, like 'at time present' (*now*), or 'this is to be expected' (*of course*), becomes cohesive when it is slipped in as an incidental or as an afterthought, since its interpretation becomes contingent on the context (and therefore on the preceding text). It is interesting that there is a general tendency in spoken English for conjunctive elements as a whole to be, phonologically, either tonic (maximally prominent) or reduced (minimally prominent), rather than anything in between. This can be explained, very simply, by reference to the function of intonation in English grammar.

Cohesive elements relate the sentence to something that has gone before it; they are normally anaphoric – there is no new content to them. Now, anaphoric items in English are phonologically non-prominent, as remarked above, and this usually extends to their syllabic structure: in other words they are 'reduced'. But if the cohesive relation itself is to be brought into focus of attention, this is marked in the usual way by tonic prominence. This takes the form of the tonic either of tone 1 (falling), if the general sense is CUMULATIVE, or (perhaps more frequently) of tone 4 (falling-rising), if the general sense is CONTRASTIVE.

We conclude this chapter with a brief discussion of the cohesive function of intonation, since this is closely related to conjunction and may be considered as expressing forms of conjunctive relation.

The FALL-RISE intonation pattern in English, TONE 4, has in many contexts a sense of reservation, 'there's a *but* about it'. This is not necessarily a cohesive factor, since the nature of the reservation may not be made explicit. But in many instances the fall-rise intonation pattern provides a clear indication, and often the only indication, that the item on which it falls is to be interpreted as contrasting with a preceding item; and in such instances, the function of the tone is specifically cohesive. We have already mentioned the falling (tone 1) and falling-rising (tone 4) intonation patterns in the discussion on the adversative in 5.5 above, illustrating the fact that these tones are characteristically associated with contexts where there are already cohesive items present. This is a very general phenomenon; the fall-rise tone pattern adds the sense of contrast, as in [5:32c], and

[5:71] a. 'Let's go back to the last remark but one.' 'I'm afraid I can't quite remember it,' Alice said very politely.
'In that case (//4 in THAT case //) we may start afresh,' said Humpty Dumpty.
b. We've been stuck in this traffic for three quarters of an hour. Another time (//4 ANOTHER time //) we'll go by train.

Very frequently, however, the tone alone shows that the item in question is cohesive; the cohesion consists just in the contrast with some preceding item. There is no doubt about the presupposing force of the fall-rise tone in the following examples:

[5:72] a. 'Seven jogged my elbow.' . . . 'That's right, Five! Always lay the blame on others!' '*You'd* better not talk!' said Five. (//4 YOU'D better not talk //)
b. People used to dress up to go to the theatre. Now (//4 NOW//) they wear any old thing.
c. 'The only difficulty is with the feet. The *head* is high enough already.' (//4 the HEAD//1 is high enough ALREADY //)
d. 'That is not said right,' said the Caterpillar. 'Not *quite* right, I'm afraid,' said Alice timidly (//4 not QUITE right, I'm afraid //)
e. Evidently Humpty Dumpty was very angry, though he said nothing for a minute or two. When he *did* speak again, it was in a deep growl. (//4 when he DID speak again //)

In (a), which can only be read //4 YOU'D better not talk //, the sense is 'you should be concerned with yourself, instead of criticizing me'. In (b) the tone 4 on *now* is cohesive because it contrasts the present with what used to happen. In (c) *the head* contrasts with *the feet*, and in (d) *not quite right* contrasts with *not right*, modifying it by reference to its original absolute form. In (e) the marked positive form *did speak* contrasts with negative *said nothing*.

The FALLING tone, TONE 1, if it is used in the context of a cohesive element, has the sense of 'and here's something more'. The additive cohesive items normally have this tone, if they carry tonic prominence at all, just as the adversative normally has tone 4 – although, as always with the English intonation system, both can be reversed, to give a flavour of the opposite meaning: for example, *moreover* can be spoken on tone 4 meaning 'there is something else, despite what you may think', and *however* on tone 1 meaning 'there is a reservation to be expressed, so wait!'

Unlike tone 4, tone 1 does not by itself carry any cohesive force. But there is a strong case for considering the LOW RISING tone (preceded by mid level), TONE 3, as the cohesive variety of tone 1, since it does function in other respects as a kind of dependent or non-autonomous equivalent of the falling tone. So for example in

[5:73] a. The little stable boy went to bed feeling very excited. In the morning (3// in the MORNING //), he packed his bag and left home.

the tone shows that *in the morning* is cohesively related to the preceding sentence, and means 'next morning'. This tone would be inappropriate, for example, in a sentence such as [5:73b] occurring initially in the discourse, where *in the morning* means 'every morning' and cannot be cohesive:

[5:73] b. In the morning I'm usually very tired.

But both tone 3 and tone 4 are also used in contexts where the relation which they signal is a structural one, to a preceding or, more often, a following clause within the same sentence. In such instances they are not cohesive in the sense in which the term is defined here.*

Naturally, the type of cohesion outlined in the last few paragraphs appears only in spoken English, since the cohesion is being expressed through the medium of intonation. Intonation, however, has a very far-reaching and pervasive function in the grammar of the spoken language, so that it is not surprising that it should play a significant part in this particular region. As we have emphasized throughout, cohesive relations are on the borders of grammar, and it is likely that some of the specific grammatical functions of the intonation system derive in the first place from its role in the expression of cohesion within a text.

---

* For a discussion of these aspects of intonation see M. A. K. Halliday, *A course in spoken English: Intonation* (Part II of *A course in spoken English*, by Ronald Mackin, M. A. K. Halliday, J. McH. Sinclair and K. H. Albrow), London: Oxford University Press, 1970.

Chapter 6

Lexical Cohesion

6.1 The class of 'general nouns'

In the previous four chapters, we have described the various types of grammatical cohesion: reference, substitution and ellipsis, and conjunction. In order to complete the picture of cohesive relations it is necessary to take into account also lexical cohesion. This is the cohesive effect achieved by the selection of vocabulary.

On the borderline between grammatical and lexical cohesion is the cohesive function of the class of GENERAL NOUN. We can speak about a borderline here because a general noun is itself a borderline case between a lexical item (member of an open set) and a grammatical item (member of a closed system).

The class of general noun is a small set of nouns having generalized reference within the major noun classes, those such as 'human noun', 'place noun', 'fact noun' and the like. Examples are:

people, person, man, woman, child, boy, girl [human]
creature [non-human animate]
thing, object [inanimate concrete count]
stuff [inanimate concrete mass]
business, affair, matter [inanimate abstract]
move [action]
place [place]
question, idea [fact]

These items are often neglected in descriptions of English; but they play a significant part in verbal interaction, and are also an important source of cohesion in the spoken language. The following examples illustrate their cohesive function:

[6:1] a. Didn't everyone make it clear they expected the minister to resign? – They did. But it seems to have made no impression on the man.

b. 'I should like to be a *little* larger, sir, if you wouldn't mind,' said Alice: 'three inches is such a wretched height to be'.
'It's a very good height indeed !' said the Caterpillar angrily, rearing itself upright as it spoke (it was exactly three inches high).
'But I'm not used to it !' pleaded poor Alice in a piteous tone. And she thought to herself, 'I wish the creatures wouldn't be so easily offended !'

c. What shall I do with all this crockery? – Leave the stuff there; someone'll come and put it away.

d. We all kept quiet. That seemed the best move.

e. Can you tell me where to stay in Geneva? I've never been to the place.

f. Henry seems convinced there's money in dairy farming. I don't know what gave him that idea.

As these examples show, a general noun in cohesive function is almost always accompanied by the reference item *the*. This *the* is anaphoric, and the effect is that the whole complex '*the* + general noun' functions like an anaphoric reference item. The most usual alternative to *the* is a demonstrative, and if a demonstrative occurs it usually carries the tonic: *cf: that idea* in example [6:1f]. This relates to the fact that the general noun itself does NOT carry the tonic, if it is functioning cohesively; a fact which holds true even when it occurs in final position, which is the unmarked location of tonic prominence. Hence in [6:1a, d, e and f] it would be highly improbable, and strongly contrastive, to assign tonic prominence to *man*, *move*, *place* and *idea*.

The above gives us some indication of the status of general nouns. From a lexical point of view, they are the superordinate members of major lexical sets, and therefore their cohesive use is an instance of the general principle whereby a superordinate item operates anaphorically as a kind of synonym (see 6.2 below). From a grammatical point of view, the combination of general noun plus specific determiner, such as *the man*, *the thing*, is very similar to a reference item. There is little difference between *it seems to have made very little impression on the man* and *it seems to have made very little impression on him*: in both instances interpretation is possible only by reference to something that has gone before. But it is not the case that there is no difference at all: the form with general noun, *the man*, opens up another possibility, that of introducing an interpersonal element into the meaning, which is absent in the case of the personal pronoun. (It may be worth stressing once again that the fact that general nouns are very general in meaning, and therefore often interpretable only by reference to some element other than themselves, does not make them unimportant in the language. Since they require recourse to another item, that item must be located earlier within the same text; and this means that they play a significant role in making a text hang together.)

The expression of interpersonal meaning, of a particular attitude on the part of the speaker, is an important function of general nouns. Essentially the attitude conveyed is one of familiarity, as opposed to distance, in which the speaker assumes the right to represent the thing he is referring to as it impinges on him personally; hence the specific attitude may be either contemptuous or sympathetic, the two being closely related as forms of personal involvement (*cf* the meaning of diminutives in many languages). There are quite a few general nouns which have this inter-personal element as an inherent part of their meaning, especially those referring to human beings, for example *idiot, fool, devil, dear;* and these are supplemented, at any one moment in time, by a host of more or less slang terms differing widely from one social group and one generation to another. But whether or not it is inherently attitudinal in meaning, a general noun in cohesive function can always be accompanied by an attitudinal Modifier. So we have examples such as *the dears, the poor dears;* and also *the stupid thing, the lucky fellow* and so on:

[6:2] a. I've been to see my great-aunt. The poor old girl's getting very forgetful these days.
   b. Alice caught the baby with some difficulty, as it was a queer-shaped little creature, and held out its arms and legs in all directions, 'just like a star-fish', thought Alice. The poor little thing was snorting like a steam-engine when she caught it...
   c. Henry's thinking of rowing the Atlantic. Do go and talk to the wretched fool.

These forms with interpersonal elements in their meaning have certain special features when they are used cohesively. The general nouns may be transcategorized up the scale inanimate–animate–human, with *creature* being used for human as well as animate, and *thing* for all three (*cf* 3.2.3 above). The adjectives cannot be submodified, by words such as *very*, nor can they be compared. Only adjectives with an attitudinal meaning can occur; it would not be possible to say *the fat man* in [6:1a] – or if one did, by virtue of its occurrence in this context *fat* would become attitudinal. A general noun in cohesive function can in fact accept only non-defining Modifiers; since it refers back to the entire nominal group with which it is to be identified for its interpretation, it carries over any defining elements from this nominal group, and hence it must itself remain undefined. Attitudinal adjectives are by their nature non-defining. Here is a Shakespearean example (*the good man*, referring to Lear):

[6:3]   All blest secrets,
        All you unpublish'd virtues of the earth,
        Spring with my tears ! be aidant and remediate
        In the good man's distress !

As a corollary of their carrying over of definiteness, general nouns of the human class are very frequently used in anaphoric reference to personal names. It is interesting that the other use of these nouns, when there is an attitudinal element present either in the noun itself or in the form of modification, is as vocatives: terms of abuse or endearment, *you crazy fool!* and the like. There they are exophoric instead of anaphoric; and this underlines the fact that the typical context in which they function is a referential one, so that like reference items they refer either to the situation or to the preceding text.

The interpersonal element of attitude, however, although it is frequently associated with the cohesive use of general nouns, is by no means always present; this kind of anaphoric reference does not necessarily embody any attitudinal meaning. The following are entirely neutral:

[6:4] a. I've just read John Smith's essay. The whole thing is very well thought out.
      b. Robert seems very worried about something. I think you ought to have a talk with the boy.

Here the items *thing* and *boy* refer anaphorically to *John Smith's essay* and *Robert* respectively; and again the identity of reference is signalled by the presence of the anaphoric reference item *the*.

6.2 Types of reiteration

Thus the use of general nouns as cohesive agents depends on their occurring in the context of reference – having the same referent as the item which they presuppose, this being signalled by the accompaniment of a reference item.

This use of general words as cohesive elements, however, when seen from the lexical point of view, is merely a special case of a much more general phenomenon which we may term REITERATION. Reiteration is a form of lexical cohesion which involves the repetition of a lexical item, at one end of the scale; the use of a general word to refer back to a lexical item, at the other end of the scale; and a number of things in between – the use of a synonym, near-synonym, or superordinate. Let us illustrate each of these in turn.

[6:5] a. There was a large mushroom growing near her, about the same height as herself; and, when she had looked under it, it occurred to her that she might as well look and see what was on the top of it.
   She stretched herself up on tiptoe, and peeped over the edge of the mushroom, . . .

   b. Accordingly . . . I took leave, and turned to the ascent of the peak. The climb is perfectly easy . . .

   c. Then quickly rose Sir Bedivere, and ran,
   And leaping down the ridges lightly, plung'd
   Among the bulrush beds, and clutch'd the sword
   And lightly wheel'd and threw it. The great brand
   Made light'nings in the splendour of the moon . . .

   d. Henry's bought himself a new Jaguar. He practically lives in the car.

In (a), there is REPETITION: *mushroom* refers back to *mushroom*. In (b) *climb* refers back to *ascent*, of which it is a SYNONYM. In (c) *brand* refers back to *sword*, of which it is a near SYNONYM. In (d), *car* refers back to *Jaguar*; and *car* is a SUPERORDINATE of *Jaguar* – that is, a name for a more general class (as *vehicle* is a superordinate of *car*, *spoon* of *teaspoon*, *cut* of *pare*, and so on). All these are cohesive in exactly the same way as the GENERAL WORDS illustrated in [6:1–4]; the latter differ only in level of generality.

All these instances have in common the fact that one lexical item refers back to another, to which it is related by having a common referent. We shall refer to this general phenomenon as REITERATION. A reiterated item may be a repetition, a synonym or near-synonym, a superordinate, or a general word; and in most cases it is accompanied by a reference item, typically *the*.

At the same time, there is no sharp dividing line between these forms, consisting of a related lexical item plus anaphoric *the*, and the personal reference forms such as *he* and *it*. We can in fact recognize a continuum, or 'cline', of cohesive elements; for example (adapting [6:5b] above):

[6:6] I turned to the ascent of the peak. $\left\{\begin{array}{l}\text{The ascent}\\\text{The climb}\\\text{The task}\\\text{The thing}\\\text{It}\end{array}\right\}$ is perfectly easy.

Here we have (1) the same item repeated, (2) a synonym, (3) a superordinate, (4) a general noun and (5) a personal reference item. Here *ascent* and *climb* are lexical items whose interpretation IN THIS INSTANCE is shown (by anaphoric *the*) to be identical with that of an earlier lexical item to which they are related either by repetition (*ascent*) or by synonymy (*climb*). The same is true of *task*, except that *task* is a more general term, higher in the lexical taxonomy; so the cohesive environment of the word *task* adds specificity to it – when we interpret *the task* by reference to *the ascent of the peak* we identify the particular kind of task referred to. The word *thing* is an even more general term which is being used in exactly the same way; but it is still more specific than *it*, because it usually excludes people and animals, as well as qualities, states and relations, and it always excludes facts and reports. Most general of all is the reference item *it*; but even *it* is not a 'pure' phoric element since it likewise embodies some specificity, though only minimal: it excludes people. The form *it* comes closest to being an alternative realization of general noun + reference item, as in *the thing*.

Hence the boundary between lexical cohesion of the type we are calling REITERATION, and grammatical cohesion of the REFERENCE type, is by no means clearcut; the class of general nouns provides a form of cohesion that lies somewhere in between the two, and is interpretable as either. Here we are interpreting it as lexical cohesion, and bringing it under the general heading of what we are calling reiteration. When we talk about REITERATION, therefore, we are including not only the repetition of the same lexical item but also the occurrence of a related item, which may be anything from a synonym or near synonym of the original to a general word dominating the entire class. Let us categorize these as above: any instance of reiteration may be (a) the SAME WORD, (b) a SYNONYM or NEAR-SYNONYM, (c) a SUPERORDINATE or (d) a GENERAL WORD. For example:

[6:7] There's a boy climbing that tree.
  a. The boy's going to fall if he doesn't take care.

b. The lad's going to fall if he doesn't take care.
c. The child's going to fall if he doesn't take care.
d. The idiot's going to fall if he doesn't take care.

In (a), *boy* is repeated. In (b), the reiteration takes the form of a synonym *lad*; in (c), of the superordinate term *child*; and in (d), of a general word *idiot*. It is typical of such general words, at least those referring to people, as we have seen, that they carry a connotation of attitude on the part of the speaker, usually one of familiarity (derogatory or intimate). Here is another example, this time with a non-human referent:

[6:8] There's a boy climbing the old elm.
  a. That elm isn't very safe.
  c. That tree isn't very safe.
  d. That old thing isn't very safe.

Here (a) repeats *elm*, (c) selects the superordinate *tree*, and (d) the general word *thing*. It is difficult to find a synonym of the same degree of specificity in this example; we could find one in a series like: *There's a boy climbing along the rafters.* (a) *Those rafters . . .* (b) *Those beams . . .* (c) *Those timbers . . .* (d) *Those things . . ..* The category of superordinate, illustrated in (c), refers to any item whose meaning includes that of the earlier one; in technical terms, any item that dominates the earlier one in the lexical taxonomy. There are often several possible superordinate terms, words that are intermediate between the lowest level, represented by (a) and (b), and the highest, represented by (d). That is to say, there may be various degrees of generality intermediate between the presupposed item itself, *eg: elm* in [6:8], on the one hand, and a very general word like *thing* on the other. Words with intermediate status are more open to modification, though still with a tendency to some evaluative meaning, *eg: this eminent author*.

The general words, which correspond to major classes of lexical items, are as we have said very commonly used with cohesive force. They are on the borderline between lexical items and substitutes. The substitutes *one* and *do* can be thought of as being as it were the highest points in the lexical taxonomy of nouns and verbs respectively; as such, they constitute a closed class, and so acquire a purely grammatical function. Next below them come the general words, such as *thing, person, make, do* and so on; these, although limited in number, are not clearly bounded and it is hardly possible to compile a definitive list of them. They do function more or less as lexical items, so when they occur cohesively we can treat them as instances of lexical cohesion. But there is no sharp line between substitutes and general words – because there is no very sharp line between grammar and vocabulary: the vocabulary, or lexis, is simply the open-ended and most 'delicate' aspect of the grammar of a language.

Not all general words are used cohesively; in fact, only the nouns are, for the reason noted above, namely that a general word is cohesive only when in the context of reference – that is, when it has the same referent as whatever it is presupposing, and when it is accompanied by a reference item. All the types of lexical cohesion that we have considered up to this point have involved identity of reference; no matter whether the reiterated item has been a repetition, a synonym, a superordinate or a general word, it has been assumed to share a common referent with the original. Keeping to this assumption for the moment we can shift our point of view from the grammatical to the lexical and look at reference from the lexical angle, interpreting it as a means of avoiding the repetition of lexical items and thus making it clear that if the lexical item had been reiterated it would have had the same referent.

The simplest illustration of this is provided by proper names. Suppose we have

[6:9] John took Mary to the dance. John was left all alone.

– how do we know whether it's the same John? The answer to this is, if you want to make it clear that it is the same John, don't call him *John*; call him *he*. In other words, we use a reference item; and this conveys the meaning 'the present sentence is related to the last one by the fact that both contain a reference to the same individual'. This does not mean that a repeated proper noun can never have the same referent as it had on its first occurrence; the second *John* COULD refer to the same person as the first – we simply do not know whether it does or not. If *John* is repeated, we need some further signal to tell us how to interpret it.

With common nouns, the means are readily available; the signal is given by a reference item, typically *the*. So for example in

[6:10] Just then a Fawn came wandering by: it looked at Alice with its large gentle eyes, but didn't seem at all frightened. . . . 'What do you call yourself?', the Fawn said at last.

the signals 'the Fawn referred to on this second occasion is the same Fawn as that referred to in the (or some) preceding sentence'.

From this it would seem that it is not the repetition of the word *Fawn* that has the cohesive effect, but only its repetition accompanied by an anaphoric reference item. This might suggest that there was no distinct category of LEXICAL COHESION; that what we are calling 'lexical cohesion' was merely the reiteration of a lexical item in a context of grammatical cohesion, the cohesion being simply a matter of reference. But that is not, in fact, the whole story. It is true that lexical reiteration, where the reference is identical, is usually made explicit by means of an anaphoric reference item. But there are other types of lexical cohesion which do not depend on identity of reference; patterns of word occurrences which by themselves give a separate, purely lexical dimension of internal cohesion to a text.

6.3 Lexical relations as cohesive patterns

The most immediately obvious type of lexical cohesion is that illustrated by *the Fawn* in [6:10], where the same word is repeated and has the same referent on both occasions. We have already seen that it is not necessary for the second instance to be an exact repetition of the same word; it may be any kind of what we have called REITERATION – synonym, superordinate, or general word. We have assumed up to this point, however, that there must be identity of reference between the two, and this suggested that 'lexical cohesion' was to be interpreted simply as an accompanying feature that may be associated with grammatical reference.

It is not necessary for two lexical occurrences to have the same referent, however, in order for them to be cohesive. Consider the following examples:

[6:11] Why does this little boy have to wriggle all the time?
    a. Other boys don't wriggle.
    b. Boys always wriggle.
    c. Good boys don't wriggle.
    d. Boys should be kept out of here.

In (a), *boys* ties with *boy* although they are not coreferential. This could be explained as cohesion by comparative reference, in view of the item *other*; but in (b) there is no identity of reference and no reference item either, yet *boys* still coheres with *boy*. It would be possible to use a personal reference item INSTEAD OF *boys* here (*they always wriggle*); this reflects the weak relation of coreference that does exist between the two – *boys* refers to 'all boys' and therefore by implication includes 'this little boy'. In (c), however, there is neither the implication of inclusion nor any form of reference whatever; yet still there is the same cohesive relation between *boys* and *boy*. Nor is this relationship in any way dependent on the presence of other items suggesting the same general referential environment; it is not the wriggling that provides the context, as (d) shows. Many instances of cohesion are purely lexical, a function simply of the co-occurrence of lexical items, and not in any way dependent on the relation of reference.

A lexical item, therefore, coheres with a preceding occurrence of the same item whether or not the two have the same referent, or indeed whether or not there is any referential relationship between them. Let us summarize the possibilities with another example. The second occurrence may be, as far as reference is concerned, (a) IDENTICAL, (b) INCLUSIVE, (c) EXCLUSIVE or (d) simply UNRELATED. So for example:

[6:12] There's a boy climbing that tree.
    a. The boy's going to fall if he doesn't take care.
    b. Those boys are always getting into mischief.
    c. And there's another boy standing underneath.
    d. Most boys love climbing trees.

In (a) *the boy* has the same referent as *a boy* has; the reference item *he* could be used instead. In (b) *those boys* includes the boy referred to previously, and others as well; here we could have a reference item *they* on the basis of the weak coreferentiality referred to in Chapter 2 (2.4.1.3), where the relation is one of inclusion; *cf* example [6:11b] above. In (c) *another boy* excludes the boy referred to in the first sentence; here there is explicit NON-identity of reference, and in such instances we cannot have a reference item to replace *boy* – we can however have a substitute or elliptical form, *another one* or *another*. In (d), *most boys* bears no referential relation at all to the boy previously mentioned; we cannot gather from (d) whether the boy in question likes climbing trees or not, and the speaker does not necessarily know, or care. This is borne out by the fact that he could make it explicit either way, by the use of a particular intonation pattern:

[6:12] d'. //1 MOST boys love climbing trees //
    d''. //4 MOST boys //1 LOVE climbing trees //

where (d') means 'just as that one does' while (d'') means 'whereas I'm not sure about that one'. Characteristically in (d), where there is no relation of reference between the two occurrences of *boy*, there is more lexical repetition overall; here not only *boy* but also *climb* and *tree* are repeated, and this compensates, as it were, for the lack of any referential connection.

Properly speaking, reference is irrelevant to lexical cohesion. It is not by virtue of any referential relation that there is a cohesive force set up between two occurrences of a lexical item; rather, the cohesion exists as a direct relation between the forms themselves (and thus is more like substitution than reference). So for example there is cohesion between the two occurrences of *wriggle* in [6:11a]; the question whether they refer to the same wriggling is one which, fortunately, does not arise. Compare:

[6:13] a. Henry presented her with his own portrait. As it happened, she had always wanted a portrait of Henry.

b. The Forthright Building Society required, apparently, that a borrower should sign, seal and deliver the mortgage deed in the presence of a solicitor, so that the solicitor would sign it as the witness. This is quite a common requirement. Where a borrower is legally represented, his own solicitor will usually be the witness to the borrower's execution of the mortgage deed.*

In (a), the second occurrence of *portrait* is indefinite; but it is still cohesive. The last sentence in (b) contains the items *borrower, witness, solicitor* and *mortgage deed*, all of which are repetitions and as such cohere with the earlier occurrences; but the whole discussion is hypothetical and the question of coreference is simply not applicable, or decidable.

6.4 Collocation

We now come to the most problematical part of lexical cohesion, cohesion that is achieved through the association of lexical items that regularly co-occur.

We have seen that lexical reiteration takes place not only through repetition of an identical lexical item but also through occurrence of a different lexical item that is systematically related to the first one, as a synonym or superordinate of it. This principle applies quite generally, irrespective of whether or not there is identity of reference; so, for example, in [6:11] we could have had *children* instead of *boys* throughout and the effect would still have been cohesive.

---

* *The Legal Side of Buying a House*, Consumers' Association, 1965.

Furthermore, we find that the cohesive effect is still present if in place of *children* we now have *girls*:

[6:14] Why does this little boy wriggle all the time? Girls don't wriggle.

Girls and *boys* are hardly synonyms, nor is there any possibility of their having the same referent; they are mutually exclusive categories. Yet their proximity in a discourse very definitely contributes to the texture.

There is obviously a systematic relationship between a pair of words such as *boy* and *girl*; they are related by a particular type of oppositeness, called COMPLEMENTARITY in Lyons' classification. We can therefore extend the basis of the lexical relationship that features as a cohesive force and say that there is cohesion between any pair of lexical items that stand to each other in some recognizable lexicosemantic (word meaning) relation. This would include not only synonyms and near-synonyms such as *climb* ... *ascent, beam* ... *rafter, disease* ... *illness*, and superordinates such as *elm* ... *tree, boy* ... *child, skip* ... *play*, but also pairs of opposites of various kinds, complementaries such as *boy* ... *girl, stand up* ... *sit down*, antonyms such as *like* ... *hate, wet* ... *dry, crowded* ... *deserted*, and converses such as *order* ... *obey*.

It also includes pairs of words drawn from the same ordered series. For example, if *Tuesday* occurs in one sentence and *Thursday* in another, the effect will be cohesive; similarly *dollar* ... *cent, north* ... *south, colonel* ... *brigadier*. Likewise with any pairs drawn from unordered lexical sets, like *basement* ... *roof, road* ... *rail, red* ... *green*. The members of such sets often stand in some recognizable semantic relation to one another; they may be related as part to whole, like *car* ... *brake, box* ... *lid*, or as part to part, like *mouth* ... *chin, verse* ... *chorus* (or *refrain*); they may be co-hyponyms of the same superordinate term, *ie* both members of the same more general class, such as *chair* ... *table* (both hyponyms of *furniture*), *walk* ... *drive* (both hyponyms of *go*); and so on.

The members of any such set stand in some kind of semantic relation to one another, but for textual purposes it does not much matter what this relation is. There is always the possibility of cohesion between any pair of lexical items which are in some way associated with each other in the language. So we will find a very marked cohesive effect deriving from the occurrence in proximity with each other of pairs such as the following, whose meaning relation is not easy to classify in systematic semantic terms: *laugh* ... *joke, blade* ... *sharp, garden* ... *dig, ill* ... *doctor, try* ...

succeed, bee . . . honey, door . . . window, king . . . crown, boat . . . row, sun-shine . . . cloud. The cohesive effect of such pairs depends not so much on any systematic semantic relationship as on their tendency to share the same lexical environment, to occur in COLLOCATION with one another. In general, any two lexical items having similar patterns of collocation – that is, tending to appear in similar contexts – will generate a cohesive force if they occur in adjacent sentences.

This effect is not limited to a pair of words. It is very common for long cohesive chains to be built up out of lexical relations of this kind, with word patterns like *candle . . . flame . . . flicker, hair . . . comb . . . curl . . . wave, poetry . . . literature . . . reader . . . writer . . . style, sky . . . sunshine . . . cloud . . . rain* weaving in and out of successive sentences. Such patterns occur freely both within the same sentence and across sentence boundaries; they are largely independent of the grammatical structure. Rather than citing a number of short passages to illustrate this we will quote one long paragraph which is a typically rich reserve of such collocational cohesion; note the importance of the title in this regard:

[6:15]   A RIDE ON AN AVALANCHE

Few Yosemite visitors ever see snow avalanches and fewer still know the exhilaration of riding on them. In all my mountain-eering I have enjoyed only one avalanche ride, and the start was so sudden and the end came so soon I had but little time to think of the danger that attends this sort of travel, though at such times one thinks fast. One fine Yosemite morning after a heavy snow-fall, being eager to see as many avalanches as possible and wide views of the forest and summit peaks in their new white robes before the sunshine had time to change them, I set out early to climb by a side canyon to the top of a commanding ridge a little over three thousand feet above the Valley. On account of the looseness of the snow that blocked the canyon I knew the climb would require a long time, some three or four hours as I estimated; but it proved far more difficult than I had anticipated. Most of the way I sank waist deep, almost out of sight in some places. After spending the whole day to within half an hour or so of sundown, I was still several hundred feet below the summit. Then my hopes were reduced to getting up in time to see the sunset. But I was not to get summit views of any sort that day, for deep trampling near the canyon head, where the snow was strained, started an avalanche, and I was swished down to the foot of the canyon as if by enchantment. The wallowing ascent had taken nearly all day, the descent only about a minute. When the avalanche started I threw myself on my back and spread my arms to try to keep from sinking. Fortunately, though the grade of the canyon is very steep, it is not interrupted by precipices large enough to cause outbounding or free plunging. On no part of the rush was I buried. I was only moderately imbedded on the surface or at times a little below it, and covered with a veil of back-streaming dust particles; and as the whole mass beneath and about me joined in the flight there was no friction, though I was tossed here and there and lurched from side to side. When the avalanche swedged and came to rest I found myself on top of the crumpled pile without a bruise or scar. This was a fine experience. Hawthorne says somewhere that steam has spiritualized travel; though unspiritual smells, smoke, etc, still attend steam travel. This flight in what might be called a milky way of snow-stars was the most spiritual and exhilarating of all the modes of motion I have ever experienced. Elijah's flight in a chariot of fire could hardly have been more gloriously exciting.

(from *The Yosemite* by John Muir, 1912)

Examples of chains of collocational cohesion are: *mountaineering . . . Yosemite . . . summit peaks . . . climb . . . ridge; hours . . . whole day . . . (sundown . . . sunset . . .) all day . . . minute; wallowing . . . sinking . . . buried . . . imbedded; ride . . . riding . . . ride . . . travel . . . travel . . . travel . . . flight . . . motion . . . flight.*

The analysis and interpretation of lexical patterning of this kind is a major task in the further study of textual cohesion. Here we shall simply group together all the various lexical relations that do NOT depend on referential identity and are NOT of the form of reiteration accompanied by *the* or a demonstrative – in other words, all lexical cohesion that is not covered by what we have called 'reiteration' – and treat it under the general heading of COLLOCATION, or collocational cohesion, without attempting to classify the various meaning relations that are involved. But it should be borne in mind that this is simply a cover term for the cohesion that results from the co-occurrence of lexical items that are in some way or other typically associated with one another, because they tend to occur in similar environments: the specific kinds of co-occurrence relations are variable and complex, and would have to be interpreted in the light of a general semantic description of the English language.*

6.5 The general concept of lexical cohesion

The suggested framework for the description of lexical cohesion is as follows:

Type of lexical cohesion: Referential relation:

1. Reiteration
    (a) same word (repetition)   (i) same referent
    (b) synonym (or near-synonym) (ii) inclusive
    (c) superordinate   (iii) exclusive
    (d) general word   (iv) unrelated

2. Collocation

The effect of lexical, especially collocational, cohesion on a text is subtle and difficult to estimate. With grammatical cohesion the effect is relatively clear: if one comes across the word *he*, for example, there is no doubt that some essential information is called for, and that the identity of the *he* must be recovered from somewhere. Reference items, substitutes and conjunctions all explicitly presuppose some element other than themselves.

In lexical cohesion, however, it is not a case of there being particular lexical items which always have a cohesive function. EVERY lexical item MAY enter into a cohesive relation, but by itself it carries no indication whether it is functioning cohesively or not. That can be established only by reference to the text.

This seems to suggest that what we are calling lexical cohesion carries no meaning; that it is simply an incidental consequence of the fact that discourse does not wander at random from one topic to another but runs on reasonably systematic lines with a certain consistency of topic and predictability of development. In general, of course, this is true; most discourse is well organized, and the patterned occurrence of lexical items is a natural consequence of this. But this does not imply that lexical co-

---

* For a more extended discussion of this point, and of lexical cohesion in general, see Ruqaiya Hasan: *Language in the Imaginative Context, a sociolinguistic study of stories told by children*, London, Routledge & Kegan Paul (Primary Socialization, Language and Education, ed Basil Bernstein), forthcoming.

hesion has no meaning. Without our being aware of it, each occurrence of a lexical item carries with it its own textual history, a particular collocational environment that has been built up in the course of the creation of the text and that will provide the context within which the item will be incarnated on this particular occasion. This environment determines the 'instantial meaning', or text meaning, of the item, a meaning which is unique to each specific instance.

In reading or listening to text, we process continuously, and therefore by the time any given lexical item is taken in, its context has already been prepared; and the preceding lexical environment is perhaps the most significant component of this context. It frequently provides a great deal of hidden information that is relevant to the interpretation of the item concerned. There are many examples of this in the long paragraph from John Muir quoted above. To consider just one of these: an inspection of the collocational environment of the item *sunset* shows that it ties with *sundown* in the preceding sentence, and less immediately, with the words *(long) time . . . hours . . . (whole) day* in the slightly less immediate context. These two collocational themes come together in the phrase *within half an hour of sundown*. This environment defines *sunset* in the context of time, as an event preceded by a fixed and limited interval, and sets the stage for the passage which serves as the immediate environment for *sunset*, namely *in time to see the sunset*. The result is twofold. On one hand, when we meet this phrase *in time to see the sunset* we interpret it with what has gone before in mind, and this defines the unique instantial meaning of the word *sunset* on this occasion. On the other hand, the fact that we do this has the effect of making the word *sunset*, when it does occur, cohesive with the related items that have preceded it, and hence of giving it a significant part in the creation of texture.

The lexical environment of any item includes, naturally, not only the words that are in some way or other related to it, in the terms discussed in this chapter, but also all other words in the preceding passage, and all of these contribute to its specific interpretation in the given instance. But it is the occurrence of the item IN THE CONTEXT OF RELATED LEXICAL ITEMS that provides cohesion and gives to the passage the quality of text. The relatedness is a matter of more or less; there is no clearly defined cutoff point such that we can say that *sunset*, for example, is related to just this set of words and no others. But we can say that it is more closely related to some than to others; and it is the closeness of the relationship that determines the cohesive effect.

The relative strength of the collocational tension is really a function of two kinds of relatedness, one kind being relatedness in the linguistic system and the other being relatedness in the text. What we are calling related lexical items are related in the linguistic system. In the linguistic system there is a closer relationship between *sunset* and *sundown* than, say, between *sunset* and *day*; the latter are, in turn, more closely related than *sunset* and *summit*, or *sunset* and *mountain*, although there is some relationship here too, less remote than, say, between *sunset* and *sight* or *sunset* and *estimate*. There are degrees of proximity in the lexical system, a function of the relative probability with which one word tends to co-occur with another. Secondly, in the text there is relatedness of another kind, relative proximity in the simple sense of the distance separating one item from another, the number of words or clauses or sentences in between. The cohesive force that is exerted between any pair of lexical items in a passage of discourse is a function of their relative proximity in these two respects.

There is a very close proximity between *sunset* and *sundown* as regards their relatedness in the linguistic system; they are morphologically related, both containing the element *sun*, and they are also near-synonyms, *sunset* referring to a particular event considered as a perceptual phenomenon, and *sundown* referring to the same event considered as defining a moment in time. If the two occur in adjacent sentences, they exert a very strong cohesive force; this would be progressively weaker the greater the textual distance between them.

There is a third factor influencing the cohesive force between a pair of lexical items in a text, and that is their overall frequency in the system of the language. A word which enters with equal readiness into collocation with words of every possible range of lexical meaning effects relatively little cohesion with any of them. Words such as *go* or *man* or *know* or *way* can hardly be said to contract significant cohesive relations, because they go with anything at all. Since, roughly speaking, words of this kind are also those with high overall frequency in the language, in general the higher the frequency of a lexical item (its overall frequency in the system) the smaller the part it plays in lexical cohesion in texts.

When analysing a text in respect of lexical cohesion, the most important thing is to use common sense, combined with the knowledge that we have, as speakers of a language, of the nature and structure of its vocabulary. We have a very clear idea of the relative frequency of words in our own language, and a ready insight (if we do not submerge it beneath the weight of the demand for formal procedures of analysis) into what constitutes a significant pattern and what does not. In assessing the lexical cohesion of a text we can safely ignore, as we certainly would do without even thinking about it, repetitive occurrences of fully grammatical (closed system) items like pronouns and prepositions and verbal auxiliaries, and also of lexical items of very high frequency like *take* and *do* and *good* and the others mentioned above. An exception to this appears just when such words occur in special senses with restricted patterns of collocation; for example *takings* in the sense of earnings, or *good* in a specifically moral context. Again, common sense needs to be brought into play. There is likely to be no significant cohesion between two occurrences of *good* of which one is in a moral sense and the other an exclamation meaning 'agree'; whereas there might be quite a significant tie between the first of these and a different but related word such as *virtue* or *judgment*.

In the coding scheme suggested in Chapter 8, we have used a single heading for all instances of collocational cohesion, making no differentiation either according to the different kinds of collocational relation or according to different degrees of cohesive force. A full interpretation of lexical cohesion would require further differentiation on both these counts: but such a treatment demands a separate study and is beyond our scope here.

There remains one point to be added to round off this limited discussion of lexical cohesion. A lexical item is not bound to a particular grammatical category, or to a particular morphological form. For example, there is just one lexical item *boy*, which has the forms *boy*, *boys*, *boy's* and *boys'*. Similarly *talk*, *talks*, *talked* and *talking* all represent a single lexical item *talk*. There are no perfectly clear criteria for deciding just how far this principle can be extended. For example, *go*, *goes*, *going*, *gone* and *went* are all one lexical item, and so are *good*, *better* and *best*; so also presumably are *noun* and (where these have the sense of 'noun') *nominal*, *nominalize* and *nominalization*. Rather more doubtful are pairs like *tooth* and *dental*, *map* and *cartographic*, *town* and *urban*; even more doubtful, perhaps, a set such as *young*, *youth* and *juvenile*. In the last resort it does not much matter, since such sets and pairs are cohesive anyway; but it is often possible to be guided by the context – the doubtful cases are generally doubtful precisely because they are sometimes the same word and sometimes not, so that pairs like *tooth* and *dental* may be used either as morphological variants of the same lexical item or as different lexical items. This, like many other linguistic points, is well brought out by forms of linguistic humour: an expression like *the archiepiscopal gaiters* is playing on the fact that *archiepiscopal* can be interpreted as simply a morphological variant of the item *archbishop*, although usually it functions as a related but separate item. On the other side of the line would be pairs like *starve* and *hunger*, or *disease* and *ill*, which are related by synonymy but probably never treated as forms of the same word.

The concept of the lexical item, therefore, is not totally clearcut; like most linguistic categories, although clearly defined in the ideal, it presents many indeterminacies in application to actual instances. Despite this indeterminacy – and it may be remarked that the term LEXICAL ITEM is rather less indeterminate than the folk-linguistic term WORD – it is an essential concept for the understanding of text. However luxuriant the grammatical cohesion displayed by any piece of discourse, it will not form a text unless this is matched by cohesive patterning of a lexical kind.

A final example:

[6:16]   Sing a song of sixpence, a pocket full of rye,
   Four-and-twenty blackbirds baked in a pie,
   When the pie was opened, the birds began to sing,
   Wasn't that a dainty dish to set before a king?

   The king was in his counting-house, counting out his money,
   The queen was in the parlour, eating bread and honey,
   The maid was in the garden, hanging out the clothes.
   Along came a blackbird and pecked off her nose.

There is reiteration of the same word, *eg: pie . . . pie, king . . . king*; of a near-synonym, *eg: eating . . . pecked*; of a superordinate, *eg: pie . . . dish, sixpence . . . money, blackbird . . . bird*; *dish* might perhaps also be interpreted as a general word in the modern sense ('anything nice'; *cf: dishy*). There is also collocational cohesion, *eg: king . . . queen, parlour . . . garden, dish . . . eat, rye . . . bread*. The rhyme provides a good illustration of the amount of lexical cohesion, and the varied nature of lexical cohesion, that is characteristic of even a very short text.★

★ In a recent unpublished paper, based on research in spoken discourse, J. McH. Sinclair suggests that patterns of lexical cohesion across utterance boundaries may be used by speakers to locate individual conceptual frames, or ORIENTATIONS. By choosing to repeat the vocabulary of a previous speaker, one signals willingness to negotiate in his terms; by using synonyms or paraphrase, one signals the opposite. Words of reference like pronouns, and elliptical syntax (*eg* one-word answers to questions) realize other selections of orientation.

Chapter 7

The meaning of cohesion

7.1 Text

In Chapter 1 we discussed what was meant by TEXT, and introduced the concept of cohesion to refer to the linguistic means whereby texture is achieved. In this chapter we resume the discussion in the light of the account that has been given of the various types of cohesion in English.

A text, we have suggested, is not just a string of sentences. In other words it is not simply a large grammatical unit, something of the same kind as a sentence but differing from it in size – a sort of supersentence. A text is best thought of not as a grammatical unit at all, but rather as a unit of a different kind: a semantic unit. The unity that it has is a unity of meaning in context, a texture that expresses the fact that it relates as a whole to the environment in which it is placed.

Being a semantic unit, a text is REALIZED in the form of sentences, and this is how the relation of text to sentence can best be interpreted. A set of related sentences, with a single sentence as the limiting case, is the embodiment or realization of a text. So the expression of the semantic unity of the text lies in the cohesion among the sentences of which it is composed.

Typically, in any text, every sentence except the first exhibits some form of cohesion with a preceding sentence, usually with the one immediately preceding. In other words, every sentence contains at least one anaphoric tie connecting it with what has gone before. Some sentences may also contain a cataphoric tie, connecting up with what follows; but these are very much rarer, and are not necessary to the creation of text.

Any piece of language that is operational, functioning as a unity in some context of situation, constitutes a text. It may be spoken or written, in any style or genre, and involving any number of active participants. It will usually display a form of consistency that is defined by the concept of register: a consistency in the meaning styles or types of semantic configuration which embody its relation to its environment. In other words, a text is usually reasonably homogeneous, at least in those linguistic aspects which most closely reflect and express its functional relationship to its setting.

7.1.1 Length of text

Text may be of any length. Since it is not a unit of the grammatical rank scale, and does not consist of sentences, it is not tied to the sentence as its lower limit. Many familiar texts in fact come out as less than one sentence in the grammatical structure. Warnings, titles, announcements, inscriptions and advertising slogans often consist of a verbal, nominal, adverbial or prepositional group only, for example

[7:1] a. No smoking
    b. Site of early chapel
    c. For sale
    d. National Westminster Bank
    e. Do not feed

Equally, there is no upper limit on the length of the text. An entire book may, and in many genres such as fiction typically does, comprise a single text; this is what is implied in the term 'a novel'. The same is true of a play, a sermon, a lecture, or a committee meeting.

The type of presupposition that provides texture in the text, in other words what we are calling cohesion, can extend over very long sequences. We find in everyday conversation elements turning up which presuppose earlier passages from which they are separated by many minutes and even hours of speaking time; and writers exploit this potential by making cohesive ties across very long stretches of text. It is clear that the awareness of text that we develop as part of the learning of the mother tongue is rather free from constraints of time, and depends much more on contextual relevance and integration of the language with the environment.

7.1.2 Definitiveness of the concept of text

It would be misleading to suggest that the concept of a text is fully determinate, or that we can always make clear decisions about what constitutes a single text and what does not. We can often say for certain that the whole of a given passage constitutes one text; and equally we can often say for certain that in another instance we have to deal with not one text but two, or more. But there are very many intermediate cases, instances of doubt where we are not at all sure whether we want to consider all the parts of a passage as falling within the same text or not.

Usually for practical purposes this does not matter very much. We are all intuitively aware of the validity of the general concept of a text; we know that there is such a thing, whether or not every instance can be unambiguously identified. What we react to, as speakers and listeners, readers and writers, in forming judgments about texture, is precisely the sort of cohesive structure the details of which we have been exploring in the preceding chapters.

Since the speaker or writer uses cohesion to signal texture, and the listener or reader reacts to it in his interpretation of texture, it is reasonable for us to make use of cohesion as a criterion for the recognition of the boundaries of a text. For most purposes, we can consider that a new text begins where a sentence shows no cohesion with those that have preceded.

Of course, we shall often find isolated sentences or other structural units which do not cohere with those around them, even though they form part of a connected passage. But usually if a sentence shows no cohesion with what has gone before, this does indicate a transition of some kind; for example, a transition between different stages in a complex transaction, or between narration and description in a passage of prose fiction. We might choose to regard such instances as discontinuities, signalling the beginning of a new text. Sometimes then the new text will turn out to be an interpolation, as in [1:8] and [1:9] in Chapter 1, after which the original text is once again resumed.

So although the concept of a text is exact enough, and can be adequately and explicitly defined, the definition will not by itself provide us with automatic criteria for recognizing in all instances what is a text and what is not. In all kinds of linguistic contexts, from the most formal to the most informal, we constantly have to do with forms of interaction which lie on the borderline between textual continuity and discontinuity. But the existence of indeterminate instances of this kind does not invalidate or destroy the usefulness of the general notion of text as the basic semantic unit of linguistic interaction.

7.1.3 Tight and loose texture

The frequent shift between narrative and verse in *Alice* provides an excellent illustration of the kind of transition that takes place between subtexts within a text. The verses are often quite outside the context of the narrative, and function as independent texts in their own right; they display no cohesion with what has preceded them. An example is *The Queen of Hearts* in the final chapter of *Alice in Wonderland*.

At the same time, the verses are often anticipated by some reference to poetry or song, or to the poem or song in question, so that the verse text as a whole is placed in an environment not unlike that of quoted speech. Here is an example:

> [7:2] 'The piece I am going to repeat,' [Humpty Dumpty] went on without noticing her remark, 'was written entirely for your amusement.'
>
> Alice felt that in that case she really *ought* to listen to it, so she sat down, and said, 'Thank you' rather sadly.
>
> 'In winter when the fields are white,
> I sing this song for your delight – . . .'.

Here there is lexical cohesion: *song* ties with *piece* in the first sentence and this in turn with *poetry* occurring a short while earlier.

This gives a fair indication of something that is a general feature of texts of all kinds. Textuality is not a matter of all or nothing, of dense clusters of cohesive ties or else none at all. Characteristically we find variation in texture, so that textuality is a matter of more or less. In some instances there will in fact be dense clusters of cohesive ties, giving a very close texture which serves to signal that the meanings of the parts are strongly interdependent and that the whole forms a single unity.

In other instances, however, the texture will be much looser. There will be fewer cohesive ties, perhaps just one or two. In *Alice* this alternation between tight and loose texture gives a very definite flavour to the whole. At one level, the whole of *Alice* is very much a single text. But when we shift our focus of attention we find that it contains portions that are less closely knit with the remainder, particularly the songs and the verses. And this is signalled by the relative cohesive independence of these from the surrounding passages – usually, however, a partial not a total independence.

Such a thing is typical of texts of many kinds. Some writers in particular seem to achieve a sort of periodic rhythm in which there is a regular alternation between tight and loose texture. In this connection we see the importance of the paragraph. The paragraph is a device introduced into the written language to suggest this kind of periodicity. In principle, we shall expect to find a greater degree of cohesion within a paragraph than between paragraphs; and in a great deal of written English this is exactly what we do find. In other writing, however, and perhaps as a characteristic of certain authors, the rhythm is contrapuntal: the writer extends a dense cluster of cohesive ties across the paragraph boundary and leaves the texture within the paragraph relatively loose. And this itself is an instance of a process that is very characteristic of language altogether, a process in which two associated variables come to be dissociated from each other with a very definite semantic and rhetorical effect. Here the two variables in question are the paragraph structure and the cohesive structure. The paragraph evolves first of all as the written symbol or representation of a periodic pattern that we might represent in the following way:

The vertical lines represent the paragraph boundaries and the wavy line represents the density of cohesive ties. Subsequently however the paragraph comes to function as a pattern maker (as distinct from being merely a pattern marker) in its own right, and something like the following picture emerges:

This represents the sort of writing in which the paragraph structure is played off against the cohesion, giving a complex texture in which the rhythm of the eye (and associated bodily rhythms of reading) is balanced against the rhythm that is engendered by the alternation between tightness and looseness of cohesive patterning.

7.1.4 Imaginary texture

Finally we may mention the type of cohesion which imposes an imaginary texture, by setting up expectations in the reader or listener which, since they are expectations of the past, by their nature, can not be satisfied. *Alice* will again serve as an example.

The very first sentence of *Through the Looking Glass* is

[7:3] One thing was certain, that the white kitten had had nothing to do with it; – it was the black kitten's fault entirely.

This sentence is clearly marked as cohesive, by the occurrence of the reference item *it*. In other words, the narrative begins as if one was already in the middle of it; it appears to presuppose a great deal that has gone before, but in fact nothing has gone before so we have to supply it for ourselves. Our interest is immediately engaged, since we inevitably start searching for some interpretation of the *it*. In this instance the reference, as often, is resolved cataphorically; we learn two paragraphs later that *it* refers to unwinding and entangling a ball of wool.

This device is commonly exploited in the opening of short stories, where it sets the tone for a genre whose meaning as a genre depends on the implications that what is in the text is not the whole story. It is also used in other contexts; the example was quoted in Chapter 1 (1.1.2) of the radio comedian who began his patter with the words *so we pushed him under the other one*.

This type of false or unresolved cohesion creates an effect of solidarity with the hearer or reader. It puts him on the inside, as one who is assumed to have shared a common experience with the speaker or writer. In its use in written fiction it is perhaps akin to the typical beginning of an oral folk narrative, which assumes prior knowledge of the matter of the tale on the part of the audience and makes allusion to the characters, the events or the circumstantial background in a form which often looks anaphoric, although there has been no previous mention, at least on the occasion in question. Similar properties are found in the oral narratives of young children, which presuppose a sharing of experience with the listener. The line between real and imaginary anaphora is not, after all, very clearcut; a great deal of news reporting depends for its interpretation on the assumption that the previous day's newspaper was part of the same text. And what is one text for one participant in a situation may not always be so for another, as appears when a person who has been day-dreaming suddenly voices one of his thoughts aloud.

7.2 The general meaning of cohesion

The general meaning of cohesion is embodied in the concept of text. By its role in providing 'texture', cohesion helps to create text.

Cohesion is a necessary though not a sufficient condition for the creation of text. What creates text is the TEXTUAL, or text-forming, component of the linguistic system, of which cohesion is one part. The textual component as a whole is the set of resources in a language whose semantic function is that of expressing relationship to the environment. It is the meaning derived from this component which characterizes a text -- which characterizes language that is operational in some context, as distinct from language that is not operational but citational, such as an index or other form of verbal inventory.

The textual component, and the place of cohesion within it, was discussed briefly in Chapter 1. The concept of a textual or text-forming function in the semantic system provides the most general answer to the question of what cohesion means. The textual component creates text, as opposed to non-text, and therein lies its meaning. Within the textual component, cohesion plays a special role in the creation of text. Cohesion expresses the continuity that exists between one part of the text and another. It is important to stress that continuity is not the whole of texture. The organization of each segment of a discourse in terms of its information structure, thematic patterns and the like is also part of its texture (see 7.4.1 below), no less important than the continuity from one segment to another. But the continuity adds a further element that must be present in order for the discourse to come to life as text.

The continuity that is provided by cohesion consists, in the most general terms, in expressing at each stage in the discourse the points of contact with what has gone before. The significance of this lies in the simple fact that there are such points of contact: that some entity or some circumstance, some relevant feature or some thread of argument persists from one moment to another in the semantic process, as the meanings unfold. But it has another more fundamental significance, which lies in the interpretation of the discourse. It is the continuity provided by cohesion that enables the reader or listener to supply all the missing pieces, all the components of the picture which are not present in the text but are necessary to its interpretation.

One of the major problems in understanding linguistic interaction – it is actually a problem in the understanding of ALL text processes, whether those of dialogue or others, though it is usually posed in the context of dialogue – is that of knowing how the listener fills in the missing information. The listener assigns meanings and interprets what is said to him; but in doing so he is himself supplying a great deal of the interpretation. The sentences and clauses and words that he hears, however perfectly formed lexicogrammatically (and, contrary to a popular belief, in most speech contexts they are very well formed indeed), are semantically full of holes. Or rather, this is the wrong metaphor. The situation is sometimes represented as if there were omissions which the listener had to supplement; as if the semantics of discourse was like a jigsaw puzzle with missing pieces in it. It would be more appropriate to describe it in terms of focus. What the lexicogrammar of the text presents is more like a picture that is complete but out of focus, with the outlines blurred and the details imperceptible. And if we take one further step and postulate that the picture to start with was not a photographic likeness but a symbolic representation, then we shall get some idea of the nature of the decoding process – for that is what it is – that the listener goes through.

What makes it possible for him to go through the process is the fact that what he hears is systematically related to its environment – it has 'textual meaning', as we have expressed it; and an essential component in this relationship is its continuity with what has preceded. The continuity is not merely an interesting feature that is associated with text; it is a necessary element in the interpretation of text. There has to be cohesion if meanings are to be exchanged at all.

This is so easy to illustrate that it is often forgotten. Consider the examples that have been cited throughout this book. The vast majority of them have been either drawn from *Alice in Wonderland* or made up. Why? This is the only way to ensure that attention would be focused on the point at issue: either to use a text that is so familiar that the reader will not pause over its interpretation, or to construct examples that are so artificial that they avoid the problem. If we had taken isolated sentences from real-life texts, they would have looked something like the following:

[7:4] a. Two rolled off it and stopped, as though arrested by a witch's wand, at Mrs Oliver's feet.
     b. This is a one with animals too, animals that go in water.
     c. Administration spokesmen were prompt to say it should not be considered any such thing.
     d. You could see them coming on him, before your very eyes.
     e. I expect you will get this but I'll send it if you want.
     f. It was the morning caught for ever.
     g. So he proposed having his discovery copied before parting with it.

These are typical examples of what people say and write – except that they do not say or write them in isolation. In interpreting them, we build in, along with other environmental factors, the continuity element; we do not even notice the indeterminacies and all the different meanings we could 'read in', because the lens is already in place before the picture comes along to be interpreted. But the process of interpretation goes on, and the patterns of cohesion have played a central part in it.

The point is perhaps obvious enough. But we often fail to realize just how much of our interpretation depends on this continuity with what has gone before. It is not only the referents that we have to supply – the meaning of *two* and *it* in (a), *this* in (b), *it* in (c), *them* and *him* in (d), *this* in (e), *it* in (f), *he* in (g). Nor is it simply information of the kind that is demanded by the *too* in (b), the *such* in (c) or the *so* in (g): 'in addition to what?', 'any thing such as what?', 'why did he propose having it done?' Taking these sentences by themselves we have no idea, or rather we have only the haziest idea, how to interpret the things – the objects, events and so forth – that are encoded in the grammatical structures and the lexical items. What kind of rolling took place? What does *with* mean, in *with animals*? In what ways are things *coming on him*? What can be made of *you will get this but I'll send it*? What sort of discovery is to be copied, how, and why? We cannot begin to visualize the morning, and we do not know whether it is a morning that has been mentioned before or one that is to be identified exophorically, as unique or at least recognizable under the circumstances. We do not know whether the spokesmen for the Administration are talking about an object, an institution or a lengthy passage of text – a fact or report. There is nothing unusual or mysterious about any of these examples; but they are out of focus, and will click into place only when we put them in their textual environment and satisfy the queries which they arouse.

It is hardly necessary to do this in order to demonstrate the point at issue. However, the reader may feel deceived if nothing further is said, so here is the immediately preceding co-text for each of the above examples:

(a) Joyce, a sturdy thirteen-year-old, seized the bowl of apples.
(b) This mobile's got fishes, yours has animals.
(c) During the hearing on Wednesday, Inouye said the questions furnished by Buzhardt 'should serve as a substitute, admittedly not the very best, but a substitute for cross-examination of Mr Dean by the President of the United States'.
(d) Spots. All over his face and hands –
(e) Nothing else has come for you except Staff Bulletin no 2.

(f) There on the rough thick paper, reduced to their simplest possible terms, were the stream, glittering and dimpling, the stone arch of the bridge flushed in morning sunlight, the moor and the hills.

(g) The nobleman, it appeared, had by this time become rather fond of Nanna and Pippa. He liked, it might be said, the way they comported themselves.

Anything approaching a 'full' interpretation is likely to need much more information than is recoverable from a preceding sentence or two. For example, in the text containing (g), two pages earlier, was the sentence *It was a highly indecent picture*.

Preceding (a), at intervals, there have occurred *It was to be a Hallowe'en party . . .* and *Mrs Oliver was partial to apples*. Moreover the whole text has, in turn, been preceded by other texts containing accounts of Mrs Oliver and her fondness for apples, as well as associated references to witchcraft. In the same way (c) has been preceded not only by six columns of detailed news but by six months of almost daily reporting centring around the Watergate affair. In (d) the chaotic absence of cohesion is used as a comic device to suggest information being extracted from someone against his will, though in fact (as the audience knows from the preceding text) the reluctance is feigned and the information is false:

Patch: Mind you, Sam, it may not be that at all. We can't tell what poor old Slivers has got –
Mellock: Who's Slivers?
  [*As they do not reply, Grindley shaking his head at Patch, Ursula cuts in.*]
Ursula: Is he the man you had locked in that cabin? [*As they do not reply*]
  He is, isn't he?
    [*They nod.*]
  Well, what's the matter with him?
Patch: It was the only thing we could do, you know. Until the doctor came.
Mellock [*not liking this*]: The doctor?
Ursula: Come on. What's the matter with him?
    [*They are obviously reluctant to answer.*]
  He was taken ill, wasn't he?
Patch: All hot and flushed. Then breaking into spots.
Gridley [*warningly*]: Bob! You know, we promised.
Ursula: Don't be idiotic. You've got to tell us.
Patch [*with feigned reluctance*]: Spots. All over his face and hands –

Gridley: You could see them coming on him, before your very eyes.
About that size. [*Indicates.*] No bigger. [*Shows them.*]★

Cohesive ties, especially those with the immediately preceding text,
are only one source for the information that the reader or listener requires. Both situational and more remote textual information are necessary
components. But it is surprising how much can often be recovered simply
from the presuppositions carried by the cohesive elements. The ongoing
continuity of discourse is a primary factor in its intelligibility.

This illustrates the meaning of cohesion as a whole. It provides, for
the text, which is a semantic unit, the sort of continuity which is achieved
in units at the grammatical level – the sentence, the clause and so on –
by grammatical structure. Like everything else in the semantic system,
cohesive relations are realized through the lexicogrammar, by the
selection of structures, and of lexical items in structural roles. Our intention in this book has been to survey the lexicogrammatical resources in
question, and show their place in the linguistic system. But the cohesive
relations themselves are relations in meaning, and the continuity which
they bring about is a semantic continuity. This is what makes it possible
for cohesive patterns to play the part they do in the processing of text by
a listener or a reader, not merely signalling the presence and extent of text
but actually enabling him to interpret it and determining how he does so.

7.3 The meaning of different kinds of cohesion

We have discussed cohesion under the five headings of reference, substitution, ellipsis, conjunction and lexical cohesion. The classification is
based on linguistic form; these are the categories of cohesion that can be
recognized in the lexicogrammatical system. In terms of the resources
which are brought into play, they are all lexicogrammatical phenomena
of one kind or another.

Reference, substitution and ellipsis are clearly grammatical, in that they
involve closed systems: simple options of presence or absence, and systems
such as those of person, number, proximity and degree of comparison.
Lexical cohesion is, as the name implies, lexical; it involves a kind of
choice that is open-ended, the selection of a lexical item that is in some
way related to one occurring previously. Conjunction is on the borderline of the grammatical and the lexical; the set of conjunctive elements
can probably be interpreted grammatically in terms of systems, but such

---

★ J. B. Priestley, *Bees on the Boat Deck* (*The Plays of J. B. Priestley*, Vol 2), Heinemann.

an interpretation would be fairly complex, and some conjunctive expressions involve lexical selection as well, *eg: moment* in *from that moment
on.*

This tells us about what form cohesion takes, what resources of the
linguistic system are drawn on in the expression of cohesive relations. But
it does not tell us about those relations themselves. If we ask what is the
NATURE of cohesive relations, as distinct from what form of EXPRESSION
they take, we get a different answer – one still in terms of the linguistic
system, but giving a different kind of explanation. We are now asking
about the nature of cohesion considered as a set of relations in language;
whereabouts in the linguistic system are these relations located? In other
words, what do the different kinds of cohesion mean?

If we look at cohesion from this point of view, we shall be able to
recognize three kinds. These are the three different kinds of relation in
language, other than the relation of structure, that link one part of a text
with another. In the most general terms they are (1) relatedness of form,
(2) relatedness of reference, (3) semantic connection.

The way these correspond to the various types of cohesion is as follows:

Nature of cohesive relation:	Type of cohesion:
Relatedness of form	Substitution and ellipsis; lexical collocation
Relatedness of reference	Reference; lexical reiteration
Semantic connection	Conjunction

7.3.1 *General principles behind the different types*

We have referred to aspects of this general picture at various places
in the discussion. It has been pointed out that reference, while it is expressed by grammatical means, is actually a semantic relation, a relation
between meanings of particular instances rather than between words or
other items of linguistic form. Substitution and ellipsis, on the other hand,
are formal relations between elements at the lexicogrammatical level.

It has also been shown that various consequences follow from this
distinction. In substitution and ellipsis it is always possible to 'restore'
the presupposed item (replacing the substitution counter, or filling out
the empty structural slot); in reference, typically, it is not. On the other
hand a substitute has to preserve the grammatical function of the presupposed item; whereas there is no such restriction on reference, which is
independent of this sort of formal constraint. Lexical cohesion has some-

thing of both types. The relation itself is a formal one, between items of the vocabulary irrespective of any referential identity; but lexical cohesion is typically used in contexts where there is identity of reference, and for this reason the cohering lexical item is usually accompanied by *the*, or other anaphoric reference item.

Why these two different types of cohesive relation, one formal the other semantic? This can be explained by the fact that there are two possible channels for the recovery of information: the situation, and the text.

The concept of SITUATION was discussed in Chapter 2. It is a very simple notion, designed to account for the fact that language takes place in social contexts and makes connections with the realities that make up those contexts. The relevant realities are by no means necessarily to be found in the surrounding stage properties, the furniture of the material environment. A social context is a much more abstract conception, a kind of semiotic structure within which meaning takes place; the 'realities' of which it is made up may be of an entirely intangible kind. But equally they may reside in the persons and the objects that figure in the imme-diate vicinity; and if so, reference will have to be made to them. This is what we have called exophoric reference.

The semantic level in the linguistic system is, among other things, an interface between language and the realities of the outside world. So the exophoric connections with the environment are connections made at the semantic level. This accounts for reference. Reference is a semantic relation linking an instance of language to its environment, and reference items are in principle exophoric. The basic meaning of *him* is 'that man out there'. We can see this clearly in the first and second person forms *me* and *you*, which refer to the roles of speaker and addressee in the communication situation; and also in the demonstratives with their sys-tem of proximity, 'near me' (*this*) or 'not near me' (*that*), with sometimes a third term 'not near either of us' (*yon*), as in

[7:5] Yon Cassius hath a lean and hungry look.

Secondly, in any connected passage of discourse it will be necessary to refer back to something that has been mentioned already, making explicit the fact that there is identity of reference between the two. There is still, no doubt, an ultimate referent beyond the language, which defines the nature of the identity between the two instances. But the immediate referent of the second instance is the first instance; and it is this imme-diate referent, the previous mention, that now constitutes the relevant environment, not the extralinguistic referent. Probably, all languages adapt their reference items to this function, extending them from exophoric to endophoric use. (This formulation is not intended to imply that such a development has taken place in the known history of languages, but rather that it is a development that has probably taken place in the evolution of human language as a whole.) Thus in English nearly all reference items are also regularly endophoric. In those types of situation in which the perceptual environment is not part of the relevant social context, uses of language which are far removed from 'language in action', endophoric reference takes precedence over exophoric as a means of establishing identity. In this way the process of identification of the referent becomes a cohesive or text-forming process.

Why do we refer to 'John' as *him* rather than as *John*? Because *John* is vague, whereas *him* is definite. *John* could be any old John; but *him* means 'that particular individual whose identity we have established and agreed upon'. We refer to John as *him* rather than as *John* in order to signal that his identity is a feature of the environment. And the same principle applies to the other reference items. The environment has been extended from the situation to include the text.

In that case, if the relation of reference may be endophoric as well as exophoric – if a reference item can refer to an element in the text as well as to an element in the situation – we may well ask why languages have evolved a second relation of a different kind, that of substitution, to relate one linguistic item to another. Here the key to the answer lies in the concept of contrast, in the sense of contrastive information. In connected discourse there are very many occasions where we need to repeat some item precisely where there is no identity of reference. For example

[7:6]   Would you like this teapot?
    – No, I want a square one.

Here the second speaker does not use the reference item *it*, because he does not, in fact, want the object referred to. But he does establish continuity of a different kind, one based not on referential identity in the given instance but on the identity of the linguistic elements involved. The continuity lies not in the meaning but in the form. The use of the substitute *one* means 'supply the lexical item that just figured as Head of the nominal group'. The relation between the two instances is a relation established at the lexicogrammatical level.

It is not, of course, without its semantic aspect; but the semantic implication is of a different kind. The general class of objects, in this case 'teapots', constitutes the link between the two. But the significance of the continuity that is established by the use of the substitute is that it is continuity in the environment of contrast. Example [7:6] is a typical instance of cohesion through substitution, where the meaning is 'a non-identical member of the identical class'.

The contrast may take many different forms. The meaning 'non-identical member of the identical class' is merely one that is characteristically associated with the use of the nominal substitute *one*. But the contrast may be in any of the systems associated with the element in which substitution occurs. With the nominal substitute, it may be found in the Deictic or Numerative element as well as in the Epithet; while a verbal substitute is typically accompanied by a contrast in polarity, in mood or in modality.

In order to express this sort of continuity in the environment of contrast, the cohesive relation that is appropriate is one that is established not at the semantic level, where there is an implication that the cohesive factor is an extralinguistic one, but at the lexicogrammatical level. Here the implication is that the continuity is essentially a linguistic continuity, that lies in the words themselves: the meaning of substitution is 'this is the same word that we had before'. It is thus inherently a textual, not a situational relation, and is used in exophoric contexts only with a special effect, that of creating the illusion that the presupposed item has occurred before.

We have used the formulation 'contrast' or 'contrastive information' to draw attention to the special feature which distinguishes substitution from reference. This might suggest that there is always some negation involved: 'not what was referred to previously, but (a different one, etc)'. This is the typical form that the contrast takes; but it is not the only form. Consider an example such as

[7:7] I want three teapots. I'll take this one, and this one, and this one.

Here the contrast simply takes the form of new information; we are talking about teapots (*one*), and the teapot in question, not specified before, is now being specified (*this*). In ellipsis, which as we have seen is closely related to substitution, this is the usual interpretation; for example

[7:8] What are you doing? – Buying a teapot.

Here the ellipsis of *I am* displays the continuity and the remainder is thereby signalled as new information. Likewise:

[7:9] How many teapots are you buying? – Three.

This is the general principle underlying the difference between reference, on the one hand, and substitution on the other. Reference is a semantic relation, in which a meaning is specified through the identification of a referent; the source of identification is the situation, so that the relation of reference is basically an exophoric one. It becomes incidentally cohesive, when the identification is mediated through the presence of a verbal referent in the preceding text; this then becomes the presupposed element, and the text replaces the situation as the relevant environment within which the relation of reference is established.

Substitution/ellipsis is a formal (lexicogrammatical) relation, in which a form (word or words) is specified through the use of a grammatical signal indicating that it is to be recovered from what has gone before. The source of recovery is the text, so that the relation of substitution is basically an endophoric one. It is inherently cohesive, since it is the preceding text that provides the relevant environment in which the presupposed item is located.

Conjunction, the third and final type of cohesive relation, differs from both of these in that it is cohesive not by continuity of form or reference but by semantic connection. Some relation is established between the meanings of two continuous passages of text, such that the interpretation of the second is dependent on the relation in which it stands to the first. This relation may be one of two kinds; either it is present in the ideational meanings, as a relation between things – for example between two events in a narrative; or it is present in the interpersonal meanings, as a relation between elements or stages in the communication process – for example between two steps in an argument. Either of these may be represented as a form of semantic connection between a pair of adjacent clauses; the former as in [7:10a], the latter as in [7:10b]:

[7:10]   a. Jack fell down and broke his crown.
                And Jill came tumbling after.
         b. For he's a jolly good fellow.
                And so say all of us.

A brief further discussion of each of the three types of cohesion is given in the following three subsections.

7.3.2 Reference

Reference is the relation between an element of the text and something else by reference to which it is interpreted in the given instance. Reference is a potentially cohesive relation because the thing that serves as the source of the interpretation may itself be an element of text.

A reference item is one whose interpretation is determined in this way. The interpretation takes one of two forms. Either the reference item is interpreted through being IDENTIFIED WITH the referent in question; or it is interpreted through being COMPARED WITH the referent – explicitly not identified with it, but brought into some form of comparison with it.

In the former case, where the interpretation involves identifying, the reference item functions as a Deictic and is always specific. Deixis is the identifying function in the nominal group; and for cohesive purposes the identification must be specific. Hence the set of reference items includes all the specific deictics (pronouns and determiners) except the interrogatives. The interrogatives cannot be cohesive since they contain only a REQUEST FOR specification, not the specification itself.

	Personal			Demonstrative
	Existential	Possessive		
Referential	*I, you, we, he, she, it, they, one*	*mine, yours, ours his, hers, (its), theirs*	*my, your, our his, her, its, their one's*	*the this, these that, those*
Interrogative	*who what*	*whose*	*whose*	*which, what*
	Specific pronouns		Specific determiners	

In other words, all reference items of this type are specific, because their interpretation depends on identity of reference. This does not imply that the referent, where it is itself an element of the text (*ie* where the reference is anaphoric), must necessarily also be specific. A reference item can relate anaphorically to any element whether specific or not; for example

[7:11] I can see a light. Let's follow it.

where *it* refers to *a light*. But the specificity is conferred by the reference relation. Since this involves identity, 'a light' thereby becomes 'the light', *ie* the light that was just mentioned – and specified in the process, so here 'the light that (I've said) I can see'. This is why it is possible to have sentences such as:

[7:12] Nobody ever believes he's going to lose.

where *he* means the person being considered as an instance, here 'the person whose belief is in question'. In this case the presupposed item is not only non-specific; it is also being said to be non-existent.

A considerable amount is now known about the rules of pronominalization, in the sense of personal reference within the sentence; but this is not a cohesive phenomenon and lies outside our scope. The question of the interpretation of reference items in contexts of potential ambiguity has also begun to be studied, and this, though not our primary concern here, does need to be briefly mentioned. Here the question is, how does the listener or reader identify which of two or more possible items in the text a reference item refers to. For example if we come across a sentence such as

[7:13] Spurs played Liverpool. They beat them.

how do we know who beat who?

Various grammatical criteria have been proposed, in terms of transitivity or of mood; suggesting that a reference item will preserve the structural function of its referent on one or another of these dimensions.

For example, if transitivity is the determining factor, a reference item functioning as Actor will refer to just that one among the possible referents that has the Actor function. If mood is the determining factor, a reference item functioning as Subject will refer to just that one among the possible referents that has the Subject function. Example [7:14] satisfies both transitivity and modal criteria:

7:14]

	The cops	chased	the robbers.	They	caught	them.
(transitivity)	Actor	Process	Goal	Actor	Process	Goal
(mood)	Subject	Predicator	Complement	Subject	Predicator	Complement

Here *they* refers to *the cops* and *them* to *the robbers*. But consider

[7:15] The cops chased the robbers. They eluded them.

Here the only possible interpretation is that *they* refers to *the robbers* and *them* to *the cops*; this involves a reversal of the roles in both structures – and yet we find no difficulty in interpreting it. Similarly:

[7:16] John wanted Bill's horse. { a. But he wouldn't give it to him.
                                    { b. But he wouldn't pay him for it.

It is clear that (a) and (b) require opposite interpretations. In (a), *he* is *Bill* and *him* is *John*, whereas in (b) it is the other way round. There is no feeling that either is more acceptable, or more cohesive, than the other.

Since reference is a semantic relation, the criteria are to be found not in the grammar but in the semantics. It is the meaning that enables us to disambiguate in such instances. If there is a grammatical tendency to be had recourse to in those instances where the meaning does not resolve the problem, it is likely to lie, as Hasan suggests elsewhere, neither in transitivity nor in mood but in theme. This again is to be expected, since it is the thematic structure which is the text-forming structure in the clause (see 7.4.1 below). The particular combination of circumstances that is required in order to produce an ambiguous reference item in precisely the kind of environment where transitivity, mood and theme are all incongruent with each other is so odd that no example of it can be very convincing; but here is an attempt:

[7:17]

i.	These ponies	the children	were given by	their grandparents.
(transitivity)				Actor
(mood)		Subject		
(theme)	Theme			

ii. They're staying here, now.

In the second sentence, *they* is Actor (in transitivity), Subject (in mood) and Theme (in theme). In the first sentence, Actor, Subject and Theme are all different items: the Actor is *their grandparents*, the Subject is *the children* and the Theme is *these ponies*. It seems that, if anything, the preferred interpretation of *they* is *these ponies* – and that in spite of the preference of English for human Subjects. If this is so, it suggests that, to the extent that there is any grammatical criterion at all, it will be found in the theme structure rather than in the transitivity or modal structure.

Note that this does not apply to substitution. If the first sentence had been followed by the question *Which ones?* or elliptical *Which?*, the more likely interpretation would have been *which grandparents?* It seems therefore that no clearcut grammatical rules can be given for assigning a reference item to one among a number of possible text referents, since the assignment is typically made on semantic grounds. If there is more than one referent for the identification of *he* or *it* or *this*, the referent is the one that makes most sense in the context. This is not to say that ambiguity cannot arise; it can, and not infrequently does. There may be no clearly predominant candidate for the status of 'making most sense'; and in that event, as a last resort, we may appeal to the grammar – probably to the theme-rheme structure. OTHER THINGS BEING EQUAL, it seems that the most probable target of a cohesive reference item is the Theme of the preceding sentence. This seems to hold even if the reference item is not itself thematic; compare:

[7:18] These ponies the children were given by their grandparents. Have you seen them?

where *them* still seems more likely to refer to *these ponies*. But given the range of POSSIBLE targets in a connected passage, it is unlikely that any purely grammatical principles could suffice for resolving the issue, and the semantic principle of 'making most sense', difficult as it may be to make explicit, is the only one that could really be expected to apply.

As regards restrictions on reference, these again are not our main concern; we are concerned with what does happen, not with what does not. But these tend also to reflect semantic considerations – often ones that are reflected in the grammar also. Here is just one example:

[7:19] a. An old man came in with his son. ⎱
       b. An old man came in with his overcoat. ⎰ They were very dirty.

The second sentence is acceptable following (a) but not, or at best doubtful, following (b). *Old man* and *overcoat* are too different to be brought within the same presupposition; and this is related to the fact that they cannot be coordinated: *an old man and his son came in*, but not *an old man and his overcoat came in*.

There are instances where a reference item is used when strictly speaking the relation is not one of reference. An example will illustrate this:

[7:20] Arthur's very proud of his chihuahuas. I don't like them.

This is ambiguous; it could mean 'I don't like Arthur's chihuahuas', or it could mean 'I don't like chihuahuas (in general; *cf: I don't like the things)*'. The second meaning is anomalous; *them* is not coreferential with the nominal group *Arthur's chihuahuas*. It is no doubt to be explained as being coreferential with the noun Head *chihuahuas* taken on its own, without the Modifier. Compare in this regard the comment on [3:52] in 3.2.6 above; and also [7:4e], *I expect you will get this but I'll send it if you want*, where *it* and *this* both refer to *Staff Bulletin no 2*, considered as an object since it is Goal of the verbs *get* and *send*), but they refer to different copies.

Finally there are instances where the reference item, because of its specificity, serves to disambiguate preceding sentences that otherwise in themselves are ambiguous; for example

[7:21] I'd rather like to see a play. It's at the Ambassador's.

Here the *it* shows that the meaning of the first sentence is 'there's a play I'd like to see'. The context of such ambiguities is very often of the kind illustrated by [7:21], namely a clause that is structured as a simple proposition but which is in fact incongruent. The congruent form of expression here would be a clause of the IDENTIFYING type, one with an equative structure such as *There's a play I'd rather like to see*.

Comparison differs from the other forms of reference in that it is based not on identity of reference but on non-identity: the reference item is interpreted, not by being identified with what it presupposes, but by being compared with it. The expression 'non-identity' is actually misleading, because one possible form of comparability is identity. But the identity is not the criterion; being identical is just one of the ways in which two things may be like or unlike each other. In the comparative type of reference, the presupposed element takes on the role of a reference POINT. It serves as a standard, to which something else is referred in terms of its likeness, in general or particular; and 'the same' is one kind of likeness. In this way the comparison provides the source of interpretation for the reference item; and where the presupposed element is also in the text, there is cohesion between the two. For example, *more* presupposing *oysters* in

[7:22] 'I like the Walrus best,' said Alice: 'because, you see, he was a *little* sorry for the poor oysters'.
'He ate more than the Carpenter though,' said Tweedledee.

When likeness takes the value of sameness, comparison resembles other forms of reference in being specific: 'same' implies 'the same'. For this reason *same* and other comparatives of identity are typically accompanied by *the*, or some other specific determiner. By contrast to this, when likeness takes the value of non-identity (similarity or difference), the reference is typically non-specific; and comparatives expressing non-identity are unlike all other forms of reference in just this respect. So we usually find *the same place* but *a similar place*, *an other place* (written as one word, *another*), *a different place*.

We can summarize the meaning of reference by using the term CO-INTERPRETATION. There is a semantic link between the reference item and that which it presupposes; but this does not mean that the two necessarily have the same referent. It means that the interpretation of the reference item DEPENDS IN SOME WAY on that of the presupposed. Co-reference is one particular form that co-interpretation may take – where the two items do, in fact, refer to the same thing. But the general concept that lies behind the cohesive relation of reference, and by virtue of which personals, demonstratives and comparatives are alike in their text-forming capacity, is that of co-interpretation. A reference item is one which is interpreted by reference to something else. It is this principle of co-interpretation that defines its role in the semantics of the text.

7.3.3 Substitution and ellipsis

With substitution there is no implication of specificity. The substitution relation has no connection with specifying or identifying a particular referent; it is quite neutral in this regard. So specific forms such as *the empty one* and non-specific ones such as *an empty one* are both equally likely. The fact that the nominal substitute *one* has evolved from the same source as the indefinite article might suggest that substitution is inherently non-specific; but the meaning of the substitute *one* is countability, not indefiniteness. This is reflected in the fact that the plural of the substitute is *ones*, while the plural of the indefinite article is *some*; and *some* is also the 'mass' form of the article, whereas there is no form of substitute available in the context of a mass noun.

We have referred already to the main distinction between substitution and nominal reference. In reference there is typically identity of referent. Substitution is used where there is no such identity. This requires a device which makes the connection at the lexicogrammatical level, at what we called the level of 'wording', since the cohesion takes the form of 'same element in the language (same wording) but different referent'. The essence of substitution therefore is contrast: a new referent is being defined – and hence there is no substitution for proper names. The contrast is not necessarily in the reference; it may be in some interpersonal element in the meaning – the modality, key, attitude etc – but the principle is the same. Reference implies that there is identity of meaning between the presupposing item and that which it presupposes, while substitution implies non-identity of meaning. This is illustrated by the use of substitution and ellipsis in responses; the function of a response is to supply missing information, or confirmation – that is to supply something that is New, and it is this that provides the environment in which the substitute or elliptical item occurs. For example,

[7:23] Did you cook the dinner? – No; John did.

The distinction between reference and substitution or ellipsis is however less clearcut with verbs and clauses than with nouns. Note the difference between [7:24a and b]:

[7:24] Are they selling the contents today?
a. No, they're doing it tomorrow. (reference)
b. No, they are (doing) tomorrow. (substitution or ellipsis)

The first, being referential, makes it an assumption that they are selling, and merely supplies the time; it parses the question as 'when are they selling the contents?', and has a thematic structure of the identifying type; it is equivalent to 'the time when they're selling=tomorrow', with the verb embedded in the Theme. An alternative form for (a) would be *It's tomorrow they're doing it*. The second does not assume the selling but states it, because the meaning which provides the contrastive environment for the substitution – namely the polarity – is New. The substitute form of the answer parses the question as 'are they selling the contents?' with 'today' either as given or as additional relevant information; its thematic organization is 'the fact=that they are selling; but tomorrow'. For this reason in a question-answer sequence with no possible focus other than the polarity, the reference form is not an appropriate form of answer; the following example shows this:

[7:25] a. Are they selling the contents? – Yes, they're doing it.
– No, they're not doing it.

The substitute or elliptical forms of the answer, on the other hand, would be entirely appropriate:

[7:25] b. Are they selling the contents? – Yes, they are (doing).
                                            – No, they're not (doing).

Conversely, when the sense requires that the focus is elsewhere (because
the process itself is not in question, but only the circumstance – locative,
temporal, etc – with which it is associated) the substitute or elliptical form
is ruled out. In [7:26], for example, the answer presents 'I sleep' as if
it was new information, and hence is rather odd:

[7:26] Do you sleep on the couch? – No; I do (do) on the sofa.

Here the reference is also ruled out, but for a different reason; we do not
say *I do it on the sofa* because *sleep* is not a verb of action. But with other
types of process, reference would be acceptable: *Do you cook every day? –
No, I do it every other day.* Two final examples:

[7:27] Does she paint for profit? { a. No, she does it for pleasure. (reference)
                                    b. No; she does (do) for pleasure. (substitution
                                       or ellipsis)

Here (b) is unlikely because it presents 'she paints' as new information,
whereas the form of the question suggests that the fact that she paints is
not at issue; the appropriate meaning is rather 'the reason she paints is for
pleasure', as expressed in (a).

This illustrates the general principle of substitution and ellipsis, with
their meaning of 'continuity in the environment of contrast'. What is
carried over is a FORM, a word or structural feature; and this happens in
an environment where the referential meanings are not identical.

The structural environment, on the other hand, tends to remain fairly
constant; examples such as [7:28a and b] are unlikely because they involve
too great a structural shift:

[7:28] a. Would you like this book to read? – I've already done so.
       b. Give me a book to read. I have (done) this one.

whereas following *Read this book!* in (a), and *Have you read these books?* in
(b), the substitute forms would be quite unexceptionable.

Why does the speaker not simply repeat the same word? He can do, of
course:

[7:29] I've had an offer for this. – I'll make you a better offer.

But notice what happens. In order to signal this as a reiteration (and if it
was not a reiteration it would not be cohesive), the speaker has to shift
the tonic away from *offer* on to *better*. But *offer* is a lexical item: hence the

placing of the focus on an earlier item is 'marked' and strongly contrastive, a function of the systemic opposition between [7:30a and b]:

[7:30] a. I'll make you a better OFFER (unmarked focus)
        b. I'll make you a BETTER offer (marked focus)

Yet this opposition is irrelevant in the context of [7:29]. There is only one possible meaning here, not two; the context requires the focus on *better*, but it also requires that it should be an unmarked focus, and this can be achieved only by the use of a structure in which there is no lexical item following *better*, so that *better* either is the last word in the information unit (ellipsis: *I'll make you a better*) or is followed only by a grammatical word, one which does not carry information focus (substitution: *I'll make you a better one*). Both these have unmarked focus. In other words, the substitute and elliptical forms are preferred because they create cohesion without disturbing the information structure of the discourse: without assigning prominence of a kind which is irrelevant in the given environment.

Between substitution and ellipsis the difference in meaning is minimal. We defined ellipsis as substitution by zero; we could equally well have defined substitution as explicit ellipsis. Ellipsis is characteristic particularly of responses: responses to yes/no questions, with ellipsis of the proposition (*No he didn't; Yes I have*, etc), and to WH- questions, with ellipsis of all elements but the one required (*In the drawer; Next weekend*, etc). But whereas there is a significant difference in meaning between elliptical or substitute forms on the one hand and the corresponding 'filled out' forms on the other, there is hardly a significant difference between the two cohesive forms themselves. For example,

[7:31] Let's see if Granny can look after the shop for us.

    a. She MIGHT look after the shop for us.
    bi. She MIGHT do.
    bii. She MIGHT.

As we saw in the last paragraph, (a) differs from (b) in that it makes explicit the Given element *look after the shop for us*, and in doing so imposes a marked information structure in which MIGHT *look after the shop for us* is specifically contrasted with *might look after* THE SHOP *for us*; whereas in (b) the distribution of information is neutral – the tonic falls in its unmarked place. This is clearly a meaningful choice on the part of the speaker. But between (bi) and (bii) there is hardly any difference in the meaning. There are many contexts in which only one or the other is possible; for numerous speakers of English, for example, only (ii) could occur here. Where both are possible, the substitute form appears slightly more explicit in its sense of 'same form in a different environment':

[7:32] Has Smith reacted to that paragraph about him in the paper?
  – No he hasn't.
  – He hasn't done yet; but when he reads it carefully he may think again.

[7:33] Have an apple. – I'll take this. – The other one's better.

The use of *do* in [7:32] and *one* in [7:33] suggests in each case a somewhat more pointed contrast than would be achieved by the elliptical form *he hasn't yet, the other's better*. And a clausal substitute may serve to disambiguate in certain reported speech contexts:

[7:34] Will Granny look after the shop for us? – She hasn't said.

The elliptical form may mean either 'she hasn't said that she will' or 'she hasn't said whether she will or not', whereas the substitute form *she hasn't said so* could only mean the former. But in many instances the distinction between substitution and ellipsis is scarcely noticeable, and can be treated for practical purposes as a matter of free variation.

7.3.4 *Lexical cohesion: reiteration and collocation*

Lexical cohesion is 'phoric' cohesion that is established through the structure of the LEXIS, or vocabulary, and hence (like substitution) at the lexicogrammatical level. To recapitulate this point:

Linguistic level at which 'phoric' relation is established		Type of cohesion
Semantic		Reference
Lexicogrammatical	⎰Grammatical	Substitution and ellipsis
	⎱Lexical	Lexical cohesion

Lexical cohesion embraces two distinct though related aspects which we referred to as REITERATION and COLLOCATION.

1. Reiteration. This is the repetition of a lexical item, or the occurrence of a synonym of some kind, in the context of reference; that is, where the

two occurrences have the same referent. Typically, therefore, a reiterated lexical item is accompanied by a reference item, usually *the* or a demonstrative. The complex consisting of *the* plus reiterated lexical item is therefore cohesive by reference. But since reiteration is itself cohesive in its own right, as shown by the fact that cohesion takes place even where there is no referential relation (*cf* next paragraph), such instances constitute a double tie and are interpreted here in this way (see Chapter 8, 8.3 and note 2 to Text 1).

2. Collocation. As remarked above, the repetition of a lexical item is cohesive in its own right, whether or not there is identity of reference, or any referential relation at all between the two. The cohesion derives from the lexical organization of language. A word that is in some way associated with another word in the preceding text, because it is a direct repetition of it, or is in some sense synonymous with it, or tends to occur in the same lexical environment, coheres with that word and so contributes to the texture.

The following passage contains illustrations of both these types:

[7:35] Soon her eye fell on a little glass box that was lying under the table: she opened it, and found in it a very small cake, on which the words 'EAT ME' were beautifully marked in currants. 'Well, I'll eat it,' said Alice, 'and if it makes me larger, I can reach the key; and if it makes me smaller, I can creep under the door; so either way I'll get into the garden, and I don't care which happens!'
She ate a little bit, and said anxiously to herself, 'Which way? Which way?' holding her hand on the top of her head to feel which way it was growing, and she was quite surprised to find that she remained the same size: to be sure, this generally happens when one eats cake, but Alice had got so much into the way of expecting nothing but out-of-the-way things to happen, that it seemed quite dull and stupid for life to go on in the common way.
So she set to work, and very soon finished off the cake.

The second occurrence of *cake*, in *when one eats cake* (second paragraph), is without reference item; there is no referential link with the first occurrence, but the repetition itself constitutes a tie. The third occurrence, in *very soon finished off the cake*, is with a reference item; here, therefore, there are two ties, one of reference, the referential identity being shown by *the*, and one of reiteration. Other instances of lexical cohesion in the passage are provided by *eat . . . eat . . . ate . . . eats; open . . . key . . . door; larger . . . smaller . . . (the same) size; makes larger . . . makes smaller . . . growing; happens . . . happen.*

The principle behind both types is the cohesive effect achieved by the continuity of lexical meaning. This may be combined with a referential relation but does not depend on this for its effect. The cohesion is a function of the relation between the lexical items themselves, which has both a semantic aspect – synonymy, hyponymy, metonymy, etc – and a purely lexical or collocational aspect, the mutual expectancy between words that arises from the one occurring frequently in the environment of the other, or (a better way of looking at it) of the two occurring in a range of environments common to both. The whole of the vocabulary of a language is internally structured and organized along many dimensions, which collectively determine 'what goes with what'; these tendencies are as much part of the linguistic system as are the principles of grammatical structure, even though they are statable only as tendencies, not as 'rules'. It is the essentially probabilistic nature of lexical patterning which makes it effective in the creation of texture; because they lie outside the bounds of structure, and are not constrained by structural relationships, the lexical patterns serve to transform a series of unrelated structures into a unified, coherent whole.

7.3.5 Conjunction

Conjunction is somewhat different from the other cohesive relations. It is based on the assumption that there are in the linguistic system forms of systematic relationships between sentences. There are a number of possible ways in which the system allows for the parts of a text to be connected to one another in meaning.

There are certain elementary logical relations inherent in ordinary language; doubtless these derive ultimately from the categories of human experience, and they figure importantly in the sociolinguistic construction of reality, the process whereby a model of the universe is gradually built up over countless generations in the course of semiotic interaction. (They can be regarded as departures from the idealized norm represented by formal logic; but it is worth remembering that in the history of human thought the concepts of formal logic derive, however indirectly, from the logic of natural language.) These logical relations are embodied in linguistic structure, in the form of coordination, apposition, modification, etc. Analogous to these are certain non-structural, text-forming relations which are what we are calling conjunctive relations. Conjunctive relations are encoded not in the form of grammatical structures but in the looser, more pliable form of linkages between the components of a text.

The specific conjunctive relations are those of 'and', 'yet', 'so' and 'then'; and each of these may occur in either an 'external' or an 'internal' context. The latter distinction, which derives from the functional basis of the semantic system, determines the locus of the conjunction; the conjunction may be located in the phenomena that constitute the content of what is being said (external), or in the interaction itself, the social process that constitutes the speech event (internal). Here is a further set of examples of each.

	External	Internal
'and'	They gave him food and clothing. And they looked after him till he was better.	They gave me fish to eat. And I don't like fish.
'yet'	They looked after him well. Yet he got no better.	That must be Henry. Yet it can't be; Henry's in Manchester.
'so'	He drove into the harbour one night. So they took his licence away.	We're having guests tonight. So don't be late.
'then'	He stayed there for three years. Then he went on to New Zealand.	He found his way eventually. Then he'd left his papers behind.

Conjunction does not depend either on referential meaning or on identity or association of wording. Conjunctive relations are not 'phoric'; they represent semantic links between the elements that are constitutive of text. There are numerous possible ways of interpreting conjunctive relations; the fourfold scheme we have adopted here is simply the one we have found most helpful in the quest for a general characterization of cohesive relations which would not be 'closed' – which would allow further subclassification as and when needed. A purely structural approach would suggest other modes of classification, based for example on the traditional categorization of subordinate clauses. As already noted, there are structural analogues of the conjunctive relations; here are some examples of the way each is expressed:

	Textual (conjunctive)	Structural (logical)	
		paratactic	hypotactic
'and'	Also, . . .	. . . and . . .	besides . . .
'yet'	However, . . .	. . . yet . . .	although . . .
'so'	Consequently, . . .	. . . so . . .	because . . .
'then'	Subsequently, . . .	. . . then . . .	after . . .

(In the same way, the 'phoric' relations of reference, and substitution and ellipsis, are also found as structure-forming relations within the sentence.) But from our present standpoint it is the nature of text, rather than the organization of grammar, that has determined the interpretation and presentation of the systems involved.

7.3.6 Summary

The semantic basis of cohesion in English texts can be summarized as follows (and cf the Table at the end of 7.3 above).

Cohesion consists (1) in continuity of lexicogrammatical meaning ('relatedness of form'; phoric)

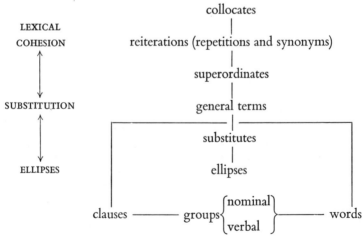

Substitution and ellipsis are relevant especially in the environment of discontinuity of reference.

(2) in continuity of referential meaning ('relatedness of reference': phoric)

REFERENCE
{
personal (communication role of referent)
|
demonstrative (proximity of referent)
|
comparative (similarity to preceding referent)
}

(3) in semantic connection with the preceding text (non-phoric)

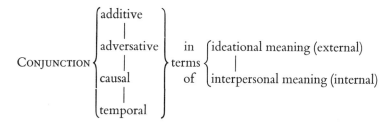

CONJUNCTION
{
additive
|
adversative
|
causal
|
temporal
}
in terms of
{
ideational meaning (external)
|
interpersonal meaning (internal)
}

These are the cohesive relations. In categorizing them in this way, it is perhaps useful to add a reminder of the difference between the cohesive relations themselves and the means by which they are represented in the linguistic system. The COHESIVE RELATIONS THEMSELVES can be interpreted as being either lexicogrammatical in nature (1) or semantic, the latter being either referential (2) or conjunctive (3). The type of cohesion, in other words, is either one that depends on semantic relations in the linguistic system or one that depends on lexicogrammatical relations. But the EXPRESSION of cohesive relations involves both the semantic and the lexicogrammatical systems in all cases: that is, both choices in meaning, and their realization in words and structures.

Thus even where cohesion is achieved through the setting up of a purely formal relationship in the text, such as the substitution of *one* for the noun expressing the Thing, the CHOICES that are involved, not only in the selection of the particular thing-meaning itself but equally in the identification of it with a preceding thing-meaning, are semantic choices. And conversely, even where the cohesive relationship is a semantic one, it has to be realized in the lexicogrammatical system; for example, identity of referential meaning as expressed through the grammatical system of third person pronouns. Here is a final summary table:

Representation in linguistic system Type of cohesive relation	Semantic	Lexicogrammatical (typically)
Conjunction	Additive, adversative, causal and temporal relations; external and internal	Discourse adjuncts: adverbial groups, prepositional groups
Reference	Identification: by speech role by proximity by specificity (only) Reference point	Personals Demonstratives Definite article Comparatives
Lexical cohesion	Collocation (similarity of lexical environment) Reiteration (identity of lexical reference)	Same or associated lexical item Same lexical item; synonym; superordinate; general word
Substitution	Identity of potential reference (class meaning) in context of non-identity of actual (instantial) reference	Verbal, nominal or clausal substitute Verbal, nominal or clausal ellipsis

7.4 Cohesion and the text

Texture involves much more than merely cohesion. In the construction of text the establishment of cohesive relations is a necessary component; but it is not the whole story.

In the most general terms there are two other components of texture. One is the textual structure that is internal to the sentence: the organization of the sentence and its parts in a way which relates it to its environment. The other is the 'macrostructure' of the text, that establishes it as a text of a particular kind – conversation, narrative, lyric, commercial correspondence and so on.

7.4.1 Texture within the sentence

The main components of texture within the sentence in English are the theme systems and the information systems (*cf* the summary at the end of Chapter 1).

These have been outlined in an article by Halliday.* The theme systems are those concerned with the organization of the clause as a message: its structure in terms of a THEME and a remainder (known as the RHEME), and a wide range of thematic variation that is associated with this structure in one way and another. The following examples give an idea of the semantic range that is involved:

[7:36] a. John's aunt | left him this duckpress
          Theme | Rheme

    b. John | was left this duckpress by his aunt
        Theme | Rheme

    c. This duckpress | John's aunt left him
        Theme | Rheme

    d. What John's aunt left him | was this duckpress
        Theme: Identified | Rheme: Identifier

    e. The way John got this duckpress | was by a legacy from his
                                               aunt
        Theme: Identified | Rheme: Identifier

    f. Bequeathing this duckpress | was what John's aunt did for
                                             him
        Theme: Identifier | Rheme: Identified

The information systems are those concerned with the organization of the text into units of information. This is expressed in English by the intonation patterns, and it is therefore a feature only of spoken English. In written English, punctuation can be used to show information structure, although it cannot express it fully, and most punctuation practice is a kind of compromise between information structure (punctuating according to the intonation) and sentence structure (punctuating according to the grammar). The intonation of spoken English expresses the information structure in a very simple way. Connected speech takes the form of an unbroken succession of intonation units, or TONE GROUPS as they are generally called; and each tone group represents what the speaker chooses to encode as one piece of information, one unit of the textual process.

---

* 'Notes on transitivity and theme in English', Part 2, *Journal of Linguistics* 3, 1967.

Each information unit is then structured in terms of two elements, a NEW element, expressing what the speaker is presenting as information that is not recoverable to the hearer from other sources; and a GIVEN element, expressing what the speaker is presenting as information that is recoverable to the hearer from some source or other in the environment – the situation, or the preceding text. The Given element is optional; the New is present in every information unit, since without it there would not be a separate information unit.

In the following examples, the information unit boundary is shown by // and the New element is printed in SMALL CAPITALS:

[7:37] a. // JOHN'S AUNT LEFT HIM THIS DUCKPRESS //
　　　　b. // JOHN'S AUNT left him this duckpress //
　　　　c. // JOHN'S AUNT // left him THIS DUCKPRESS //
　　　　d. // John WAS LEFT THIS DUCKPRESS // by HIS AUNT //
　　　　e. // JOHN was left this duckpress // by HIS AUNT //
　　　　f. // JOHN // WAS LEFT THIS DUCKPRESS BY HIS AUNT //
　　　　g. // THIS DUCKPRESS // JOHN'S AUNT left him //

The number of possibilities is very large indeed, and the combination of thematic systems with information systems gives a paradigm which, with a clause of average length, runs into the tens and hundreds of thousands. Since each one has a different textual meaning this might seem unmanageably complex – until it is realized that this enormous number of different textual structures within the sentence is the result of combining a number of related but independent choices each one of which is by itself very simple. If there are only twenty different choices, each of only two possibilities, this already yields over a million forms. In fact, of course, things are not quite as simple as that; the number of possibilities depends on the structure of the sentence, the choices are not fully independent, so that not all the theoretically possible combinations occur, and not all choices are limited to two options. But it is this principle on which the sentence is structured internally in its role as the realization of text; and this internal texture is the structural counterpart of cohesion. Neither cohesion alone, nor internal textual structure alone, suffices to make of a set of sentences a text. Texture is a product of the interaction between the two.

7.4.2 The texture of discourse

The third and final component of texture is the structure of discourse. By this we mean the larger structure that is a property of the forms of discourse themselves: the structure that is inherent in such concepts as narrative, prayer, folk-ballad, formal correspondence, sonnet, operating instructions, television drama and the like.

It is safe to say that every genre has its own discourse structure. It might seem as if informal, spontaneous conversation had no structure of its own over and above the internal organization of each sentence and the cohesion between the sentences. But the work of Harvey Sacks and Emanuel Schegloff has shown beyond question that conversation is very highly structured. There are definite principles regulating the taking of turns in conversation, and one of the functions of some of the items operating cohesively as conjunctives (Chapter 5) is that of marking and holding turns. There are several types of what Sacks and Schegloff call 'adjacency pairs', ordered sequences of two elements in a conversation that are related to each other and mutually presupposing, like greetings, invitations, or question-answer sequences. The discourse structure of a conversation is in turn reinforced by the cohesion, which explicitly ties together the related parts, bonding them more closely to each other than to the others that are not so related; hence Goffman's observation that 'there tends to be a less meaningful relationship between two sequential interchanges than between two sequential speeches (*ie* turns) in an interchange' (*Interaction Ritual, p* 37).

Other forms of discourse are more obviously structured than conversation; and some, notably narrative, have been studied in considerable detail in a variety of different languages. There is no need here to labour the point that the presence of certain elements, in a certain order, is essential to our concept of narrative; a narrative has, as a text, a typical organization, or one of a number of typical organizations, and it acquires texture by virtue of adhering to these forms. Literary forms, including the 'strict' verse forms – culturally established and highly-valued norms such as those of metre and rhyme scheme, defining complex notions such as the sonnet, iambic pentameter blank verse, and the like – all fall within the general category of discourse structures. They are aspects of texture, and combine with intrasentence structure and intersentence cohesion to provide the total text-forming resources of the culture.

7.4.3 *The role of. linguistic analysis*

The linguistic analysis of a text is not an interpretation of that text; it is an explanation. This point emerges clearly, though it is often misunderstood, in the context of stylistics, the linguistic analysis of literary texts.

The linguistic analysis of literature is not an interpretation of what the text means; it is an explanation of why and how it means what it does.

Similarly, to the extent that linguistic analysis is concerned with evaluation, a linguistic analysis of a text is not an evaluation of that text; it is an explanation of how and why it is valued as it is. A linguistic analysis of a literary text aims at explaining the interpretation and evaluation that are put upon that text. The role of linguistics is to say how and why the text means what it does to the reader or listener, and how and why he evaluates it in a certain way.

This point can be generalized to the study of texts as a whole. The analysis of cohesion, together with other aspects of texture, will not in general add anything new to the interpretation of a text. What it will do is to show why the text is interpreted in a certain way; including why it is ambiguous in interpretation wherever it is so. It will explain the nature of conversational inferences, the meanings that the hearer gets out of the text without the speaker having apparently put them in – presuppositions from the culture, from the shared experience of the participants, and from the situation and the surrounding text. It is the text-forming or 'textual' component of the semantic system that specifically provides the linguistic means through which such presuppositions are made. Similarly the analysis of cohesion will not tell you that this or that is a good text or a bad text or an effective or ineffective one in the context. But it will tell you something of WHY YOU THINK it is a good text or a bad text, or whatever you do think about it.

It is in this perspective that in the final chapter we suggest means for describing the cohesive patterns of a text. The intention is to provide for a reasonably comprehensive picture of this aspect of texture; and in this way to offer an insight into what it is that makes a text a text.

Chapter 8

The analysis of cohesion

In this concluding chapter we suggest a method for the analysis of cohesion in a text. First there is a brief discussion of the principles of analysis (8.1); next, a coding scheme for the various types of cohesion (8.2), and finally an analysis of seven short passages of text.

8.1 General principles

The basic concept that is employed in analysing the cohesion of a text is that of the TIE, already discussed in Chapter 1. A tie is a complex notion, because it includes not only the cohesive element itself but also that which is presupposed by it. A tie is best interpreted as a RELATION between these two elements.

A tie is thus a relational concept. It is also DIRECTIONAL; the relation is an asymmetric one. It may go either way: the direction may be anaphoric, with the presupposed element preceding, or cataphoric, with the presupposed element following. The typical direction, as has been illustrated throughout the discussion, is the anaphoric one; it is natural, after all, to presuppose what has already gone rather than what is to follow. But this is not to say the presupposition will necessarily be aimed at the immediately preceding sentence. It often is, and this is perhaps the simplest form that cohesion takes: a single tie between a pair of elements in adjacent sentences, with the second of the pair presupposing the first while the first does not presuppose anything else in its turn. Most of the examples we have cited have been of this kind, if only for the sake of brevity. But although this can reasonably be regarded as the paradigm form of a cohesive tie, actual instances of cohesion are typically somewhat more complex.

In the first place, as has frequently been brought out, any sentence may have more than one tie in it. This is in fact the usual pattern in connected texts, of whatever variety. Even such a short sentence as the second one in [8:1], which at first sight seems to contain only one tie, has in fact two, since in addition to the reference item *it*, presupposing *the plan*, there is lexical cohesion of *succeed* and *try*:

> [8:1] A little provoked, she drew back and, after looking everywhere for the Queen (whom she spied out at last, a long way off), she thought she would try the plan, this time, of walking in the opposite direction.
> It succeeded beautifully.

In the second place, however, the form of cohesive ties may diverge from the simple, idealized type in either, or both, of two ways. (i) The presupposed item may be not in the immediately preceding sentence, but in some sentence that is more distant in the past. (ii) The presupposed item may itself be cohesive, presupposing another item that is still further back; in this way there may be a whole chain of presuppositions before the original target item is reached. The following passage exemplifies both these points:

> [8:2] The last word ended in a long bleat, so like a sheep that Alice quite started (1). She looked at the Queen, who seemed to have suddenly wrapped herself up in wool (2). Alice rubbed her eyes, and looked again (3). She couldn't make out what had happened at all (4). Was she in a shop (5)? And was that really – was it really a *sheep* that was sitting on the other side of the counter (6)? Rub as she would, she could make nothing more of it (7).

In sentence (2), the *she* refers to *Alice* in sentence (1). This is the simplest form of presupposition, relating the sentence to that which immediately precedes it; we shall refer to this as an IMMEDIATE tie. Similarly the *she* in (4) refers to the *Alice* in (3). But the *she* in (5) has as the target of its presupposition another instance of *she*, that in (4); and in order to resolve it we have to follow this through to the occurrence of *Alice* in sentence (3). We shall call this type a MEDIATED tie. It is not necessary that the mediating items should always be the same, although in this case the item mediating between *she* in (5) and *Alice* in (3) is, in fact, another instance of *she*. It might have been another form of the personal (*eg: her*), or another type of cohesive element altogether (*eg: the poor thing*).

Now consider the clause *Rub as she would*, in (7). Here we have an instance of lexical cohesion, and it is interesting to note that it is necessary to resolve this tie in order for the passage to be understood. Taken by itself, *rub as she would* is uninterpretable; if one met it out of context, one would probably expect something to follow such as *she could not get it to shine*. Here it must cohere with *Alice rubbed her eyes*. This, however, is in sentence (3), and there are no intermediate references to the rubbing of the eyes. Here we have what we shall call a REMOTE tie; and the distance between the two items can be very much greater than this, especially in spoken language where a tie often spans large numbers of intervening sentences.

Finally, a tie may be BOTH mediated AND remote. For example, the *she* in sentence (7) presupposes nothing in (6) but refers back to sentence (5); hence the tie is remote. At the same time the presupposed item in (5) is again *she*, which has to be followed through to the *she* in (4) and finally to the *Alice* in (3), so it is also mediated. This again is quite typical of both speech and writing, with a tendency for the more informal modes of discourse to be the more complex, as they are also in sentence structure.

When analysing a text for cohesion, it is useful to note not only the type of tie – whether immediate or not; and if not immediate, whether mediated, remote, or both – but also the distance separating the presupposing from the presupposed. Hence if an instance is coded as mediated, this can be accompanied by a figure indicating the number of intermediate sentences which participate in the chain of cohesion, having in them an item which is both presupposed and presupposing, like the *she* in (4). If an instance is coded as remote, there can again be an accompanying figure, this time showing the number of sentences separating the presupposing from the presupposed while not themselves participating in the presupposition. So the *she* in sentence (7) would be coded as 'mediated: 2', the number 2 referring to sentences (5) and (4) both of which have *she* in them, and also as 'remote: 1', where the 1 refers to sentence (6) which has no part in the resolution of the *she*. The two figures can simply be added together to show the overall distance, the total number of sentences occurring in between the presupposing element and that by which it is ultimately resolved.

It should be stressed that in all cases it is the number of intervening SENTENCES that is being counted, and not (in the case of a mediated tie) the number of occurrences of a mediating cohesive element. This is because our interest lies in the way in which cohesive relations build up a text. As far as texture is concerned, the important question is, is this sentence related by cohesion or not; and if it is, in how many different ways? Which items in the sentence enter into cohesive relations, and what is the type and distance of the cohesion in each instance? Once we have established that *she* (= 'Alice') is functioning in the sentence as a cohesive agent by personal reference, we have established the salient fact; it does not much matter for cohesive purposes (however interesting it might turn out to be in other respects) whether *she* occurs once or half a dozen times within the sentence.

For any sentence, therefore, we shall indicate, first of all, how many cohesive ties it contains: how many instances of a cohesive element that are not resolved by presupposition within the sentence. This shows the total extent of the demands it makes on the preceding (or rather the surrounding) text. Secondly, for each of these ties we shall specify what type of cohesion is involved, in terms of reference, substitution and so on; this can be specified up to a varying degree of delicacy, as suggested in 8.2 below. Finally, for each tie we shall specify whether it is immediate or non-immediate, and if non-immediate, whether mediated, remote (non-mediated), or both; and we shall assign numerical values to each instance of a non-immediate tie, showing the number of intervening sentences. This figure is the index of cohesive distance, and it shows both the number of mediating sentences – those containing an element that forms a link in a chain – and the number of non-mediating sentences, those that do not contribute to the tie in question.

In presenting a framework for the analysis and notation of a text, however, we should emphasize the fact that we regard the analysis of a text in terms of such a framework as a means to an end, not as an end in itself. There are numerous reasons why one might undertake such an analysis, and the enquiry will lead in all kinds of different directions; it is likely to mean one thing in the context of the teaching of composition, another thing in the context of the automatic analysis of text by computer, and something different again in the context of stylistic studies. Whatever the ultimate goal, one will almost certainly wish not only to codify the text in terms of cohesive categories but also to inspect the individual instances of cohesion, to look closely at the actual words and phrases that enter into cohesive ties and see what patterns of texture then emerge. A particular text, or a genre, may exhibit a general tendency towards the use of certain features or modes rather than others: for example, in certain types of narrative, where the continuity is provided by the doings or the personality of one individual, it would be interesting to know whether this is reflected in a predominance of reference to that individual as a cohesive device. Other questions that arise are: Does a particular speaker or writer favour one type of cohesion over others? Does the density of cohesive ties remain constant or vary, and if it varies, is the variation systematically re-

lated to some other factor or factors? What is the relation between cohesion and the division of a written text into paragraphs?* There are many
fundamental questions which can be approached by taking the systematic
· of cohesion as a point of departure.

Summary of cohesion, and coding scheme

ſpe of cohesion

		Coding R
REFERENCE		
1. Pronominals		1
(1) singular, masculine	*he, him, his*	11
(2) singular, feminine	*she, her, hers*	12
(3) singular, neuter	*it, its*	13
(4) plural	*they, them, their, theirs*	14
1(1–4) functioning as:		
(a) non-possessive, as Head	*he/him, she/her, it, they/them*	6
(b) possessive, as Head	*his, hers, (its), theirs*	7
(c) possessive, as Deictic	*his, her, its, their*	8
2. Demonstratives and definite article		2
(1) demonstrative, near	*this/these, here*	21
(2) demonstrative, far	*that/those, there, then*	22
(3) definite article	*the*	23
2(1–3) functioning as:		
(a) nominal, Deictic or Head	*this/these, that/those, the*	6
(b) place adverbial	*here, there*	7
(c) time adverbial	*then*	8
3. Comparatives (not complete lists)		3
(1) identity	*eg: same, identical*	31
(2) similarity	*eg: similar(ly), such*	32
(3) difference (*ie:* non–identity and dissimilarity)	*eg: different, other, else additional*	33

* A very interesting study of this question was made some years ago by Colin C. Bowley, of
the University of Wellington, New Zealand, in an early application of the concept of cohesion
to the analysis of text. Bowley suggested that the cohesive status of the paragraph might differ
markedly from one writer to another (for example along the lines discussed in 7.1.3 above),
but remain fairly constant within one writer, or at least within one work. See Colin C.
Bowley, *Cohesion and the Paragraph*, University of Edinburgh Diploma in General Linguistics
Dissertation, 1962.

		Coding
(4) comparison, quantity	*eg: more, less, as many*; ordinals	34
(5) comparison, quality	*eg: as*+adjective; comparatives and superlatives	35

3(1–5) functioning as:
(a) Deictic	(1–3)	6
(b) Numerative	(4)	7
(c) Epithet	(5)	8
(d) Adjunct or Submodifier	(1–5)	9

Note: Not all combinations of (1–5) with (a–d) are possible; the usual functions are those indicated here in the last table.

SUBSTITUTION		S
1. Nominal substitutes		1
(1) for noun Head	*one/ones*	11
(2) for nominal Complement	*the same*	12
(3) for Attribute	*so*	13
2. Verbal substitutes		2
(1) for verb	*do, be, have*	21
(2) for process	*do the same/likewise*	22
(3) for proposition	*do so, be so*	23
(4) verbal reference	*do it/that, be it/that*	24
3. Clausal substitutes		3
(1) positive	*so*	31
(2) negative	*not*	32

3(1–2) substitute clause functioning as:
(a) reported	6
(b) conditional	7
(c) modalized	8
(d) other	9

ELLIPSIS	E
1. Nominal ellipsis	1
(1) Deictic as Head	11
i. specific Deictic	1
ii. non-specific Deictic	2
iii. Post-deictic	3

	Coding
(2) Numerative as Head	12
i. ordinal	1
ii. cardinal	2
iii. indefinite	3
(3) Epithet as Head	13
i. superlative	1
ii. comparative	2
iii. others	3
2. Verbal ellipsis	2
(1) lexical ellipsis ('from right')	21
i. total (all items omitted except first operator)	1
ii. partial (lexical verb only omitted)	2
(2) operator ellipsis ('from left')	22
i. total (all items omitted except lexical verb)	1
ii. partial (first operator only omitted)	2

Note: Where the presupposed verbal group is simple there is no distinction between total and partial ellipsis; such instances are treated as 'total'. Where it is above a certain complexity there are other possibilities intermediate between the total and partial as defined here; such instances are treated as 'partial'.

3. Clausal ellipsis	3
(1) propositional ellipsis	31
i. total (all Propositional element omitted)	1
ii. partial (some Complement or Adjunct present)	2
(2) modal ellipsis	32
i. total (all Modal element omitted)	1
ii. partial (Subject present) [rare]	2

Note: Lexical ellipsis implies propositional ellipsis, and operator ellipsis implies modal ellipsis, unless all clause elements other than the Predicator (verbal group) are explicitly repudiated.

(3) general ellipsis of the clause (all elements but one omitted)	33
i. WH- (only WH- element present)	1
ii. yes/no (only item expressing polarity present)	2
iii. other (other single clause element present)	3
(4) zero (entire clause omitted)	34
3(1–4) elliptical clause functioning as:	
(a) yes/no question or answer	6

		Coding
(b) WH- question or answer		7
(c) 'reported' element		8
(d) otherwise		9

Note: Not all combinations of (1–4) with (a–d) are possible.

CONJUNCTION (items quoted are examples, not complete lists)		C
Note: (E) = external, (I) = internal.		
1. Additive		1
(1) simple: (E/I)		11
i. additive	*and, and also*	1
ii. negative	*nor, and . . . not*	2
iii. alternative	*or, or else*	3
(2) complex, emphatic: (I)		12
i. additive	*furthermore, add to that*	1
ii. alternative	*alternatively*	2
(3) complex, de-emphatic: (I)	*by the way, incidentally*	13
(4) apposition: (I)		14
i. expository	*that is, in other words*	1
ii. exemplificatory	*eg, thus*	2
(5) comparison: (I)		15
i. similar	*likewise, in the same way*	1
ii. dissimilar	*on the other hand, by contrast*	2
2. Adversative		2
(1) adversative 'proper': (E/I)		21
i. simple	*yet, though, only*	1
ii. + 'and'	*but*	2
iii. emphatic	*however, even so, all the same*	3
(2) contrastive (avowal): (I)	*in (point of) fact, actually*	22
(3) contrastive: (E)		23
i. simple	*but, and*	1
ii. emphatic	*however, conversely, on the other hand*	2
(4) correction: (I)		24
i. of meaning	*instead, on the contrary, rather*	1
ii. of wording	*at least, I mean, or rather*	2

		Coding
(5) dismissal: (I)		25
i. closed	*in any/either case*	1
ii. open-ended	*in any case, anyhow*	2
3. Causal		3
(1) general: (E/I)		31
i. simple	*so, then, therefore*	1
ii. emphatic	*consequently*	2
(2) specific: (E/I)		32
i. reason	*on account of this*	1
ii. result	*in consequence*	2
iii. purpose	*with this in mind*	3
(3) reversed causal: (I)	*for, because*	33
(4) causal, specific: (I)		34
i. reason	*it follows*	1
ii. result	*arising out of this*	2
iii. purpose	*to this end*	3
(5) conditional: (E/I)		35
i. simple	*then*	1
ii. emphatic	*in that case, in such an event*	2
iii. generalized	*under the circumstances*	3
iv. reversed polarity	*otherwise, under other circumstances*	4
(6) respective: (I)		36
i. direct	*in this respect, here*	1
ii. reversed polarity	*otherwise, apart from this, in other respects*	2
4. Temporal		4
(1) simple: (E)		41
i. sequential	*then, next*	1
ii. simultaneous	*just then*	2
iii. preceding	*before that, hitherto*	3
(2) conclusive: (E)	*in the end*	42
(3) correlatives: (E)		43
i. sequential	*first . . . then*	1
ii. conclusive	*at first/originally/ formerly . . . finally/now*	2
(4) complex: (E)		44
i. immediate	*at once*	1
ii. interrupted	*soon*	2

Coding

iii. repetitive	*next time*	3
iv. specific	*next day*	4
v. durative	*meanwhile*	5
vi. terminal	*until then*	6
vii. punctiliar	*at this moment*	7
(5) internal temporal: (I)		45
i. sequential	*then, next*	1
ii. conclusive	*finally, in conclusion*	2
(6) correlatives: (I)		46
i. sequential	*first . . . next*	1
ii. conclusive	*in the first place . . . to conclude with*	2
(7) here and now: (I)		47
i. past	*up to now*	1
ii. present	*at this point*	2
iii. future	*from now on*	3
(8) summary: (I)		48
i. summarizing	*to sum up*	1
ii. resumptive	*to resume*	2
5. Other ('continuative')	*now, of course, well, anyway, surely, after all*	5
6. Intonation		6
(1) tone		61
(2) tonicity		62

LEXICAL	L
1. Same item	1
2. Synonym or near synonym (incl hyponym)	2
3. Superordinate	3
4. 'General' item	4
5. Collocation	5
1–5 having reference that is:	
(a) identical	6
(b) inclusive	7
(c) exclusive	8
(d) unrelated	9

Coding

B. Direction and distance of cohesion

IMMEDIATE   O

Not immediate:

MEDIATED [number of intervening sentences]   M[n]

REMOTE NON-MEDIATED [number of intervening sentences]   N[n]

CATAPHORIC   K

Note: Any cohesive instance, or 'tie', may be 'immediate' (presupposing an item in a contiguous sentence) or not immediate. If not immediate, it may be 'mediated' (having one or more intervening sentences that enter into a chain of presupposition) or 'remote' (having one or more intervening sentences not involved in the presupposition), or both. Finally it may be anaphoric or cataphoric; cataphoric ties are relatively infrequent and almost always immediate. A tie is assumed to be anaphoric unless marked 'K'.

The coding scheme provides a means of representing the cohesive patterns in a text in terms of the present analysis. Each sentence is given an index number, and the total number of ties in that sentence is entered in the appropriate column. Then for EACH TIE we specify (A) the type of cohesion and (B) its distance and direction.

The coding is designed to allow for variation in the delicacy of the analysis. For example, suppose we had

What is Mary doing? – Baking a pie.

we could code the second sentence as any of the following:

Ellipsis	E
Clausal ellipsis	E 3
Clausal ellipsis: modal	E 3 2
Clausal ellipsis: modal: total	E 3 2 1

and with any of these we could specify 'functioning as answer to WH-question' simply by adding a '7': E7, E37, E327 or E3217. (There is also verbal ellipsis, type E221, but this can be predicted from the clausal ellipsis.) In the coding of all types of cohesion except conjunction, the numbers 1–5 are used for subcategorization and 6–9 for cross-categorization. In conjunction there is no cross-categorization, but there is more subcategorization, so all the numbers 1–8 are used for this purpose. The primary types of cohesion are shown by their initial letters: R (reference), S (substitution), E (ellipsis), C (conjunction), L (lexical). Letters are also used to indicate the direction and distance.

In the final section we present an analysis of seven sample texts.

8.3 Sample texts

Text I: (as example [8:2])

... The last word ended in a long bleat, so like a sheep that Alice quite started (1).

She looked at the Queen, who seemed to have suddenly wrapped herself up in wool (2). Alice rubbed her eyes, and looked again (3). She couldn't make out what had happened at all (4). Was she in a shop (5)? And was that really – was it really a *sheep* that was sitting on the other side of the counter (6)? Rub as she would, she could make nothing more of it (7) ...

Sentence number	No. of ties	Cohesive item	Type	Distance	Presupposed item
1	1	*last*	R 34.7	0	*Be-e-ehh!* (in preceding sentence)
2	3	*She*	R 12.6	0	*Alice*
		the Queen	L 1.6	N.2	*the Queen* (in preceding text)
		wool	L 5	0	*sheep*
3	3	*Alice*	L 1.6	N.1	*Alice*
		looked	L 1.9	0	*looked*
		again	C 44.3	0	*looked at the Queen*
4	1	*She*	R 12.6	0	*Alice*
5	1	*she*	R 12.6	M.1	*she → Alice*
6	5	*And*	C 11.1	0	(S.5)
		really	C 22	N.4	*so like a sheep* (S.1)
		a sheep	L 1.9	N.4	*a sheep* (S.1)
		the (counter)	R 23.6	0	*a shop*
		counter	L 5	0	*shop*
7	5	*Rub*	L 1.6	N.3	*rubbed* (S.3)
		she (2×)	R 12.6	M.2+ N.1	*she → Alice*
		more	R 34.9	K	(than what follows)
		it	R 13.6	0	(SS. 5, 6)

Notes

1 Sentence 1: *last* is ambiguous. If it means 'the last of those just uttered', it is as coded here; if it means 'preceding', it should be coded C ᴖ1.3. There seems no way of telling, and it may rather be a blend of both.

2 Sentence 6: *the* shows *counter* to be referentially related to *shop:* ('what counter?' – 'the one in the shop just mentioned'). This is one tie; the cohesion provided by the collocational link between the lexical items *counter* and *shop*, which is independent of reference, constitutes another.

3 Possibly a 'past in past' tense such as *what had happened* in Sentence 4 could be treated as an instance of conjunction, presumably C 41.3. We have not attempted to include tense in the present treatment.

4 Sentence 3: *Alice* is coded as N.1, not M.1, since strictly speaking the repetition of a proper name is lexical not referential cohesion, and therefore the *she* in the intervening sentence is irrelevant.

5 Sentence 7: The two occurrences of *she* are both entered. It could be argued that two occurrences of a reference item constitute only a single tie; but this would be difficult to apply, and we adopt the simpler solution.

Text II (conversation) (*cf* example [1:28])

Can I tell you about the time when I screamed (1)?
Yes, do (2).
Well, I met a thief in my house (3). I had one of those nice old houses – I was very lucky (4). It was about thirty years old, on stone pillars, with a long stone staircase up and folding doors back on to a verandah (5). And I came through the door from the kitchen, and a thief carrying my hand-bag emerged through my bedroom door into the living room at the same moment (6).
Splendidly timed (7)!
I couldn't believe my eyes for a minute (8). I gave a little sort of gulp, and it flashed through my mind 'this won't do', and d'you know what I did (9)? I screamed (10)! And my scream went wafting out on the night air (11)! And some neighbours who – they were my nearest neighbours, but they were still some distance away – came rushing along (12). They were awfully good, and they said afterwards they thought I'd been being murdered (13). Well, I couldn't've made more noise if I had been (14). But I'd surprised myself (15). Really, the sound that went floating out on the air I didn't know I had it in me, and they said it would make my fortune if I sent it to Hollywood (16). And I may say it surprised the thief sufficiently that he dropped my handbag and fled (17). Fortunately I wasn't between him and the door (18). So there was no harm done, and I didn't lose anything (19).

Fortunately for him, or fortunately for you (20)?

Oh, for me (21). They generally carry knives (22).

I know (23). Someone was murdered in the main hotel quite recently (24).

Oh yes, yes (25). Though people did say that there were wheels within wheels in that (26). But you get between a fleeing thief and his exit and he's bound to be carrying a knife (27). But anyhow, the only thing I lost was my voice (28). I couldn't speak for a week afterwards (29).

(recorded by Afaf Elmenoufy)

Sentence number	No. of ties	Cohesive item	Type	Distance	Presupposed item
2	2	*Yes*	E 33. 2.6	0	(S.1)
		do	S 21	0	(S.1)
3	1	*Well*	C 5	M.1	(S.2 → S.1)
4	1	*houses*	L 1.7	0	*house*
5	2	*It*	R 13.6	0	*one of those nice old houses*
		thirty years old	L 1.6	0	*old*
6	4	*And*	C 11.1	0	(SS. 4–5)
		a thief	L 1.6	N.2	*a thief*
		door (2×)	L 1.7	0	*doors*
7	2	*Splendidly timed*	E 22.1; 32.1.9	0	(S.6)
		timed	L 5	0	*moment*
8	1	*minute*	L 5	N.1	*moment*
9	1	*this*	R 21.6	N.2	(S.6)
10	1	*screamed*	L 1.6	N.8	*screamed*
11	2	*And*	C 11.1	0	(S.10)
		scream	L 1.6	0	*screamed*
12	1	*And*	C 11.1	0	(S.11)
13	3	*they* (2×)	R 14.6	0	*neighbours*
		murdered	L 5	0	*scream*
14	4	*Well*	C 5	0	(S.13)
		more	R 34.7	N.2	*scream*
		noise	L 3.8	N.2	*scream*
		I had been	E 21.2	0	*I'd been being murdered*
15	1	*But*	C 23.1	N.1	(S.13)

Sentence number	No. of ties	Cohesive item	Type		Presupposed item
				Distance	
16	5	sound	L 2.8	N.1	noise
		the	R 23.6	N.4	scream
		floating out	L 2.6	N.4	wafting out
		air	L 1.6	N.4	air
		they	R 14.6	N.2+ M.1	→ they → neighbours
17	6	And	C 11.1	0	(S.16)
		it	R 13.6	0	sound
		the	R 23.6	N.10	a thief
		thief	L 1.6	N.10	a thief
		dropped	L 5	N.10	carrying
		handbag	L 1.6	N.10	handbag
18	2	him	R 11.6	0	the thief
		door	L 1.8	N.11	door (S.6)
19	1	So	C 31.1	0	(S.18)
20	1	Fortunately (2×)	L 1.6	N.1	fortunately
		him	R 11.6	N.1+ M.1	→ him → the thief
21	1	Oh, for me	E 33.3. 6/7	0	(S.20)
22	1	They	R 14.6	N.2+ M.2	→ him → him → the thief
23	1	I know	E 34.8	0	(S.22)
24	1	murdered	L 1.8	N.10	murdered
25	1	Oh yes, yes	E 33.2.9	0	(S.24)
26	2	Though	C 21.1	0	(S.23)
		that	R 22.6	N.1	(S.24)
27	5	But	C 21.2	0	(S.26)
		fleeing	L 1.9	N.9	fled (S.17)
		thief	L 1.9	N.9	thief
		exit	L 3.9	N.8	door (S.18)
		(carry) knife	L 1.9	N.4	carry knives (S.22)
28	3	But anyhow	C 25.2	0	(S.27)
		(thing) lost	L 1.8	N.8	I didn't lose anything (S.19)
		voice	L 5	N.16	scream (S.11)

Sentence number	No. of ties	Cohesive item	Type	Distance	Presupposed item
29	2	*speak*	L 5	0	*voice*
		afterwards	C 41.1	N.27	*the time when I screamed*

Notes

1 Sentence 10: The form of texture provided by a Question-and-Answer sequence is regarded as a discourse feature (here the structure of conversation; see 7.4.2). Since there is no ellipsis here, this is not an instance of cohesion.

2 Sentence 16: The *the* in *the sound that went floating out* is primarily cataphoric; but the lexical relation between *sound* and *scream* suggests that it may also be referring anaphorically.

3 Sentence 18: It is likely that *the door* here refers to the main door of the house; if so, *the* is exophoric and not cohesive.

4 Sentence 20 is an alternative question; these are mixed in type, being partly yes/no and partly WH- (hence the mixed intonation pattern, with first part rising and second part falling). The response is coded as a response to both.

5 Sentence 22: *They* here means 'thieves in general', having the sort of anomalous reference mentioned in 7.3.2 (example [7:20]).

Text III (sonnet)

> The Bad Thing (1)
> Sometimes just being alone seems the bad thing (2).
> Solitude can swell until it blocks the sun (3).
> It hurts so much, even fear, even worrying
> Over past and future, get stifled (4). It has won,
> You think; this is the bad thing, it is here (5).
> Then sense comes; you go to sleep, or have
> Some food, write a letter or work, get something clear (6).
> Solitude shrinks; you are not all its slave (7).
>
> Then you think: the bad thing inhabits yourself (8).
> Just being alone is nothing; not pain, not balm (9).
> Escape, into poem, into pub, wanting a friend
> Is not avoiding the bad thing (10). The high shelf
> Where you stacked the bad thing, hoping for calm,
> Broke (11). It rolled down (12). It follows you to the end
> (13).
>
> (John Wain)

Sentence number	No. of ties	Cohesive item	Type	Distance	Presupposed item
2	1	*The bad thing*	L 1	0	(S.1)
3	1	*Solitude*	L 2.9	0	*being alone*
4	1	*It*	R 13.6	0	*solitude*
5	5	*It* (2×)	R 13.6	M.1	*it → solitude*
		think	L 2.7	N.2	*seems*
		the	R 23.6	N.2	*the bad thing*
		bad thing	L 1.6	N.2	*bad thing*
6	1	*Then*	C 41.1	0	(S.5)
7	2	*Solitude*	L 1.9	N.3	*solitude*
		shrinks	L 5	N.3	*swell*
8	4	*Then*	C 41.1	0	(S.7)
		think	L 1.8	N.2	*think*
		the	R 23.6	N.2	*the bad thing*
		bad thing	L 1.6	N.2	*bad thing*
9	2	*(just) being alone*	L 1.9	N.6	*(just) being alone*
		pain	L 2.9	N.4	*hurts*
10	2	*the*	R 23.6	N.1	*the bad thing*
		bad thing	L 1.6	N.1	*bad thing*
11	2	*the*	R 23.6	0	*the bad thing*
		bad thing	L 1.6	0	*bad thing*
12	1	*It*	R 13.6	0	*the bad thing*
13	2	*It*	R 13.6	M.1	*it → the bad thing*
		follows	L 5	N.2	*avoiding*

Note

The continued use of *the* in *the bad thing* may be interpreted as anaphoric as well as cataphoric, suggesting a specific entity which stays around and contrasting with the general qualities of solitude and being alone; for the same reason *bad thing* is analysed as L 1.6, *solitude* and *being alone* as L 1.9. The cohesive pattern reflects and reinforces the interplay of localized and generalized imagery; and so contributes to the impression of something that is complex, both abstract and intangible, and at the same time concrete and very tangible.

Text IV (autobiography)

I had found when a boy in Dublin on a table in the Royal Irish Academy a pamphlet on Japanese art and read there of an animal painter so remarkable that horses he had painted upon a temple wall had slipped down after dark and trampled the neighbours' fields of rice (1). Somebody had come into the temple in the early morning, had been startled by a shower of water drops, had looked up and seen painted horses still wet from the dew-covered fields, but now 'trembling into stillness' (2).

I had soon mastered Mathers' symbolic system, and discovered that for a considerable minority – whom I could select by certain unanalysable characteristics – the visible world would completely vanish, and that world, summoned by the symbol, take its place (3). One day when alone in a third-class carriage, in the very middle of the railway bridge that crosses the Thames near Victoria, I smelt incense (4). I was on my way to Forest Hill; might it not come from some spirit Mathers had called up (5)? I had wondered when I smelt it at Madame Blavatsky's – if there might be some contrivance, some secret censer, but that explanation was no longer possible (6). I believed that Salamander of his but an image, and presently I found analogies between smell and image (7). That smell must be thought-created, but what certainty had I, that what had taken me by surprise, could be from my own thought, and if a thought could affect the sense of smell, why not the sense of touch (8)? Then I discovered among that group of students that surrounded Mathers, a man who had fought a cat in his dreams and awakened to find his breast covered with scratches (9). Was there an impassable barrier between those scratches and the trampled fields of rice (10)? It would seem so, and yet all was uncertainty (11). What fixed law would our experiments leave to our imagination (12)?

(W. B. Yeats)

Sentence number	No. of ties	Cohesive item	Type	Distance	Presupposed item
2	6	the	R 23.6	0	a temple wall
		temple	L 1.6	0	temple
		the (early morning)	R 23.6	0	after dark
		painted	L 1.7	0	painted
		horses	L 1.7	0	horses
		fields	L 1.9	0	fields
3	3	Mathers	L 1.6	N.3	Mathers (preceding text)
		symbol (2×)	L 1.7	N.3	symbol (preceding text)

Sentence number	No. of ties	Cohesive item	Type	Distance	Presupposed item
4	I	*smelt incense*	L 1.9	N.59	*smell . . . incense* (preceding text)
5	2	*it*	R 13.6	o	*incense*
		Mathers	L 1.6	o	*Mathers*
6	3	*smelt*	L 1.8	o	*smelt*
		it	R 13.6	o	*incense*
		censer	L 5	o	*incense*
7	6	*that*	R 22.6	N.7	*Salamanders* (preceding text)
		Salamander	L 1.6	N.7	*Salamanders* (preceding text)
		his	R 11.7	N.1	*Mathers*
		image (2 ×)	L 1.7	N.8	*images* (preceding text)
		smell	L 1.8	o	*smelt (it at Madame B's)*
8	3	*That*	R 22.6	o	*smell*
		smell (2 ×)	L 1.6 (7)	o	*smell*
9	4	*Then*	C 41.1	o	(S.8)
		that	R 22.6	N.18	*a little group . . . students* (preceding text)
		group of students	L 1.6	N.18	*a little group . . . students* (preceding text)
		Mathers	L 1.6	N.1	*Mathers*
10	5	*those*	R 22.6	o	*scratches*
		scratches	L 1.6	o	*scratches*
		the	R 23.6	N.8	*the . . . fields of rice*
		trampled	L 1.6	N.8	*trampled*
		fields of rice	L 1.6	N.8	*fields of rice*
11	I	*so*	S 31.8	o	(S.10)
12	I	*fixed*	L 5	o	*uncertainty*

Note

The repetition of the lexical item *smell* provides an interesting illustration of the different referential relations that may be involved in lexical reiteration. The incident referred to in S.4 stands in no explicit relationship to that in which the word had last occurred 59 sentences earlier; hence L 9. In S.6 *smelt* refers to that earlier incident in a context in which it is explicitly contrasted with the present one; hence L.8. In S.7 we are back to the present, so L.8 again. In S.8 it occurs twice: first in reference to the present (*that smell*), so L.6; secondly in a general context *the sense of smell*, which therefore includes the preceding instance and hence is represented as L.7. There is considerable indeterminacy among these categories, which are probably the most difficult to apply with any consistency; but they are not irrelevant to patterns of text construction.

Text V (dramatic dialogue) (*cf* example [3:59])

Mrs Birling: I think we've just about come to an end of this wretched business – (1)

Gerald: I don't think so (2). Excuse me (3).

[*He goes out. They watch him go in silence. We hear the front door slam.*]

Sheila [*to Inspector*]: You know, you never showed him that photograph of her (4).

Inspector: No (5). It wasn't necessary (6). And I thought it better not to (7).

Mrs Birling: You have a photograph of this girl (8)?

Inspector: Yes (9). I think you'd better look at it (10).

Mrs Birling: I don't see any particular reason why I should – (11)

Inspector: Probably not (12). But you'd better look at it (13).

Mrs Birling: Very well (14). [*He produces the photograph and she looks hard at it.*]

Inspector [*taking back the photograph*]: You recognize her (15)?

Mrs Birling: No (16). Why should I (17)?

Inspector: Of course she might have changed lately, but I can't believe she could have changed so much (18).

Mrs Birling: I don't understand you, Inspector (19).

Inspector: You mean you don't choose to do, Mrs Birling (20).

Mrs Birling [*angrily*]: I meant what I said (21).

Inspector: You're not telling me the truth (22).

Mrs Birling: I beg your pardon (23)!

Birling [*angrily, to Inspector*]: Look here, I'm not going to have this, Inspector (24). You'll apologize at once (25).

Inspector: Apologize for what – doing my duty (26)?

Birling: No, for being so offensive about it (27). I'm a public man – (28)

Inspector [*massively*]: Public men, Mr Birling, have responsibilities as well as privileges (29).

Birling: Possibly (30). But you weren't asked to come here to talk to me about my responsibilities (31).

Sheila: Let's hope not (32). Though I'm beginning to wonder (33).
Mrs Birling: Does that mean anything, Sheila (34)?
Sheila: It means that we've no excuse now for putting on airs and that if
we've any sense we won't try (35).

(J. B. Priestley)

Sentence number	No. of ties	Cohesive item	Type	Distance	Presupposed item
2	1	*so*	S 31.6	0	(S.1)
3	0				
4	2	*photograph*	L 1.6	N.600 approx.	*photograph* (preceding text)
		her	R 12.6	N.43+ M.20	→ *her* (→ . . .) → *Daisy* (preceding text)
5	1	*No*	E 33.2.6	0	(S.4)
6	1	*It*	R 13.6	N.1	(*to*) *show him that photograph of her*
7	2	*And*	C 11.1	0	(S.6)
		not to	E 21.1; 31.1.9	N.1+ M.1	*it* (S.6) → *show him that photograph of her*
8	2	*photograph*	L 1.7	N.3	*photograph*
		this	R 21.6	N.46+ M.21	→ *her* (→ . . .) → *Daisy*
9	1	*Yes*	E 33.2.6	0	(S.8)
10	1	*it*	R 13.6	N.1	*a photograph*
11	1	*I should*	E 21.1; 31.2.8	0	*you'd better look at it*
12	1	*Probably not*	S 32.8	0	(S.11)
13	3	*But*	C 21.2	0	(S.12)
		it	R 13.6	N.3+ M.1	→ *it* → *a photograph*
		look at	L 1.6	N.2	*look at*
14	1	*Very well*	E 33.3.9	0	(S.13)
15	0	*her*	R 12.6	N.52+ M.22	→ *her* (→ . . .) → *Daisy*
16	1	*No*	E 33.2.6	0	(S.15)

Sentence number	No. of ties	Cohesive item	Type	Presupposed Distance	item
17	1	*Why should I?*	E 21.1; 31.2.9	N.1	*recognize her* (S.15)
18	4	*Of course*	C 5	0	(S.17)
		she (2×)	R 12.6	N.54+ M.23	→ *her* (→ . . .) → *Daisy*
		so much	R 34.9	N.1	(S.16)
19	0				
20	1	*to do*	S 21	0	*understand me*
21	1	*meant*	L 1.6	0	*mean*
22	1	*tell . . . truth*	L 5	0	*meant . . . said*
23	0				
24	1	*this*	R 21.6	N.1	(S.22)
25	0				
26	2	*Apologize for what?*	E 22.1; 32.1.7	0	(S.25)
		apologize	L 1.6	0	*apologize*
27	4	*No*	E 33.2.6	0	*apologize . . . for doing my duty?*
		for being so offensive about it	E 33.3.7	0	*apologize for what?*
		so	R 35.8	N.4	(S.22)
		it	R 13.6	0	*doing your duty*
28	0				
29	1	*Public men*	L 1.7	0	*public man*
30	1	*Possibly*	E 33.3.9	0	(S.29)
31	2	*But*	C 21.2	0	(S.30)
		responsibilities	L 1.7	N.1	*responsibilities*
32	1	*not*	S 32.6	0	(S.31)
33	2	*Though*	C 21.1	0	(S.32)
		to wonder	E 34.8	N.1	(S.32)
34	1	*that*	R 22.6	0	(S.33)
35	2	*It*	R 13.6	M.1	*that* → (S.33)
		means	L 1.6	0	*mean*

Notes

1 Dramatic dialogue may be interpreted in two ways: either as read, or as acted. The former would take account of stage directions, and treat all reference as endophoric; in the latter

perspective, which is that adopted here, stage directions are excluded and reference to situational features is treated as exophoric, and thus not cohesive.

2 Sentence 4: Both *him* and *that* (in *that photograph*) are exophoric here. The *her*, however, is at least partially endophoric: the only appearance of Daisy on the stage is in the form of the photograph. The same consideration applies to Sentence 15.

Text VI (informal interview, adult; reported)

I harked back to his school years, and he confessed that he had never liked school (1). 'I remember it very well, and particularly my dislike of it, which has never died to this very day (2). And I am now 68 (3)!'

Whenever he visited schools, the smell of the chalk or the plasticine always gave him a sinking feeling (4). He hated it so much (5).

'Then we moved into the country, to a lovely little village called Warley (6). It is about three miles from Halifax (7). There are quite a few about (8). There is a Warley in Worcester and one in Essex (9). But the one not far out of Halifax had had a maypole, and a fountain (10). By this time the maypole has gone, but the pub is still there called the *Maypole* (11). Perhaps they were the happiest days of my life, in the country (12). I was there for about seven or eight years and I loved it (13).'

Even the village school proved less odious than its predecessor in his life (14). 'I started to take a little bit of a liking to school then (15).'

(from 'Meeting Wilfred Pickles', by Frank Haley)

Sentence number	No. of ties	Cohesive item	Type	Distance	Presupposed item
1	4	*his*	R 11.8	N.2+ M.6	→ 'I' (→ ...) → *Wilfred* (preceding text)
		he (2×)	R 11.6	N.2+ M.6	→ 'I' (→ ...) → *Wilfred* (preceding text)
		school	L 1.9	N.13	*school* (preceding text)
2	5	'I'	R 11.6	M.7+ N.2	*he* (→ ...) → *Wilfred*
		it (2×)	R 13.6	0	*school*
		'my'	R 11.8	M.7+ N.2	*he* (→ ...) → *Wilfred*
		dislike	L 2.6	0	*never liked*

Presence number	No. of ties	Cohesive item	Type	Distance	Presupposed item
3	3	*And*	C 23.1	0	*never . . . to this very day*
		'*I*'	R 11.6	M.8+ N.2	'*I*' (→ . . .) → *Wilfred*
		now	R 21.8	0	*to this very day*
4	2	*he/him*	R 11.6	M.9+ N.2	'*I*' (→ . . .) → *Wilfred*
		schools	L 1.9	N.2	*school*
5	3	*he*	R 11.6	M.10+ N.2	*he* (→ . . .) → *Wilfred*
		it	R 13.6	N.2+ M.1	→ *it* → *school*
		so much	R 34.9	0	(S.4)
6	3	*Then*	C 41.1	N.26	*Then* (preceding text)
		'*we*'	R 11.6	M.11+ N.2	*he* (→ . . .) → *Wilfred*
		moved to	L 1.8	N.26	*moved to Brighton*
7	2	*It*	R 13.6	0	*village called Warley*
		Halifax	L 1.6	N.32	*Halifax* (preceding text)
8	1	*quite a few*	E 12.3	0	*village called Warley*
9	1	*Warley*	L 1.8	N.2	*Warley*
10	4	*But*	C 23.1	0	(S.9)
		one	S 11	0	*Warley*
		not far out of	L 5	N.2	*about three miles from*
		Halifax	L 1.6	N.2	*Halifax*
11	4	*By this time*	C 44.6	N.4	*Then we moved* (S.6)
		the	R 23.6	0	*a maypole*
		maypole	L 1.6	0	*maypole*
		Maypole	L 1.8	0	*maypole*

Presence number	No. of ties	Cohesive item	Type		Presupposed Distance item	
12	2	*the country*	L 1.6	N.5	*the country*	
		'*my*'	R 11.8	N.7+	→'*we*'(→ …)→	
				M.11	→ *Wilfred*	
13	3	'*I*' (2×)	R 11.6	M.12+	'*my*' (→ …)→	
				N.7	*Wilfred*	
		there	R 22.7	0	*in the country*	
14	5	*village*	L 1.6	N.7	*village* (S.6)	
		school	L 1.8	N.9	*schools* (S.4)	
		odious	L 2.8	N.11	*dislike* (S.2)	
		his	R 11.8	M.13+	'*I*' (→ …)→	
				N.7	*Wilfred*	
		life	L 1.6	N.1	*life* (S.12)	
15	4	'*I*'	R 11.6	M.14+	*his* (→ …)→	
				N.7	*Wilfred*	
		take a liking	L 2.6	0	*less odious*	
		school	L 1.7	0	*school*	
		then	R 22.8	N.1	(S.13)	

Notes

1 The first person forms *I* etc (in the speech of the interviewee) are anaphoric and cohesive, functioning in this context as conditioned variants of the third person reference item *he* etc.

2 Sentence 4: *the chalk, the plasticine* refer to *schools* within the same sentence, and are therefore not treated as cohesive.

3 Sentence 12: *they* here is cataphoric to (*those*) *in the country*, which is within the same sentence.

4 Sentence 13: *it* refers to '*being there*', *ie: was there* in the same sentence.

Text VII (informal interview, children; transcribed)*

We've made so far a boat, garden dibber, teapot stand . . . (1)
What else (2) ?
A seed marker (3).
I think our nail box was the best one that we made (4).
Yes (5) ?
The nail box (6). We just made this little box out of wood (7). It's very

* Recorded by Ruqaiya Hasan; Nuffield Foreign Languages Teaching Materials Project, Reports and Occasional Papers No 29 (slightly adapted).

useful as something else than a nail box (8). My father's friend went out, he brought two packs of seeds back and he gave them to my father (9). And we keep my sister's pack in one half of the box and my pack in the other half (10).

What did it look like (11)?

Yes what did it (12)?

Well, we had a base, and then an end, and the two sides, with a piece of wood across the middle (13). And no lid (14). We left the lid off (15).

Did you paint it (16)?

We didn't (17). Not in school (18). But we could have done at home (19). I painted the boat at home, all different colours (20).

Sentence number	No. of ties	Cohesive item	Type	Distance	Presupposed item
2	2	*What else?*	E 33.1.7	0	(S.1)
		else	R 33.9	0	*a boat, garden dibber, teapot stand*
3	1	*A seed marker*	E 33.3.7	0	(S.2)
4	1	*one*	S 11	N.2	(list in S.1 (→ *one → thing* in prec. text))
5	1	*Yes?*	E 33.2.6	0	(S.4)
6	3	*The nail box*	E 33.3.6	0	(S.5)
		the	R 23.6	N.1	*our . . . that we made*
		nail box	L 1.6	N.1	*nail box*
7	3	*made . . . box*	L 1.6	N.2	*made . . . box*
		this	R 21.6	K	
		box	L 3.6	0	*nail box*
8	2	*It*	R 13.6	0	*this little box*
		nail box	L 1.9	N.1	*nail box*
9	0				
10	4	*And*	C 11.1	0	(S.9)
		pack	L 1.6	0	*packs of seeds*
		the (box)	R 23.6	N.1+ M.1	→ *it* → *this little box*
		box	L 1.6	N.1+ M.1	→ *a nail box* → *this little box*

Sentence number	No. of ties	Cohesive item	Type	Distance	Presupposed item
11	1	*it*	R 13.6	0	*the box*
12	2	*what did it?*	E 21.1; 31.2.7	0	(S.11)
		it	R 13.6	M.1	*it* → *the box*
13	5	*Well*	C 5	M.1	(S.12 → S.11)
		base	L 5	N.2	*box* (S.10)
		end	L 5	N.2	*box* (S.10)
		sides	L 5	N.2	*box* (S.10)
		wood	L 1.9	N.5	*wood* (S.7)
14	2	*And*	C 23.1	0	(S.13)
		no lid	E 33.3.9	0	*we had . . .* (S.13)
15	2	*the*	R 23.6	0	*no lid*
		lid	L 1.6	0	*lid*
16	1	*it*	R 13.6	N.3 + M.2	→ *it* → *it* → *the box* (S.10)
17	1	*We didn't.*	E 21.1; 31.1.6	0	(S.16)
18	1	*Not*	S 32.9	M.1	(S.17 → S.16)
19	3	*But*	C 21.2	0	(S.18)
		could have done	S 21	M.2	*paint it* (S.16)
		at home	L 5	0	*in school*
20	4	*painted*	L 1.8	N.3	*paint* (S.16)
		the	R 23.6	N.18	*a boat* (S.1)
		boat	L 1.6	N.18	*boat* (S.1)
		at home	L 1.6	0	*at home*

Note

It is perhaps questionable whether the lid that was 'left off' (*ie* not made; Sentence 15) is referentially identical with the lid that did not exist (Sentence 14). But this is a harmless assumption that is required for interpretation of the *the*.

Bibliography

The Bibliography contains selected items related in various ways to the main theme.

1. Standard grammars of English, such as those of Curme, Fries, and Jespersen, figure both as general background and for their discussion of particular elements that enter into the expression of cohesion. Also listed are some other works that contain relevant background material, for example by Abercrombie, Ullmann, and Gleason.

The major source of up-to-date information on English grammar (up-to-date both in terms of the English language and in terms of linguistic scholarship) is provided by *A Grammar of Contemporary English*, by Quirk and others, and its shorter version *A University Grammar of English* (American title *A Concise Grammar of Contemporary English*). Both contain treatments of the areas of the grammar that are involved in cohesion.

2. Other general works on English have been included where they throw light on the theoretical background of the present account; for example Hudson, *English Complex Sentences*; Sinclair, *A Course in Spoken English: Grammar*.

Two large-scale studies of English texts are of special relevance: that by Huddleston and others, on grammar, and that by Sinclair and others, on lexis. (It is unfortunate that these were written at a time when text studies were heretical in linguistics, and so they were not published; but they were distributed in the form of reports.)

3. Many articles have appeared particularly in transformational grammar dealing with cohesive relations within the sentence, especially pronominal reference and conjunction. A selection of these has been included; see for example Lees and Klima, George Lakoff, Robin Lakoff, and Postal.

4. Discourse structure in languages other than English, typically non-

Indo-European languages, has been described in numerous studies inspired particularly by the theoretical work of Pike and Gleason. These studies have not been cited here; bibliographies are readily available.

5. Cohesion in literary texts is treated in a recent book by Gutwinski (which had not yet appeared at the time of writing). Aside from this, as far as literary studies are concerned, the list includes some general works on style and the linguistic study of literature, such as Leech's *A Linguistic Guide to English Poetry*; and also some recent collections of essays, such as Chatman's *Literary Style: a symposium*. Stylistic studies of particular prose or verse texts have not been listed; for references to these, see Richard W. Bailey and Dolores M. Burton, *English Stylistics: a bibliography* (Cambridge, Mass: MIT Press, 1968).

6. Some recent works have been cited from the field of rhetoric and composition, where there is systematic treatment of discourse structure in a primarily educational context.

From the newer, related field of language variety (register) studies are included one or two general treatments, such as that of Benson and Greaves; and certain papers which relate particularly to cohesion in this context, for example those by Jean Ure.

7. Finally reference is made to selected books and articles dealing with particular aspects of the English language that in one way or other relate to cohesion: either topics falling directly under the main headings (reference, substitution and ellipsis, conjunction, lexical cohesion), or parts of the grammar that figure prominently in cohesive patterns (such as the noun phrase, or nominal group; see for example Peter Fries).

Abercrombie, David. *Elements of General Phonetics*. Edinburgh: University Press, 1967.

Allan, Keith. 'In reply to "There₁, there₂"' *Journal of Linguistics* 8, 1972.
– 'A note on the source of *there* in existential sentences' *Foundations of Language* 7, 1971.

Allen, Robert L. 'The classification of English substitute words' *General Linguistics* 5, 1961.

Allerton, D. J. 'The sentence as a linguistic unit' *Lingua* 22, 1969.

Arapoff, Nancy. 'The semantic role of sentence connectors in extra-sentence logical relationships' *TESOL Quarterly* 2, 1968.

Ballard, Lee, Conrad, Robert J. and Longacre, Robert E. 'The deep and surface grammar of interclausal relations' *Foundations of Language* 7, 1971.

Barthes, Roland. 'L'ancienne rhétorique' *Communications* 16, 1970.

Becker, Alton L. 'Symposium on the paragraph' *College Composition and Communication*, May 1966.

Behre, Frank. 'On the principle of connecting elements of speech in contemporary English' G. A. Bonnard (ed), *English Studies Today*. Bern: Francke Verlag, 1961.

Benson, James D. and Greaves, William S. *The Language People Really Use*. Agincourt, Ontario: The Book Society of Canada, 1973.

Bolinger, Dwight L. *That's that*. The Hague: Mouton, 1972.

– 'Entailment and the meaning of structures' *Glossa* 2, 1968.

– *Degree Words*. The Hague: Mouton, 1972.

Bouton, Lawrence. 'Identity constraints on the *Do So* rule' *Papers in Linguistics*, Tallahassee: Florida State University, 1969.

Buyssens, Eric. *La Communication et l'Articulation Linguistique*. Bruxelles: Presses Universitaires de Bruxelles, 1967.

Cartledge, H. A. 'The articles in English' *English Language Teaching* 14, 1959–60.

Centro Internazionale di Semiotica e di Linguistica, Università di Urbino: Working Papers and Prepublications, 1971—.

Chafe, Wallace L. 'Directionality and paraphrase' *Language* 47, 1971.

Chatman, Seymour. 'English sentence connectors' *Studies in Languages and Linguistics in Honor of Charles C. Fries*. Ann Arbor, Michigan: University of Michigan English Language Institute, 1964.

– (ed). *Literary Style: a symposium*. New York & London: Oxford University Press, 1971.

Christiansen, Francis. *Notes Toward a new Rhetoric*. New York: Harper & Row, 1967.

Christophersen, Paul. *The Articles: a study of their history and use in English*. Copenhagen: Munksgaard, 1939.

Crymes, Ruth. *Some Systems of Substitution Correlations in Modern American English*. The Hague: Mouton, 1968.

Crystal, David. 'Specification and English tenses' *Journal of Linguistics* 2, 1966.

Crystal, David and Davy, Derek. *Investigating English Style*. London: Longman (*English Language Series*), 1969.

Curme, George O. *A Grammar of the English Language III: Syntax*. Boston: Heath, 1931.

Daneš, František. 'Zur linguistischen Analyse der Textstruktur' *Folia Linguistica* 4, 1969.

– 'One instance of Prague school methodology: functional analysis of utterance and text' Paul L. Garvin (ed), *Method and Theory in Linguistics*. The Hague: Mouton, 1970.

– (ed). *Papers on Functional Sentence Perspective*. Prague: Academia, 1974.

Davies, Eirian C. 'Some notes on English clause types' *Transactions of the Philological Society*, 1967.

Dik, Simon. *Co-ordination: its implications for the theory of general linguistics*. Amsterdam: North Holland, 1968.

– 'Referential identity' *Lingua* 21, 1968.

Dixon, Robert M. W. *What IS Language? a new approach to linguistic description*. London: Longman (*Longman Linguistics Library*), 1965.

Dorfman, Eugene. *The Narreme in the Medieval Romance Epic: an introduction to narrative structures*. Toronto: University Press (*Romance Series* 13), 1969.

Doughty, Peter S., Pearce, John J. and Thornton, Geoffrey M. *Exploring Language*. London: Edward Arnold (*Schools Council Programme in Linguistics and English Teaching*), 1972.

Dressler, Wolfgang U. 'Textsyntax' *Lingua e Stile* 5, 1970.

– 'Towards a semantic deep structure of discourse grammar' *Papers from the Sixth Regional Meeting of the Chicago Linguistics Society*. Chicago: University of Chicago Department of Linguistics, 1970.

Eaton, Trevor. 'The foundations of literary semantics' *Linguistics* 62, 1970.

Elmenoufy, Afaf. *A Study of the Role of Intonation in the Grammar of English*. University of London PhD thesis, 1969.

Enkvist, Nils Erik, Spencer, John and Gregory, Michael. *Linguistics and Style*. London: Oxford University Press (*Language and Language Learning*), 1968.

Firbas, Jan. 'On defining the theme in functional sentence analysis' *Travaux Linguistiques de Prague* 1, 1964.

– 'On the interplay of means of functional sentence perspective' *Proceedings of the Tenth International Congress of Linguists*. Bucharest: Rumanian Academy of Sciences, 1970.

Fries, Charles C. *American English Grammar: the grammatical structure of present-day American English with especial reference to social differences or class dialects*. New York: Appleton-Century-Crofts, 1940.

– *The Structure of English: an introduction to the construction of English sentences*. New York: Harcourt Brace, 1952. London: Longman, 1957.

Fries, Peter H. *Tagmeme Sequences in the English Noun Phrase*. Norman, Oklahoma: University of Oklahoma Summer Institute of Linguistics, 1970.

Gleason, H. A., Jr. *Linguistics and English Grammar*. New York: Holt, Rinehart & Winston, 1965.

– 'Contrastive analysis in discourse structure' *Monograph Series on Languages and Linguistics* 21. Washington, DC: Georgetown University Press, 1968.

Gleitman, Lila R. 'Co-ordinating conjunctions in English' *Language* 41, 1965.

Green, Georgia M. 'On *Too* and *Either*; and not just *Too* and *Either*, either' *Papers from the Fourth Regional Meeting of the Chicago Linguistics Society*. Chicago: University of Chicago Department of Linguistics, 1968.

Greenbaum, Sidney. *Studies in English Adverbial Usage*. London: Longman (*Longman Linguistics Library*), 1969.

Grimes, Joseph E. 'Kinds of information in discourse' *Kivung* 4, 1971.

Gunter, Richard. 'Elliptical sentences in American English' *Lingua* 12, 1963.

– 'On the placement of accent in dialogue: a feature of context grammar' *Journal of Linguistics* 2, 1966.

Gutwinski, Waldemar. *Cohesion in Literary Texts: a study of some grammatical and lexical features of English discourse*. The Hague: Mouton, 1974.

Halliday, M. A. K. 'The linguistic study of literary texts' Seymour Chatman and Samuel R. Levin (eds), *Essays on the Language of Literature*. Boston: Houghton Mifflin, 1967.

– 'Lexis as a linguistic level' C. E. Bazell, J. C. Catford, M. A. K. Halliday and R. H. Robins (eds), *In Memory of J. R. Firth*. London: Longman (*Longman Linguistics Library*), 1966.

– *Intonation and Grammar in British English*. The Hague: Mouton, 1967.

– 'Notes on transitivity and theme in English, Part 2' *Journal of Linguistics* 3, 1967.

– 'Language structure and language function' John Lyons (ed), *New Horizons in Linguistics*. Harmondsworth: Penguin Books, 1970.

– *A Course in Spoken English: Intonation*. London: Oxford University Press, 1970.

– *Language and Social Man*. London: Longman (*Schools Council Programme in Linguistics and English Teaching*, Papers, Series II, 3), 1974.

– *The Meaning of Modern English*. London: Oxford University Press (forthcoming).

Harris, Zellig S. *Discourse Analysis Reprints* (*Papers on Formal Linguistics* 2). The Hague: Mouton, 1963.

Hartmann, Peter. 'Textlinguistik als neue linguistische Teildisziplin' *Replik* I, 12, 1968.

Hasan, Ruqaiya. *A Linguistic Study of Contrasting Features in the Style of Two Contemporary English Prose Writers*. University of Edinburgh PhD thesis, 1964.

– 'Linguistics and the study of literary texts' *Études de Linguistique Appliquée* 5, 1967.

– *Grammatical Cohesion in Spoken and Written English Part I*. London: University College London Department of General Linguistics (Communication Research Centre) and Longman (*Papers of the Programme in Linguistics and English Teaching*, Series I, 7), 1968.

– *Language in the Imaginative Context: a socio-linguistic study of stories told by children*. London: Routledge & Kegan Paul (*Primary Socialization, Language and Education*) (forthcoming).

Hausenblas, Karel. 'On the characterization and classification of discourses' *Travaux Linguistiques de Prague* 1, 1964.

Hays, Daniel G. and Lance, Donald M. *From Soundstream to Discourse: papers from the 1971 Mid-America Linguistics Conference*. Columbia, Missouri: University of Missouri Linguistics Area Program, 1972.

Hendricks, William O. 'On the notion "beyond the sentence"' *Linguistics* 37, 1967.

– 'Current trends in discourse analysis' Braj B. Kachru and H. W. Stahlke (eds), *Current Trends in Stylistics*. Edmonton, Alberta: Linguistic Research Inc, 1972.

Hill, Archibald A. 'A re-examination of the English articles' *Monograph Series on Languages and Linguistics* 19. Washington, DC: Georgetown University Press, 1966.

Hlavsa, Zdenek. 'On the operators of reference' *Travaux Linguistiques de Prague* 3, 1968.

Huddleston, Rodney D. 'Rank and depth' *Language* 41, 1965.

Huddleston, Rodney D., Hudson, Richard A., Winter, Eugene and Henrici, Alick. *Sentence and Clause in Scientific English*. London: University College London Department of General Linguistics (Communication Research Centre), 1968.

Hudson, Richard A. 'Constituency in a systemic description of the English clause' *Lingua* 17, 1967.

– *English Complex Sentences: an introduction to systemic grammar*. Amsterdam: North Holland (*North Holland Linguistic Series* 4), 1971.

Jakobson, Roman. *Shifters, Verbal Categories, and the Russian Verb*. Cambridge, Mass.: Harvard University Press, 1957.

Jespersen, Otto. *A Modern English Grammar on Historical Principles I–VII*. London: Allen & Unwin, 1909–49.

– *Essentials of English Grammar*. New York: Holt, 1933.

Karlsen, R. *Studies in the Connection of Clauses in Current English: zero, ellipsis and explicit forms*. Bergen: Eides, 1959.

Karttunen, Lauri. 'Discourse referents' Bloomington, Indiana: Indiana University Linguistics Club (mimeo.), 1971.

Kiefer, Ferenc (ed). *Studies in Syntax and Semantics. Foundations of Language Supplements* 10, 1970.

Kinneavy, James L., Cope, John A. and Campbell, J. W. *The Design of Discourse*. Englewood Cliffs, NJ: Prentice-Hall, 1969.

Kiparsky, Paul and Kiparsky, Carol. 'Fact' Manfred Bierwisch and K. Heidolph (eds), *Progress in Linguistics*. The Hague: Mouton, 1968.

Knapp, Donald S. *Formal Factors affecting Paragraph Division in Expository Writing*. Columbia University PhD thesis, 1967.

Koch, Walter A. 'Preliminary sketch of a semantic type of discourse analysis' *Linguistics* 12, 1965.

– 'Einige Probleme der Textanalyse' *Lingua* 16, 1966.

Kruisinga, E. *A Handbook of Present-day English, Parts I & II*. Groningen: Noordhoff, 5th edn, 1931–32.

Lakoff, George. *Irregularity in Syntax*. New York: Holt, Rinehart & Winston, 1970.

– 'Pronouns and reference' Bloomington, Indiana: Indiana University Linguistics Club (mimeo.), 1969.

Lakoff, Robin, 'If's, and's and but's about conjunctions' C. J. Fillmore and D. T. Langendoen (eds), *Studies in Linguistic Semantics*. New York: Holt, Rinehart & Winston, 1971.

Leech, Geoffrey N. *English in Advertising: a linguistic study of advertising in Great Britain*. London: Longman (*English Language Series*), 1966.

– *Towards a Semantic Description of English*. London: Longman (*Longman Linguistics Library*), 1969.

– *A Linguistic Guide to English Poetry*. London: Longman (*English Language Series*), 1969.

Lees, Robert B. and Klima, E. S. 'Rules for English pronominalization' *Language* 39, 1963.

Longacre, Robert E. 'Taxonomy in deep and surface grammar' *Proceedings of the Eleventh International Congress of Linguists*. Bologna: Il Mulino, 1975.

Lowe, Ivan. 'An algebraic theory of English pronominal reference' *Semiotica* 1, 1969.

Lyons, John. *Introduction to Theoretical Linguistics*. Cambridge: University Press, 1969.

McIntosh, Angus. 'Patterns and ranges' Angus McIntosh and M. A. K. Halliday, *Patterns of Language: papers in general, descriptive and applied linguistics*. London: Longman (*Longman Linguistics Library*), 1966.

Morgan, James O. 'English structure above the sentence level' *Monograph Series on Languages and Linguistics* 20. Washington, DC: Georgetown University Press, 1967.

Nickel, Gerhard. 'Some contextual relations between sentences in English' *Proceedings of the Tenth International Congress of Linguists*. Bucharest: Rumanian Academy of Sciences, 1970.

Olney, J. C. and Lande, D. L. 'An analysis of English discourse structure, with particular attention to anaphoric relations' *Proceedings of the Tenth International Congress of Linguists*. Bucharest: Rumanian Academy of Sciences, 1970.

Padučeva, E. V. 'Anaphoric relations and their manifestations in the text' *Proceedings of the Tenth International Congress of Linguists*. Bucharest: Rumanian Academy of Sciences, 1970. Also in Bierwisch and Heidolph (eds), *Progress in Linguistics*. The Hague: Mouton, 1968.

Palek, Bohumil. 'Cross-reference: a contribution to hyper-syntax' *Travaux Linguistiques de Prague* 3, 1968.

Palmer, Harold E. 'English article usage' *English Language Teaching* 2, 1947–48.

Pike, Kenneth L. 'Discourse analysis and tagmemic matrices' *Oceanic Linguistics* 3, 1964.

– 'A linguistic contribution to composition' *College Composition and Communication*, May 1964.

– 'Beyond the sentence' *College Composition and Communication*, October 1964.

Postal, Paul M. 'On so-called "pronouns" in English' David Reibel and Sandford Schane (eds), *Modern Studies in English: readings in transformational grammar*. Englewood Cliffs, NJ: Prentice-Hall, 1969.

– 'Anaphoric islands' *Papers of the Fifth Regional Meeting of the Chicago Linguistics Society*. Chicago: University of Chicago Department of Linguistics, 1969.

– 'Problems in linguistic representation of reference' Danny D. Steinberg and L. A. Jakobovits (eds), *Semantics: an interdisciplinary reader in philosophy, linguistics and psychology*. Cambridge: University Press, 1971.

Quirk, Randolph. 'Descriptive statement and serial relationship'
   Language 41, 1965.
– *Essays in the English Language, Medieval and Modern*. London: Longman
   (*Longman Linguistics Library*), 1968.
Quirk, Randolph, Greenbaum, Sidney, Leech, Geoffrey and Svartvik,
   Jan. *A Grammar of Contemporary English*. London: Longman, 1972. New
   York: Seminar Press, 1972.
Quirk, Randolph and Greenbaum, Sidney. *A University Grammar of
   English*. London: Longman, 1973. (*A Concise Grammar of
   Contemporary English*. New York: Harcourt Brace Jovanovich, 1973.)
Robbins, B. L. *The definite article in English transformations*. The Hague:
   Mouton: 1968.
Ruhl, Charles. 'Prerequisites for a linguistic description of coherence'
   Language Sciences 25, 1973.
Sachs, Harvey, Schegloff, Emanuel A. and Jefferson, Gail. 'A simplest
   systematics for the analysis of turn-taking in conversation' *Language*
   50, 1974.
Sampson, Geoffrey. 'There$_1$, there$_2$' *Journal of Linguistics* 8, 1972.
Scott, Charles T. 'On defining the riddle: the problem of a structural
   unit' *Genre* 2, 1969.
Sebeok, Thomas A. (ed). *Style in Language*. Cambridge, Mass: MIT
   Press, 1960.
Sinclair, J. McH., 'Beginning the study of lexis' C. E. Bazell, J. C.
   Catford, M. A. K. Halliday and R. H. Robins (eds), *In Memory of
   J. R. Firth*. London: Longman (*Longman Linguistics Library*), 1966.
– *A Course in Spoken English: Grammar*. London: Oxford University
   Press, 1972.
Sinclair, J. McH. Jones, S., and Daley, R. *English Lexical Studies*.
   University of Birmingham Department of English, 1970.
Sinclair, J. McH. and Coulthard, R. M. *Towards an Analysis of Discourse:
   the English used by teachers and pupils*. London: Oxford University Press,
   1975.
Smith, Carlotta S. 'Determiners and relative clauses in a generative
   grammar' *Language* 40, 1964.
– 'Sentences in discourse: an analysis of a discourse by Bertrand Russell'
   Journal of Linguistics 7, 1971.
Sommerstein, Alan H. 'On the so-called Definite Article in English'
   Linguistic Inquiry 3, 1972.
Sørensen, H. 'The function of the definite article in Modern English'
   English Studies 40, 1959.

Staal, J. F. 'Some semantic relations between sentoids' *Foundations of Language* 3, 1967.

Stockwell, Robert P., Schachter, Paul and Partee, Barbara Hall. *The Major Syntactic Structures of English*. New York: Holt, Rinehart & Winston, 1973.

Strang, Barbara M. H. 'Types and tokens in language' *Proceedings of the University of Durham Philosophical Society* I, B, 3, 1958.

– *Modern English Structure*. London: Edward Arnold, 1962; 2nd ed, revised, 1968.

Sumpf, J. and Dubois, J. Problèmes de l'analyse de discours. *Langages* 13, 1969.

Svartvik, Jan. *On Voice in the English Verb*. The Hague: Mouton, 1966.

Todorov, Tsvetan. La grammaire du récit. *Langages* 12, 1968.

Turner, Geoffrey J. and Mohan, Bernard A. *A Linguistic Description and Computer Program for Children's Speech*. London: Routledge & Kegan Paul (*Primary Socialization, Language and Education*), 1970.

Ullmann, Stephen. *Language and Style*. Oxford: Blackwell, 1964.

Ure, Jean N. 'Practical registers' (Parts 1 & 2) *English Language Teaching*, 1969.

– 'Lexical density and register differentiation'. G. E. Perren and J. L. M. Trim (eds), *Applications of Linguistics: selected papers of the Second International Congress of Applied Linguistics* (Cambridge, 1969). Cambridge: University Press, 1971.

Van Dijk, Teun A. 'Sémantique générale et théorie des textes' *Linguistics* 62, 1970.

– *Some Aspects of Text Grammars: a study in theoretical linguistics and poetics*. The Hague: Mouton, 1972.

Vendler, Zeno. *Adjectives and Nominalizations*. The Hague: Mouton, 1968.

Waterhouse, Viola. 'Independent and dependent sentences' *International Journal of American Linguistics* 29, 1963.

Williams, Joseph M. *Some Grammatical Characteristics of Continuous Discourse*. University of Wisconsin PhD thesis, 1966.

Winbourne, John. 'Sentence sequence in discourse' *Proceedings of the Ninth International Congress of Linguists*. The Hague: Mouton, 1964.

Winterowd, W. Ross. 'The grammar of coherence' *College English* 31, 1970.

Young, Richard E., Becker, Alton L. and Pike, Kenneth L. *Rhetoric: discovery and change*. New York: Harcourt, Brace and World, 1970.

Zandvoort, R. W. *A Handbook of English Grammar*. London: Longman, 3rd edn, revised, 1965.

Index